Therefore every scribe trained for the Kingdom of Heaven is like a householder who brings out of his treasury what is new and what is old.

MATTHEW 13:52

BREVARD SPRINGS CHILDS

THEOLOGICAL EXEGESIS

• •

Essays in Honor of
BREVARD S. CHILDS

Edited by

Christopher Seitz *and* Kathryn Greene-McCreight

WILLIAM B. EERDMANS PUBLISHING COMPANY
GRAND RAPIDS, MICHIGAN / CAMBRIDGE, U.K.

© 1999 Wm. B. Eerdmans Publishing Co.
255 Jefferson Ave. S.E., Grand Rapids, Michigan 49503 /
P.O. Box 163, Cambridge CB3 9PU U.K.

Printed in the United States of America

03 02 01 00 99   7 6 5 4 3 2 1

Library of Congress Cataloging-in-Publication Data

Theological exegesis: essays in honor of Brevard S. Childs /
edited by Christopher Seitz and Kathryn Greene-McCreight.
p.   cm.
Includes bibliographical references.
ISBN 0-8028-4198-8 (pbk.: alk. paper)
1. Bible — Canonical criticism.
I. Childs, Brevard S.   II. Seitz, Christopher R.
III. Greene-McCreight, Kathryn, 1961-
BS521.8.T44   1999
220.6 — dc21   98-37775
                                           CIP

Contents

II. CANONICAL READINGS AND THE OLD TESTAMENT

Contents

III. CANONICAL READINGS AND THE NEW TESTAMENT

Abbreviations

ANF	Ante-Nicene Fathers
BDB	F. Brown, S. R. Driver, and C. A. Briggs, *A Hebrew and English Lexicon of the Old Testament* (Oxford: Clarendon, 1907)
CBQ	*Catholic Biblical Quarterly*
ET	English translation
JBL	*Journal of Biblical Literature*
JSOT	*Journal for the Study of the Old Testament*
JTS	*Journal of Theological Studies*
KJV	King James Version
MT	Masoretic Text
NEB	New English Bible
NJB	New Jerusalem Bible
NJPS	New Jewish Publication Society Version
NPNF	Nicene and Post-Nicene Fathers
NRSV	New Revised Standard Version
NTS	*New Testament Studies*
OBT	Overtures to Biblical Theology
REV	Revised English Bible
RSV	Revised Standard Version
THAT	*Theologisches Handwörterbuch zum Alten Testament*
TDOT	*Theological Dictionary of the Old Testament*
UBS	*Greek New Testament* (United Bible Societies)
VT	*Vetus Testamentum*
ZAW	*Zeitschrift für die Alttestamentliche Wissenschaft*

I. CANONICAL METHOD

The Work and Witness of Brevard S. Childs: Comprehension, Discipline, Obedience

Kathryn Greene-McCreight and Christopher Seitz

Festschriften typically celebrate a milestone in the life of an influential scholar and teacher by gathering essays from former students and colleagues. Brevard S. Childs was honored with such a volume on the occasion of his sixty-fifth birthday. The present volume has been prepared to mark his seventy-fifth birthday and to pay tribute to his published work and classroom presence over the past forty years. While some of the following essays are contributed by his students, the majority are from those who wish they could have been Childs's students or who understand themselves to have been influenced by his work. All of the essays are attempts to engage in some constructive way aspects of Childs's thinking and writing.

This collection seeks to be faithful to the comprehensive vision of biblical and theological studies that Childs has never ceased to outline, illustrate, and defend throughout the corpus of his scholarship. Childs paid only modest institutional attention to the working classifications typical of the field and sought in his published work and teaching to pursue a much more holistic project. In teaching at Yale's Divinity School and Graduate School alike, Childs ranged out beyond the usual Old Testament offerings into the areas of Theology, History of Interpretation, and New Testament. A colleague once quipped that Childs was considering offering a course on the canonical shape of the patristic literature. While the colleague meant it as a joke, others of us wondered where we could sign up.

The essays in this volume can in fact be classified according to the usual technical division into the areas of Old Testament, New Testament, Theology,

3

and History of Interpretation. However, as the reader will discover, each essay draws on and contributes to more than just its own discipline. The wide range of scholarly interests represented in this collection of essays is itself tribute to the fact that Childs himself did not think and write according to inherited categories, but constantly reached for a comprehensive goal for biblical studies. In Commentary, there was History of Biblical Interpretation.[1] In Introduction, there was Hermeneutics, Critical Analysis, and Exegesis.[2] In Exegesis there was Constructive Theology; in Constructive Theology there was Exegesis. Alongside technical monographs on Biblical Theology[3] or History[4] there was a book to aid pastors and teachers in assembling a helpful working library.[5] Finally, the very division of scholarship on Christian Scripture into a discrete study of the Old Testament and a discrete study of the New Testament was called into question.[6] And at each point along the path of Childs's writing one saw the capacity to adjust and reconsider, so that later writing did not consist of mere recapitulation or repetition — even as the agenda stayed the same — but always exposed some fresh new angle on an old problem. Who else, in a volume announcing the demise of the Biblical Theology Movement, would attempt to breathe new life into the very "movement" being declared dead by offering normative suggestions on sexual ethics and practical theology?[7] In Childs's published work, one witnessed the demolition of older genres of scholarly writing and their replacement with fresh forms to challenge and instruct.

Yet, at the same time, Childs was the consummate *Fachman*. Alongside the drive for comprehension stood discipline and close attention to the constraints of scholarly publication. Who else would (or could) follow up a massive volume on Biblical Theology, in which matters seemingly so peripheral to the discipline of Old Testament Studies were considered, such as Ethics, Preaching, and Patristics, with the sort of technical writing typical of stan-

1. Brevard S. Childs, *The Book of Exodus* (Philadelphia: Westminster, 1972).

2. Brevard S. Childs, *Introduction to the Old Testament as Scripture* (Philadelphia: Fortress, 1979).

3. Brevard S. Childs, *Myth and Reality in the Old Testament* (Studies in Biblical Theology, 27; Naperville: Allenson, 1960); *Memory and Tradition in Israel* (London: SCM, 1962).

4. Brevard S. Childs, *Isaiah and the Assyrian Crisis* (Studies in Biblical Theology, 3; Naperville, Allenson, 1967).

5. Brevard S. Childs, *Old Testament Books for Pastor and Teacher* (Philadelphia: Westminster, 1977).

6. Brevard S. Childs, *Biblical Theology of the Old and New Testaments: Theological Reflection on the Christian Bible* (Minneapolis: Fortress, 1993[1]).

7. Brevard S. Childs, *Biblical Theology in Crisis* (Philadelphia: Westminster, 1970).

dard scholarly journals?[8] And those of us who were his doctoral students, who may have been privately dubious of or even openly antagonistic toward his challenges to the field, knew him to be the most formidable controller of those disciplines he was challenging. No one in the field would have entertained his more comprehensive proposals had they not been grounded in exegesis of the most careful, technical, and judicious sort and in the fullest possible conversation with historical-critical endeavor. And, to our horror, we knew that we were held to the same high standards that he held for himself.

Yet Childs was immune to egocentric rigidity on the one hand and to the winds of changing doctrine on the other because of a character of humility grounded in the desire for, above all else in his life and work, obedience to God's Word. For example, Childs rarely ever assigned his own writings as course material, almost never presented his published views in lectures or seminars, and avoided any self-referentiality in both style and content. As fits the logic of the gospel, this humility unleashed in Childs not caution or scrupulosity, but an entire poetic range of response freed from concern for either self-protection or politesse. This, of course, made both his introductory lectures and technical exegesis equally adventuresome and memorable for the student. But above all, we witnessed in his classroom presence how prayer, preaching, and exegesis depend fundamentally on obedience to the Word.

It has been a curiosity to witness in recent years the publication of several volumes devoted entirely to discussing Childs's work as though he were a figure from the past, even though he yet remains among us as colleague and mentor. Here we step into the rarest of possible spaces: between an author's own perceptions of his intentions and proposals, on the one hand, and the perceptions of others about his intentions and proposals, both triangulated against the third entity of his public writing in its present "canonical shape." Ironically, one here senses what is at stake in Childs's most basic claim about Holy Scripture: to read the Bible as the Word of God means an encounter with a dimension of reality fully grounded in concrete life that nevertheless transcends the original moments of utterance and individual intention. It is in an analogous transcending of the original utterance that Scripture allows its readers to listen in on God's ever-contemporaneous speech.

In his life and in his work, Brevard S. Childs has proclaimed and pointed to a Word that does not return empty, but accomplishes that which God has purposed (Isa. 55:11). While Childs himself has always insisted that we are not prophets or apostles, we are fortunate to know the prophets and

---

8. Brevard S. Childs, "Retrospective Reading of the Old Testament Prophets," *ZAW* 108 (1996) 362-77.

apostles more deeply because of his work and teaching, which have enabled us, despite our one-tiered universe and age of electric lights, to glimpse small points of continuity with those ancient witnesses nonetheless. For this glimpse, which makes us shudder at the grandeur and magnificence of what God has done in Israel and in Christ Jesus, the Word behind all words, we who are the students, colleagues, and friends of Brevard Childs here pay him tribute.

What I Believe My Old Schoolmate Is Up To

Roy A. Harrisville

At the outset, I admit my inability to give anything like a thorough analysis of the work of my old friend and schoolmate, Brevard Springs Childs. But I take comfort in the fact that I am not alone in that. For one thing, the majority of Bible interpreters in this country are not able to match Childs in the extent of territory traversed. He has simply read more than we have! For another, Childs's interest in the questions of systematic or dogmatic theology, engined by his conviction respecting the biblical interpreter's task, is not shared by the members of his guild. For still another, we will have to reach into an era long gone to discover another with sufficient lung power to plunge into the waters of both Testaments. Still, when this modest piece is done I hope to have shown that what a majority of Childs's readers have missed, overlooked, or ignored, anyone with average intelligence could have recognized — the heart and soul of his work.

I. The Irritant

As far as I can see, what has irritated Childs all his life is the separation between the descriptive and constructive elements of biblical interpretation, that is, the distance between "Biblical Theology" as a primarily historical task *and* subsequent theological reflection, a distance celebrated, for example, by Krister Stendahl in his article on "Biblical Theology" in *The Interpreter's Dictionary of the Bible.* There, Stendahl wrote that the "first and crucial task of biblical theology" was to limit the original text to what it meant. This was the "new phenomenon in biblical studies," a "mature growth of the historical and critical study of the scriptures." The following makes clear to what extent Stendahl had separated the two tasks:

> This descriptive task can be carried out by believer and agnostic alike. The believer has the advantage of automatic empathy with the believers in the text — but his faith constantly threatens to have him modernize the material. . . . The agnostic has the advantage of feeling no such temptations, but his power of empathy must be considerable. . . . The meaning for the present — in which the two interpreters are different — is not involved.[1]

Childs totally rejected the separation, and early on. In an article written for the journal *Interpretation,* he asked,

> Does not theology need normative as well as descriptive categories in order to execute its task? . . . Can the theological task of a commentator be exhausted when he remains on the level of the witness? Is there not a responsibility to penetrate to the substance toward which the text points?[2]

In his first major piece, *Biblical Theology in Crisis,* Childs answered his own question:

> To the extent that the use of the critical method sets up an iron curtain between the past and the present, it is an inadequate method for studying the Bible as the church's Scripture.[3]

In his commentary on Exodus he gave the reason for his answer:

> The rigid separation between the descriptive and constructive elements of exegesis strikes at the roots of the theological task of understanding the Bible.[4]

Separation between the two tasks belonged to that "sterile impasse" that resulted from a setting of limits in the nineteenth century.

Childs acknowledged he was not alone in his irritation, but shared it with others, with, for instance, James Smart, Floyd Filson, or his colleague Paul Minear. Minear, for example, had argued that a method designed to

---

1. Krister Stendahl, "Biblical Theology," *The Interpreter's Dictionary of the Bible* (Nashville: Abingdon, 1962) I, 422; cf. 418 and 425.

2. Brevard Childs, "Interpretation in Faith," *Interpretation* 18 (1964) 433, 436.

3. Brevard Childs, *Biblical Theology in Crisis* (Philadelphia: Westminster, 1970) 141-42; cf. Childs's remarks concerning the Uppsala University faculty as well as Stendahl on 26 and 79.

4. Brevard Childs, *The Book of Exodus* (Philadelphia: Westminster, 1974) xiii.

treat events of the "old age" according to the operation of the laws of that age was incapable of understanding biblical history, that the task of the biblical theologian was to study the biblical point of view with "eyes of faith," to be addressed by God himself in a "final, ever-repeated act of creation, judgment and redemption."[5] Childs stated that the irritation and the prescription for its removal in the use of biblical criticism coupled with a robust theological perspective was a peculiarly American phenomenon.[6] The discovery that it was not came later, in encounter with theologians of Europe — some of whom were heard in his student days but ignored. For example, in a 1969 symposium held at Yale on Karl Barth's theology, Childs admitted he had been typical of most biblical scholars and had not taken Barth seriously, but that he had now had a change of heart. Perhaps that discovery, more than what Childs shares with others this side of the sea, fired his attempt at a new way of biblical interpretation.

II. The Prescription

In his prescription for removal of the irritant, that is, in his "Biblical Theology," Childs did not pay lip service to the historical task. Rather, he asserted that the descriptive lay at the heart of the theological task — that the fundamental criticism of Luther's or Calvin's exegesis, or even of the exegesis of Karl Barth, was that they did not execute the descriptive task with sufficient precision.[7] In the volume on Exodus, he wrote that serious theological exposition of the biblical text required attention to the entire range of problems involving text and source criticism, syntax and grammar, history and geography. In his *New Testament as Canon* he affirmed the entire set of procedures to which the biblical text must be subjected before it could be understood, procedures involving the determination of milieu, date, authorship, addressees, literary growth, etc. His criticism of Paul Ricoeur and his disciples was that their understanding of the Bible as a deposit of metaphors containing inherent powers by which to interpret present experience irrespective of their source, and thus their concern to illuminate what lies "ahead" of rather than behind the text, displayed little or no interest in the text's historical development.[8] For that reason, Childs's reference to the reader's "religious stance" as playing a legitimate

5. Quoted in *Biblical Theology in Crisis*, 44.

6. *Ibid.*, 21.

7. "Interpretation in Faith," 438, 440.

8. Brevard Childs, *Introduction to the Old Testament as Scripture* (Philadelphia: Fortress, 1979) 77.

role "after" the descriptive task had been attended to, when the reader chooses whether or not to identify with the perspective of the text he is studying,[9] was not intended to distance the religious from the descriptive task. A century earlier, Adolf Schlatter had asserted the legitimacy of a "methodological atheism," which in the interest of begetting pure, genuine observation tabled the question of God "for a time" *(nur zeitweilig)*. But to exclude the question of God altogether, wrote Schlatter, rendered science a caricature and led to polemic against rather than submission to its object.[10]

Of course, in that wedding of criticism to theological reflection Childs gives priority to the latter. In the 1969 symposium, he cited with approval Barth's giving the lion's share to theological reflection.

> Barth came to the Bible, from the outset, from a confessional standpoint. He confessed that the Old and New Testaments were Scriptures of the Church, that they contained the prophetic and apostolic Witness, that this was the normative Witness, and that in this context (as the Church had received it) one remembered how the Church fathers and the Church had heard the Word, and yet waited in expectation that the Word of God would become alive through the Holy Spirit for them.[11]

Childs conceded that the attempt at combining criticism and reflection was fraught with risk, a risk that some of his critics suggest has landed him in the fundamentalist aversion to critical method. In a review of *Biblical Theology in Crisis*, J. A. Sanders hinted at what he called Childs's latent "biblicism."[12] In a testy review of *Introduction to the Old Testament as Scripture*, James Barr referred to Childs's "deep disillusionment with historical study," an attitude "deeply welcome to conservative opinion." Childs, wrote Barr, created a vacuum into which reactionary notions would naturally flow, since he removed "the extrinsic critical effect of modern biblical study which was the main obstacle to these convictions."[13] In a volume written in 1987 and

---

9. *Ibid.*, 72-73.

10. Adolf Schlatter, *Atheistische Methoden in der Theologie*, ed. Heinz-Peter Hempelmann (Wuppertal: Brockhaus, 1985) 38, 46.

11. *Karl Barth and the Future of Theology: A Memorial Colloquium Held at the Yale Divinity School, January 28, 1969*, ed. David L. Dickermann (New Haven: YDS Association, 1969) 33.

12. "Childs' position might easily sponsor a kind of biblicism of its own, which he himself regrets in the early Biblical Theology Movement," James A. Sanders, review of *Biblical Theology in Crisis* in *Union Seminary Quarterly Review* 26 (1971) 303.

13. James Barr, review of *Introduction to the Old Testament as Scripture* in *JSOT* 16 (1980) 15, 23.

covering "all" contemporary biblical theologies, Manfred Oeming referred to the "two phases" in Childs's biblical-theological sojourn, the first marked by attention to critical method, the second and latest by aversion to tradition-historical inquiry, or by "dogmatic flight" from the difficulties of historical work. Oeming wrote:

> In recent years, the rejection and criticism of historical criticism, long since widespread in evangelistic-evangelical circles, has received support from well-known representatives of the exegetical science. Stuhlmacher [i.e. Prof. Peter Stuhlmacher of Tübingen University] and Childs are merely exponents of the discontent or helplessness abroad in wide circles toward the value and results of historical-critical work.[14]

According to Oeming, that aversion may root in "good old American respect for positivism."[15] According to Childs, however, it was precisely the wedding of the descriptive and constructive tasks that preserved the integrity of the descriptive task. In fact, the whole point of emphasizing the canon was "to stress the historical nature of the biblical witness."[16]

At any rate, for Childs "canon" is the locus at which the descriptive and constructive aspects of interpretation combine, the term "canon" functioning as cipher for that process by which the church's sacred writings were formed and by which they exercised their roles in the life of each generation of believers.

Choice of the term "process" is deliberate, since "canon" denotes the interpretive activity of those who not merely sought to identify with the received tradition but also to appropriate its message, who for this reason structured the received tradition so as to enable it to perform a role in the life of each generation. Thus, while Childs concedes, as per adherents of the "newer criticism" in English literature, that an interpreter "can" use only the final stage of literature as a legitimate context, his intention is to focus on that final stage as culminating or gathering up each level of the tradition's collection and of the reflection upon it, since at each level the hearer or reader has been confronted with its power.[17]

For lack of attention to this idea, some of Childs's reviewers contend that he focuses rigidly on the last stage of the process, that is, on the "final literary

---

14. Manfred Oeming, *Gesamt biblische Theologien der Gegenwart* (Stuttgart: Kohlhammer, 1987) 215-16; cf. 195-96.

15. *Ibid.*, 208.

16. *Introduction to the Old Testament as Scripture*, 71.

17. *Biblical Theology in Crisis*, 98; cf. Childs's response in *JSOT* 16 (1980) 52-60; idem, *The New Testament as Canon: An Introduction* (Philadelphia: Fortress, 1985) 27, and *Old Testament Theology in a Canonical Context* (Minneapolis: Fortress, 1985) 11, 14.

text" apart from its antecedents. James Sanders expresses hesitation at Childs focusing so much on the "final literary text," adding that although the traditions attained stability at points along the way, they were nevertheless adapted to the needs of succeeding generations.[18] Another reviewer queries, "Why must one necessarily designate the final transmitted form of a biblical book as intentional?" adding that Childs's approach "shrinks" the biblical witness by restricting the scope of God's action in history.[19] Manfred Oeming sees in Gerhard Maier, ultra-conservative head of Tübingen's Bengel House, a striking analogy to Childs, for whom "the obligatory norm can only be the present text, the text actually given into our hand."[20] Other reviewers simply set Childs down as one more redaction critic. The author of a review in the *Expository Times* writes that the term "canonical" adds nothing to the sense, that "we are within the field of redaction criticism, although Childs frequently distinguishes his approach from that."[21] Of the reviewers consulted, precious few caught the connotation of process. One was Rudolf Smend of Göttingen, whose theological sojourn bore striking resemblance to that of Childs, and who wrote:

> Childs is far from restricting [canon] to the collection of Biblical books in their more or less present form. He uses it in large measure of the prehistory of these books.[22]

"Process" and nothing else explains Childs's preference for the Masoretic Text of the Old Testament, in which more than one critic believes he detects a chink in his armor.[23] First, he insists that the history of the Old Testament text participates in the canonical process. Second, he asserts that the Masoretic Text is not the canonical text but rather the "vehicle for its recovery" — it gives access to the text "held in common by ongoing religious communities." Or again, because taking the canon seriously means to establish the level of the biblical literature "in accordance with its historical stabilization by the Jewish community," this "mutilated MT text" has the priority due to its standing in that community.[24]

---

18. James A. Sanders, "Biblical Criticism and the Bible as Canon," *Union Seminary Quarterly Review* 32 (1977) 163.

19. *JSOT* 16 (1980) 168, 170.

20. Oeming, 217.

21. Review of *The New Testament as Canon* in *Expository Times* 4/97 (1986) 99.

22. Rudolf Smend, *JSOT* 16 (1980) 47-48.

23. R. E. Murphy, *JSOT* 16 (1980) 41: "One fails to see why a later generation of the People of the Book should be pinned down to a doubtful, if not erroneous, form of the text as normative." Cf. Sanders, *Horizons in Biblical Theology* 2 (1980) 187, 188.

24. *Introduction to the Old Testament as Scripture*, 100, 101, 104, 106.

Childs has never abandoned the term "process." In 1985 he wrote that the formation of the canon involved a series of decisions affecting the shape of the literature. In fact, such distinctions as Albert Sundberg and Theodore Swanson drew between "Scripture" and "canon" limited "canon" to the final stages of a long and complex process begun in the preexilic period.[25] Agreed, the "final form" of the text had the lion's share, but that was because the total process could only be perceived when it had reached its goal. Or again, it was the "final form" that reflected the entire history of the believing community's interaction with its traditions.[26] For this reason, methods that concentrated on the preliterary shape of the biblical traditions and whatever "situation-in-life" in the Jewish or Christian community that shape reflected came under attack. Of tradition-historical work on the Old Testament Childs wrote:

> To seek to give theological autonomy to a reconstructed Yahwist source apart from its present canonical context is to disregard the crucial theological intention of the tradents of the tradition, and to isolate a text's meaning from its reception.[27]

To all of this Childs refuses to attach the designation "method." He specifically avoids such terms as "canon criticism" or "canonical criticism" precisely because they suggest the formulation of a method to supplement or replace others of its kind. The term "canon" (without the article) suggests not a new exegetical technique but a *context* from which the literature is to be understood and interpreted. Attention to this point could have saved his critics space and effort.[28]

III. Canon and Church

Essential to Childs's definition of "canon" is the fact of its reception by the church. For if "canon" is where the descriptive and constructive meet, the locus for that meeting is the church as recipient of the canon. This involves a certain restriction, that is, a restriction to a discrete collection recognized by

25. *Ibid.*, 58-59.
26. *Ibid.*, 75-76; *JSOT* 16 (1980) 54.
27. *Old Testament Theology in a Canonical Context*, 11.
28. *Introduction to the Old Testament as Scripture*, 16. In Childs's response to his reviewers in *JSOT* 16 (1980) he wrote: "Some of the misunderstanding of parts of my book stem from replacing my broad use of the term with a much narrower, traditional usage, and thus missing the force of the argument" (p. 53).

the Christian community as sacred Scripture. For although the church's "hearing of the text" may not be divorced from "that other community of faith which lives from the same Bible," or from the "countless other stances outside of any commitment to faith or tradition," it nonetheless gives priority to a particular corpus because it believes that that corpus testifies to the transcendent reality to which it owes its life.[29] On the other hand, the church as context spells extension, for by juxtaposing the Old and New Testaments the church has created something that is not restricted to the one or the other. Childs writes:

> The formation of a canon of Scriptures is a recognition of the need for a context, different from both Testaments, in which the Christian church continues to wrestle in every new age with the living God who continues to confront his people through the ancient testimony of the prophets and apostles.[30]

This concept of "canon" in "context" has one eminent consequence for interpretation. In the "classical" period of Biblical Theology, that period "in crisis," exposition of each testament was carried out independently of the other. Let the biblical theological work of the century's two great interpreters, Gerhard von Rad of the Old Testament and Rudolf Bultmann of the New Testament, stand in evidence. For Childs, the church as the context of "canon," the place of meeting for the descriptive and the constructive, requires a relation between Old and New Testaments, precisely because the church confesses that it encounters the transcendent reality to which it owes its life through the testimony of the apostles *and* the prophets.[31] In 1964, Childs wrote of the "ontological relation" or "ontological correspondence" between the two Testaments — both functioning as vehicles for the divine revelation.[32]

IV. Canon and Confession

There is more. Childs faulted the "Biblical Theology Movement" for assuming that one came to the biblical text from a vantage point outside it, for fail-

---

29. *The Book of Exodus,* ix; Brevard Childs, *Biblical Theology of the Old and New Testaments* (Minneapolis: Fortress, 1993) 8.
30. *Biblical Theology in Crisis,* 113; cf. 112.
31. *Ibid.,* 113, 159.
32. "Interpretation in Faith," 440, 442.

ing to take the text seriously in its "canonical form,"[33] "canonical form" in this instance serving as logarithm for sharing the church's confession. Childs saw nothing illegitimate in such activity. He wrote:

> The role of the Bible is not being understood simply as a cultural expression of ancient peoples, but as a testimony pointing beyond itself to a divine reality to which it bears witness. To speak of the Bible now as scripture further extends this insight because it implies its continuing role for the church as a vehicle of God's will. Such an approach to the Bible is obviously confessional. Yet the Enlightenment's alternative proposal which was to confine the Bible solely to the arena of human experience is just as much a philosophical commitment. . . . The basic hermeneutical issue at stake turns on the fact that no modern biblical theology can function without some other conceptual framework.[34]

At the 1969 Symposium, Childs referred to Barth's continual complaint that one could not get *behind* the text, could not get at Scripture from a context other than the "canonical," since there was no neutral position from which to begin and from which to move from neutrality to commitment.[35]

Thus, Childs insists, there is no unbridgeable chasm between "hard-nosed" critical exegesis and the "ecclesiastical form" assigned the sacred writings. In fact, "penetrating theological exegesis" is rare among those who share little or nothing of the faith reflected in the literature.[36] The preface to Childs's commentary on Exodus is as succint a statement as he gives anywhere respecting the descriptive and interpretive task as joined at the locus of "canon" within the "context" of the church:

> The purpose of this commentary is unabashedly theological. Its concern is to understand Exodus as scripture of the church. The exegesis arises as a theological discipline within the context of the canon and is directed toward the community of faith which lives by its confession of Jesus Christ.[37]

---

33. *Biblical Theology in Crisis*, 102.
34. *Biblical Theology of the Old and New Testaments*, 9, 42.
35. *Karl Barth and the Future of Theology*, 32.
36. *The New Testament as Canon*, 21, 39.
37. *The Book of Exodus*, ix.

V. The Text and Nothing but the Text

Childs is adamant: The canonical approach, with its requirement that the interpreter share the faith reflected in the literature, does not divert attention from the text. The reverse is true: The interpreter is bound to the text since it is the text that reflects the transcendent reality. On the other hand, the fundamentalist and the liberal seek to ground biblical truth on propositions *apart from the text,* while the *Heilsgeschichtler* searches for continuity between the Testaments in events *behind the text,* requiring a process of critical reconstruction to extract the theological data from the text.[38]

Childs expresses appreciation for the "experiential-expressive category" used by his colleague George Lindbeck to sketch Bernard Lonergan's theory of religion. According to Lonergan (as interpreted by Lindbeck) the objectivizing of common core experiences in biblical religions is not merely a symbolizing of those experiences, but has its source in the revealed will of God, thus ensuring its status as norm. Childs finds the category "full of insight" for distinguishing his position from the liberal model.[39]

Childs may entertain the greatest reservation toward the so-called literary approach. For example, in his reference to an exegesis free of dogmatics or of faith as capable of being "equally" stifling and superficial, he cites with obvious approval George Steiner's "devastating" review of the Alter-Kermode volume. In that review Steiner had written:

> The separation . . . between a theological-religious experience of Biblical texts and a literary one is radically factitious. It cannot work. This is to say that the plain question of divine inspiration . . . must be faced squarely and unflinchingly. . . . The author of Job . . . was not producing "literature." Nor were those who bore witness to the "darkness upon the earth" the evening of Good Friday. A literary elucidation of such texts is legitimate and can be helpful, but only . . . if it tells us that that which it omits is the essential.[40]

Or again, when colleague Lindbeck offers his own "cultural-linguistic" approach in opposition to that of Lonergan, which he describes as creating a nest of problems, he draws Childs's fire:

---

38. *Biblical Theology of the Old and New Testaments,* 17-18.

39. *The New Testament as Canon,* 543; cf. Lindbeck's *The Nature of Doctrine* (Philadelphia: Westminster, 1984) 31-32.

40. George Steiner, "The Good Books," *Religion and Intellectual Life* 6 (1989) 15-16; cf. Childs, *Biblical Theology of the Old and New Testaments,* 12, and *The Literary Guide to the Bible,* ed. Robert Alter and Frank Kermode (Boston: Harvard University, 1987).

The attempt of many literary critics to by-pass the problem of biblical reality and refuse to distinguish between the text and the reality of its subject matter severely cripples the theological enterprise of Biblical Theology. It is basic to Christian theology to reckon with an extra-biblical reality. . . . [Lindbeck's] proposal of the text creating its own world — some would call it fictive world — into which the reader is drawn has its origins far more in high church liturgical practice than from the Bible.[41]

But if it is the text and nothing but the text that mirrors the divine reality, no single text or cluster of texts may be assigned that function in preference to others. Again, Childs is adamant: To seek a relation between the Old and New Testaments means to take seriously the church's confession of a *canon of Scripture,* thus to reject any appeal to a "canon within the canon."[42]

The rejection of a canon within the canon does not mean that all texts are treated on the same level, or that inherited tradition is uncritically appropriated. Childs states that it is precisely the function of "canonical shaping" to render the received material in "different critical ways."[43] And again Childs's reviewers furnish contradictory appraisals. Norman Porteous questions whether Childs's critical handling of the biblical witness is compatible with his insistence on canonical authority, and Luke Timothy Johnson refers to his inability to "let go of the historical and engage the theological," while Oeming and Hübner concur that ultimately Childs flees the problems of historical criticism.[44]

VI. Canon and Encounter with God

We have arrived at the heart of Childs's concern, the nerve of his project: to render transparent the reality reflected in the text. In each piece he has turned to print, Childs has recited, repeated, accented, trumpeted, elucidated, adumbrated this concern — as if it were some elusive thing his reader were forever apt to miss or overlook. In the midst of the bulk of criticism and analysis, of historical recollection and dogmatic reflection, of exegesis and

---

41. *Biblical Theology of the Old and New Testaments,* 20-21; cf. Lindbeck, 32ff.

42. *Biblical Theology in Crisis,* 159.

43. *The New Testament as Canon,* 41-42.

44. Cf. N. W. Porteous, review of *Biblical Theology in Crisis* in *Scottish Journal of Theology* 25 (1971) 494; Luke Timothy Johnson, review of the same volume in *Commonweal* 120 (1993) 21; Oeming, 195; Hans Hübner, *Biblische Theologie des Neuen Testaments* (Göttingen: Vandenhoeck und Ruprecht, 1990) 70, note 172.

interpretation, Childs's single perduring theme is that of the canon as vehicle to encounter with God.

In one of the first pieces to come from his pen he wrote that the final task of exegesis was to seek to hear the Word of God; that since the divine reality to which the Bible witnesses is not confined to the historical past, historical tools are inadequate to exhaust the material.[45]

In *Biblical Theology in Crisis,* he wrote:

> The canon marks the area in which the modern issues of life and death are defined in terms of what God has done and is doing, and what he demands as a response from his people. . . . The God of the Bible is not a theological system, but a living and acting Lord, the one with whom we have to do — now. *We are confronted, not just with ancient witnesses, but with our God who is the Eternal Present.*[46]

In *The New Testament as Canon,* he wrote:

> The theological issue turns on the Christian church's claim for the integrity of *a special reading which interprets the Bible within an established theological context and toward a particular end, namely the discerning of the will of God.*[47]

Or again, in the same volume:

> The canonical interpreter stands within the received tradition, and, fully conscious of his own time-conditionality as well as that of the scriptures, strives *critically to discern from its kerygmatic witness a way to God which overcomes the historical moorings of both text and reader.*[48]

In *Biblical Theology of Old and New Testaments,* Childs wrote:

> A major thesis of this book is that this basic problem in Biblical Theology can only be resolved by *theological reflection which moves from a description of the biblical witnesses to the object toward which these witnesses point, that is, to their subject matter, substance, or res.*[49]

And again, in the same volume:

---

45. "Interpretation in Faith," 440, 443-44.
46. *Biblical Theology in Crisis,* 219; cf. 101-2; italics mine.
47. *The New Testament as Canon,* 37; italics mine.
48. *Ibid.,* 51-52; italics mine.
49. *Biblical Theology of the Old and New Testaments,* 80; italics mine.

Scripture . . . points beyond itself to the reality of God. The ability to render this reality is to enter the "strange new world of the Bible."[50]

Of course, making the "subject matter," the "substance," or *res* transparent was not a matter left to criticism. For if the text itself was not the "generative force of truth," then its hearing, exposition, or criticism required confirmation by that very reality it intended to reflect. So, Childs wrote:

A canonical context includes not only the scope of the sacred literature, but the means by which the reader engages the scriptures, namely an expectation of understanding through the promise of the Spirit.[51]

Again:

Through the Spirit the reality to which the text points . . . is made active in constantly fresh forms of application.[52]

Thus, when Childs refers to the "process" by which the canon achieved its authoritative form, or speaks of the "historical and theological forces" at work in the canon's growth, he has more than immanence in mind. It is the Spirit of God that renders the Scripture a medium of encounter with God in each new generation of faith. For this reason, there is no avenue to the Christ worshiped by the Christian church apart from the biblical testimony. And for this reason Childs approves James Sanders's broadening of the definition of canon to include a process, but opposes his explanation of the canon's growth as a search for identity in times of crisis. He challenges Walter Brueggemann's substitution of the interpreter for the text as the decisive tradent of the norm. And his quarrel with Peter Stuhlmacher of Tübingen has to do with the latter's substitution of the Old Testament's "vertical, existential dimension" for its construal as a "horizontal stream of tradition from the past," its witness limited to its effect on subsequent writers.[53] James Barr, as others, argued that the "actual biblical period," not the later world of canonization, should be the interpretive basis.[54] In the parlance of the sixteenth century, there is something *schwärmerisch* about these attempts to anchor the normative in the existential or the interpretive, in the history of the tradi-

---

50. *Ibid.*, 721; italics mine.

51. *The New Testament as Canon*, 40.

52. *Biblical Theology of the Old and New Testaments*, 724.

53. *Introduction to the Old Testament as Scripture*, 57; *Biblical Theology of the Old and New Testaments*, 72 and 77.

54. *JSOT* 16 (1980) 14.

tion's effects or in "the actual biblical period," presumably recoverable by means of historical science.

VII. Forbears

If the irritation was shared, so was the goal. Childs admitted that in his 1970 sketch of the problems of Biblical Theology he "had not thrown the net wide enough," that it had only slowly begun to dawn on him that everything turned on how the material was to be understood.[55] Just as slowly or gradually may have dawned the consciousness that there had been others ahead of him moving toward the same goal. For example, Irenaeus had formulated a framework for interpretation which sought to join the church with the living voice of God according to the truth of its apostolic content. And Origen sought to relate the two Testaments theologically in terms of the selfsame divine reality that was its subject matter. Augustine understood the impact of the biblical message as evoking an existential dimension to faith. For Luther, the application of the gospel to the hearer was not an additional level of meaning, but an integral part of the one transforming word of the gospel. But of these "ancients" Childs seemed to prefer Calvin as clearest:

> God, to instruct the church, not merely uses mute teachers but also opens his own most hallowed lips. Not only does he teach the elect to look upon a god, but also shows himself as the God upon whom they are to look. . . . God, the Artificer of the universe, is made manifest to us in Scripture. . . . The highest proof of Scripture derives in general from the fact that God in person speaks in it. . . . Above human judgment we affirm with utter certainty . . . that [Scripture] has flowed to us from the very mouth of God by the ministry of men.[56]

As for the "moderns," it was chiefly Barth with whom Childs stood together in the fight — as his reviewers were never slow to point out. In fact, wrote Patrick Miller, Childs's indebtedness to Barth and the Reformers was even greater than his explicit references suggested. The ever-critical Oeming stated that Childs's notion of the entire canon as the one, equally valid Word of God within the one, unified community of faith, was more suggestive of a piece of Barthian dogmatics than of any kind of tenable historical judg-

---

55. *Biblical Theology of the Old and New Testaments*, xv.
56. *Calvin's Institutes: A New Compend*, ed. Hugh T. Kerr (Louisville: Westminster, 1989) 28, 30, 31; *Biblical Theology of the Old and New Testaments*, 32, 35, 38, 44-46.

ment.[57] And, in fact, Barth's exposition of Genesis in *Church Dogmatics* III/1 illustrated what Childs was after, that tendency always to "move down, to move through, and talk about the transparency," to confront the reality of the material in such a massive way as to confront God. In the midst of his exegesis of the Genesis "saga" Barth wrote:

> If we do not know the God of Israel, the Father of Jesus Christ, who is Himself Jesus Christ in concealment, how can we possibly understand the speaking and acting Subject of the biblical creation saga? How can we realise what it means that the reference here is to a real Creator and real creation? How can we differentiate between myth and saga, or between this saga and others? But to know this God, and in this way to realise the absolute uniqueness of the saga which speaks of Him, is to know Him as one's own God. . . .[58]

VIII. The Misapprehension

Once upon a time an entire generation sang requiem for an epoch in which the Bible was read objectively, loosed from the commitment for or against it. At that time, Adolf Schlatter insisted that the act of thinking followed living, for which reason one's own life-situation had to be incorporated into the historical putting of the question. As far as Schlatter was concerned, that life-situation was given beforehand, in the context of the effects of the history of Jesus Christ.[59] Theology, wrote Rudolf Bultmann, required a mode appropriate to its object. It could not be carried on "out of curiosity" or for the purpose of earning a living, but as a "venture in which we ourselves are at risk." For if God was the object of faith and accessible only to it, then a science apart from or merely alongside faith saw neither God nor faith.[60] And Hans-Georg Gadamer, whose notion of "process" in the transmission of the tradition Manfred Oeming found "closely related" to that of Childs, had written:

57. Patrick Miller, review of *Biblical Theology in Crisis* in *JBL* 90 (1971) 210; cf. Susan E. Schaeffer's review of *Biblical Theology of the Old and New Testaments* in *Lutheran Forum* 29 (1995) 58; Oeming, 204.

58. Karl Barth, *Church Dogmatics* III/1, ed. G. W. Bromiley and T. F. Torrance (Edinburgh: Clark, 1958) 92.

59. Cf. Ulrich Luck's introduction to Adolf Schlatter, *Zur Theologie des Neuen Testaments und zur Dogmatik* (Theologische Bücherei, 41, Munich: Kaiser, 1969) 13, 17-19, 24-25.

60. Rudolf Bultmann, *What Is Theology?* tr. Roy A. Harrisville (Minneapolis: Fortress, 1997) 20, 22, 84, 102, 155, 160.

The gospel does not exist in order to be understood as a merely historical document, but to be taken in such a way that it exercises its saving effect. This implies that the text, whether law or gospel, if it is to be understood properly — i.e., according to the claim it makes — must be understood at every moment, in every concrete situation, in a new and different way. Understanding here is always application.[61]

This insistence on the Bible as requiring a decision on its behalf derived from the conviction that one encountered its "Object," God, through it. And for that idea, the older generation of rebels had harked back to forbears to whom Childs appeals.

Now, biblical research is being attempted as if that earthquake of the "teens" and "twenties" never occurred. For this reason, almost all of Childs's critics have either misunderstood, half understood, or ignored, clumsily or artfully, what has persistently served as his primary concern. In what he may imagine to be a partial concession to Childs's program, Porteous writes that "one can readily agree that the Bible provides the classic and indispensable witness to God's concern and action."[62] Terence Fretheim, a Lutheran, whose acquaintance with the notion of *viva vox evangelii* (the living voice of the gospel) could justly have been assumed, summarizes Childs's position respecting the Bible as "most fundamentally a witness to God's word and action, supremely embodied in Jesus of Nazareth."[63] In one review, Sanders writes of Childs's call for a new Biblical Theology movement "on the basis of a biblical understanding of the ways one might contemporize the church's essential traditions." In another he describes canonical criticism as stressing the Bible's ontology as a "paradigm of God's work" from which we may construct paradigms for our own.[64] Johnson writes that Childs has not grasped that what theology engages is the living God "encountered in human experience."[65]

For Childs the Bible is more than a classic and indispensable witness to God's concern and action, however embodied; its understanding more than a contemporizing of the church's traditions; its ontology more than a para-

---

61. Hans-Georg Gadamer, *Truth and Method,* translation revised by Joel Weisheimer and Donald G. Marshall (New York: Crossroad, 1990) 309.

62. Porteous, 494.

63. Terence Fretheim, review of *Biblical Theology of the Old and New Testaments* in *CBQ* 56 (1994) 326.

64. Sanders, review of *Biblical Theology in Crisis,* 304, and "Biblical Criticism and the Bible as Canon," 164.

65. Johnson, 21.

digm, and more than a documenting of the human experience. For Childs
the Bible, in the context of the church's confession, is the instrument of encounter with the living God. Sanders's statement to the effect that "Childs
sees canon as God's Word,"[66] though imprecise, is as close to Childs's primary concern as his reviewers will get.

What would it have cost his critics to take note of that goal on which he
has forever had his eye? How would such attention have spelled compromise?
Or were the references to Childs's indebtedness to Barth, or the disclaimer that
he had produced anything new,[67] a screening or a bowdlerizing of what in less
discrete company would have been a forthright frontal attack: "This fellow believes that the Bible not merely talks about God but actually mediates encounter with God, and has gone and attempted a scheme calculated to facilitate that
encounter"? Why not "give the dog a bad name and hang it," that is, simply
characterize the notion as an absurdity? Fretheim may be the least squeamish.
He writes that Childs's formulations of the Bible's witness "so often reflect a
world other than the one in which I live."[68] They do indeed! But does life in the
one world render impossible an apprehension of life in the other, within range
of accuracy? As a matter of fact, that "other world" has more than one inhabit-
ant. One of the most provocative thinkers of the age speaks of the notion of a
"spirit" in or "behind" the letter as a "relevant presumption." Just this presumption, he asserts, underwrites the concept of the "iconic," the belief that
the icon is not so much a representation of the sacred person or scene as its
"immediate manifestation," its "epiphany." And as for "canon," whatever mediates that immediacy or epiphany to the reader to the point of altering the "texture of consciousness" is "canonical."[69]

IX. The Question of Method

Where the "guild" should, might have attacked, was at the point of whether
or not any construal in biblical interpretation can facilitate encounter with
God. Over against Barth, who despite his rampant exegesis disparaged critical method, Schlatter and Bultmann assigned critical method the capacity

66. *Horizons in Biblical Theology* 2 (1980) 181.
67. Cf. Miller, 210; James Barr, *JSOT* 16 (1980) 12.
68. Fretheim, 326.
69. *George Steiner: A Reader* (New York: Oxford, 1984) 85, 91; cf. Steiner's *Real Presences* (Chicago: University of Chicago, 1989) with its advocacy of the "logocentric" view throughout, that is, the view according to which words have referents beyond them-selves.

for at least setting the scene for, if not actually creating, encounter with God. Like Childs, Schlatter insisted that historical research, rather than putting faith in question, actually uncovered its effectiveness. And in his review of Barth's commentary on Romans, Bultmann wrote:

> When in exegeting Romans I detect tensions and contradictions, places high and low; when I take pains to show how Paul is dependent on Jewish theology or popular Christianity . . . I am not just carrying on historical-philological criticism, but am doing it from the viewpoint of *showing where and how the subject matter is expressed, in order to lay hold of the subject matter* which is greater even than Paul.[70]

Of course, for all his commitment to method, Schlatter was damned as a pietist whose faith in the Bible rendered him unfit for scientific work, and Bultmann's method appeared to reduce the biblical text to one long, elongated, and pendulous disquisition on self-understanding, to the point where he was unable to speak of God apart from human existence.

It may be that Childs has erred in supposing that his prescription for alleviating the irritation could render the divine reality transparent. It may be, with the "guild's" centuries-long preoccupation with perspectives, stances, postures, methods, and methodologies, that the resulting contemporary malaise and the dizzying number and variety of solutions served up to us now is nothing but the tale of a pursuit of something that can never be caught. It may be that the passion and power of exposition can never be communicated, at least not to the point where "epiphany" occurs. It may be that exegesis, interpretation, is not a science, a *Wissenschaft* that allows some space to intuition or divination, but a *Kunst*, an art that uses rules only to fuel or focus its passion. George Steiner asks, "Can a logic of immanence account for the coming into being of the fact of meaningful form?" and he answers:

> A triple echo may be of help. The precept is in Augustine; the rephrasing is by Boehme; it is Coleridge who transcribes: "I warn all Inquirers into this hard point to *wait* — not only to plunge forward before the Word is *given* to them, but not even to paw the ground with impatience. For in a deep stillness only can this truth be apprehended." . . . There is no mysticism in this monition; only the elusive light of common sense.[71]

---

70. "Karl Barths 'Römerbrief' in zweiter Auflage," *Anfänge der dialektischen Theologie,* ed. Jürgen Moltmann (Theologische Bücherei, 17, Munich: Kaiser, 1962-63) 141-42, italics mine.

71. Steiner, *Real Presences,* 224.

Isaiah Berlin echoed the sentiment in an essay on "political judgment." When we speak of statesmen, Berlin wrote, we resort to metaphors; we speak of a good political eye, or nose, or ear — "a species of direct acquaintance" distinct from description, calculation, or inference. Refuting Freud's dictum that while science cannot explain everything, nothing else does, Berlin stated that in ordinary life,

> those are Utopian who place excessive faith in laws and methods derived from alien fields, mostly from the natural sciences, and apply them with great confidence and somewhat mechanically.[72]

Childs is hardly unaware of any of this! In his response to reviewers in *Horizons in Biblical Theology* he includes a telling concession calculated to make liars of all who attack him for his rigidity:

> Slowly I began to realize that what made von Rad's work so illuminating was not his method as such, but the theological profundity of von Rad himself. The same observation holds true for Wolff and Zimmerli. I am convinced that no amount of methodological refinement will produce a quality of interpretation which that generation achieved whose faith in the God of Israel was hammered out in the challenge to meet the Nazi threat against the life of the church.[73]

Brevard Childs would scarcely apply the same observation to himself. The question, however, is whether or not anyone else in this generation has achieved what Childs has achieved by virtue of passionate commitment to the Scriptures as the instrument of encounter with the living God.

Apart from that commitment, thus by inference apart from Childs — alone and solitary, at least in terms of an approach throbbing with a commitment that one can see in print this side of the Atlantic — we are left only with immanence, deprived of whole dimensions of thought and creativity, indifferent to theology and metaphysics, dead to aesthetic creation and reception, and ultimately dead to God.

72. Isaiah Berlin, "On Political Judgment," *New York Review of Books* 43 (1996) 30.
73. *Horizons in Biblical Theology* 2 (1980) 208.

Postcritical Canonical Interpretation: Three Modes of Retrieval

George A. Lindbeck

I. Introduction

Brevard Childs is first among the scriptural scholars engaged in the postcritical retrieval of classic scriptural hermeneutics.[1] Other retrievalists do not rival him in quantity and quality of exegetical work. They in some cases differ, however, in mode of procedure, in what they primarily look for, and these differences need to be critically assessed. This essay undertakes that task by comparing Childs's work (which, because of its familiarity to readers of this volume is only briefly characterized) to two other modes or models of retrieval practiced both inside and outside the biblical guild. The argument is that all three are needed and that when taken in isolation, as is done by Childs and others, they wrongly appear mutually exclusive or contradictory.

---

1. The language is not his, but the appropriateness of the description seems undeniable in view of, e.g., his discussion of "Classic Earlier Approaches to Biblical Theology" in *Biblical Theology of the Old and New Testaments* (Minneapolis: Fortress, 1992) 30-31, cf. 725. To keep this conversation with Childs contemporary, in this essay I cite none of his publications earlier than *Biblical Theology*.

Childs grants on at least one occasion that his own work can be called "postcritical" (*ibid.*, 99). The difficulty of speaking simply of "critical retrieval," as some might prefer, is that this risks seeming oxymoronic to those for whom modern biblical criticism is by definition opposed to premodern interpretation and therefore also to its retrieval. In addition to avoiding this confusion, "postcritical" has the advantage of being the more common label for the kind of enterprise this essay discusses.

As a theologian, I lack the competence to deal with specifically exegetical isssues and shall therefore limit myself to theory or second-order reflection. Theory, however, only partially reflects actual practice, and in biblical studies as elsewhere, good scholars do better and poor scholars worse than what is mandated by the models they think of themselves as following. Yet while weakness in models does not necessarily translate into exegetical deficiency, it nevertheless hinders communication with those whose *forte* is theory. It is, then, the desire for better communication between theologians and biblical scholars that prompts the present critique. This critique has to do with theory and does not help with first-order interpretation in the absence of the appropriate exegetical skills and training, but perhaps it will contribute to the wider theological diffusion of the work of retrieval done by Prof. Childs and by the others whom we shall consider.

The three models we shall compare share a common commitment to recovering the premodern interpretation of the Old and New Testaments as a canonical whole while at the same time maintaining the modern critical awareness of their internal diversity and of their differences from each other. Despite their similar aim, however, these modes differ sharply in primary focus. What each chiefly interprets Scripture for is, respectively, (1) witness, (2) narrationally structured symbolic worlds, and (3) authorial discourse.

For reasons that have already been indicated, Brevard Childs is the inescapable example of the first mode, that is, of interpretation of Scripture in its canonical wholeness for its witness to God's reality. In reference to the second mode, canonical interpretation for narrationally structured symbolic worlds, Richard Hays's *The Moral Vision of the New Testament*[2] is the most comprehensive available illustration. It typifies the problems Childs thinks are present in whole or in part in the works of (to mention only those with Yale connections) Hans Frei *(requiescat in pacem)*, David Kelsey, Wayne Meeks, Stanley Hauerwas, and myself.[3] These authors differ and sometimes disagree among themselves and with Richard Hays, but they nevertheless contribute in various ways and degrees to his hermeneutical approach. The choice of Nicholas Wolterstorff as representative of the third mode, that of canonical interpretation for authorial discourse, is also inevitable, though for different reasons. His book *Divine Discourse: Philosophical Reflections on the Claim that God Speaks*[4] is the first and so far the only

2. San Francisco: Harper, 1996.

3. For Childs's references in his most recent relevant work to each of these authors (including Hays) see especially the index of *Biblical Theology*.

4. Cambridge/New York: Cambridge University Press, 1995.

articulation of this model, which, neverthless, may in practice be the classically dominant one.

II. Classic Hermeneutics

If all data is theory-laden, as is now commonly said, there can be no description of the classic hermeneutics which is equally compatible with each of the modes of canonical interpretation we have just listed. This difficulty may be diminished, however, by the use of a description dating from before the time when canonical interpreters began thinking of their differences as disagreements. This was not very long ago; Childs indicates that in the early eighties, in contrast to his present views, he "greeted largely as an ally the growing twentieth-century appeal to narrative theology as at least a move toward recovering a holistic reading of the Bible" (*Biblical Theology,* 722f.).

The description I shall use is drawn from unpublished lectures of mine delivered in 1988, that is, during the years to which Prof. Childs refers in the quotation just cited. This description is both more homiletical and more schematic than is usual in a scholarly article, but it has the merit of being unaffected by later controversies. Its initial section outlines under numbered heads and subheads a variety of interpretive strategies which were traditionally discussed separately but which need to be considered jointly when retrieval is the goal. "Classic hermeneutics" was at that time a neologism but now seems reasonably familiar as a term of art. This ten-year-old description constitutes the remainder of this section.

Before defining "classic hermeneutics," an introductory remark may be helpful. Whatever else we know or do not know about the original or classic Christian way of interpreting Scripture, we are all aware that it developed before there was a New Testament. All Christians had at first was the Jewish Bible, which they now call the Old Testament. It was to this that Paul referred when he said that Scripture was written for our learning so that through it we might have hope (Rom. 15:4); and it was these sacred writings that, according to 2 Timothy, are able to make us wise unto salvation through the faith in Christ Jesus and are profitable in their entirety for teaching, reproof, correction, and instruction in righteousness (3:15-16). The Jewish Bible, needless to say, could do these things for Christians only if it was read in a special way: only if it was read in the light of what were at first the unwritten stories of Jesus. In sum and substance, this is what the classic heremeneutics consisted of: the use of the stories about Jesus as the interpretive key. Jesus was first, of course, the key to the Old Testament, but when the New Testament canon was formed, he was the center of that also. Let us see in more detail how this worked.[5]

My first heading is that the Bible was read as a single book, a unified canon. Whenever we read a book as a unified work, however, we in effect treat it as self-interpreting: we understand one part by reference to other parts. This was done on a massive scale with Scripture: it functioned as an interlocking, inter-glossing, self-referential whole.

In the second place, it was the realistic narrative meaning of Scripture that was the main unifying ingredient, the glue that held the whole together. The overarching unity of the Bible was its story of God's dealings with his world and his people from the beginnings until the end, from Genesis to Revelation. It was within this framework, this story-shaped universe, that the prophetic protests, the wisdom literature, and the poetry (or, as many people now say, the symbols and myths) were understood.

Third, the stories of Jesus were central. It was in the accounts of his life, death, and resurrection taken in their plain sense that the meaning of the whole was most fully manifest. They were the interpretive key. Any way of using Scripture that contradicted the identity and character of Jesus and Jesus' God as depicted in these focal narratives was to be rejected.

Fourth, the main device for unifying the story of Jesus with the Old Testament tales of Israel was typological interpretation. Israel is said in the New Testament, you remember, to be a type of Christ and, in a rather different way, of the church. What happened to Israel is the type, what happened to Christ is the antitype; Israel is the promise, Christ is the fulfillment.

Here two subheads need to be introduced. Under subhead (a) it needs to be emphasized that in the earliest period it was Christ alone together with the final kingdom he proclaimed that is the antitype or fulfillment of the type and promise, which is Israel. Christians as individuals and as the church live in the time between the times when the kingdom has begun in Christ but is not yet fully manifest. Thus Christians now participate in the fulfillment in anticipatory and incomplete ways. Unlike the incarnate, crucified, and resurrected Lord, they are not, to repeat, the antitype or fulfillment of Israel. Forgetting this point has been the source of much antisemitism and of other forms of Christian triumphalism.

Under the next subheading (b), it must be stressed that the type-

---

5. The following sentences were part of the lecture as originally delivered: "Those of you, by the way, who are familiar with the work of my colleague at Yale, Mr. Hans Frei, will notice how deeply indebted I am to his understanding of the classic interpretive pattern. I think he would agree with what I am about to say, but I do spell it out rather differently."

antitype or promise-fulfillment relationship is interpretively a two-way street. Not only does one need Jesus in order to understand the Old Testament, but one needs the Old Testament to understand Jesus. A fulfillment is meaningless without a promise. A prize cannot be received if one does not know about raffles and unless the bit of paper in one's pocket is the winning ticket. Simlarly, the Jewish Bible was essential to the early Christians. It told them who Jesus was; it provided them his fundamental and abiding identity description. It was not a ladder that could be disposed of once the goal was reached in Christ.

These first four main points have to do with explicating the internal meaning of the text. One does this by treating the Bible, in sum, as a single book, unified by narratives, of which the story of Jesus is central, and by typological interpretation. Now we come to a fifth point: the application of the text to things outside it.

Under this fifth point, there are again two subheadings. Subhead (a) is a reminder that application for the early Christians was a matter of absorbing all reality into the text. They lived imaginatively in the world projected by Scripture and interpreted everything they were and knew within that framework. One can also say that their applications were intratextual, a matter of inscribing external realities into the text. Or one could use Calvin's metaphor and speak of the Bible as the glasses or lenses through which the eyes of faith perceive the universe. For the early Christians, not to mention many later ones, the stories of Israel and Israel's God interpreted in the light of Christ defined the cosmos in which they dwelled. They read Scripture in order to hear the blessings and the curses, the warnings and the consolations of Israel's God, whom they understood as also, and definitively, Jesus' God. The circumstances and ways of thinking of the early Christians were vastly different from those of Sarah and Abraham, Moses and Miriam, Ruth and her great-grandson David, but they reenvisioned their own thoughts and situations from the perspective of the dealings of Jesus' God with these Old Testament figures. Thus the Bible interpreted them perhaps even more than they interpreted the Bible. Scripture absorbed them and their world into itself.

Under subhead (b) we note that although this reenvisioning of all things present and future in heaven and earth in the light of the biblical stories of God's dealings with his people and his world has historically been given such special names as "tropological" and "anagogical," it is a mistake to separate it sharply from typological interpretation. To be sure, when Old Testament types are applied to later Christians, these Christians are not to be understood as antitypical, as fulfillment. As we earlier noted, only Jesus Christ is that. As far as Christians were concerned, the Old Testament stories and personages, when interpreted in Christ, are prototypical. They function in any number of figural modes as examples, models, paradigms, parables, and analogies for self, situation, and action. They provide indispensable guidance for life's way. Traditionally expressed, one could perhaps say that typological tropology or tropological typology was the chief interpretive strategy for making the Bible contemporary, for absorbing one's own world into the world of the text.

All of these interpretive devices are to some extent familiar even in contemporary practice. They are to be found in the liturgical and devotional uses of Scripture. Much preaching, especially black preaching, is full of them. But in the early church they were employed much more massively and at times expertly than in any of our contemporary Christian traditions. The theological retrieval of the classic hermeneutics is much to be desired if it is at all possible.

III. Interpreting for Witness

Interpreting Scripture for its witness to God in his dealings with his creatures is an inseparable part of premodern Bible reading, and no responsible attempt at retrieval can exclude it. It can be amply accommodated, as we shall have occasion to note, in both of the other postcritical modes of classic hermeneutics with which we are concerned.

Its role and importance vary, however; only the first mode makes this aspect of scriptural interpretation primary. In acknowledged dependence on Karl Barth, Prof. Childs holds, if I understand him rightly, that all the biblical writings are to be construed theologically first of all as witnesses, although that might not be their literary genre. Moreover, each is a fallible witness in no way distinguishable in this respect from all other products of the human hand and mind. Yet they bear in their canonical unity reliable "testimony to divine reality" (*Biblical Theology*, 98) found fully "in Jesus Christ in the combined witness of the two testaments" (85). It is primarily by interpreting Scripture as witness that "those who confess Christ" struggle "to understand the nature and will of the One who has already been revealed as Lord" (86).

As is suggested by this initial statement, Scripture is conceived as witness in this outlook in such a way as to make possible the double affirmation that the Bible is an entirely human book fully subject to historical criticism and yet one whose content or message is divine. Thus is overcome "the legacy of Enlightenment . . . the theological impasse reached at the end of the nineteenth century" by being "more critical than the critics! . . . all Scripture

31

suffers from human frailty; there is no untainted position . . . the church approaches its scripture in the confidence that in spite of its total time-conditionality the true witness of the gospel can be heard in the sacred text through the continuing work of the Spirit" (*Biblical Theology*, 215).

Two other reasons for favoring the primacy of witness are dogmatic rather than apologetic; they are part of the inner logic of the faith rather than replies to objections from outside. First, God's freedom in making Jesus Christ the only fully true Word of God is compromised unless one is clear that other human words, including the biblical ones, are not truly, not literally, divine. To say that "the Bible has the attribute of being the Word of God" is "to violate the Word of God which is God himself — to violate the freedom and sovereignty of God" (Barth, *Church Dogmatics* I/2, 513). This is Barth's main reason for insisting on the wholly nondivine, the wholly human character of the Bible. Childs does not disagree, but he does not have occasion to stress this point. A second consideration, however, is important for both authors. Witnesses are those who point outward to something other than themselves. To take this pointing seriously, as every retrievalist must, is to escape the anthropocentric and/or subjectivist reductionism of contemporary hermeneutical strategies, which make God dependent on human needs and desires. Unless Scripture is read as fundamentally testimony, it will not lead us to encounter God as did our ancestors in the faith, namely, as utterly objective, the reality independent of human needs and desires, on whom, conversely, human beings and all creatures are completely dependent.

Childs's chief complaint against the mode of retrieval we shall next consider is that it does not sufficiently maintain this objectivity. But before turning to that mode, we need first to note a problem internal to interpreting the Bible primarily for witness.

It is not clear that doing so is anywhere near as successful in providing guidance to Christian communities as its proponents would like to think. To the extent Scripture is construed as pointing Godward, it does not directly address human beings. It becomes rather a means God uses to create the conditions in which he speaks commands that are specific to each individual in his or her particular circumstances. It is true that similar commands will generally be issued under similar circumstances and that departures from the Decalogue or the Sermon on the Mount, for example, are not to be lightly undertaken, but in view of God's freedom, exceptions are possible. No general principles can be formulated, it seems, on the basis of which exceptionalist claims can be communally approved or disproved.

Childs is aware of this difficulty. In explicit agreement with Barth, he observes that the Bible is "the unique vehicle by which we are brought face-to-face with the person of God and the revelation of his will." This implies that it "can never function as a source to the will of God apart from his own active living communication."[6] From this follows a "major criticism. . . . Is there only a vertical, punctiliar dimension? Is the appeal to a direct, charismatic experience? Above all, does this approach not rule out of court any attempt to formulate normative ethics?" Correctives can be offered in response to these objections, not least among which would be "more careful attention to the role [as Childs develops it] of the canon's shaping of scripture" (*Biblical Theology,* 713-14). One may readily grant the importance of such modifications for exegetical practice, however, and yet doubt that they help save the theory. Indeed, from the perspective of the second mode of interpretation, to which we now turn, the theory is superfluous; its values, which are significant, can also be derived as well or better from other sources.

IV. Interpretation for Narrationally Structured Symbolic Worlds

For Prof. Hays, whom we are taking as representative of the second mode, Barth's often admirable first-order contributions are not at all dependent on the primacy in his second-order thought of interpreting Scripture for witness; the kind of narrative interpretation for which Barth is preeminent could have been developed in some other framework, or perhaps could itself serve as the canonically unifying category (as it indeed does in the classic hermeneutics as this was earlier described). Biblical narrative is fundamental for the shaping of Christian life. "By virtue of his attentiveness to narrative patterns, Barth values the biblical stories as paradigms. . . . In particular, the story of Jesus Christ functions in Barth's theology as the single definitive template for obedience and authentic humanity. The 'identity of authority

---

6. As could be expected, much the same point regarding the exegetically crucial role of personal encounter with God that is here made in reference to ethics also holds for dogmatic construals such as the christological interpretation of such Old Testament passages as Isaiah 53. "Crucial to this reading is the recognition that the interpreter's fuller grasp of God's reality which he brings to the biblical text is not a collection of right doctrine or some moral idea, but a response to a living God who graciously lets himself be known. Much of the success of such an exegesis depends on how well God's presence has been understood. There is no objective criterion by which this knowledge can be tested beyond the reality of God himself. If the church confesses that the spirit of God opens up the text to a perception of its true reality, it also follows that the Spirit also works in applying the reality of God in its fullness to an understanding of the text" (*Biblical Theology,* 382).

and freedom' that is accomplished in the person of Jesus Christ 'becomes normative for what is demanded of us.'" This centrality of narrative leads to an understanding of the symbolic world projected by Scripture that lends itself, speaking metaphorically, to indwelling. "One might describe Barth's whole theological project as a resolute effort to place himself and his readers in 'the strange new world within the Bible'" (Hays, *Moral Vision*, 237). The result is "a powerful account of the identity and action of God, who claims us through Jesus Christ for covenant partnership" (238). Looked at from this angle, it was Barth's methodological commitment to describing the biblical world from the inside that enabled him to perceive the centrality of stories, especially those telling of Jesus, for identifying and characterizing the biblical God. This identifying and characterizing function of stories is describable as a witnessing or testifying, but could it not be equally well described in other ways, and are these the most helpful terms to apply to Scripture as a whole?

Answering the last question in the negative need not lead to a derogation of witness, but to its relocation and redescription. It can be motivationally rather than interpretively primary. Searching the Bible to find the God to whom it testifies may be the motivation without being the mode of interpreting Scripture. Thus interpreters as diverse as Machen and Bultmann, as fundamentalists and existentialists, may share the motive but not the mode of Barth's and Childs's approach. In short, from Hays's perspective, to push him a bit farther than he actually goes, it is better to describe Barth's practice (though not his theory) as that of interpreting Scripture for the symbolic world or worlds that it projects rather than for its witness. Discerning the content of the Bible's witness to God may prove to be materially central to the interpretive task, but that is a result, not a presupposition, of interpretation; it is, in other words, methodologically secondary.[7]

A clarification is in order before we proceed. "Symbolic" refers in the present discussion to representations of all kinds whether conceptual or imaginative, factual or fictive. It is not limited to expressive or idealistic sym-

---

7. Given Childs's unhappiness with the proliferation of what both he and Hays regard as misuses of narrative interpretation in recent theology and biblical studies, it is not surprising that he, unlike Barth, is not notable as a narrative exegete; his primary vocation is to interpret Scripture for the canonical shaping of its content. To lump this highly diverse content together under the rubric "witness," however, does not add clarity to his task.

It should also be observed that the Bible on the verbal level is for Barth chiefly "God's word in written form" rather than "witness." That this verbalization is not in accord with the content of Barth's position is, however, strongly argued by Wolterstorff (*Divine Discourse*, 63-74).

bolisms as happens, for example, in David Kelsey's *The Uses of Scripture in Recent Theology*,[8] where Tillich is contrasted with Barth as interpreting Scripture for its symbols rather than for its realistic narratives. From the perspective of the second mode, both Tillich and Barth are engaged in describing the symbolic world or worlds of the Bible, though in partly contradictory ways. One could equally well say, however, that they differ in their notions of the biblical universe of discourse, or semiotic or cultural-linguistic system, or projected world. The last term has the advantage (at least as used by Wolterstorff) of being precise and free of the expressivist overtones of "symbolic."[9] An example may help.

For those acquainted with the relevant train schedules, the sentence, "She left at 6:45 and arrived in the big city an hour and thirty-seven minutes later," projects the world of early morning commuters from New Haven to New York, but whether the projected world is here a part of a detective story or belongs to a veridical account of my neighbor's life (who in fact does make this daily commute) is left undecided. In going through the hypothetical manuscript in which this sentence occurs, readers will almost certainly encounter claims, usually implicit ones, about the projected world's ontological status, but that does not settle the issue of whether these claims are truthful and how they apply to either the details or the whole of the story.

The same considerations apply *mutatis mutandis* to interpreting the Bible for its projected world or worlds; such a program does not in principle either favor or oppose that emphasis on the objective reality of God that Brevard Childs fears it will diminish or deny. Everything depends, not on whether interpreters construe their task as that of describing a symbolic world from the inside, but on what they find once they have entered, and on whether that world is for them the most comprehensive of outlooks, which alone has within it the criteria for determining what is ultimately right or wrong, real or unreal. From the perspective of practitioners of the mode of interpretation we are now considering, this is an adequate response to the most troubling of the theological objections to it.

Among the nondefensive or positive reasons for adopting this interpretive mode, three in particular have to do with retrieval. First, retrieval is radically incomplete in the absence of attention to Scripture's symbolic worlds.

---

8. Philadelphia: Fortress, 1975.

9. Not that "projected" and "symbolic" worlds are synonymous. Wolterstorff has suggested in personal conversation that the latter term as it is used here in the description of the second mode tends to blur "projected world" with "projecting rhetoric." Even if this ambiguity were eliminated, however, the major difficulties with the second mode of interpretation as these are later described would still persist.

These worlds constitute the perceptual categories by means of which a believer apprehends reality, and they provide the concepts and images utilized both in describing realities outside the text and in responding to them. Jesus' Jewish contemporaries, for example, reacted to him, whether negatively or positively, in the context of first-century versions of the Old Testament universe they imaginatively and behaviorally inhabited. The approval or disapproval of non-Jews such as Pilate, on the other hand, was shaped by very different symbolisms and forms of life. Similarly, when contemporary Christians read the morning paper in the light of the Bible — as Barth and, by extension, Calvin recommend[10] — they place the news within the framework of the biblical world to the degree that they participate in it. This participation is for the most part implicit rather than explicit or, to use Polanyi's terms, tacit rather than focal. Like glasses, the Bible, to the extent that it functions as a symbolic world within which believers dwell, shapes and corrects their vision (and therefore also influences how they act), even when they do not know how the lenses are ground or, on occasion, are not aware of looking through them. To neglect these tacitly present projected worlds and focus only on what texts explicitly say or witness to is to ignore a major dimension of their meaning. (All good exegetes, needless to say, do in fact pay attention to symbolic worlds even when they profess not to, but inadequate theories, it may be surmised, do sometimes hinder practice.)

It follows, in the second place, that the meaning ascribed to texts is underdetermined to the extent that their use in shaping life and thought is unspecified. Or, to put it another way, the same sentences, concepts, and images say very different things and help project very different worlds depending on their use to shape thought and behavior. Their meanings are as numerous as the universes in which one can imagine them being significantly employed; and, conversely, what one thinks the life world and symbolic world of a text is will determine how one understands it. Wayne Meeks makes a similar though more limited point when he says that ascertaining the meaning of a text "entails the competence to act, to use, to embody" in particular social settings "the universe rendered or signalled by the text." Thus "the hermeneutical circle is not completed until it finds a fitting social setting."[11]

10. Calvin seems to be the first to coin what is now the commonplace phrase about viewing everything through the spectacles of Scripture.

11. See Wayne Meeks, "The Hermeneutics of Social Embodiment," *Harvard Theological Review* 79 (1986) 183-85. Cf. Nicholas Lash's thesis that "the fundamental form of the Christian interpretation of scripture is the life, activity, and organization of the be-

Thirdly, interpreting for symbolic worlds in correlation with forms of life increases the possibilities for scriptural guidance of the contemporary church. For those who read the Bible as projecting a narrationally structured world, analogical reasoning is of central applicative importance; it is the means by which the storied past becomes paradigmatic for the present. This is illustrated by the role, for example, of exodus imagery in the Old and New Testaments (e.g., Jesus as the lamb of God, etc.) not to mention its significance in postbiblical times down to present-day liberationists. Troped by the exodus, the story of Jesus becomes supremely normative for later Christians. Because God's will for Jesus depicted in the canonical narratives (and commented on in the epistles, etc.) is God's will for us, knowledge of the first gives knowledge of the second to the extent we make the proper analogical connections between Jesus in his symbolic and life-world setting and ourselves in our vastly different situation. Analogy is an integral part of what were classically called the spiritual senses of Scripture (now usually referred to by such names as figures, tropes, and metaphors), but such reasoning has fallen into disrepute, and not without reason. Protection against arbitrary analogizing was insufficient in premodern exegesis. Thomas Aquinas, joined in this by the Reformers, insisted on the primacy of the literal sense; but then in modern times, as we recall from Hans Frei's *Eclipse of Biblical Narrative*,[12] the meaning of the literal sense became hopelessly confused by, among other things, neglect of canonical meaning and the ignoring of symbolic in favor of purely ostensive referents.[13] In the view of someone like Hays, however, interpreting for narrationally structured symbolic worlds has now come to the rescue. Because of its modern historical-critical dimension, this approach makes possible more accurate analogizing, and the better the analogies the more powerful the guidance Scripture can provide. The second postcritical mode of interpretation, in other words, not only retrieves but also enhances the spiritual senses of the classic hermeneutics in their guiding function for the church.

The role of historical criticism in correcting and thus empowering the hermeneutical use of the analogical imagination needs illustration. A convenient example is Hays's critique of one of Barth's more far-fetched exegetical

---

lieving community." Lash, *Theology on the Way to Emmaus* (London: SCM, 1986) 42. This insight, which seems undeniable, implies that symbolic and life worlds are inseparable; or, to use different terminology, one cannot properly interpret a text for the cultural-linguistic system it instantiates without inquiring about the form of life with which it is correlated, and vice versa.

12. New Haven: Yale University Press, 1974.

13. Readers will recognize that this is in part interpretation rather than simple reiteration of Frei's thesis.

flights. Barth holds that Christian ethics is constrained by a mandate comparable to that "given to Israel to occupy the land of Canaan. . . . The Word of
God has invaded the world, and human reason can only bow before it. The
task . . . must be to proclaim and explicate the Word, 'taking every thought
captive to obey Christ'" (Hays, *Moral Vision*, 226-27, cf. 237). For Barth, this
is a direct rather than analogically mediated scriptural injunction; but Hays
understandably thinks this is a mistaken classification and treats the appeal to
the conquest of Canaan as an intriguing bit of analogical reasoning. He dis-
agrees with its prescription, but not because there is anything wrong in the
logic of thus using the conquest of Canaan interpreted through Jesus Christ,
the one on whom the canon centers, as a metaphor with which to trope Christian ethics, but because Barth's description of the biblical universe is flawed.
Barth does not sufficiently allow for the diversity of the biblically projected
symbolic worlds, some of which accord a greater role in ethics to reason and
experience than Barth admits. His error — with which Childs, by the way,
cannot be charged — is that "because he did most of his writing before the development of redaction criticism, he gives little attention to the individual
theological perspectives" of the biblical writers (*Moral Vision*, 235). Thus he
confuses the unity of the canon with uniformity and, despite his, in Hays's
view, marvelously innovative exegetical imaginativeness, he makes scriptural
directives less flexible, less contextually adaptable, than they really are. He has
to appeal to what Hays regards as, in effect, arbitrary private revelations (232)
in order to introduce the necessary exceptions into what otherwise are impos-
sibly exceptionless divine commands. Modern biblical scholarship, it seems,
can correct both the arbitrariness in origin and rigidity in use of analogical insights and can thus help in the recovery of classic hermeneutics.

This is possible, however, only if the problem of canonical diversity, of
which redactional criticism has made us vividly aware, can be solved. If it can
be solved, the troping of our contemporary embattled worlds by the common symbolic universe of Scripture could generate for Christians a realm of
discourse in which polarizations are attenuated, consensus-building facilitated, and conversation becomes civil even when disagreements remain.

Few think, however, that this happy outcome is in the offing. Hays himself points out that Wayne Meeks, the most highly regarded expositor of
Scripture for its symbolic and correlative life worlds,[14] denies that the vari-

14. Meeks's three books, *The First Urban Christians: The Social World of the Apostle
Paul* (New Haven: Yale University Press, 1983); *The Moral World of the First Christians*
(Philadelphia: Westminster, 1986); and *The Origins of Christian Morality: The First Two
Centuries* (New Haven: Yale University Press, 1993), all illustrate this approach.

ous New Testament worlds, not to mention the Old Testament ones, can be "synthesized" into some kind of "unity of ethical perspective" (Hays, *Moral Vision,* 4); and given the inseparability of the symbolic and life worlds on which he insists, Meeks would be equally skeptical about descriptively synthesizing their theological perspectives. Without a synthesis, however, it becomes impossible to appeal to Scripture as a whole for the contemporary guidance of the church. The canon threatens to become a grab-bag in which searchers pick and choose according to whim[15] or, less pejoratively, in accordance with extrabiblical principles. The choices tend to range between the three poles of ecclesiastical magisterium, unchanging communal tradition, and private interpretation or, more concretely and inaccurately expressed, Rome, Constantinople, and Wittenberg/Geneva. Representatives of each of these tendencies often claim in our ecumenical age to adhere to *sola scriptura* in the sense of the Bible being the ultimate authority, but this may simply imply a commitment (which may or may not have significant procedural consequences) to finding some kind of biblical legitimation for whatever is decided on other grounds. The nineteenth-century theological impasse to which, it will be recalled, Brevard Childs refers has not disappeared. Scripture continues to have a wax nose. Extrabiblical factors determine the direction in which it points, and the Reformation wish to read the Bible as the self-interpreting guide of the church remains a dream. As is evident from such considerations, much hinges on whether the diverse biblical symbolic worlds can be persuasively synthesized.

Nor does it help to distinguish, as Meeks does, between "normative" (which would include theologically based) syntheses and "historical" or "descriptive" ones and concede the possibility of the first but not the second (Meeks, *Origins of Christian Morality,* 3-4). The contemporary difficulty is greater than this observation suggests; those who largely agree in doctrine, theology, ethics, and even ecclesiology are regularly at odds on how to interpret Scripture. Hays approvingly quotes from an unpublished paper I wrote evaluating his synthetic proposal, which says that it is "'dependent on the

---

15. In a personal conversation Krister Stendahl once used this language (except for the word "whim") to explain why maintaining the wholeness of the canon is important; unlike Kaesemann's "canon within the canon," it maintains rather than limits the range of options available to Christians. Ray Brown's book, *The Churches the Apostles Left Behind* (New York: Paulist, 1984) is a parade example of this approach to canonical unity, except that in the case of the Roman Catholic Brown, in contrast to the Lutheran Stendahl, it is the magisterium rather than personal or popular opinion that determines which of the biblically authorized and unharmonizable (though not directly contradictory) options need to be utilized in given circumstances.

mainstream Christian tradition of canonical reading that goes back to Irenaeus' and that it articulates a theological framework 'fully consistent with the christological, trinitarian, and anti-Marcionite decisions of the church'" (*Moral Vision*, 198-99). What I said about Hays applies equally well to the work of Brevard Childs; nor are the two authors far apart on the major practical or ethical issues of our day (except, perhaps, for pacifism). Yet they disagree fundamentally in their theological devices for unifying canonical outlooks and on the scriptural warrants for the contemporary guidance of Christian life and thought, even when they largely agree on what that guidance should be (as they seem usually to do). Agreement on *what* Scripture says combined with disagreement on *how* to derive it from Scripture was once exceptional but is now widespread across the spectrum of Christian opinion from right to left. Such methodological chaos, however, shifts authority, contrary to the intentions of ecclesially-oriented interpreters, from the Bible to private preference. It seems that disagreements over interpretive modes even more than over doctrinal content are at the heart of the present crisis of biblical authority.

V. Interpreting for Authorial Discourse: Diagnosis

Nicholas Wolterstorff suggests a fresh though not unparalleled diagnosis of the crisis, and makes a proposal for its solution which he rather ruefully admits has no precedents. The diagnosis depends on two theses that, while not without antecedents when considered separately, have not before, as far as I know, been joined together. The first thesis, directed against Ricoeur (Wolterstorff, *Divine Discourse*, 130-52), has affinities to Derrida and deconstructionism; it holds that "there's no such thing as the sense of a text" (171). To explicate this thesis (which in its outcome is not in the least Derridian) would unduly prolong this essay, but its general character is conveyed by a summarizing sentence: "If the only requirement for arriving at the sense of a text is that, given the meanings of the sentences *per se* and their position in the text, one arrives at a consistent meaning which can in principle function as the neomatic content of someone's discourse, then no text has one sense, but all have a huge number of senses" (173).

In attempting a nontechnical explanation, I shall use my own example. Instead of reading Swift's *Modest Proposal* as satire, one might take it as a serious recommendation to cannibalize Irish infants. In this case, the neomatic content (which in the terminology of the second mode of interpretation includes the projected or symbolic world) would change radically even while

40

the dictionary meaning of every word and sentence is accounted for. Any number of deconstructive interpretations can also be generated simply by mixing serious and satirical senses so that each subverts the other in a variety of ways. Nor is it difficult to imagine IRA fanatics supposing that the *Proposal* was at one time official policy; and, if so, they would treat it as a source of historical information about British atrocities. The possibilities seem endless, just as the thesis maintains.[16]

Wolterstorff's difference from the deconstructionists is that he grants only that their interpretive mode is just as possible as others; he does not go on, as they do, to give this mode privileged or hegemonic status (*Divine Discourse,* 169). If all interpretation is text-immanent, there is no reason to regard one type of interpretation, whether deconstructionist or nondeconstructionist, as superior to others. Wolterstorff's conclusion is that decision between interpretations requires exiting the text. It is only by considering such extratextual factors as the particular use of a text in particular circumstances for particular purposes that one can discover its determinate signification. The problem of how to get out of the text is the crucial one that needs to be solved, but before discussing that difficulty and Wolterstorff's solution, the second step preparatory to his diagnosis needs to be looked at.

This step is Wolterstorff's analysis of what is involved in interpreting for "a" rather than "the" meaning of a text. It is to engage in what he calls "performance interpretation" on analogy with the interpretation of, for example, a musical score by the way in which it is played or performed (*Divine Discourse,* 171-82). It is helpful to think of the suggested construals of Swift's *Proposal* as distinctive performances of one and the same score, and as therefore comparable to, for example, spritely or solemn renderings of a given piece.[17] In abstraction from extratextual considerations such as use, no one type of literary construal (that is, no performance interpretation) is privileged over the others, just as is the case for musical performance interpretations. In both genres, to be sure, particular performances (or, to use the musical term, "realizations") of a given interpretation may vary greatly in quality, but the distinction here, it will be observed, is between good and bad rather than true or false. This is a logically crucial point that is understandably easier to overlook in the case of texts than of musical scores. Auditors

---

16. Another illustration, once again my own, is too intriguing to omit. Satan twists Scripture to his own ends, the Bible tells us. To the degree that this implies that he can consistently interpret the canon as a whole for his evil purposes, Wolterstorff's thesis is scripturally supported.

17. This oversimple example is not Wolterstorff's, but his elaborately precise illustrations are not fully intelligible to those, like myself, who are not musical *cognoscenti*.

who knew nothing of history, Swift, or standard ways of interpreting his works might very well be persuaded by a verbally faithful and particularly eloquent reading of the *Proposal* that it was not satire but a serious recommendation that had been brutally enacted. They would have made the fatal mistake of supposing that a performance interpretation based, as it by definition is, on only one of the many possible senses of a text can be true or false rather than simply felicitous or infelicitous.

A third consideration not discussed by Wolterstorff[18] is needed before we turn to the implied diagnosis of the crisis in biblical authority. Correspondence or lack of correspondence to extratextual reality can decide the truth or falsity of some performance interpretations of some texts, but not of others. The Swiftian example just cited belongs to the first type; the reading of the *Proposal* as a brutal recommendation rather than as a satire is decisively falsified for most people by its irreconcilability with extratextual history. Similarly, to switch examples, those who save biblical inerrancy by construing Jonah as a parabolic story rather than a report do so because performing the text as a report involves projecting what they regard as a false picture of the ancient Near East (not to mention whales). There are also instances of the second type, however; there are some performances of some texts that project worlds so comprehensive that there is nothing outside with which to compare them; each one absorbs, so to speak, all relevant reality.

Performance interpretations of sacred writings provide examples of this type, but so also may performances of such texts as Shakespeare's *Hamlet*. Its scope and complexity, among other things, lend themselves to performance interpretations which project all-embracing worlds. Classic, romantic, and psychoanalytic traditions of performing this play have developed over the centuries, and each of these traditions incorporates and projects a distinctive and comprehensive vision of reality in which the influence of text and interpretive perspective is reciprocal; the vision is, for example, both romanticized Shakespeare and Shakespeareanized romanticism. Some realizations of each of these visions skillfully interpret Shakespeare's text, while others do so clumsily, and this makes it possible to compare the quality of individual realizations (that is, performances) from the different traditions providing they agree sufficiently on extratextual standards of dramatic excellence. When it comes to truth, however, there are no shared criteria. Dramas

18. And for good reason. Agreement on a correspondence view of truth, on which this third consideration depends, is itself intentional. Appeal to it when discussing interpretation cannot be separated from appeals to authorial intention; and it is only because we have not yet discussed these that it here appears as a distinct, a third, consideration.

are praised for being "true to life," but the Aristotelian, Wordsworthian, and Freudian worldviews embedded and projected in their respective performance interpretations shape notions of what is morally, experientially, and ontologically true into sometimes radically different concrete forms. Thus what is advanced as a truth claim in one of these interpretive traditions registers as a value preference from the perspectives of the others. There is no world outside the text common to the three perspectives we have been considering to serve as a criterion for judging whether Hamlet played as a classic tragic hero is "true to life." Unless some fourth perspective or framework is agreed upon, the question of what is true to life has to be decided from within the tradition of classic performance interpretations.

The picture that results from applying this analysis to Scripture is not without parallels, as was earlier mentioned. For David Kelsey, as cited approvingly by Hays, a *discrimin,* as he calls it, does much the same work in much the same way as a performance interpretation. "Every theological reading of Scripture depends on 'a single synoptic, imaginative judgment' in which the interpreter 'tries to catch up what Christianity is basically all about'" and which "not only shapes 'decisions about how to construe and use particular passages of scripture' but also governs 'the sort of wholeness each [theologian] concretely ascribes to Scripture.' In other words, the unity and sense of Scripture can be grasped only through an act of metaphorical imagination that focuses the diverse contents of the texts in terms of a particular 'imaginative characterization'" (Hays, *Moral Vision,* 194).[19] The conceptual vocabulary is different, but the resemblances of a *discrimin* to a performance interpretation are obvious. In both cases, the picture that emerges is one of apparently self-enclosed hermeneutical universes isolated not only from each other but from extratextual reality. In such approaches, "talk about 'text' stands in place of talk about 'God.'"[20]

It is because of such considerations, it will be recalled, that Childs rejects the second mode of interpretation we are considering. Wolterstorff is also unhappy with it, but this does not entail agreement with Childs. The reply to Childs from the perspective of the second mode is one that Wolterstorff could adopt; practitioners of the first mode, such as Barth and

---

19. Hays is quoting here from Kelsey's *The Uses of Scripture in Recent Theology* (Philadelphia: Fortress, 1975) 163, 167, 197 in support of his synthesizing of diverse biblical symbolic worlds. The notion of performance interpretation, he observes, can be utilized to the same end (*Moral Vision,* 189), though he had not had opportunity to read Wolterstorff's book (cf. *ibid.,* 191, note 3).

20. R. Thiemann, "Reponse to George Lindbeck," *Theology Today* 43 (1986) 378, cited in Childs, *Biblical Theology,* 22.

Childs, are enclosed in a performance interpretation (that is, symbolic world or *discrimen*) of their own that construes the whole of Scripture as "witness," and they are therefore in fact performing in accordance with the second mode without knowing it. Hans Frei, according to Wolterstorff, was in a similar predicament up until shortly before his death, when he recognized that interpreting the Gospels for their "literal sense," that is, for the stories that, when understood as realistic narratives "present to us the enactment by Jesus of Nazareth of his identity as Messiah" (*Divine Discourse,* 231, cf. 229-36), is simply one option among others. Wolterstorff approves of Frei's choice of realistic narrative, as he does of Barth's choice of witness, as hermeneutically appropriate for some though not all parts of Scripture; but this leaves untouched the issue of how one decides. Neither mode of interpretation helps in answering that question. For both, choices between alternative patterns of canonical construal are intratextually arbitrary; one must exit the text in order to find grounds for decision; and as to how one does that they seem to have no hermeneutically usable answers.

The problem of hermeneutical arbitrariness or undecidability is not confined to sacred texts, but it is there that it is most acute. In reference to the arts, most people resist exclusive preferences between types of performance. They may be convinced Freudians or Aristotelians and yet enjoy performances that depict Hamlet as neither oedipal nor classical but as a romantic tragic hero. As was earlier mentioned, what counts aesthetically is whether a given rendition is skillful (that is, among other things, "true to the text"), not whether the interpretation it renders is true *per se.* In canonical construals of the Christian Scriptures, in contrast, decision is imperative. If the primary aim is the moral guidance of communal and personal life rather than aesthetic enrichment, something much worse than literary pluralism ensues when choice is not made among contrary interpretative traditions; community itself disintegrates and the breach with the mainstream hermeneutical tradition becomes irreparable. That tradition cannot be retrieved apart from settling on which performance interpretations of Scripture in its canonical wholeness are compatible with the truth of the gospel; but it is the chaos of opinion on how to answer precisely that question that is at the heart of the contemporary crisis of biblical authority.

This crisis, it scarcely needs to be said, is primarily on the level of theory, but it has practical repercussions. While these are troubling for all ecclesially oriented interpreters, they are especially severe among Protestants of Reformation persuasion who, like Childs and Hays, are concerned about postcritical retrieval for the sake of the church. They want to maintain that the Bible is in some significant sense self-interpreting, that it corrects rather than simply serving church and tradition, and that it resists being taken captive by culture or philosophy (which remain now, as in the days of early Gnosticism, the main sources for the proliferation of interpretations). Others have hermeneutical reasons for failing to exit the text, but such Protestants have theological reasons as well. How can Scripture be self-interpreting if something outside the text decides how it is to be interpreted? This dilemma was always a problem for the heirs of Luther and Calvin, but now it seems unresolvable. The theoretical crisis threatens to become a practical cataclysm, as the decline of the historically mainline denominations suggests.

VI. Interpreting for Authorial Discourse: Appropriation

Unlike the diagnosis implied by his work, Wolterstorff's solution has no parallels or precedents. He argues that Scripture should be thought of as God's word, God's discourse, in a sense more direct, more literal, than that conceived by plenary-inspiration inerrantist fundamentalists, not to mention such cautious formulators of the concept as Karl Barth. That is the theological scandal of his position. On the hermeneutical side, he scandalizes the theorists by contending that meaning is determined by the author's intentions, thus in their eyes committing the mortal sin of affirming the intentional fallacy.

He considers himself justified in perpetrating the first of these outrages by one of the ordinary-language meanings of speech that was somehow overlooked down through the centuries when theologians discussed what might be meant by God, an incorporeal being, speaking, uttering words, engaging in discourse. Instead of formulating complicated theories of inspiration or revelation, why not simply utilize the commonplace notion of appropriated discourse?[21] The ancients were as familiar with this notion as we moderns. Plenipotentiaries sent abroad to speak in the name of their monarch issued promises, demands, threats, and reassurances formulated in words that were entirely their own and with no other guidance from their ruler than the general instruction to promote the welfare of the realm; yet both those addressed and the emissary's monarch treated those words as if they issued directly from

21. Wolterstorff, *Divine Discourse*, 51-54. For the sake of brevity, I give my own examples in what follows. Further, "complicated theories" are ultimately needed if one undertakes to answer philosophical questions about the created means (i.e., "second causes") whereby God appropriates human discourse, but in this approach, the theories come later rather than at the beginning.

her majesty's mouth. Similarly, the president's signature makes documents and letters conceived and written by others into his very own words. Or to take a more complex and not wholly fictitious example, someone tells me I can know what he has to say about the pseudo-Dionysius if I read Gerson's *Anagogicum* as commented by Combes in conjunction with Derrida's *Of Grammatology*, which, despite the author's often mistaken views, illuminates some otherwise opaque aspects of the Areopagite's thought. Finally, hypothesizing once again within the realm of verisimilitude, one of the woman members of the *Weisse Rose*, a student resistance group in Nazi Germany, lost her life because she told her questioner, when asked what she thought of the Final Solution, to go and read the book of Esther. Why not say, Wolterstorff in effect suggests, that Esther, the least explicitly godly book in the Bible, was and is God's word, appropriated by him through the process by which the canon was formed beginning over two thousand years ago, and now appropriated anew by a German girl scarcely in her twenties?[22]

How to circumvent one major obstacle to considering the Bible divine discourse is illustrated by these examples. It is often objected that God cannot literally speak by means of a book replete with factual, moral, and even theological falsity. The notion of appropriation, however, solves the difficulty. In the last of the above examples, "read the story of the queen of Persia, which comes just after Ruth" could perfectly well replace "read Esther" even though the two books are separated by three hundred pages in the Bible I have in front of me. Moreover, much that is in Esther, such as the royal marriage customs or the pogrom against the enemies of the Jews, was not what the young woman had in mind; and her Nazi questioners, however stupid they may have been, had no difficulty distinguishing what she herself was saying from what she was not saying by means of her appropriated discourse. One must always ask what the appropriator intends to say by means of the discourse he or she has appropriated.

VII. Interpreting for Authorial Discourse: Intention

This brings us, then, to the second scandal, Wolterstorff's apparent embrace of the intentional fallacy. Isn't it an obvious error to try to determine the

22. Note that when appropriated by the student, Esther again becomes human rather than divine discourse; her appropriation turned the book into her own human message about what she thought of the extermination of the Jews. On the other hand, however, her human act was done in obedience to what she, as a member of a fervently Catholic group, regarded as a scripturally mediated divine command.

meaning of texts by reference to what their authors intended, especially when they are not available for questioning? To speculate about authorial intention in distanciated speech or writing is to plunge into endless and fruitless speculation. Much better to stick to the sense of the text. Not to do so is to commit the mortal sin beyond repair, which is the intentional fallacy for much modern literary theory.

Wolterstorff employs speech action theory to deal with this dilemma (*Divine Discourse*, 75-94, 197-99). The theory goes back some forty years and is philosophically familiar, but it, like the notion of appropriated discourse, has not been applied before to biblical hermeneutics. Yet its import even if not its defense can perhaps be presented briefly by the use of commonsense examples (chiefly my own).

Two distinctions suffice to explain the difference between licit and fallacious interpretive appeals to authorial intention. The first distinction is between intending to act and an intentional action; there is all the difference in the world between Amy intending to put the kettle on and her actual performance of that act (*Divine Discourse*, 197). In reference to the particular kind of intentional action known as "speaking," a further distincton is needed, this time between speech acts proper, "illocutionary" actions, and the locutions or "locutionary" actions by which they are performed. Vast numbers of different locutions may be used to perform one and the same speech act; the illocutionary action of urging that a gladiator's life be spared, for example, can be performed in any natural or artificial language from English to Esperanto and beyond by making sounds, marks on paper, or gestures such as "thumbs up" at the arena in ancient Rome. In this schema, licit interpretation seeks the meaning of locutions in the intentional speech actions performed by means of locutions, while illicit interpretation seeks their meaning in acts of intending which may motivate or cause speech actions.

The fallaciousness of the latter strategy is sometimes blatant. Imagine Herod, for example, claiming that his order to behead John the Baptist had been misinterpreted. His deepest intention was to save John from death, and the true meaning of his command to kill was simply that he did not want to be shamed in front of his guests. Herod's wickedness was not quite of Nero-like proportions; if it had been, he would have executed the executioner for disobeying the true meaning of his original command to kill John. As can be seen from this example, interpreting for authorial intention when unprotected from the intentional fallacy results in much the same dilemma as does its opposite extreme, interpreting for the sense of the text. Meaning becomes undecidable, in one case because subjective intentions are endlessly debatable and, in the other, because there is no such thing as the sense of the text.

Yet the logic that prompts the intentional fallacy is pervasive in modern Romanticist interpretive theory,[23] and is largely responsible by way of reaction for the contemporary attempts to interpret without any reference of any kind to what authors or speakers intend. Even biblical scholars such as Childs and Hays assume that the canonical sense of Scripture is to be determined as much as possible without reference to what was intended by either God or its human authors. Fear of the intentional fallacy, it seems, prevents them from recognizing that their exegetical practice is (fortunately) full of appeals to authorial intention. They have no usable way of distinguishing between licit and illicit appeals; and in the absence of these, they are unable to explain how to exit the text to determine its meaning. What they need, it can be argued, are the distinctions provided by speech action theory; only thus can they escape the current crisis in biblical interpretation.

Escape is possible if the only appeals to authorial intention admitted into the interpretive process are those that help interpreters decide what speech acts are being performed by the locutions (the utterances or texts) that are being interpreted. "Could you pass the salt?" for example, is ambiguous; it is normally used to perform the speech act of asking someone to pass the salt, but grammatically it is an inquiry about the salt-passing ability of the person addressed. How resolve the doubt? By reference, so the answer goes, to which illocutionary act the speaker intended to perform by uttering those words. That intention and that alone determines the interpreter's choice of the first of the two speech acts as the one performed by the utterance in question. It would be a very abnormal speaker indeed who would intend any other speech act in the circumstances appropriate for the uttering of these words. Thus the appeal to intention is limited; it refers not to the speaker's acts of intending but only to her intentional acts. Perhaps she wanted to ask for sugar, but misspoke herself, or perhaps she intended to strike up a conversation; but such motivating or causal intentions are irrele-

---

23. According to "the expressionist (Romanticist) view" as described by Wolterstorff, speaking consists "in the intentional expression of inner states by way of uttering or inscribing some bit of language." After noting some major objections to this view, Wolterstorff says that it is not "devastated by these few brief and quick remarks"; if it were, it "wouldn't have been around so long" (*Divine Discourse*, 76). The same applies in spades to my far briefer comments. For an extended theological critique of the expressivist theories of revelation which have largely monopolized the scene in modern times see Ronald Thiemann, *Revelation and Theology: The Gospel as Narrated Promise* (Notre Dame: University of Notre Dame Press, 1985).

vant to interpreting what she actually said.[24] To suppose otherwise is to fall victim once again to the intentional fallacy. In short, the distinction to be maintained is between why and what, between the speaker's act of intending a speech act (why she spoke) and the speech act's intentionality (what she intended to say). Appeal to authorial intention in the first sense is illicit, an intentional fallacy, while in the second, it is not only legitimate but necessary; without this appeal there is no exit from the text, that is, no nonarbitrary way of discerning which of its many possible senses is the true or most plausible one.

VIII. Conclusion

The meager hints we have given as to what is involved in interpreting Scripture for authorial intention will have to suffice for the purposes of this essay. Its aim has been to suggest a possibility rather than to persuade or make fully intelligible. We would have to go into much more detail in what has already been said in order to make possible responsible assessment of this mode of interpretation, and, more than that, additional topics that have not even been mentioned would have to be dealt with. This is especially true of the understanding of language as a public and normative system in which speaking is primarily a matter of acquiring rights and responsibilities toward others rather than of expressing inner thoughts or states (Wolterstorff, *Divine Discourse*, 82-94) and, together with this, of the distinction between the neomatic and designative meaning or content of speech acts (138-39, 150-52). Further, the use of speech action theory in clarification and defense of traditional scriptural interpretation would need to be reviewed. Wolterstorff is clearly committed to what we have called the postcritical retrieval of classic hermeneutics, but he says little of the role of that hermeneutics in making of the Bible, to repeat Calvin's metaphor, the spectacles through which believers perceive and interpret the world.[25] For those who think of premodern inter-

---

24. Prof. Wolterstorff, who kindly read a draft of this essay, suggested that it might be helpful to insert in the above text some such sentence as the following: "We appeal to her intentionally implemented action plan while acknowledging that she might fail to implement it; the appeal is not to what motivated her attempt."

25. He touches on this role when he says "that the significance of the Bible goes beyond its being an instrument of divine discourse . . . the church has wanted to be so formed by the very phrases and images of scripture, the narratives and songs, the preachments and visions, that it sees reality and imagines possibilities through those phrases and images, through those narratives and songs, through those preachments

pretation in terms of the description at the beginning of this essay, this is a serious deficiency, but an easily correctable one on the theoretical level, as we shall shortly see. Beyond theory, however, is the decisive test, the usefulness of interpreting for authorial intention in actual scriptural exegesis, and on this work has yet to begin. Wolterstorff's comments in this regard are, as he would be the first to admit, philosophical suggestions not biblical scholarship. In short, the third mode of interpretation is at present a possible project rather than a reality.

Yet it is an intriguing possibility, one that those committed to retrieval would do well to take seriously. The theses it defends are integral to traditional practice: the Bible is literally God's word, divine discourse, and it must be interpreted for God's authorial intention; but the first has been denied in theory even by the tradition (which had no notion of appropriated discourse), and as far as postcritical enthusiasts for premodern interpretation are concerned, they have in theory even if not in practice ignored the second thesis because of their fear of the subjective abysses into which the intentional fallacy leads. The difficulties of understanding and accepting Wolterstorff's rehabilitation of authorial intention are great, but this, it seems to me, is because of its unfamiliarity. In principle, advocates of the first and second modes of interpretation we have considered should welcome it.

They should welcome it because, among other things, it accommodates and clarifies their own concerns. Childs's interpretation of Scripture for its witness is not denied but rather placed in a wider context that decreases its ambiguity and increases its force. No longer is the concept of witness stretched to the breaking point and beyond in order to cover Scripture as a whole, and it gains clarity by being restricted to that which is ordinarily thought of as witness. Nor does this restriction result in disempowerment; authorial intention in combination with appropriation makes it possible to understand those portions of Scripture that are literally human witnesses to God as also, in their appropriated form, quite literally God's self-witness. Further, on analogy with the New Testament appropriation of the Old (not to mention nonbiblical examples), what God says by the appropriated dis-

and visions." Like a poem, the Bible "offers stuff for our meditation, offers words for our voice, gives form to our consciousness, shapes our interpretation of life and reality" (*ibid.*, 185-86). This, however, is an isolated passage and does not begin to do justice, it seems to me, to the historical importance of living imaginatively within the world of the Bible; or, more precisely, within worlds which have been to one degree or another transformed by and absorbed into the biblical "symbolic universe" (which, be it noted, is never available in any pure or original form).

course is at times quite different from anything that the original writers had in mind; and yet what they intended is indispensable in seeking to understand what God intends by his use of them. Thus Childs's basic enterprise of canonical interpretation can be fully accommodated, as far as I can see, as well as being clarified and perhaps strengthened.

In reference to the second mode of interpretation, that also can be embraced and enhanced from the perspective of the third. If interpreting for symbolic worlds is a species of performance interpretation, as was earlier suggested, then the only way of escaping from pluralistic chaos is to seek to discern which of the available performances by which scripture can be synthesized into a whole is God's will for the church in particular times and places. Discernment is often difficult and always debatable, but interpreting for authorial intention provides criteria on how to proceed with the discussion where there was none before. It can help solve the problems of diversity inside and outside the canon by generating a realm of discourse for Christians in which polarizations are attenuated, consensus-building facilitated, and conversation becomes civil even when disagreements remain.

Finally, as Brevard Childs frequently reminds us, theologically fruitful interpretation does not happen apart from the guidance of the Holy Spirit. On the other hand, as he no less emphatically insists, the Holy Spirit enlightens the mind as well as warms the heart. All three of the authors we have taken as representative of three different modes of interpretation would like their work to be used by God both to enlighten and to warm; and it is in the hope that these wishes will be fulfilled that this essay is dedicated to Prof. Childs.

The Significance of Context in Theology: A Canonical Approach

Paul C. McGlasson

As Thomas Kuhn once forcefully argued,[1] it is a characteristic of brilliant new paradigms that they not only explain the specific problems they are designed to address; they likewise become the basis for a fresh grasp of broader issues in related fields of inquiry. Such is the nature of the work of Brevard S. Childs on canon. It is already clear that its significance reaches well beyond the field of biblical studies and includes dogmatics and ethics as well. It is my purpose here to argue that it is essential for a proper understanding of church history as well.

The present essay contains a theological argument concerning the much-debated issue of the significance of context in theology. The premise of the argument is that common approaches to the question of context are derived elsewhere than from the very theological reality that they are meant to explain; that is, they are usually derived from a philosophical or sociological base, and then applied to theology. The predictable outcome is that the history of theology is then "construed" to meet the requirements of the philosophical schema, with the result that no actual light is shed on the true understanding of context in theology. The argument here seeks, on the contrary, to follow the theological method of faith-seeking-understanding. First, we will investigate a series of six patterns of context in the history of theology. In each pattern, we will present an example of success and an example of

---

1. Thomas Kuhn, *The Structure of Scientific Revolutions* (Chicago: University of Chicago, 1970).

52

failure in theological response to context. Second, we will offer a theological argument concerning the significance of context in theology in the light of the patterns we have observed. The heart of the argument will be the indispensable role of canon for a true understanding of the actual dynamics of context in the history of theology. Third, we will conclude by offering a brief refutation of competing paradigms. The point here will be that apart from canon, the church's actual life with Scripture is completely misunderstood, whether on the theological left, the theological right, or from a mediating position.

I

The first pattern to be observed concerns the changing contexts during the lifetime of an individual theologian. In my judgment, the most striking case of an individual theologian who responded successfully to changing contexts was Martin Luther. Luther had a brilliant grasp of the change in theological fronts throughout his life, which necessitated a different response; and yet he was able at the same time to hold and articulate with enormous power the selfsame theological substance. From the wealth of material that could be adduced in this regard, the prefatory material from the 1519 *Lectures on Galatians* will be compared and contrasted with the prefatory material from the 1535 *Lectures on Galatians*.[2]

In the brief preface to the 1535 lectures it is clear that Luther himself is aware of changing contexts. On the one hand, the substance of the book of Galatians remains the same: the doctrine of faith. Moreover, Luther's estimation of its importance remains unchanged: "If it is lost and perishes, the whole knowledge of truth, life, and salvation is lost and perishes at the same time."[3] On the other hand, the danger is "clear and present" that the doctrine of faith will be lost to the church.[4] The flesh continues to live; therefore "temptations of every sort attack and oppress us on every side."[5] Consequently, the doctrine of faith must be taught afresh.

While the differences between the 1519 lectures and the 1535 lectures can be rightly studied in terms of the development of Luther's thought, they can also be studied as a perfect example of the challenge of changing con-

---

2. *Luther's Works* (hereafter *LW*), ed. Jaroslav Pelikan (Saint Louis: Concordia, 1963-4) XXVI and XXVII.

3. *LW* XXVI, 3.

4. *Ibid.*, 3.

5. *Ibid.*

texts successfully met. Several differences can be observed. In the 1519 lectures there is only one enemy: Rome. The "power of the pope and the privileges of the Roman church" are the one topic upon which theologians are forbidden to speak critically, while it is fully permissible to "wink at and consent to all the swamps of shame and corruption" in the church.[6] The threat of the abuse of power by the Roman curia is related specifically to the church in Germany. Moreover, Luther criticizes directly the role of specific individual theologians, namely Cardinal Cajetan and Sylvester Prierias. Resistance to the Roman curia is more important than resistance to the Turks. Such resistance is necessary even at the cost of personal suffering of bloodshed.

What is the issue that calls forth such a vehement and uncompromising response? The Roman curia have abused the name of Christ, compromised the authority of Scripture, and threatened the unity of the church through their false teaching. The proper response is to expound the letter of Paul to the Galatians, in which Paul teaches "trust in Jesus Christ alone" and warns the Galatians against "legalistic righteousness."[7] The error of the Galatians was to confuse adiaphora with that which is necessary for salvation. So, too, the Roman Curia have perverted the gospel, have ridiculed God's commandments by their human laws, and seek to cover up the heinous sins that are commonplace among them. The prefatory material in the 1519 lectures is laced with brilliant irony. The style of the commentary itself is characterized by Luther as "not so much a commentary as a testimony of my faith in Christ. . . ."[8]

But by 1535 the context had changed, and so had Luther's response. On the one hand, the same subject matter was at issue: the doctrine of faith taught in the apostle Paul. And yet the fronts had shifted. No longer was the enemy simply Rome. Now, it was the misunderstanding of law and gospel that characterized "Jews, Mohammedans, papists, (and) sectarians."[9] In particular, Luther now accuses the "fanatical sectarians" of twisting his own words and reproducing the very error of the papists; the words and names have changed, but "the content remains the same."[10] Luther's style no longer draws heavily on irony; rather, he operates as a "dialectician"[11] who insists upon absolute clarity on the issue of active and passive righteousness. Clarity is necessary because the temptations to lose the distinction, which would be

6. *LW* XXVII, 154.
7. *Ibid.,* 161.
8. *Ibid.,* 159.
9. *LW* XXVI, 10.
10. *Ibid.*
11. *Ibid.,* 11.

tantamount to a loss of the gospel itself, are so numerous and persistent. Finally, the personal context of the theologian has shifted; in 1519 the threat was actual bloodshed, but now the threat has become the struggle of faith against "temptation."[12]

In summary, Luther represents in brilliant fashion a pattern of response to shifting contexts in the lifetime of a single theologian. The early, focused debate with Rome shifted to the wide-ranging debate with Rome, the Anabaptists, and others. Luther does not abandon his earlier attack on Rome; he does not seek a "middle way." Quite the opposite; he continues his vehement attack, and yet recognizes that now more than one front calls for a wider range of critical response. Luther responded with changes in style, argumentation, and emphases; and yet the subject matter remained the Pauline doctrine of justification by faith.

A significant example of the failure to meet the challenge of changing contexts in the lifetime of an individual theologian is Karl Barth. First was Barth's failure to observe and adjust to the changing circumstances. One can only be impressed, indeed astonished, at the crucial role that Barth played during the church struggle in Germany. His biography[13] reveals an uncanny ability to participate in events of momentous importance in the life of the church and in the political life of Germany and yet to continue academic work of amazing brilliance and superior quality. Perhaps most significant of all was his leadership in the confessing church, in particular his role in the construction of the Barmen Declaration.[14] However, after the war, there was a change in his public role, both in the life of the church and in political life. He held to the position against the rearmament of Germany as a confessing position, that is, as if it were identical to the church's opposition to Hitler. For example, in the late Autumn of 1954 he delivered an address in Wiesbaden espousing German neutrality and opposing rearmament, in opposition to Adenauer. Even the Social Democrats distanced themselves from Barth's position. His position not only did not attract the consensus among church leaders that his position at Barmen had; he became increasingly alienated, precisely on the grounds of the confessional nature of his opposition to Adenauer. In his retort to his opponents in the church, he resorted to questioning of personal "commitment."[15]

Second, there is the change in his theological direction, best seen in the

---

12. *Ibid.,* 10.
13. Eberhard Busch, *Karl Barth* (Philadelphia: Fortress, 1976).
14. *Ibid.,* 245-48.
15. *Ibid.,* 404-5.

lecture he gave in Aarau in 1956 entitled "The Humanity of God."[16] He interprets his earlier opposition to the anthropocentrism of the nineteenth century as a tactical move made necessary by the times rather than as a criticism grounded in the truth of the theological subject matter itself. The theocentric dimensions of his earlier and middle period give way to emphasis on human "partnership" with God.[17] Finally, he espouses a position of universalism and, significantly, resorts to attacking the motives of those who oppose it theologically: "One question should for a moment be asked, in view of the 'danger' with which one may see this concept [universalism] gradually surrounded. What of the 'danger' of the eternally skeptical-critical theologian who is ever and again suspiciously questioning, because fundamentally always legalistic and therefore in the main morosely gloomy? Is not his presence among us currently more threatening than that of the unbecomingly cheerful indifferentism or even antinomianism, to which one with a certain understanding of universalism could in fact deliver himself?"[18]

Where Luther exhibits a pattern of adjusting to the changing circumstances while still holding firm to the selfsame theological substance, Barth moved in the opposite direction. In a sense, Barth's weaknesses are the mirror-image of Luther's strengths. Barth held intransigent on issues that called for fresh approaches in the light of the changing context; and he changed his theological position in ways that compromised the very theological substance for which he had once fought so hard.

The second pattern to be observed is the change of context in the movement of theological ideas from one generation to the next. A good example of the successful shift of context from one generation to another is to be found in the man who understood Luther better than anyone else, John Calvin. Though Calvin's explicit references to Luther are few, his debt to Luther is massive. Nevertheless, it is also clear that Calvin avoided the trap of Melanchthon; there is no hint in Calvin of an attempt to teach "Luther's theology." Rather, Calvin inherited from Luther a vision of Scripture, in two dimensions. First, he inherited Luther's adherence to the authority of Scripture alone for the work of theology. Second, he inherited Luther's brilliant use of dialectic in the study of Scripture: on the one hand, there is one subject matter in both Testaments of Scripture, Jesus Christ; and yet on the other hand, the full complexity of the witness of Scripture is to be preserved rigorously. Calvin inherited Luther's vision of Scripture, but his role was clearly different

16. Karl Barth, *The Humanity of God* (Atlanta: John Knox, 1960) 37-65.
17. *Ibid.*, 45-46.
18. *Ibid.*, 62.

from Luther's. To the end of his life, Luther's role necessarily had a constantly polemical edge, as he rightly sought to preserve the gains that had been won and to defend them against ever-increasing threats. Calvin, on the other hand, had a more pedagogical role. Eventually laboring in the supportive environment of Geneva, his stated aim in the *Institutes* was the training of a new generation of pastors in the study of Scripture: "Moreover, it has been my purpose in this labor to prepare and instruct candidates in sacred theology for the reading of the divine Word, in order that they may be able both to have easy access to it and to advance in it without stumbling. For I believe I have so embraced the sum of religion in all its parts, and have arranged it in such an order, that if anyone rightly grasps it, it will not be difficult for him to determine what he ought especially to seek in Scripture, and to what end he ought to relate its contents."[19]

Calvin's treatment of the issue of law and gospel[20] is a good example of the successful shift in context in the movement of theology from one generation to another. The theological substance and rigor of Luther's formulation in the Galatians commentary is preserved; and yet different nuances emerge in Calvin's treatment. Calvin begins by asserting the ontological unity of the old and new covenants in the one mediator, Jesus Christ. Nevertheless, while there is a unity of substance in the old and new covenants, there is a different "mode of dispensation." This unity in difference is then carefully mapped out by Calvin. The ontological unity of the substance in both Old and New Testament is manifested in three dimensions, which both Testaments share alike: the hope of immortality, the grounding of salvation in divine mercy rather than human merit, and the knowledge of the person of Christ, through whom reconciliation with God is received. Then Calvin moves to consider five differences of the Old Testament from the New in the mode of administration: the representation of spiritual blessings by material blessings, the role of the ceremonial law as a type of Christ, the literal nature of the Old Testament in contrast to the spiritual nature of the New, the bondage of the Old in contrast to the freedom of the New, and finally the limits of the Old to one nation in contrast to the universal reference of the New.

A good example of the failure to respond to the shifts in generational context is to be found in the theology of Phillip Melanchthon. Melanchthon was the friend and younger colleague of Martin Luther at the University of Wittenberg. Many of the themes of Luther's theology are echoed in Melanch-

---

19. John Calvin, *The Institutes of the Christian Religion,* ed. John T. McNeill (Philadelphia: Westminster, 1960) 4.
20. *Institutes* II.10-11.

thon; however, the enormous power of Luther is missing. Moreover, it is not convincing to characterize Melanchthon's work as an effort to bring clarity to matters that Luther was content to leave complex, with the resulting loss of brilliance;[21] in my judgment, Luther's theology is far more clear than Melanchthon's, while at the same time far more complex. Rather, it appears that themes in the theology of Luther, which were articulated in the context of heated debate with Rome, are lifted out of that context into a basically humanistic concern for pedagogy. That is to say, the theological stance of Luther had subtly but drastically shifted in Melanchthon, with the result that the same themes were transformed into a very different theological substance.

Several examples of the difference can be given. Where Luther was clearly critical of the failure of late medieval exegesis, Melanchthon turns this theme into an attack on the very genre of commentary: "For on the whole I do not look very favorably on commentaries, not even those of the ancients. Far be it from me to call anyone away from the study of canonical Scripture by too lengthy a composition of my own!"[22] Luther's brilliant dialectical offensive against reason is transformed into a concern for "spiritual judgment" through "suppression of the mental faculties."[23] Luther's affirmation of *sola Scriptura* is expressed in the form of affirmation of the pristine purity of Pauline doctrine in comparison with the speculative doctrine of the scholastics.[24]

The difference runs deeper than the overall characterization of the theology of Melanchthon. On the details of theology, Melanchthon clearly meant to reproduce the basic thrust of Luther's teaching. However, the differences at times are glaring. An example is Melanchthon's treatment of the relation of law and gospel. Melanchthon, like Luther, taught that the law is abrogated through faith in Christ: "But [the law] is abrogated by the new preaching, now that the message concerning his Son Christ is begun. If nothing is preached but that Christ is the Son of God, it follows that the righteousness of the law, or works, are not demanded, nor is anything else; and all that is commanded is that we embrace that Son."[25] But his further treat-

---

21. Cf. the judgment of Wilhelm Pauck: "However, Melanchthon is much less profound and paradoxical, but generally much clearer, than Luther . . ." *Melanchthon and Bucer,* ed. Wilhelm Pauck (Philadelphia: Westminster, 1969) 15.

22. *Ibid.,* 19.

23. *Ibid.*

24. "In his letter to the Romans when he was writing a compendium of Christian doctrine, did Paul philosophize about the mysteries of the Trinity, the mode of incarnation, or active and passive creation?" *Ibid.,* 22.

25. *Ibid.,* 122.

ment falls well short of Luther's view. The law is abrogated, but the reason is that the Christian, renewed by the Spirit of Christ, now does "spontaneously" what the law used to demand.[26] Freedom from the law means the necessary observance of the law by those in whom the Spirit dwells: "The Spirit of God cannot be in the human heart without fulfilling the Decalogue. The Decalogue is therefore observed by necessity."[27] The Decalogue is therefore to be understood as requiring the "righteousness of the heart" rather than any "definite work."[28] Gone entirely from Melanchthon is Luther's rigorous dialectic of law and gospel. Justification and sanctification have simply been fused; there is no sign of *simul justus et peccator;* gone is the passionate struggle of faith; and there is no theological grounding for Luther's own detailed exposition of the Decalogue as the eternal expression of God's concrete will for the Christian life.[29]

In summary, Melanchthon failed to respond to the changing contexts of theology across generational lines, even generations so close together as his and Luther's. Luther's clear ability to respond to rapidly shifting contexts stands in sharp contrast to Melanchthon's misguided effort to teach Lutheran theology. The issue cannot rightly be gauged in psychological terms. Melanchthon clearly had the highest respect for Luther, and made every effort to reproduce his teaching.[30] Indeed, no less a judge than Luther himself thought he had.[31] Rather, it must be understood in terms of the failure to adjust to the shifting contexts that even a generational difference can bring. Calvin and Melanchthon shared a similar pedagogical interest; they likewise shared a similar humanistic training; finally, they shared alike a deep indebtedness to Luther. Nevertheless, it seems clear in hindsight that Calvin, not Melanchthon, constructed a second-generation body of theological work in essential continuity with the first-generation labor of Luther.

A third pattern of shifting contexts occurs in the movement of theolog-

---

26. *Ibid.,* 123.

27. *Ibid.,* 127.

28. *Ibid.*

29. "There is, in addition to these, yet another righteousness, the righteousness of the Law or of the Decalog, which Moses teaches. We too, teach this, but after the doctrine of faith." *LW* XXVI, 4. Cf. Luther's exposition of the Ten Commandments in the *Catechisms.*

30. E.g., in his treatment of law and gospel, Melanchthon refers to *Against Latomus* as definitive.

31. Cf. Luther's well-known assessment of the *Loci Communes* in *The Bondage of the Will:* ". . . a book, in my judgment, worthy not only of being immortalized, but of being included in the ecclesiastical canon." *The Bondage of the Will,* tr. Henry Cole (Grand Rapids: Baker, 1976) 14.

ical ideas across wide or extended theological eras. A good example of success in the shift of cultural context across several centuries is the relation of Dietrich Bonhoeffer to Martin Luther. Bonhoeffer first learned Luther's theology from Seeberg and Holl; however, his understanding of Luther transcended, and even contradicted, the Protestant liberal approach to Luther common to his theological environment. There is no attempt in Bonhoeffer to repristinate Luther; indeed, Bonhoeffer's appreciation of Luther is sharply distinguished from the hero-worship of Luther common to Germany at the time. Rather, the influence of Luther on Bonhoeffer is measured by the critical stimulus that Luther provided in Bonhoeffer's opposition to theological liberalism. One dimension of Bonhoeffer's successful use of Luther is in his approach to homiletics, especially during the years of teaching at the illegal seminary in Finkenwalde. Bonhoeffer learned from Luther that the preaching of the Word is God's very Word, the *viva vox Christi,* to the specific congregation in the specific time and place. The impression that his lectures on preaching made upon his students testifies to the extraordinary freshness of his approach.[32] A second dimension of Bonhoeffer's relation to Luther is in his exegesis of Scripture. A good symptom of the influence of Luther can be seen in the astonishing preface to *Creation and Fall.* Bonhoeffer writes: "Theological interpretation accepts the Bible as the book of the Church and interprets it as such. . . . When Genesis says 'Yahweh,' historically or psychologically it means nothing but Yahweh. Theologically, however, i.e. from the Church's point of view, it is speaking of God. God is the one God in the whole of Holy Scripture: the Church and theological study stand and fall with this faith."[33] The extraordinary power of these words is only magnified when one recalls that they were spoken by a young *Privatdozent* in Germany during the early 1930s.

A good example of failure in the shifting of cultural context across theological eras is the misappropriation of Calvin by the Princeton orthodoxy. We will consider the views of B. B. Warfield as expressed in his article on Calvinism for *The New Schaff-Herzog Encyclopedia of Religious Knowledge.*[34] Calvinism, argues Warfield, is to be understood as an "entire body of conceptions, theological, ethical, philosophical, social, political, which under the influence of the master mind of John Calvin, raised itself to dominance in the Protestant lands of the post-Reformation age, and has left a perma-

32. See the description in Eberhard Bethge, *Dietrich Bonhoeffer* (New York: Harper and Row, 1967) 361-63.

33. Dietrich Bonhoeffer, *Creation and Fall* (New York: Macmillan, 1959) 12.

34. Benjamin Breckenridge Warfield, *Calvin and Augustine* (Philadelphia: Presbyterian and Reformed, 1956) 287-300.

nent mark not only upon the thought of mankind, but upon the life-history of men, the social order of civilized peoples, and even the political organization of states."[35] The entire outworking of Calvinism is but a manifestation of its underlying "religious consciousness." According to Warfield, Calvinism is the highest form of theism, piety, and evangelical religion. It does not differ in kind, but merely in degree, from other religious experiences and conceptions; that is, it brings to representative perfection the less developed forms of human religion. For this reason, it is fully irenic, having no difficulty "recognizing the theistic character of all truly theistic thought, the religious note in all actual religious activity, the evangelical quality of all really evangelical faith."[36]

Now, one approach to Warfield would be to isolate and highlight the influences of the nineteenth century, especially of Schleiermacher. However, although such influences are obviously there, they do not strike at the heart of the matter. Rather, the failure of Warfield was in seeking to repristinate an earlier theology without any awareness of shifting cultural contexts. At the outset, his stated intention is to reproduce the ideas of Calvin. And yet the result of Warfield's approach is exactly the opposite. Incidental features of Calvin's theology are raised to the level of basic assumptions. Critical dimensions of Calvin's theology are ignored entirely. Calvin would never measure the truth of theology by its cultural influence, but rather by Scripture alone. Calvin would never argue that true faith in the gospel is different only in degree from all other religious "conceptions," for salvation is by faith in Jesus Christ alone. Warfield misses entirely the radically christological nature of Calvin's theology. He is irenic where Calvin is combative: for Calvin, human piety is nothing but a "factory of idols."[37] Warfield is combative and rigid where Calvin is subtle and flexible; in his well-known views on inspiration and inerrancy Warfield holds a number of critical positions that Calvin himself either expressly denies or leaves open. In summary, Warfield attempted to embrace and champion Calvin's theology; and yet the result was that the real force of Calvin's work was lost, and on some life-or-death issues, radically contradicted.

A fourth pattern of context in theology is the difference between cultural variables and the constancy of the subject matter, and the relation between the two. Some features of the witness of Scripture are once-for-all, while other features are given as historically representative. Thus, in the

35. *Ibid.*, 287.
36. *Ibid.*, 290.
37. *Institutes*, 108.

church's reception of the witness of Scripture a key issue in context is the observation of the difference between the constant subject matter, which is Jesus Christ, and the shifting historical appropriation. And yet the two cannot be separated; it is in the historically concrete moment that the once-for-all subject matter is appropriated. Holy Scripture itself is the authoritative guide, both to the once-for-all and to the culturally variable appropriation. Both the variable and the once-for-all are expressions of God's one eternal will for his people.

Luther serves as an example of the successful observation of this difference over the lifetime of a theologian. First, Luther affirmed the radically christological subject matter of Scripture as a theological constant. As he states in the 1535 *Commentary on Galatians,* the subject matter of the letter is the doctrine of faith, the one pure gospel; and the duty of the church's teachers is to teach the one pure gospel, which they have learned from Scripture.[38] But, second, Luther shifted several times in his appropriation of that subject matter in given cultural-historical circumstances. That is not to say that Luther considered the question of appropriation unimportant or theologically immaterial; the historical context varies over time, but it is by no means inconsequential or "contingent." On the contrary, it is only in the concrete historical moment that the one true subject matter of Scripture is rightly appropriated, and the truthful appropriation in the given moment is decisive. Third, Luther turned to Scripture itself as the authoritative guide both to the theologically constant subject matter and to the historically variable appropriation. Scripture teaches the once-for-all subject matter; but it likewise teaches by representation the true appropriation of that subject matter in a given historical moment. In the 1535 *Commentary on Galatians,* for example, Luther reads Paul's attack on the heretical party in the church at Galatia figuratively, as applying to the papacy, the Anabaptists, the Turks, and so forth.[39] There is in Luther no sense that the attack on heresy is less important than, or unattached to, the affirmation of the theologically constant subject matter. On the contrary, it is not possible to teach the one doctrine of faith without attacking the church's contemporary enemies.

A good negative example of the fourth pattern of context in theology is the cultural Christianity of Albrecht Ritschl. First, Ritschl displaced the radically christological subject matter of Scripture with a Kantian notion of the universal ethical imperative, which he called "the Kingdom of God." The kingdom of God, according to Ritschl, is the "imperative of the moral associ-

38. *LW,* XXVI, 13-17.
39. *Ibid.,* 14-15, and throughout.

ation of all men as men."[40] All other Christian doctrines, including christology, are filtered through the doctrine of the kingdom, defined in the manner of the Enlightenment ethical idealism of the nineteenth century. But, second, according to Ritschl the ethical imperative of the kingdom surpasses "ethical forms of society" such as marriage, family, vocation, and the state.[41] According to Ritschl these are "conditioned by natural endowment" and are hence "occasions for self-seeking."[42] Thus, those issues that Luther treated as historically variable in Scripture, but nevertheless absolutely necessary in the articulation and defense of the gospel in a given time and place, Ritschl redefines as beneath the ethical concerns of the church. And third, the concrete imperatives of the law of Christ in Scripture are replaced in Ritschl by a series of reflections on "character" and "virtue" in the Christian life, all of which bear the imprint of post-Kantian moralism.[43]

A fifth pattern in the study of context in theology is the use of new tools for the purpose of fresh articulation of the one gospel, which nevertheless remains self-identically the same since the beginning. A good positive example of this pattern is the use of the new humanistic learning by Calvin and Luther.[44] While there are some differences in formulation, the approach of both is the same. Both were deeply learned in the tools of humanism, and yet both are sharply distinguished from Erasmus and Reuchlin in their use of those tools. The approach of Luther and Calvin was intensely dialectical. On the one hand, human reason is sinful and is absolutely excluded as a source of our knowledge of God. As Oberman states it: "justification by faith alone not only excludes human merit; 'faith alone' is another spearhead aimed at the claims of reason *(ratio).*" And yet on the other hand, both Luther and Calvin used the new humanistic tools of logic, rhetoric, and literary analysis in their study of Scripture. But simply describing their approach as dialectical is not sufficient. Rather, their approach must be seen against the backdrop of the eschatological tension of the Christian life, which both Reformers embraced. In reference to the old world of sin and evil, reason is excluded from theology as a product of sinful humankind. Faith is in no

40. "Instruction in the Christian Religion," par. 19, in Albrecht Ritschl, *Three Essays* (Philadelphia: Fortress, 1972) 228.

41. *Ibid.,* 223.

42. *Ibid.*

43. *Ibid.,* 240-54.

44. For Luther, see the summary in Heiko A. Oberman, *The Reformation: Roots and Ramifications* (Grand Rapids: Eerdmans, 1994) 12-16. For Calvin, see Quirinus Breen, *John Calvin: A Study in French Humanism* (Grand Rapids: Eerdmans, 1931); and Ford Lewis Battles, *Calvin's Commentary on Seneca's* De Clementia (Leiden: Brill, 1969) 1-140.

sense the exercise of a human capacity, but is a gracious divine gift. But in reference to the new person in Christ, the mind has a role in the service of Christ with one's whole being, under the guidance of the Spirit. The tools of the Renaissance were used by the humanists in the service of worldy ideology, which must be exposed and strongly criticized. But the same tools are now to be used in the service of Christ, in the work of Christian theology. The tools are the same; the radical difference is that the tools are now used in a way that is subordinate to the sole authority of Scripture and to the subject matter of which Scripture speaks.[45]

A good negative example of this fifth pattern is the theology of Paul Tillich.[46] The failure of Tillich was not in using cultural resources in the enterprise of theology. We have seen that Calvin and Luther successfully used humanistic tools. Rather, the failure of Tillich was in the "method of correlation,"[47] which failed to subordinate the tools of twentieth-century philosophy and psychology to the authority of Scripture. The relation between the reader and Scripture is clearly in some sense dialectical; every reader brings certain tools and resources to the study of Scripture. The vast difference between Tillich and the Reformers is the *aim* of theological exegesis. For the Reformers, the aim was the transformation of the reader into the likeness of the subject matter of Scripture, by subordinating the resources of the reader to the world of Scripture. For Tillich, it was the correlation of the situation of the reader with the world of Scripture. The massive difference in results are palpable: for the Reformers, Scripture functions as the instrument by which the risen Lord trains each new generation of the church in the knowledge of the truth through the guidance of the Spirit; in Tillich, Scripture becomes a collection of images, metaphors, and stories that theology must symbolically

45. Here I must disagree with the general characterization of the Reformers in Hans Frei's *The Eclipse of Biblical Narrative* (New Haven and London: Yale University Press, 1974) 18-37. Despite many useful insights, Frei misuses the category of narrative as an overall description of the Reformers. On the contrary, the Reformers used a wide variety of logical, rhetorical, and historical tools; Luther's use of dialectic, or Calvin's use of the rhetorical categories of metonymy and synecdoche, are examples among dozens of others. Moreover, Frei's use of narrative entails a collapsing of the subject matter of Scripture and the texts that bear witness to it in a way that is foreign to the Reformers. According to Frei, the reader has only to "comprehend" the meaning (p. 37). Missing from his description is the necessary response of faith, which entails intense struggle in moving from the witness of the text to the subject matter of which it speaks. Luther once spent three years on a single verse; and Calvin berated those who claimed to preach from Scripture without careful study of church scholarship.

46. Paul Tillich, *Systematic Theology* (Chicago: University of Chicago, 1967).

47. *Ibid.,* 59-66.

"reinterpret." The results clearly place the theology of Tillich outside the confessing heritage of the church in numerous ways: in christology, creation, the trinity, soteriology, anthropology, and so forth. Indeed, in many respects Tillich simply reproduced the Gnostic errors already decisively refuted by Irenaeus.[48]

Finally, a sixth pattern in the study of context in theology is the strategy of theology in relation to theological opposition. A good example of this pattern is the great work of Irenaeus, *Against All Heresies*.[49] Several features must be noted. First, Irenaeus is constantly on the offensive in his trenchant criticism of the Gnostics, never on the defensive. Nor does Irenaeus ever hint at a "middle way." There is no common ground shared with the Gnostics; hence, the genre of theological criticism is confessional in nature rather than disputational. Second, Irenaeus bases his criticism of the Gnostics on the authority of Scripture, as received by the church. His refutation is fully objective: the Gnostics "disregard the order and the connection of the Scriptures, and so far as in them lies, dismember and destroy the truth."[50] They distort the true subject matter of Scripture into the image of a "dog."[51] While his critique is objective in nature, Irenaeus makes it from a particular theological stance in relation to Scripture, which he shares with the whole of Christendom: "The Church, though dispersed throughout the whole world, even to the ends of the earth, has received from the apostles and their disciples this faith. . . ." Thus, the criticism of the Gnostics is not of one party by another party, but brings with it the full weight of the universal church.[52] Third, his

48. Here again, I must differ with Frei's grounds for dispute with modern theology. I fully agree with his negative assessment of the whole range of modern theology, which includes Butler, Semler, Schleiermacher, Ritschl, Herrmann, Brunner, Bultmann, Rahner, Pannenberg, and Moltmann (see Frei's treatment, *ibid.*, 124-30 — which curiously omits Tillich). I also fully agree with Frei's criticism of the natural theology of these theologians, which argues that "there is an area of human experience on which the light of the Christian gospel and that of natural, independent insight shine at the same time, illumining it in the same way." This is the negative side of the dialectic in the Reformers, which absolutely rejects reason and common human experience as a source of our knowledge of God. However, what is missing in Frei is the positive side of the dialectic; the use of the tools of culture, not for the sake of establishing a natural theology, but in subordination to the sole authority of Scripture and its subject matter.

49. In *The Ante-Nicene Fathers* I (Grand Rapids: Eerdmans, reprinted 1993).

50. *Ibid.*, 326.

51. *Ibid.*

52. As we shall see, this clearly distinguishes Irenaeus from the "evangelicals." But it also distinguishes him from George Lindbeck, in his *The Nature of Doctrine* (Philadelphia: Westminster, 1984). Lindbeck writes in order to give an account of the meaningfulness of ecumenical discussion, an account that is itself "ecumenically neutral." That is

criticism is grounded in theological reflection on the christological subject matter of Scripture. There is never a question of the theological difference between Irenaeus and the Gnostics, for his presentation manifests clearly the decisive confrontation of the truth against falsehood.

A good negative example of this pattern is the work of J. Gresham Machen; the contrast between Machen's criticism of the heresy of liberalism[53] and Irenaeus's criticism of the heresy of Gnosticism could hardly be greater. First, Machen in fact agrees with liberalism in the need for a defensive apologetic in relation to modernity. He shares with liberalism the basic question: "whether first-century religion can ever stand in company with twentieth-century science";[54] he differs only in relation to the method of defense. Both Machen and the heresy of liberalism are in stark contrast to the offensive stance of Irenaeus, and for that matter the Reformers. Second, unlike Irenaeus, whose critique of Gnosticism is grounded christologically in the substance of the faith, Machen pits the cultural principle of "conservatism" over against the cultural principle of "liberalism."[55] Doctrinal issues such as creation, the Bible, Christ, salvation, and the church are *illustrations* of the conservative principle. But so also are a wide range of cultural issues, from music, to art, education, politics, poetry, and sculpture — all of which suffer the need for a return to "conservatism." Indeed, Machen's view is not different in kind from the cultural Christianity of Ritschl; Machen laments the loss of the "spiritual realm" in modern culture;[56] there is no longer any "appreciation of the glories of the past" in modern history;[57] there is a "narrowing of the range of personality" in the modern world;[58] Machen speaks of a "limitation of the realm of freedom for the individual man" in modern life;[59] in summary, Machen complains that "great men are non-existent."[60] In all these ways, Machen clearly shares with Ritschl the pagan ideology of

---

to say, the "rule theory" that he proposes is "doctrinally neutral," and therefore useful for both orthodox and unorthodox Christians (p. 9). By sharp contrast, Irenaeus adopts a particular theological stance in relation to Scripture. His criticism is grounded in the true subject matter itself and seeks to distinguish without ambiguity catholic Christianity from heresy.

53. J. Gresham Machen, *Christianity and Liberalism* (Grand Rapids: Eerdmans, 1946).

54. *Ibid.,* 4.

55. *Ibid.,* 15.

56. *Ibid.,* 10.

57. *Ibid.*

58. *Ibid.*

59. *Ibid.*

60. *Ibid.,* 15.

the Enlightenment; the difference is only in the matter of how best to defend Christianity in respect to the Enlightenment. Finally, again in sharp contrast to Irenaeus, Machen writes as an independent critic, one whose views encompass church doctrine but also extend beyond to broader cultural issues. He speaks not as a church theologian but as a freelance cultural observer.[61]

II

We have observed six patterns in the history of theology concerning the role of context and have considered successes and failures of theological response to context. Our aim now is to offer a theological argument concerning the significance of context in the history of theology that will shed light on the patterns which we have observed. The thesis of the present essay is that *canon is ontologically necessary* for the true understanding of the issue of context in Christian theology.

Firstly, by canon here we mean the shape, purpose, and subject matter of Scripture, which has been convincingly shown by Brevard S. Childs.[62] According to Childs, Scripture serves as the vehicle by which the risen Lord governs his church with absolute authority. The work of the Spirit is to guide the church in a continuing encounter with the risen Lord through the witness of the prophets and the apostles. Scripture is the result of a process of shaping for this purpose of addressing each new generation of the community of faith with the eternal will of God. The work of shaping was done by canonical editors, who left their witness not in the form of self-referencing the process, but in the form of bearing witness to the subject matter that evoked their witness, namely Jesus Christ. The various elements of canonical shaping vary from book to book and must be determined with the help of the tools of historical criticism. Nevertheless, the purpose of canonical shaping is common to both Testaments and both warrants and necessitates a holistic reading of the Christian Bible. The miraculous work of the Spirit is to under-

---

61. Unfortunately, the errors of Machen are shared by the whole school of conservative evangelicalism, including Charles Hodge, B. B. Warfield, Carl F. H. Henry, J. I. Packer, Mark Noll, David Wells, and Alister McGrath. For example, in his recent article, "Why Evangelicalism is the Future of Protestantism," McGrath states: "Liberalism has thus lost its credibility in the area of apologetics; that mantle has passed to evangelicalism" (*Christianity Today* 39 [June 19, 1995] 22). From the point of view of canon, evangelicalism is not different in kind from the heresy of liberalism.

62. Brevard S. Childs, *Biblical Theology of the Old and New Testaments* (Philadelphia: Fortress, 1992).

cut evasions of the subject matter of the text and to evoke from the church a fresh proclamation of the Word of God based on the sole authority of Scripture.[63]

The patterns of context that have been treated here show that canon is not a "construal" of modern theological imagination. On the contrary, the patterns of context clearly show that the church has, from the beginning, built its theology on the basis of canon. Already in Irenaeus, the refutation of the Gnostics turned on the proper understanding of the shape and purpose of the books of Scripture and of their christological subject matter. The Reformers' appeal to the authority of Scripture is distinguished from humanism by the various canonical elements of their exegesis: the emphasis on the literal sense, the affirmation of the one christological subject matter of both Testaments of Scripture, the attention to the variety of ways in which the witnesses of Scripture bear witness to that subject matter, and the critical role of Scripture as the sole means by which the church is judged and reformed under the guidance of the Spirit. Finally, the work of Bonhoeffer demonstrates that despite the onslaughts of historical criticism in dismantling canon, the modern confessing church continues to live out of the context of its theological stance in relation to Scripture. Different words have been used to express the reality of canon: *scopus Scripturae, regula fidei, regula veritatis;* nevertheless, an understanding of canon has been the true basis of the scholarship of the church since its inception.

Here even the errors of the church are instructive. The various negative examples that have been adduced here all share one fact in common: an ignorance of canon. For this reason, the customary division of theology into conservative and liberal only conceals the underlying problem. For in fact both left and right are a departure from the confessing faith of the church built on the reality of canon. Neither is the answer a retrieval of "classical" theology in opposition to all "modern" theology. On the one hand, the work of Melanchthon exemplifies the fact that "classical" is not coextensive with an understanding of canon; there were theologians in the classical era who nevertheless, despite their best intentions, failed to grasp the true significance of canon. On the other hand, the example of Bonhoeffer illustrates the opposite point: that Scripture has continued to be read as canon in pockets of the confessing church in modernity as well. Moreover, the Reformers ex-

---

63. Childs's work on canon is similar in name only to that of J. A. Sanders, which properly belongs under the category of liberalism. The same must be said for the work of Paul Achtemeier, Elizabeth Achtemeier, Raymond Brown, James Luther Mayes, Walter Brueggemann, James Barr, et al.

emplify the continuing need to use the tools at one's disposal and not to retreat into the past. Consequently, the argument of the present essay is not that canon is now one example among others of the way in which the church has read Scripture. Rather, the argument is that canon is now the one true basis for the scholarship of the church, to the exclusion of all other bases, and that canon is the one and only link in the present to the true confessing heritage of the church in the past.

In the light of the church's confession of canon, we now return to the question of context; what light is shed on the issue of context by our consideration of the six patterns that we have observed? Three answers must be given, all of which bear evidence of the basic eschatological tension in which the church lives:

1. There is only one gospel. Canon is not to be confused with erroneous efforts of "reinterpretation" of the Christian faith. Rather, in the shifting contexts of the church's life, the response of faith is to hold to the truth of the one gospel against the many threats of heresy. Indeed, canon requires the church to take the offensive against heresy, exposing claims to new, revelatory experience as demonic. The Reformers correctly held in their debate with Rome that it was Rome that had departed from the heart of the church's confession; the Reformation proclamation of justification by faith was an affirmation of the one gospel, held by the church catholic. Moreover, it was necessary that both Luther and Calvin would go on to criticize the "radical reformation" on the same theological grounds as their criticism of Rome, for Reformation theology was a direct contradiction of the claims to revelatory experience by the left wing.

And yet, on the other hand, each generation must respond afresh to the witness of Scripture. It was Melanchthon, not Luther, who sought to "retrieve" the first five centuries. Similarly, despite Calvin's obvious respect for and indebtedness to Augustine, not even Augustine is Holy Scripture. While the dogmatic tradition of the church, including its creeds and confessions, is an indispensable aid in recognizing the lines of right doctrine beyond which the gospel is not rightly preached, the true subject matter of theology is to be sought and found in the witness of Scripture alone.

2. The church lives in dialectical tension with culture. On the one hand, the cross of Christ is the end of all cultural values, whether on the left or on the right. Reason and common human experience are not a source of our knowledge of God. Efforts of natural theology to base theology on reason and experience always lead to heresy and idolatry, for the scope of sin is universal. Again, it makes no difference whether the natural theology is based on the resources of high culture or counterculture; all natural theology is utterly

false. Canon means that Holy Scripture alone is the source of our knowledge of God.

And yet the church continues to live in the world, including the world of human culture. While the efforts of human culture are not a source of our knowledge of God, they provide useful tools for the scholarship of the church. The failure to observe this rule simply opens the door for a countercultural Christianity, which is theologically indistinguishable from cultural Christianity. Here we must again assert the continuing role of historical criticism in the church's study of Scripture. On the one hand, it provides a negative check against the many heretical claims that truth is found in Scripture through its "images," "metaphors," and so forth. On the other hand, the proper use of historical criticism in a canonical context has sharpened the church's reading of Scripture and has indeed helped to correct mishearing of the text carried over from ecclesiastical tradition.[64]

3. Faith is a free gift of the Spirit and in no sense whatsoever the exercise of a human capacity. It is the miraculous work of the Spirit to evoke a response of faith in the church. The presence of the Spirit is both sovereign and mysterious. In no sense whatsoever is faith the exercise of free will, human capacity, the human spirit, or spirituality, all of which are the idolatrous products of human arrogance. The greatest threat to the reality of canon is piety, and the worst heretics are usually supremely pious. The critical role of the Spirit is to undercut all subterfuges of piety and spirituality, guiding the church to hear in Scripture the direct existential address of the risen Lord.

And yet the required response of faith, engendered by the Spirit, is disciplined reflection on the subject matter of Scripture. Canon is opposed to all forms of biblicism, whether on the theological left or on the theological right. The role of the Spirit is to lead the reader of Scripture from the witness of the text, in astonishment and joy, to the true subject matter of which it speaks, which is Jesus Christ himself. Canon embraces the reality of the analogy of faith, which calls for rigorous attention to the rich variety of the witnesses of Scripture in its testimony to the one substance of the faith.

III

We have now articulated the view that canon is the sole and exclusive basis for a true understanding of the church's life with Scripture in the past, in-

---

64. See Brevard S. Childs, *Introduction to the Old Testament as Scripture* (Philadelphia: Fortress, 1979), and *The New Testament as Canon* (Philadelphia: Fortress, 1984).

cluding the subtle and complex issue of context. The competing paradigms of Protestant liberalism and propositionalism, as well as mediating positions combining elements of both, are not only false theologically; they are also bankrupt as useful explanatory tools for the critical assessment of church history. A brief refutation of those competing paradigms will now be given.

David Kelsey's widely influential book *The Uses of Scripture in Recent Theology*[65] represents the liberal Protestant, functionalist approach to context and reproduces the many heresies of theological liberalism. First, Kelsey limits his analysis to a narrow range of nineteenth- and twentieth-century theologians. It is little wonder therefore that the prescriptive statements on context that he derives from this analysis bears the obvious imprint of Protestant liberalism, and in particular the theology of Paul Tillich.[66] Second, Kelsey forces the theological texts with which he works into a simplistic schema of "ordinary" logic. The result is that the more dialectical and rigorous theological questions involved in the issue of context are eliminated at the outset. Third, Kelsey reverses the relation between canon and context; he seeks to approach the reality of canon from the question of context, rather than approaching context from the point of view of canon. The result is that Kelsey has no room in his analysis for reckoning with actual constraints that Scripture itself has exercised on the history of theology. And yet, how can a view of context be theologically adequate if it fails to describe the actual presence of Scripture in the church? While he clearly intends otherwise, Kelsey has in fact separated Scripture from the church. Finally, Kelsey replaces the sovereign and mysterious work of the Spirit with a variety of anthropological appeals to "imagination," "experience," and so forth. It is not surprising that Kelsey's views are widely held in the many factions of the heresy of liberation theology, which appeal to various modes of revelatory "consciousness" and "spirituality."

But we must also criticize just as sharply the approach to context on the right, represented by the understanding of the history of theology in the propositionalist orthodoxy of Warfield.[67] Indeed, the errors of Warfield are closely parallel to those of Kelsey. While Warfield sought to study a wider range of theologians than Kelsey, his approach to those theologians employed a heavy-handed, nineteenth-century idealistic notion of theological "principles." Again, the result was that the more subtle theological questions of context were eliminated at the outset. Second, Warfield also separated

---

65. Philadelphia: Fortress, 1975.
66. The subject of Kelsey's dissertation.
67. See his *Calvin and Augustine*.

Scripture from the church by his doctrines of inspiration and inerrancy, whose apologetic purpose opened the door for a natural theology of reason and experience. Consequently, the rich and dialectical theological reflection on the subject matter of Scripture by the Reformers and Augustine was altogether missed by Warfield, who reduced everything to a lifeless series of theological propositions. Finally, while he affirmed the sovereign work of the Spirit, he eliminated the mystery of the Spirit's work by mediating it through an arid Enlightenment rationalism; the result was a failure to discern the time-conditionality in which the history of theology has taken place.

Finally, we must criticize equally as sharply the "middle way" as represented in the position of John Leith.[68] Leith seeks to avoid the extremes, while encompassing both conservative and liberal elements in a mediating concept of "tradition." However, the result is that the views of both the left and the right are simply combined in a position that shares the errors of both. Paradoxically, despite his affirmation of "tradition," Leith shows no grasp of the reality of canon that is actually operative in the Christian tradition itself. For Leith, the driving force of church history is not the theological reality of canon but the psychological and sociological constraints of "ethos." But above all, Leith fails to recognize the canonical function of Scripture as the vehicle by which the risen Lord stands in judgment over the church itself. Despite an honest attempt to be reformed, Leith ignores the very reality by which the church is reformed.

68. See, e.g., John H. Leith, *An Introduction to the Reformed Tradition* (Atlanta: John Knox, 1977).

II. CANONICAL READINGS AND THE OLD TESTAMENT

Canon and Tradition: The Limits of the Old Testament in Scholastic Discussion

Corrine Patton

Inspired Scripture is precisely Scripture in that it has been recognized by the Church as the rule of faith. Hence the significance, in this light of both the final form in which each of the books of the Bible appears and of the complete whole, which all together make up as canon. Each individual book only becomes biblical in the light of the canon as a whole. It is the believing community that provides a truly adequate context for interpreting canonical texts.

The Interpretation of the Bible in the Church (Rome: Pontifical Biblical Commission, 1993) §C.1

In a recent article in *Commonweal,* Luke Johnson poses the question, what is "Catholic" about Catholic biblical scholarship.[1] Probably in the minds of most Catholics and Protestants, the answer would be the incorporation of "tradition," however that is defined. In Catholic teaching "tradition," manifested through a variety of vehicles within the church, stems from the continuing work and presence of the Holy Spirit in the church clarifying those things that are necessary for salvation, which Scripture contains implicitly.[2]

1. "So What's Catholic about It?: The State of Catholic Biblical Scholarship," *Commonweal* 16 (1998) 12-16.
2. For influential discussions within Catholicism of the relationship between Scrip-

Although Johnson speaks only briefly of "tradition,"[3] his description of a biblical exegesis that focuses on "testing and reconnecting" is most certainly interpreting within a communal interpretive tradition.[4] He proposes that what makes a distinctly Catholic interpretation is loyalty to "the church's teaching and practices," that is, an interpretation that is responsible to both the text and the community.[5] His proposal resonates in many ways with the canonical approach to the Bible described by Brevard Childs, which also aims to take the interpretive history of a community of faith seriously, especially when interpretation explores the theological significance of the text.[6] For some Catholics, however, "tradition," in the sense of a "deposit of faith," constitutes a more authoritative parameter for matters of theology than I believe are envisioned by either Childs or Johnson. Within the history of the Catholic Church, at times of theological controversy, usually some appeal is made, on one side or the other, not only to Scripture, but also to a sense of tradition, whether that is located in a consensus of church practice (the rule of faith), decretal or conciliar statements, or the teaching of noted scholars. Often theological controversy over issues such as the call of the church to apostolic poverty in the late Middle Ages, or the question of women's ordination in this decade, revolve around the weight given to these various elements.[7] One such dispute in the history of the church was the delineation

---

ture and tradition, see K. Rahner, *Inspiration in the Bible* (Quaestiones Disputatae; New York: Herder and Herder, 1961); G. Tavard, "The Authority of Scripture and Tradition," in *Problems of Authority*, ed. J. Todd (Baltimore: Helicon, 1962) 27-42; K Rahner and J. Ratzinger, *Revelation and Tradition* (Quaestiones Disputatae; New York: Herder and Herder, 1965) 26-66; Y. M.-J. Congar, *Tradition and Traditions: An Historical and a Theological Essay* (London: Burns and Oates, 1966); F. A. Sullivan, *Magisterium: Teaching Authority in the Catholic Church* (New York: Paulist, 1983); and, recently, R. R. Gaillardetz, *Teaching with Authority: A Theology of the Magisterium in the Church* (Theology and Life; Collegeville: Liturgical, 1997). The issue is addressed in a number of church documents as well, especially *Dei Verbum* II, 8-10, and "The Interpretation of the Bible in the Church" III, B.

3. "So What's Catholic about It," 15.

4. *Ibid.*, 13.

5. *Ibid.*, 15-16.

6. "The term canon points to the received, collected, and interpreted material of the church and thus establishes the theological context in which the tradition continues to function authoritatively for today" (B. S. Childs, *Biblical Theology of the Old and New Testaments: Theological Reflection on the Christian Bible* [Minneapolis: Fortress, 1992] 71). Although Childs goes on to critique the Catholic view of canon, he does not quote the church documents of this century, which do advocate a stable and normative canon as a primary vehicle for revelation.

7. Modern appeals to a concept of the "magisterium" are of only limited help, since on most questions, especially with respect to biblical interpretation, there is no "magiste-

and authority of the Old Testament canon itself. Although for Catholics this matter was settled at Trent,[8] an examination of the debates in the Middle Ages about which books are "canonical" reveals the same probing over the locus and authority of the community of faith's "tradition" as is seen in current theological debates within Catholicism.[9]

Canonical criticism, in the sense of the examination of the formation and continuing function of the canon,[10] presumes a community of faith that has determined both the contemporary communal context for interpretation and the canon itself. Criteria for the determination of the canon do not evolve primarily from historical methodology, but flow directly from the community's determination of the interplay and locus of that tradition which preserves the text. In fact, in some ways the whole notion of the importance of tradition evolves as subsidiary to the notion of canon. The New Catechism, for instance, defines tradition's primary function as "transmit[ting] in its entirety the Word of God which has been entrusted to the apostles by Christ the Lord and the Holy Spirit. It transmits it to the successors of the apostles so that, enlightened by the Spirit of truth, they may faithfully preserve, expound, and spread it abroad by their preaching."[11] The canonical context entails not just the limits of the canon itself, but the status of

---

rial" position. Even more problematic is the question of the degree, nature, and extent of the magisterium's authority. On these issues, see recently, Gaillardetz (esp. 230-46) and Sullivan (esp. 4-23 and 174-218).

8. Although dissent from the canon outlined at the fourth session of Trent (April 8, 1546) was declared "anathema," Catholics still defend the longer canon in various ways. See, for instance, P. Benoit, "La Septante est-elle inspirée?" *Exegèse et théologie* I (Paris: Cerf, 1961) 3-12; K. Rahner, *Inspiration in the Bible,* esp. 46-47, and, most recently, J. Lienhard, *The Bible, the Church, and Authority: The Canon of the Christian Bible in History and Theology* (Collegeville: Liturgical, 1995). There seems to be an increase of Protestants also examining the question of the Old Testament canon. See, for instance, R. T. Beckwith, *The Old Testament Canon of the New Testament Church and Its Background in Early Judaism* (Grand Rapids: Eerdmans, 1985); E. E. Ellis, *The Old Testament in Early Christianity: Canon and Interpretation in the Light of Modern Research* (Tübingen: Mohr, 1991); J. W. Miller, *The Origins of the Bible: Rethinking Canon History* (Theological Inquiries; Mahwah: Paulist, 1994); P. R. House, "Canon of the Old Testament," *Foundations for Biblical Interpretation: A Complete Library of Tools and Resources,* ed. D. S. Dockery, et al. (Nashville: Broadman and Holman, 1994) 134-55; and L. M. McDonald, *The Formation of the Christian Biblical Canon* (rev. ed.; Peabody: Hendrickson, 1995).

9. In fact, what separates Catholics and Protestants on this very issue today is that each chose different options voiced within their community of faith.

10. J. A. Sanders, *Canon and Community: A Guide to Canonical Criticism* (Guides to Biblical Scholarship; Philadelphia: Fortress, 1984), esp. p. 18.

11. Pt. I, ch. 2, art. II, para. 81.

these texts as inspired, authoritative, and canonical.[12] The question itself of which books and which version comprise the canon hints at the rich variety of mechanisms for the interplay of Scripture and tradition.

The variability of this interplay can be demonstrated by the late medieval antecedents to the debates about the canon in the Reformation period. While a great deal of scholarly focus has been directed to the question of the initial formation of the canon within both Judaism and Christianity,[13] less notice has been taken of the degree of variation within Christian tradition up until the Reformation concerning this issue. While these variations suggest a nonfixed or at least fluid canon, the criteria by which medieval exegetes determined the authority of different biblical books and versions reveals that at root is a more fundamental assumption about the location and determination of tradition within the church. This variability in the determination of the warrants within tradition continued trends seen as early as Jerome and Augustine, which remained evident in the debates between Protestants and Catholics during the Reformation period. This paper will examine three different determinations of the Old Testament canon in the work of three prominent medieval theologians, Hugh of St. Victor, Thomas Aquinas, and Nicholas of Lyra, in an attempt to explore the broader theological issues at play in the determination of a canonical context.

I. Background for the Medieval Positions: Jerome and Augustine

The factors that led to the formation of the Old Testament canon remain obscure. While early research posited a Jewish closure of the canon at Jamnia in reaction to nascent Christianity, recent work has decisively shown that the "closure" of the Hebrew Scriptures was not an event but a process.[14] While

12. See, for instance, R. Gnuse, *The Authority of the Bible: Theories of Inspiration, Revelation and the Canon of Scripture* (New York: Paulist, 1985).

13. In addition to the works on canon by Catholics and Protestants cited above, see also I. Baldermann, ed., *Zum Problem des biblischen Kanons* (Jahrbuch für biblische Theologie 3; Neukirchen-Vluyn: Neukirchener, 1988), esp. the articles by H.-G. Link, H. P. Rüger, and G. Stemberger and the review of American discussions on the canon by P. D. Miller; A. Ziegenaus, *Kanon: Von der Väterzeit bis zur Gegenwart* (Handbuch der Dogmengeschichte 1: Das Desein im Glauben 3a [2]; Freiburg: Herder, 1990) 65-179.

14. See especially Sanders, *Canon and Community*; C. Theobald, "Le canon des Écritures: L'enjeu d'un 'conflit des facultés,'" in *Le canon des Écritures. Études historiques, exégétiques et systématiques,* ed. C. Theobald (Lectio Divina 140; Paris: Cerf, 1990) 13-73; and J. W. Miller, *Origins of the Bible,* 68-82.

the basic proto-Masoretic text received the widest approval, variant traditions remained in use throughout Judaism and Christianity; especially noteworthy are the omission of Esther from various early canonical lists and the inclusion of Sirach in others.[15] Christian churches, to be sure, adopted their Old Testament canon from current communal use, but since that use varied among Jewish communities, so, too, did Christian appropriation of the delineation of the canon.

It was not until the church began to codify and standardize both the contents of the canon and its translation that these competing views came to a head.[16] Ellis traces the vitality of the tradition of the shorter canon in early Christianity, noting that those early Christians who accepted a shorter canon had a three-tiered view of authority: fully canonical texts, texts with religious value but not binding in certain types of theological arguments, and noncanonical, nonauthoritative texts. Those who opted for the longer canon had only two categories: canonical and noncanonical.[17] It is this latter view that there is only one "level" or mode of canon, corresponding to one revelation, that in part is assumed in the later Catholic teaching on the unity of all modes of revelation.[18]

By the period of late antiquity, the debates over canonical determination had crystallized into clearly defined arguments. These arguments can be seen most clearly in the debates between Jerome and Augustine on this very issue.[19] Ziegenaus identifies three different arguments used in late antiquity to determine the full canonical authority of a given text.[20] First is that represented by Jerome, who employs a historical argument to substantiate the exclusion of certain Jewish texts from the Christian canon. The second argument hinges on liturgical use of the longer canon within the

15. J. Trublet, "Constitution et clôture du canon hébraïque," in *Le canon des Écritures*, 77-187.

16. For discussion of early church councils on the canon, see A. C. Sundberg, *The Old Testament of the Early Church* (Cambridge: Harvard University, 1964) 130-31; Miller, *Origins of the Bible*, 97.

17. Ellis, *The Old Testament in Early Christianity*, 6-36. Ellis claims that those who opt for the longer canon "confuse" categories meant to remain separate. However, most Catholics would not agree with his assessment of the historical variations.

18. The principle of the unity of revelation, whether mediated through Scripture, through tradition, or through God's creative works, is at the heart of all Catholic teaching on revelation.

19. For a brief comparison of Jerome and Augustine on the canon, see P. Vullin, "La formation de la Bible chrétienne," in *Le canon des Écritures*, 189-236.

20. Ziegenaus, *Kanon*, 162-79. See also Vullin, "La formation de la Bible chrétienne."

church.[21] The third basis for canonical limits depends on the majority consensus of various Christian communities, again leading to the longer canon. The second and third of these arguments can be found in Augustine.

Jerome's attitude toward the apocryphal books vacillated throughout his writings.[22] However, his explicit statements about their authority had far more influence than his sporadic citation of them as "Scriptures." While Jerome does not explicitly state why he rejects the canonicity of the apocryphal texts,[23] the historical argument he implies assumes that the oldest texts are the best. For Jerome the biblical authors were more reliable witnesses to the events that they related than were secondary interpreters and translators. It is these historical moments that have authority. This implies that inspiration of an author reveals a historical truth or event to which we are given access through the text of the inspired eyewitness. The Holy Spirit works to preserve this text, and therefore this event, in an authoritative form, which then speaks directly to each generation.

While it appears that the issue is one of historical reliability, on closer examination of Jerome's discussions of the Septuagint it becomes clear that the ultimate criterion for determining the canon is the question of the limitations of prophetic revelation and, ultimately, of inspiration, understood in this context as either prophetic or apostolic experience of God.[24] For Jerome, prophetic interaction between God and humanity was a thing of the past. The activity of interpretation, whether individual or collective, did not involve revelatory experience, as did inspired authorship.[25] Similarly, Jerome explicitly rejects the view that the translators of the Septuagint were divinely

---

21. Both Jerome and Augustine maintain that the LXX can be used in liturgy. See S. Kamin, "The Theological Significance of the Hebraica Veritas in Jerome's Thought," *Sha'arei Talmon: Studies in the Bible, Qumran, and the Ancient Near East Presented to Shemaryahu Talmon,* ed. M. Fishbane and E. Tov (Winona Lake: Eisenbrauns, 1992) 243-53. However, for Augustine, this use has larger implications for the text's authority than it did for Jerome.

22. See, among others, D. Brown, *Vir Trilinguis: A Study in the Biblical Exegesis of Saint Jerome* (Kampen: Pharos, 1992) 55-71.

23. For general discussion of Jerome's view of the canon, see, for example, Sundberg, *The Old Testament of the Early Church,* 148-53; J. N. D. Kelly, *Jerome: His Life, Writings, and Controversies* (New York: Harper and Row, 1975) 159-61; A. Kamesar, *Jerome, Greek Scholarship, and the Hebrew Bible: A Study of the Quaestiones Hebraicae in Genesim* (Oxford: Clarendon, 1993); and J. W. Miller, *Origins of the Bible,* 87-93.

24. See, most recently, Kamin, "The Theological Significance of the Hebraica Veritas in Jerome's Thought."

25. B. Vawter, *Biblical Inspiration* (Theological Resources; Philadelphia: Westminster, 1972) 39-40.

inspired.[26] His historical argument presumes a theological understanding of the relationship between God and the church. While the Holy Spirit may be guiding the church, it does so only insofar as the church derives its teachings from the primary revelation in the past. The church only has access to revealed truth via the ancient revelation contained in the pristine text or autograph, handed down in an unbroken line, not through any secondary recension of that text in either another language or a later version. Jerome, then, would reject the Septuagint both because, as a translation, it was not inspired and because there was no singular version handed down in an unbroken tradition.[27] For Jerome, the action of the Holy Spirit preserving a reliable text cannot be detected in the Greek traditions.

Augustine, on the other hand, locates the source for the determination of the canon primarily in the use of and esteem for texts within the majority of churches, with preference given to those churches founded by apostles.[28] Although he admits this "rule of faith" could lead to conflict, in which particular apostolic churches would disagree with the majority of churches, he doubts this is likely and merely states that equal weight should be given to both positions. The activity of the Holy Spirit is evident in the actions of the community of faith, the worldwide church, not in a text known by historical investigation. The historical events remain, but it is only the church's witness that reveals where the Holy Spirit resides. Church use alone makes evident the reliable text tradition. Augustine's conclusions allow a much fuller role for the Holy Spirit in the continuing life and teaching of the church. The authority and teaching of the Scriptures is not separate from its use and appropriation in the church, evidenced not in theological reflection but in church use, especially in the oldest Christian communities. Thus, while Augustine's conclusions appear to be theological, they, too, are historically based.

Respect for history is even more evident in Augustine's discussions of the Septuagint. Accepting the legend preserved in the *Letter of Aristeas*, Augustine maintains that the original translators of this text were themselves

---

26. See his Prologue to Genesis and the discussion by Kamin.

27. See E. F. Sutcliffe, "Jerome," *Cambridge History of the Bible* II: *The West from the Fathers to the Reformation*, ed. G. W. H. Lampe (Cambridge: Cambridge University Press, 1969) 95-96.

28. See especially *De doctrina Christiana* II.viii.12: "In the matter of canonical Scriptures, one should follow the authority of the majority of catholic churches, among which are those which have deserved to have apostolic seats and to receive epistles." For a general discussion of Augustine's view of the canon, see Sundberg, *The Old Testament of the Early Church*, 155-57; Miller, *Origins of the Bible*, 94-96. Similar views on the "rule of faith" are seen as early as Irenaeus, *Against Heresies*, esp. III.2.

directed by the "Spirit."[29] Canon is not simply the result of a later decision or experience of the church. The decision itself involves the secondary recognition of the original inspired nature of the text. Both the process of the original production of these translations, which renders them authoritative, and the anterior de facto recognition of their authoritative status by communal use stem from the presence and activity of the Spirit throughout history.

What differs, then, between Jerome and Augustine is the location of the "defining" history or tradition for the church. Is it in the biblical authors or in ecclesiastical use and appropriation? If both men accept the dual revelation for the church in Scripture and tradition, where does tradition lie? This is a both theological and historical question, one that assumes that God works in history, although the means of that divine activity remain obscure. This debate about the definition and locus of tradition stands at the core of the various attitudes toward the Old Testament in the Middle Ages.

II. The Canon of Hugh of St. Victor

Hugh of St. Victor (d. 1141) advocates a rather eclectic canon.[30] On the one hand he holds to the shorter canon for the Old Testament, quoting the con-

---

29. See especially *City of God* XVIII.42-43. Augustine's views are discussed by Vawter, *Biblical Inspiration*, 33-38.

30. General treatments of the work of Hugh of St. Victor can be found in B. Smalley, *The Study of the Bible in the Middle Ages* (Oxford: Clarendon, 1941); J. P. Kleinz, *The Theory of Knowledge of Hugh of St. Victor* (Catholic University of America Philosophical Studies 87; Washington, D.C.: Catholic University Press, 1945); J. Taylor, *The Origin and Early Life of Hugh of St. Victor: An Evaluation of the Tradition* (Texts and Studies in the History of Medieval Education; Notre Dame: University of Notre Dame Press, 1956); R. Baron, *Science et sagesse chez Hugues de Saint-Victor* (Paris: Lethielleux, 1957); *Études sur Hugues de Saint Victor* (Paris: Desclee de Brouwer, 1963); S. Ernst, *Gewissheit des Glaubens: Der Glaubenstraktat Hugos von St. Viktor als Zugang zu seiner theologischen Systematik* (Beitrage zur Geschichte der Philosophie und Theologie des Mittelalters, n.f., 10; Münster: Aschendorff, 1987); and P. Sicard, *Hugues de Saint-Victor et son école* (Témoins de notre histoire; Turnhout: Brepols, 1991).

The variety of canonical lists in the early Middle Ages has been demonstrated in R. Gameson, ed., *The Early Medieval Bible: Its Production, Decoration and Use* (Cambridge Studies in Paleography and Codicology; Cambridge: Cambridge University Press, 1994); this variety is confirmed by P. G. Remley, *Old English Biblical Verse* (Cambridge Studies in Anglo-Saxon England 16; Cambridge: Cambridge University Press, 1996), esp. for the text of Daniel. However, the majority of the Bibles studied have at least some of the deuterocanonical books, sometimes with the addition of prologues and prayers, but not with tractates by Christian scholars or ecclesiastical documents.

clusions of Jerome's *Praefatio in Salamonem* and *In libros Samuel et Malachim.*[31] On the other hand, he expands the New Testament canon to include the decretals, as well as the writings of the "fathers and doctors" of the church. The clearest access to this canon is in the *Didascalicon.*[32] Hugh parallels the three divisions of the Hebrew Bible (law, prophets, and writings) with three divisions in the New Testament (Gospels, apostles, and fathers). He excludes from the canon Wisdom, Sirach, Judith, Tobit, and Maccabees, as well as 2 and 3 Esdras. Nowhere does he mention Baruch. He also accepts the shorter version of Daniel, but does not discuss the text of Esther. Further, he does not enumerate what should be included among "the fathers." While Berndt claims that this is a complete innovation of Hugh's, Congar's work shows clear precedents for Hugh's conclusions.[33]

Several theological issues are at play in Hugh's delineation of the canon. First, the primary warrant for the determination of the Old Testament canon is the position of Jerome, whom he includes among the authoritative fathers. From Jerome he derives the principle of a return to the Hebrew canon as the basic text for the Old Testament. This leads not just to the denigration of the apocryphal works but to a reordering of the books within the Old Testament as well. Thus, while the Vulgate, following the LXX order, divides the text into law, history, wisdom, and prophets, to which the New Testament corresponds with Gospels, Acts, epistles, and prophecy (Revelation), the Hebrew divisions of law, prophets, and writings require a different understanding of the order of the New Testament to correspond to the Old. As Berndt shows, since the present order of the New Testament would have nothing to parallel the Hebrew section of writings, there would either have to be a complete reshuffling of the order of the New Testament texts, or the addition of traditional authorities to the canon.[34]

The historical patterning that is a prominent element in Hugh's theology reflects his understanding of history as the primary arena for God's activity. While history is a sequence that is varied and changing, sacred history

31. *Didascalicon* IV.2.

32. A similar view of canon can be found throughout Hugh's work. See also *De Scripturis,* chapter 6 (Patrologia Latina 175, 15A-16C) and *De sacramentis,* prologue and chapter 7 (Patrologia Latina 176, 186D). For further citations of the "Fathers" in Hugh's work see R. Berndt, "Gehören die Kirchenväter zur Heiligen Schrift? Zur Kanontheorie des Hugo von St. Viktor," in *Zum Problem des biblischen Kanons,* ed. I. Baldermann (Jahrbuch für biblische Theologie 3; Neukirchen-Vluyn: Neukirchener, 1988) 192.

33. Congar, *Tradition and Traditions,* 89-93. See also L. Ott, "Hugo von St. Viktor und die Kirchenväter," *Divus Thomas* 3/27 (1949) 184; R. Baron, *Science et sagesse,* 104.

34. Berndt, "Gehören die Kirchenväter zur Heiligen Schrift?" 196-97.

has a unified message provided by its divine source. Knowledge of God can be discerned through history, which is one of the primary loci of God's revelation.[35] Berndt points out that Hugh's reading of history asserts that the revelation of Christ in history is embedded in the Jewish texts themselves, even though the Jewish authors were unaware of such implications. Even more than that, however, the patterning assumes and furthers the belief that the church is the true arena for God's continued activity in history. The church then is not just playing out the effects of a past revelation in history, as implied by Jerome, but is the vehicle for continued revelation through the teaching of accepted Christian theologians. Unlike Augustine's concept of continuing divine activity, however, Hugh locates the evidence for this activity in the continued writings and interpretations of Scripture by Christian scholars, not in communal use.

Hugh's discussion of the canon can in no way be separated from the broader context of the *Didascalicon*. Written as a monastic guide for reading and study, this work is concerned not with interpretation in the abstract but with biblical reading as the basis for spiritual growth. Hugh was well aware of the varieties of interpretations that could be derived from the biblical texts. He warns his students against idle study of the Bible in an attempt to "multiply meanings." The use of patristic tradition prioritizes various interpretations in view of the final goal of biblical reading, which is spiritual growth. The importance of tradition within the project of the *Didascalicon* becomes most apparent in books 5 and 6. Hugh assumes a threefold method of interpretation: literal or historical, allegorical, and moral or tropological. In his discussion of the aim and order of reading, a literal reading should proceed in chronological order, from Old Testament to New, since its main purpose is knowledge, primarily of the historical sense, while reading for allegory should commence with the New Testament, which makes manifest what is hidden in the Old Testament. However, Hugh maintains that biblical interpretation should be aimed not just at the acquisition of knowledge but even more at the development of the moral life. The moral implications are not

35. See Hugh's periodization of history, which permeates *De sacramentis Christianae fidei*. See further M.-D. Chenu, *Nature, Man, and Society in the Twelfth Century: Essays on New Theological Perspectives in the Latin West* (Chicago: University of Chicago Press, 1968) 165-73; G. A. Zinn, "*Historia fundamentum est:* The Role of History in the Contemplative Life according to Hugh of St. Victor," in *Contemporary Reflections on the Medieval Christian Tradition: Essays in Honor of Ray C. Petry,* ed. G. H. Shriver (Durham: Duke University Press, 1974) 135-58; and J. W. M. van Zweiten, "Jewish Exegesis within Christian Bounds: Richard of St. Victor's *De Emmanuele* and Victorine Hermeneutics," *Bijdragen, tijdschrift voor filosofie en theologie* 48 (1987) 327-35.

isolated to the development of ethical principles by which certain moral decisions are made, but rather lead to the ultimate activity and aim of humanity, which is experiential knowledge of God through mystical union. This latter task is thoroughly dependent on a correct interpretation of the Scriptures, defined as one that leads to a deeper experience of God. The path to this meaning is provided by the interpretations contained in the fathers and doctors of the Church.[36] When reading to understand the moral sense, reading commences with the writings of the "saints." For Hugh these writings are more directly related to the moral life, are "simpler" than the Scriptures, and as such lead to less confusion on the part of the reader in directing human action and spiritual growth. The Bible by itself does not provide a guide for human behavior. This comes through the correct interpretation of that text preserved in the "saints."

For Hugh, then, reading of Scripture is ultimately directed by three considerations. First is the primary goal of all religious education: knowledge of God best exemplified in mystical experience. Second, the interpretation of Scripture reaches its fullest realization in a communal interpretation going back to the church fathers. Third, Scripture itself is part of a continuing line of God's revelation in history, a line that continues into the life of the contemporary church. Therefore, both the shorter Old Testament canon that Hugh adopts from Jerome and the expansion of the New Testament canon by the very addition of scholars such as Jerome belie the same understanding of the relationship between Scripture and tradition. While both contain the "truth," the truth is most fully revealed by the unity of both sources of revelation.

III. The Canon of Thomas Aquinas

Thomas Aquinas (d. 1274) adhered to the longer canon of the Old Testament of the Vulgate and LXX traditions, circulating widely in the form of the "Paris Bible" of the thirteenth century.[37] This acceptance is clearly apparent in the fre-

---

36. Congar (*Tradition and Traditions*, 89-93) assumes that Hugh subordinates the fathers to the Scriptures, since they merely interpret Scripture.

37. For a discussion of medieval Bible production, see esp. R. Loewe, "The Medieval History of the Latin Vulgate," *Cambridge History of the Bible* II, 145-54; and L. Light, "Versions et révisions du texte biblique," *Le Moyen Age et la Bible*, ed. P. Riché and G. Lobrichon (Bible de tous les temps 4; Paris: Beauchesne, 1984) 75-93. For discussion of how Thomas's century altered and "fixed" the order of biblical books, see L. Light, "French Bibles c. 1200-30: A New Look at the Origin of the Paris Bible," *The Early Medieval Bible*, ed. R. Gameson, 159-63.

quent citations of deuterocanonical texts throughout his works, which belie an intimate knowledge of and esteem for these books. Within the *Summa Theologiae,* however, little attention is paid to the defense of this canon. While this tractate commences with a discussion of scriptural use and authority, the delineation of the canon itself is not addressed; the issue is a moot point, requiring no defense or explanation.[38] Although the issue of the delineation of the canon is ignored, however, the question of the authority of both pontifical statements represented by councils and decretals and of the opinions of early exegetes is raised time and again. Like the work of Hugh of St. Victor, Thomas's assumptions about the canon cannot be understood apart from his views on the locus of traditional authority for the determination of this question.[39]

Thomas recognizes the need for the church to have some access to an authoritative interpretation, or extension, of biblical revelation, both for ecclesiastical governance and for those not learned in Scripture.[40] While Thomas maintains that the Holy Spirit can be detected in the practices of the "faithful" for matters of church governance and customs,[41] he notes that everyone, even the unlearned, needs a sure access to the truths necessary for salvation. The source for these truths is not the writings of the doctors, who disagree on many points of interpretation,[42] but the official statements of the church pronounced under the auspices of the papacy.[43] Thomas spells these

38. Ziegenaus discusses a text that may be from Thomas which states that the Apocryphal books have authority specifically because they have been received by the church (*Kanon,* 196-97).

39. On Aquinas's view of the relationship between canon and tradition see, among others, G. Geenen, "The Place of Tradition in the Theology of St. Thomas," *The Thomist* 15 (1952) 110-35; P. de Vooght, *Le course de la doctrine chrétienne d'après les théologiens du XIVe siècle et du début du XVe* (Paris, 1954); G. Tavard, *Holy Writ or Holy Church* (London: Burns and Oates, 1959) 12-66; Y. M.-J. Congar, "Traditio und Sacra Doctrina bei Thomas v. Aquin," in *Kirche und Überlieferung. Gestgabe J. R. Geiselmann,* ed. H. Fries (Freiburg, 1960) 170-210; Congar, *Tradition and Traditions,* 91-94.

40. *Summa Theologiae* II-II.1.9. All further Aquinas references are to the *Summa Theologiae.*

41. III.25.3. ad 4.

42. R. E. McNally notes scholasticism's growing awareness of discrepancies among patristic writers (*The Bible in the Early Middle Ages* [Woodstock Papers 4; Westminster: Newman, 1959] 23; "Christian Tradition and the Early Middle Ages," *Perspectives on Scripture and Tradition,* ed. J. Kelly [Notre Dame: Fides, 1976] 50-54).

43. I am not suggesting that Aquinas is the first to state these opinions. He clearly shares the scholastic skepticism of patristic "unanimity." See the discussion of medieval views toward tradition in Congar, *Tradition and Traditions,* 86-94; Tavard, *Holy Writ or Holy Church,* 12-21; and the critique by B. Tierney, "'Sola Scriptura' and the Canonists," *Studia Gratiana* 11 (1967) 347-66. However, his clear statements on the topic are a good example of this common view.

out as the decretals, councils, and synods of the church. Although he recognizes that many of these statements go back to the opinions of various scholars,[44] he states that the opinions of these fathers do not become authoritative until recognized as such by the church. The activity of the Spirit in the official statements of the church makes explicit what is necessary for salvation, derived from the "first truth," which is Scripture.

These conclusions depend on Thomas's precise determination for the recognition of the activity of the Holy Spirit in the continued life and teaching of the church.[45] "The universal Church cannot err, since it is governed by the Holy Spirit, who is the spirit of truth."[46] The locus of the Spirit's activity differs from Hugh, who locates it in the fathers, and from Augustine, who himself asserts that the Spirit can be found in the activity of the universal church. Instead, Aquinas unequivocally rejects the notion that the doctors of the church had authority equivalent to Scripture.[47] While Scripture contains everything necessary for salvation, divinely revealed to the "apostles and prophets" and written in the canonical Scriptures,[48] the opinions of the church doctors attempt to derive the truths from Scripture necessary for salvation. Although these may be the result of divine revelation,[49] they could only be a truth already contained in the text. More important, they only function as truth when recognized as such by official ecclesiastical assent through decretals, councils, and synods. For Aquinas, the inability to identify any other location with certainty renders the work of the Holy Spirit through either the fathers or majority consensus ultimately unreliable.[50] Such unreliability would make the correct interpretation of Scripture necessary for salvation functionally inaccessible to "those not learned," a result incompatible with God's aid in salvation. Aquinas's views on scriptural tradition, then, like Hugh's, cannot be separated from his assessment of the vehicles leading to the final goal of studying Scripture, which is salvation.

The implications for Thomas's understanding of canon are obvious.

44. III.25.3. ad. 4. For a discussion of various views of the "inspiration" of these pronouncements at this time, see Congar, *Tradition and Traditions,* 119-37.

45. See Ziegenaus, *Kanon,* 190-205.

46. II-II.1.9.

47. I.1.8. ad. 2.

48. See, for instance, I.1.8. ad. 2; II-II.1.5-7, 9; II-II.5.3; III.25.3. ad.4; and III.60.8. ad.1.

49. I.1.8. He also notes that the doctors can disagree on matters not necessary for faith or on matters not yet determined by the church without threat of error (II-II.11.3).

50. Y. Congar ("St. Thomas and the Infallibility of the Papal Magisterium," *The Thomist* 38 [1974] 97) comes to a similar conclusion.

While many texts of the Old Testament may have been in circulation or endorsed by various scholars at various points in the history of the church, what determines the final canon is not the question of which texts are historically more pristine, older, or more authentic, as it was for Jerome. Nor does the issue concern which texts have been used by most worshiping communities, as it was for Augustine. The determining factor is not even which texts have more support among church scholars, as it was for Hugh. The only determining factor for the definition of the canon is the official statements issued under the authority of the pope.[51] Using this criterion of going back to councils in the patristic period, the longer canon has a more clear endorsement.

Aquinas also posits a distinct type of inspiration and prophecy by which the biblical authors wrote, not shared by later interpreters. He does not address the inspiration of biblical authors apart from the question of prophetic knowledge, indicating that biblical authorship is a form of prophetic revelation. Prophetic knowledge of a revealed truth results from the inspiration of the prophet, an action of sanctifying grace that elevates the mind to receive the revealed truth.[52] Although he does not address the question of whether the translators of the Septuagint were inspired, it must be conjectured that Thomas would at least maintain that the authors of the material contained in the longer canon also wrote from prophetic knowledge or under the sway of inspiration. It must be noted, however, that Aquinas focuses on the activity of the Holy Spirit not as the instrument involved in the production of the Bible, but as God's presence in some sure way in the church. While this does not necessarily subordinate Scripture to ecclesial decisions, it certainly adumbrates attempts to precisely locate God's role in the original production of Scripture, since this criterion can add or subtract nothing from the list defined by the official statements. No matter how the texts were produced, the knowledge that their authors were inspired is determined only because of the later church decrees that these texts are canonical.

---

51. See Ziegenaus, *Kanon*, 196-97.

52. Most studies on Aquinas's view of inspiration focus on his description of the interplay of human and divine causality in the act of inspiration, without discussing the secondary recognition of this activity by the church. See, for instance, A. Desroches, *Jugement pratique et jugement spéculatif chez l'Écrivain inspiré* (Ottawa: Éditions de l'université d'Ottawa, 1958) 17-38; P. Synave and P. Benoit, *Prophecy and Inspiration: A Commentary on the* Summa Theologica II-II, *Questions 171-178* (New York: Desclee, 1961) esp. 61-83; Congar, 119-37; P. Benoit, *Aspects of Biblical Inspiration* (Chicago: Priory, 1965) 36-64; and B. Vawter, *Biblical Inspiration*, 52-57.

For Aquinas, God's continued action in the present church is functionally more accessible than divine action in the past.

For Thomas, tradition is not located in a historical moment or among a consensus of churches or scholars. It rests in the sure and unequivocal decrees of a clearly defined ecclesiastical body.[53] Although Aquinas defines the canon as those things written by the "apostles and prophets," neither authorship[54] nor historical claims nor majority assent ultimately determine the shape of the canon. Such conclusions allowed for more flexibility in interpretation in the face of growing historical awareness, freeing biblical scholars to explore a variety of meanings since the ultimate determination of the "authority" of given interpretations lies not with the exegete but with the official institutions of the church.

IV. The Canon of Nicholas of Lyra

A different assessment of tradition is exhibited in the work of Nicholas of Lyra (d. 1349).[55] In the prologue to the *Postilla litteralis super totam Bibliam,* Lyra advocates the shorter canon of the Old Testament, citing as his authority both the opinions of Jerome and the superior textual witness of the Hebrew text.[56] Thus, Lyra neither grants previous scholars the same status as does Hugh, nor does he view official decrees to be as determinative as

53. This is closer to modern definitions of the magisterium, which primarily concern the teaching office of the bishops.

54. The recognition of who was inspired is ultimately a secondary activity of recognition.

55. For general introduction to Lyra, see H. Labrosse, "Sources de la biographie de Nicolas de Lyre," *Études Franciscaines* 16 (1906) 383-404; "Biographie de Nicolas de Lyre," *Études Franciscaines* 17 (1907) 489-505; "Ouevres de Nicolas de Lyre," *Études Franciscaines* 19 (1908) 41-52, 153-75, and 368-79; 35 (1923) 100-32 and 171-87; C. Langlois, "Nicolas de Lyre, Frère Mineur," *Histoire littéraire de la France* 36 (1927) 355-400; A. S. Wood, "Nicholas of Lyra," *Evangelical Quarterly* 33 (1961) 196-206; H. A. Oberman, *Forerunners of the Reformation: The Shape of Late Medieval Thought* (New York: 1966) 286-92; H. Ruthing, "Kritische Bemerkungen zu einer mittelalterlichen Biographie des Nikolaus von Lyra," *Archivum Franciscanum Historicum* 60 (1967) 42-57; E. A. Gosselin, "A Listing of the Printed Editions of Nicolaus de Lyra," *Traditio* 26 (1970) 399-403; J. G. Kiecker, "The Hermeneutical Principles and Exegetical Methods of Nicholas of Lyra, O.F.M. (ca. 1270-1349)" (Ph.D. dissertation, Marquette University, 1978); and P. D. Krey, "Nicholas of Lyra: Apocalypse Commentary as Historiography" (Ph.D. dissertation, University of Chicago, 1990).

56. This shorter canon is also evident in the writing of Ockham, his contemporary and fellow Franciscan. For the background to their position, see Ziegenaus, *Kanon,* 190-99.

Thomas. Before analyzing the connection between tradition and canon in Lyra, however, it is important to define more precisely his attitude toward both ecclesiastical authority and previous scholarship.

Lyra provides a commentary to the books he deems "apocryphal," namely Judith, Tobit, the two books of Maccabees, 2 Esdras, Ecclesiasticus, Wisdom, Baruch, and the additions to Daniel and Esther. While most analyses of Lyra's position on the canon depend on his general prologue to the *Postilla litteralis,* the subject is broached more fully in his prologues to these various biblical books, especially Tobit. Lyra's discussion of the canon focuses on which texts can be used in theological debate.[57] Only the Hebrew canon can provide a sure warrant for determining "what must be held for faith" and "for proving things which come into contention."[58] Just as philosophical reasoning proceeds through arguments appealing to first principles, so, too, theological reasoning ultimately depends on God, who is revealed primarily in the "canonical" texts, here defined as the Hebrew text. Lyra grants that the correct interpretation of these texts is located in the "doctors" of the church, but his wording emphasizes the fact that their conclusions are only considered valid if they do indeed lead back to the Scriptures. Even more noticeable, unlike Aquinas, Lyra never mentions the authority of official church statements on this issue, not even to refute or limit them. The prologue to Tobit also contains a discussion of the status of the apocryphal books, which do in fact have a "moral" purpose, guiding individuals to proper action, but for Lyra, unlike Hugh, this purpose of reading Scriptures is subordinated to that of reasoning and argumentation, rendering these texts less "worthy."[59]

Several factors may be at work in his approach to the locus and importance of tradition. On the one hand, Lyra, like Hugh and Jerome, is influenced by his intimate knowledge of and high regard for the Hebrew text.[60]

57. His clearest discussion of this very issue can be found in his anti-Jewish tractate, *Quaestiones Iudaicam perfidiam improbantes.* Here he outlines that Christians who wish to dispute the Jews must start with the shorter Hebrew canon in the Hebrew order, then move to the targumim, the Talmud, and other "Hebrew doctors," in that order. He notes that the Septuagint may also be useful for clarification, but does not grant it the same importance as either the Hebrew text or the targumim.

58. This focus on the function of the canon in debate itself reflects Jerome.

59. Congar notes a similar limitation of authority in Ockham, who asserts above all else the primacy of Scripture (*Tradition and Traditions,* 94-95; see also Tavard, *Holy Writ or Holy Church,* 30-31 and 35-37). However, within this list Ockham does not distinguish the status of the deuterocanonical books.

60. The interplay of Hebrew learning and the tendency to support a shorter canon is stressed in Ziegenaus, *Kanon,* 191-92, 198-99.

The very fact that all three scholars learned Hebrew belies a prior commitment to the Hebrew text.[61] As a mendicant writing at the height of the disputations with the Jews in northern France, Lyra also belonged to a community for whom the impetus to learn Hebrew stemmed in part from the desire to refute and convert Jews.[62] At the heart of these disputations was the question of the best text of the Old Testament: Had the Jews changed the Hebrew text to obscure references to Christ, or, to take a different approach, was the Septuagint an inspired translation and therefore superior to the Hebrew text for matters of faith? Lyra grants the Hebrew text, although he asserts that matters mentioned in the New Testament dependent on the Septuagint text provide a secondary theological warrant for Christian exegesis. Thus, while the Hebrew text of Isa 7:14 refers to a young woman, which is the literal meaning of the passage in Isaiah, the New Testament reference to her as a virgin provides a second literal sense to the text, even though it is based on the Greek. To what extent this double literal interpretation reflects disputes with Jewish communities is unclear, but it would not be surprising that the intellectual tradition of the mendicant orders, which were forced to take seriously the Hebrew text, would contribute to a higher estimation of the independent integrity of the Hebrew text even within Christianity.

Lyra also writes at a time when the Franciscans were involved in debates with the papacy specifically over the limits and extensions of papal authority.[63] The Franciscan teaching of the virtue of poverty ultimately derived from an attempt to return to the status of Jesus and the "primitive church," as depicted in the Gospels' account of the commission of the apostles (Matt 10:9-10; Mark 6:8-9; Luke 9:3; 10:4). At the heart of the issue was the relationship between Scripture and tradition. Pope John XXII, while accepting

---

61. On Lyra's use of Jewish exegesis in addition to the Hebrew text see, among others, H. Halperin, "Nicolas de Lyra and Rashi: The Minor Prophets," in *Rashi Anniversary Volume* (Texts and Studies 1; New York: American Academy for Jewish Research, 1941) 115-47; *Rashi and the Christian Scholars* (Pittsburgh: University of Pittsburgh Press, 1963); "De l'utilisation par les chrétiens de l'oeuvre de Rachi (1125-1300)," in *Rachi*, ed. M. Sperber (Paris: Service technique pour l'éducation, 1974) 163-200; E. H. Merrill, "Rashi, Nicholas de Lyra and Christian Exegesis," *Westminster Theological Journal* 38 (1975) 66-79.

62. See esp. J. Cohen, *The Friars and the Jews: The Evolution of Medieval Anti-Judaism* (Ithaca: Cornell University Press, 1982) esp. 170-95. I do not think the references to settling disputed matters in the prologue to Tobit, however, concern Jewish-Christian debates specifically. Rather, the context suggests that Lyra is concerned with inner-Christian discussions.

63. For the effects of this controversy on notions of tradition see B. Tierney, "'Sola Scriptura' and the Canonists."

the authority of the scriptural text as supporting poverty as a virtue,[64] rejected the Franciscan interpretation of the superior quality and normative claim of the virtue of poverty in the church, in part because there was no warrant in the "fathers" for such an interpretation of these texts.[65] Franciscans, however, rejected this dependence on interpretations by the fathers as binding and argued for the possibility of new interpretations based on the anterior and more authoritative historical person and message of Jesus.[66]

Throughout the exegesis of the Old Testament, Lyra clearly discerns the activity of God in biblical history. For instance, Lyra provides a positive assessment of the function of the Law in ancient Israel. Krey, studying Lyra's interpretation of Revelation, demonstrates Lyra's willingness to see God's activity in human history through the periodization of the text; yet, Krey also notes Lyra's reluctance to identify or define present history.[67] Clearly, Lyra believes that the Holy Spirit continues to act in history and in the church, but, unlike Aquinas, he remains skeptical about humanity's ability to define and locate that activity, especially for the current community. In addition, Lyra avoids limiting God's activity to a defined vehicle of revelation and leaves ambiguous the precise interplay of the historical event, the account of that event in the text, and the location of the correct interpretation of that text "for faith."[68]

64. C. Condren notes that both sides were claiming scriptural support and citing their return to the biblical past as their authority. See "Rhetoric, Historiography, and Political Theory: Some Aspects of the Poverty Controversy Reconsidered," *Journal of Religious History* 13 (1984) 15-34. See also G. Leff, *The Dissolution of the Medieval Outlook: An Essay on the Intellectual and Spiritual Change in the 14th Century* (New York: New York University Press, 1976) 130-33.

65. See M. D. Lambert, *Franciscan Poverty: The Doctrine of the Absolute Poverty of Christ and the Apostles in the Franciscan Order, 1210-1323* (London: SPCK, 1961); B. Tierney, *Origins of Papal Infallibility, 1150-1350: A Study on the Concepts of Infallibility, Sovereignty and Tradition in the Middle Ages* (Studies in the History of Christian Thought, 6; Leiden: Brill, 1988, 2nd ed.) 171-204; and J. Heft, *John XXII and Papal Teaching Authority* (Texts and Studies in Religion, 27; Lewiston: Mellen, 1986) 94 and 150-52.

66. As Tierney has shown, the controversy also concerned the limits of the authority of papal statements. The Franciscans maintained that Nicholas III's support of their community rule could not be refuted by a later Pope, while John maintained that papal statements had no such force. As will be seen below, at least regarding the relative authority of Scripture, Lyra is closer to the position represented by John XXII than to his contemporary Franciscans.

67. "Apocalypse Commentary as Historiography," esp. 140-203.

68. The degree to which this position may represent a typical Franciscan critique of Thomas is ambiguous. In particular, Franciscan stances to the relative authority of the Bible seem to contrast sharply with the view represented by Nicholas. Prominent Francis-

Lyra clearly exhibits the belief that exegesis can be innovative and can contradict or augment traditional interpretations. This is seen over and over again in his work. For instance, if one compares Lyra's commentary on Jonah with that of Jerome, many places can be found where Lyra merely ignores the conclusions of the older scholar. He was subsequently criticized for this liberal attitude toward scholarly tradition.[69] While Lyra bases his argument for the canon nominally on Jerome,[70] what Jerome provides is a warrant to prefer the historical moment of the text's inception, a warrant that assumes that the "better text" was that text which is older and closer to the autograph. For Lyra, this text was the Hebrew text, not the later Greek translation, as well as the shorter, "more pristine" canon as reflected by its unbroken use by the Jewish community. Thus, Lyra's arguments for the shorter canon are not based on a tradition that is defined as the conclusions of earlier doctors. Instead, the best tradition is that which takes one back to the original event as closely as possible, back to the prophets, back to the apostles, back to the Christ event. Scripture remains the primary witness for faith, a stance that minimizes, but does not relinquish, the authoritative nature of ecclesiastical statements or interpretations by earlier Christian scholars.[71]

V. Conclusion

For these three exegetes, then, the determination of the limits of the Old Testament canon rests ultimately on their determination of the locus of an authoritative tradition that defines that canon. All three accept that there is something besides the scriptural text itself that is authoritative for determining both the canon itself and its meaning in matters necessary for faith and salvation. How that authority operates remains the crucial question. For

---

cans such as Duns Scotus and William of Ockham seem to support a secondary locus of authority in ecclesial statements, a position closer to Thomas than to Nicholas. For the Franciscan context, see B. Tierney, *Origins of Papal Infallibility*, 171-237; and H. A. Oberman, "Fourteenth-Century Religious Thought: A Premature Profile," *Speculum* 53 (1978) 80-93.

69. See, for instance, the critiques of Lyra by Jean Gerson, found in J. S. Preus, *From Shadow to Promise: Old Testament Interpretation from Augustine to the Young Luther* (Cambridge: Harvard University Press, 1969) 79-84, and by Erasmus, quoted in H. A. Oberman, *Forerunners of the Reformation: The Shape of Medieval Thought* (New York: Holt, Rinehart, and Winston, 1966) 311-12.

70. See Ziegenaus, *Kanon*, 198-99.

71. See R. Wood, "Nicholas of Lyra and Lutheran Views on Ecclesiastical Office," *Journal of Ecclesiastical History* 29 (1978) 451-62.

Hugh, tradition consisted in the majority witness of Christian scholars. For Aquinas, tradition was clearly defined as the official decrees of the papacy via decretals, councils, and synods. For Lyra, tradition was that which provided best access to the historical events witnessed to in the Bible. This question of tradition and canon was alive in the earliest stages of the determination of the canon. It was played out in the Middle Ages and was ultimately an issue separating Christian communities after the Reformation.

Canonical criticism takes place within a community, then, for whom the determination of canon itself is based on theological presuppositions that are often left unexpressed. It is not enough for a community of faith, or for two scholars, to state that their biblical theology takes place within the confines of a canon determined by their own community. It is not enough to transfer the criteria by which a text became canonical to the present question of what factors give a text continued status as canonical.[72] Even more, it is not enough to say that theological interpretation itself is limited by the parameters set by a given community of faith. The experience of the Middle Ages demonstrates that behind such statements are assumptions of how one defines that community of faith, how communal limitations are determined, and who determines limitations for interpretation.

Ultimately, canonical criticism leads the biblical theologian to face the fundamental questions of both biblical and communal authority within theological discussion. To return to Johnson's proposal for a "Catholic" biblical theology, each of the medieval exegetes would have defined themselves as "loyal to the church's teaching and practices." Each would have defended their view as responsible to both the text and the community. It appears that for approximately 1500 years the church was comfortable with the kind of

---

72. Sanders's argument in *Canon and Community*, 30-36 that canon formation is a process not identifiable with any given historical point is irrelevant to a later community that wishes to trace the roots of its current canon, recognizing the presence of variant traditions. Although Sanders recognizes that the historical process of canon formation matters little to later communities, he tends to underestimate the theological presuppositions of the discussion of the canon, especially within a Roman Catholic context, in which the community experiences a continuous, unified, singular presence of God in the midst of human, historical variations. Quoting the Pontifical Commission, "Should the interpretive process which led to the formation of the Canon be recognized as the guiding principle for the interpretation of Scripture today?" Clearly for this document, which represents a community that ultimately accepted Aquinas's view that the Holy Spirit is found best in ecclesial institutions such as councils, the answer is a resounding "no." For Roman Catholicism, even if the primary determination of the canon was a historical accident, the church's consistent approval of the longer canon, especially in "official" statements, itself demonstrates that God has provided these texts for the church.

fluidity of interpretation over this issue that Johnson extols at the end of his article.[73] The reality of life within a community of faith, however, is that at points in the community's history, decisions must be made about contemporary church practice and teaching. At those points, when the rubber hits the road, so to speak, fluidity fades into conflict.[74] What makes Catholic biblical theology Catholic, then? Perhaps simply this: that this community of faith has been wrestling with what it means to interpret a text both within the canon as a whole and within a particular community of faith throughout its history. This task can be either exhilarating for its "playful variety" or frustrating in times of increased conflict, experiences seen even within the debates over the canon itself.

73. See his discussion of the parallels between Jewish and Catholic exegesis on pp. 15-16.

74. To apply the issue to a recent theological issue, both sides of the debate over women's ordination appeal to "tradition," variously defined as the pristine historical, the rule of faith, or official church teaching. For instance, the papal decree *Ordinatio Sacerdotalis* shows careful appeal to each of these loci of tradition, demonstrating the importance of the definition of authoritative tradition within Catholic theological debate.

Is Eve the Problem?

Gary A. Anderson

The story is a familiar one. Adam and Eve sin and then seek, in a futile fashion, to hide from their Maker. Upon discovery, God asks Adam to account for himself. He declares that the woman God bestowed on him gave him the fruit and he ate. God then turns to Eve for her version of the story. She declares that *"the snake deceived me and I ate"* (Gen 3:13). And in these few words, only three in the original Hebrew, reside the case that was to be made both against and on behalf of Eve.

The verse had a large impact on early Christian thought about original sin, in part because of what happened to the word *"deceive"* when it made that short but treacherous journey from its original home in the Hebrew text to its exile within the Greek and Latin Bibles. In Hebrew the verb is somewhat rare but hardly ambiguous.[1] It refers to an act of representing something as what it is not. But when it was translated the sense of deception remained but far more dangerous cargo was taken on board. The Greek and Latin Bibles allow us to construe the verse as an act of sexual seduction.[2] This fateful accident of overlapping semantic fields allowed for the creation of a far more pernicious picture of the deed Eve had wrought. Not only did she consume the forbidden fruit but she was seduced by the Evil Serpent and engendered the demonic figure of Cain.[3]

1. The expression used is *hiššiʾani,* from the root *n-š-ʾ*. Its very pedestrian sense of "to deceive" can be found in Jer 29:8; 37:9.

2. The term in the LXX is *exapataō;* in the Old Latin the term is *seducta.* These terms can mean both "to deceive" and "to seduce."

3. The idea seems to be presumed already in *Protoevangelium of James* 13. In this document, Joseph laments, on finding Mary pregnant, that just as Adam's wife was se-

Frequently, Eve's conception of Cain was not construed as the result of sexual reproduction, in the conventional sense of the term. Rather, Eve conceived Cain through her disobedient act of hearing. This notion of *conceptio per aurem* had a dramatic life in many early Christian texts and iconography.[4] For it provided the impetus for the immensely popular notion that Mary, the Second Eve, undid this sordid act through an unparalleled act of obedience. Indeed, Mary, who was also approached by an angel unawares, was repelled by his provocative and forward suggestion regarding her womb.[5] The reservations of Mary are strikingly evident in iconographic representation. In nearly every rendering of the annunciation Mary is shown turning away from Gabriel, demonstrating strong reservations about the message he brings. Perhaps one of the most famous of these would be that of S. Martini, housed in the Uffizi Museum in Florence. In this painting, Mary's time of prayer is interrupted by the surprise appearance of the angel Gabriel. Mary, rather than responding with immediate approbation to his request,

---

duced and defiled while he was away, so was his. The obvious irony here is that the child conceived by Mary did come by way of angelic mediation, but this time in order to undo what had come about through Eve. One should also compare the peculiar descriptions of Cain's birth in the Armenian and Georgian versions of *Life of Adam and Eve* 21:3 (see G. Anderson and M. Stone, *A Synopsis of the Books of Adam and Eve* [Atlanta: Scholars, 1994]). These versions, which go back to very ancient Greek originals (most likely at least to the fourth century c.e.), describe Cain as having an appearance like the stars and causing infertility and other unpleasantries to arise on earth. This idea of Eve's defilement by the snake is also attested in Jewish sources — see *Targum pseudo-Jonathan* on Gen 4:1 and the discussion in L. Ginzberg, *Legends of the Jews* (Philadelphia: JPS, 1925) V, 133, note 3.

4. See the discussion of this point in the fine article of R. Murray, "Mary, the Second Eve in the Early Syriac Fathers," *Eastern Churches Review* 3 (1971) 372-84. N. Constas is preparing a more detailed manuscript on the problem in Eastern Christendom in general. I would like to thank him for sharing his work with me.

5. For an excellent example of Mary's suspicion of Gabriel see pseudo-Chrysostom, *In annuntiationem* (Patrologia Graeco-Latina 60:775D). In this text Mary takes umbrage at Gabriel's very "forward" suggestions about her womb. After politely asking the visitor to desist from such talk and be gone, she turns quite hostile and asserts that things will turn much worse when her beloved, Joseph, returns and discovers this gross impropriety. Mary's vigilance in this matter, her concern not to be "duped" as Eve was, underscores the strength of her character and the shrewdness of her intellect. For the representation of the annunciation in early Christian art see K. Urbaniak-Walcak, *Die Conceptio per Aurem. Untersuchung zum Marienbild in Ägypten unter besonderer Berücksichtigung der Malereien in El-Bagawat* (Alternberge: Oros, 1992). The typical portrayal of Mary giving some sign of unease as the angel Gabriel approaches cannot be understood without the corresponding patristic data, which document Mary's worry that she would succumb to the devil's wiles (while he is dressed like an angel) as Eve did.

Simone Martini, *Annunciation*. Uffizi, Florence, Italy.
Alinari / Art Resource, NY.

turns hesitatingly to the side, in an expression that suggests modesty. But at
origin, this posture of modesty belies more serious reservations about the
nature of this visit. Only after diligent and shrewd interrogation does Mary
relent to the suggestion of this angel. It is this act of intelligent, or dare I say,
well-conceived, obedience that occasions the birth of the Savior. This second
act of *conceptio per aurem* subverted the first.

But as important as this curious Marian inversion of the sin of Eve is,
its long-term effect on Christendom has been negligible. Excluding its
perdurance as an iconographic feature in Western art, it was quickly dropped
from our growing corpus of commentaries on the subject. The most significant thing that happened to this verse was its incorporation within a letter
attributed to the apostle Paul. In 1 Tim 2:14-15 we find those fateful lines
that have proved such a problem in our modern age: *"Adam was not deceived,
but Eve, having been deceived, came into transgression. So she will be saved
through childbirth, if she remains in faith, love, and sober chastity."*

98

It would be hard to overstate the difficulty these verses have provided modern readers. The noted New Testament scholar Richard Hays has summarized the matter thus:

> The assertion that women will be saved through bearing children clashes flagrantly with Paul's profound conviction that all human beings are saved only by virtue of the death of Christ. The lame exoneration of Adam (2:13-14) also sits oddly in conjunction with Paul's portrayal in Romans 5:12-21 of Adam as the source of sin and typological representative of sinful humanity. The peculiarity of the passage has given rise to various imaginative exegetical attempts at damage control, but the overall sense of the text is finally inescapable: women (or perhaps wives) are to be silent and submissive and to bear children.[6]

For Hays, the danger of this text can be cordoned off by noting its peculiarity within the larger New Testament canon.[7] Believing that a text must resonate across a broad spectrum of New Testament writings in order to have a compelling moral voice,[8] Hays is able to isolate and defuse this potentially combustive and incendiary text. But his methods are, of course, peculiarly modern in that they involve setting the biblical text against itself. Paul is set in contrast to deutero-Paul; and deutero-Paul is set in contrast to the rest of the New Testament.

6. Richard Hays, *The Moral Vision of the New Testament* (San Francisco: HarperCollins, 1996), 67-68.

7. Consider the observation of Jürgen Roloff, *Der erste Brief an Timotheus* (Evangelisch-Katholischer Kommentar, 15; Neukirchen: Neukirchener, 1988), 140: "Um diese für den heutigen Leser außerordentlich befremdliche Argumentation zu beurteilen, muß man erkennen, daß sie nicht nur die ursprüngliche Intention von Gen 2 und 3 verfehlt, sondern auch in Distanz zur paulinischen Interpretation der Sündenfallgeschichte (Röm 5:12-21; 7:7-25) und damit zum Sündenverständnis des Apostels steht. In dem Maße, in dem sie sich von Paulus entfernt, nähert sie sich der Tradition jüdischer Interpretation wieder an. Für Paulus ist Adams Tat unteilbar, und ihre Folge ist von unüberbietbar Totalität. Durch den Ungehorsam des ersten Menschen ist die Sünde in die Welt gekommen und damit ein Unheilszusammenhang geschaffen, der die gesamte Menschheit unterschiedslos umfasst (Röm 5:12-14)." It is not clear to me that the tradition of 1 Timothy represents a "Jewish tradition," but Roloff has put in bold relief the problems and uniqueness of this verse when set against the rest of the Pauline corpus.

8. Hays makes the argument (*Moral Vision*, 195) that for any theme from the New Testament to be morally compelling for Christians it must satisfy three criteria: (1) it must have a textual basis in all the canonical witnesses; (2) it must not stand in serious tension with another major point of emphasis; and (3) it must highlight some substantial or central moral concern. The theme of the subordination of women as propounded in 1 Timothy may, for a small minority, meet the concerns of 3, but it certainly cannot do so for 1 or 2.

This is not an answer that would have resonated with patristic readers. Yet for many of these readers — and here I am anticipating my conclusions — this text from 1 Timothy was equally difficult and troubling. I urge some caution here, for I use the phrase "many of these readers" advisedly, for the tradition of reading we are about to examine is not shared by all. One should consult the *Wirkungsgeschichte* of Jürgen Roloff for other patristic voices on this issue.[9] Yet curiously, none of the texts we will adduce are cited in his overview of the subject. And these texts are hardly a minor voice from the patristic period. Quite the contrary. We shall consider the three most important biblical commentators of the Patristic age: Origen, St. Ephrem, and St. Augustine. And just as important, the reading of Augustine will have an illustrious *nachleben*. It will live on in the work of Milton and Michelangelo. What we are to witness is not some blind alley in the history of Christian thought.

I. Patristic Evidence

A. The Allegorical Approach

Let us begin with Origen, who writes in the first half of the third century and is certainly to be considered the most important Christian Biblical exegete prior to Augustine. We are fortunate to have Origen's exegesis of 1 Tim 2:14 embedded in a commentary on the Song of Songs.[10] The text that concerns us follows upon the lemma of 1:6, *"The Sons of my mother have fought in me, they have made me the keeper in the vineyards; my vineyard I have not kept."* For Origen, the central topic of this verse is the church, otherwise known as the bride of Christ. This identification of the church as the bride of Christ puts the individual members of this sodality in the role of a woman; it constrains the pious believer to think of himself as a woman. *"They have made me the keeper in the vineyard"* refers to the divine inheritance or patrimony of the church, defined by Origen as sacred Scripture, the testimony of God's public revelation to his people. On the other hand, the claim that *"my vineyard I have not kept,"* is understood as referring to those poisonous doctrines that both Jews and Gentiles must jettison before joining the church. This point prods Origen to embark on a rather lengthy digression as to what we

9. J. Roloff, *Der erste Brief an Timotheus,* 143-45.

10. We have used the translation of R. P. Lawson, *Origen: The Song of Songs, Commentary and Homilies* (Westminster: Newman, 1957) 113-17. For the original Latin (the Greek is no longer extant) see L. Brésard and H. Crouzel, *Origine: Commentaire sur le Cantique des Cantiques* (Paris: Cerf, 1991) 322-24.

must be prepared to cast overboard when preparing for membership in God's Holy church.

> But you should not be surprised that she who is gathered out of the dispersion of the nations and prepared to be the Bride of Christ, has sometimes been guilty of these faults. Remember how the first woman *was seduced and was in the transgression* (I Tim 2:14) and could find her salvation, so the scripture says, only in bearing children; which for our present purpose means those who *continue in faith and love with sanctity* (I Tim 2:15). The Apostle, therefore, declares what is written about Adam and Eve thus: *This is a great mystery in Christ and in the church* (Eph 5:32); He so loved her that He gave Himself for her, while she was yet undutiful, even as he says: *When as yet we were ungodly according to the time, Christ died for us* (Rom 5:6); and again: *When as yet we were sinners, Christ died for us* (Rom 5:8).

Here we see a very curious interpretation of 1 Tim 2:14. Understanding this verse spiritually, Origen has extended the metaphor of the church as bride back to the beginning of time. The church takes its point of origin in Eve, the *"mother of all living"* (Gen 3:20). Just as we can be subsumed under the category of the feminine for the purpose of mapping out the contours of our mystical espousal to Christ, so we must imagine ourselves as feminine in order to consider the story of our primal transgression.

But this should give pause. Did not Adam sin? Unfortunately we do not have Origen's entire view on this complicated question. Much to our misfortune, due to the vagaries of text transmission and the unfortunate postmortem usage of a few of Origen's more speculative ideas, we no longer have extant his full commentary on Genesis 1–3. We do, however, possess the commentary of a near disciple, Didymus the Blind.[11] And it is possible to use the evidence of Didymus to fill in what Origen has not left us.[12] Didymus also understood this text from Timothy allegorically. Adam was not deceived, he observes, because, like Christ, he innocently went into exile to rescue God's espoused bride, Israel. Adam's venturing forth from Eden to Earth was typologically suggestive of the incarnation, wherein God the Son left heaven to come to earth to redeem humankind.

11. P. Nautin and L. Doutreleau, *Didyme l'Aveugle, Sur Genèse* (Paris: Cerf, 1976) I, 220

12. The problem of reconstructing Origen's views on the sin of Adam are many and well-known. For an excellent discussion of the issue see C. P. Bammel, "Adam in Origen," in R. Williams, ed., *The Making of Orthodoxy: Essays in Honor of Henry Chadwick* (Cambridge: Cambridge University Press, 1989) 62-93. Her discussion of the value of Didymus, especially his commentary on Genesis, is addressed directly on p. 69.

What is striking here is the fact that in this myth, Eve is no more feminine than Christ is masculine. The sexual attributes of both are demanded not by the nature of the deity but by the needs of the erotic metaphor, bride and bridegroom. Consider the words of Gregory of Nyssa on this question: "The divine power, though it is exalted far above our nature and inaccessible to all approach, like a tender mother who joins in the inarticulate utterances of her babe, gives to our human nature what it is capable of receiving; and thus in the various manifestations of God to humanity, God both adapts to humanity and speaks in human language."[13]

If we presume that Origen followed a similar line of thinking to that of Didymus, then we can understand how easily and naturally he could take the more problematic part of our Timothy text — that women are saved by childbirth — in a completely nongendered way. For Origen the soteriology here was that of a life of virtue: to be saved by childbirth was nothing other than to be saved by perduring in faith, love, and sanctity. In this case, the gendered aspect of the biblical verse is deconstructed by Origen and then writ large over all humankind. That Adam is for Origen not so much the progenitor of all males but the typological pointer to our Redeemer is indicated by his very next comment: "The Apostle, therefore, declares what is written about Adam and Eve thus: *This is a great mystery in Christ and in the Church* (Eph 5:32); He so loved her that He gave Himself for her, while she was yet undutiful."

In sum, we could say that what is striking about Origen is that his allegorical stance allows him to be quite literal about the text in Timothy. Because Adam represents Christ and Eve the Church, Origen can affirm, without the slightest blush, the text's simple sense: *"Adam was not deceived, but Eve having been deceived came into transgression."* But amid this affirmation of the simple sense of the text is an allegorical deconstruction of its gendered implications. Adam is no cipher for all males nor Eve for all females. Adam points solely to God's Christ, a person who stands over and above all gender, whereas Eve is representative of all God's church, both male and female.

B. The Citation Approach

The second patristic writer I would like to examine is the fourth-century Syriac theologian St. Ephrem. Though less well known in the West, he was a

---

13. The reference is from *Against Eunomium* II.419. The translation is from J. Pelikan, *Mary through the Centuries* (New Haven: Yale University Press, 1996) 220.

figure of untold importance in the East.[14] Besides being the intellectual giant of Syrian Christianity, he also loomed very large in Armenian and Russian Christianity. As one scholar notes, "The writings of Ephrem remained so popular that for the medieval Russian Church, they, along with those of John Chrysostom, comprised the entire patristic tradition."[15]

The first thing worth noting is that Ephrem does not introduce 1 Timothy when he reaches that portion of Genesis that treats the transgression (Gen 3:6-7). He tells the story of the transgression without any reference to this New Testament text. For Ephrem, and he is quite emphatic on this point, the transgression is shared equally by Adam and Eve.[16]

St. Ephrem's concern to treat both Adam and Eve as equally culpable is obvious from the way in which he puzzles over the chronological order of the transgression and its effects (Gen 3:6-7). Since Ephrem believed, as did nearly all other patristic writers, that Adam and Eve were *clothed* in glory prior to their sin, this meant that the moment of transgression was marked by an *observable physical transformation*. The discovery of nakedness was no metaphorical allusion to an internal transformation; it marked the loss of something real. Because transgression led to visible change, a real problem would be created if Eve sinned first and was so transformed. For if Eve transgressed first and so lost her garment of glory, Adam would have seen this vis-

14. For a fine introduction to his thought and significance see S. Brock, *The Luminous Eye: The Spiritual World of St. Ephrem the Syrian* (Kalamazoo: Cistercian, 1985).

15. E. Mathews, "St. Ephrem, *Madrashe* on Faith, 81-85; Hymns on the Pearl, I-V," *St. Vladimir's Theological Quarterly* 38 (1994) 45.

16. Because Ephrem believed that Adam and Eve lost *visible* "garments of glory" when they sinned, he puzzled over the chronological order of transgression. If Eve sinned first and so lost her garment of glory, then Adam would enjoy an unfair advantage: he would have empirical proof of the effect of sin that was not available to Eve. About this Ephrem writes (translation from S. Brock, *St. Ephrem the Syrian, Hymns on Paradise* [New York: St. Vladimir's Press, 1990] 213):

> Having once eaten, Eve did not die as God had said, nor did she find divinity, as the serpent had said. For had she been exposed, Adam would have been afraid and would not have eaten, in which case, even though he would not have been guilty in that he did not eat, yet he would not have been victorious either, seeing that he would not have been tempted. It would have been the exposing of his wife that would have restrained him from eating rather than love for, or fear of, Him who gave the commandment. It was so that Adam might for a moment be tempted by Eve's blandishments — just as she had been by the counsel of the serpent — that she had approached and eaten, but had not been exposed.

Ephrem concludes, then, that both lose their garments at the same time because both were tempted and sinned in a state of *comparable* innocence.

ible change and would have known the results of eating the fruit. In order to forestall any such advantage given to Adam, Ephrem observes:

> Having once eaten, Eve did not die as God had said, nor did she find divinity, as the serpent had said. For had she been exposed, Adam would have been afraid and would not have eaten, in which case, even though he would not have been guilty in that he did not eat, yet he would not have been victorious either, seeing that he would not have been tempted. It would have been the exposing of his wife that would have restrained him from eating rather than love for, or fear of, Him who gave the commandment. It was so that Adam might for a moment be tempted by Eve's blandishments — just as she had been by the counsel of the serpent — that she had approached and eaten, but had not been exposed.[17]

Adam's act of transgression was every bit the act of disobedience Eve's was.

Matters turn worse when Adam must account for his actions before the Deity. At this point he casts the blame on Eve: *"The woman with whom you provided me gave of the tree and I ate."* Adam's self-righteous tone is emphasized in Ephrem's paraphrase of these lines: "I *myself* did not approach the tree, nor was it *my* hand which presumed to stretch out for the fruit." Then Ephrem adds: "This is why the Apostle too says, '*Adam himself did not sin, but Eve [did sin and so] transgressed the commandment*' (I Tim 2:14)."[18] By the very way Ephrem cites 1 Timothy, we can see he understands Paul's assertion *"Adam himself did not sin,"* in an ironic manner. 1 Timothy is not telling us anything new about the *nature* of the transgression; Ephrem presumes we all know that Adam most definitely did sin. Instead, Ephrem understands 1 Timothy as alluding to Adam's cowardly act of dissembling before the Deity![19] It is as though the fact that Adam did not, himself, take from the tree

---

17. Brock, *Hymns on Paradise*, 213.

18. *Ibid.*, 218.

19. What I have labeled the "citation" approach also occurs in Greek and Latin writers. By limiting the meaning of 1 Timothy to "a citation" of the Old Testament, the intention of the words are reduced from a more general state of affairs (Adam was not, in fact, deceived) to a specific reference in another writer (in Genesis we read that only Eve's sin was characterized by the term "deception"). If 1 Timothy is a mere citation of Genesis, then it by no means lets Adam off the hook. It merely tells us what we already knew: Eve's sin was characterized by the term "deception," leaving us free to imagine another term to characterize the sin of Adam. Compare the comment of Hugh of St. Victor (Patrologia Latina 175:598) on this: "Doctores Novi Testamenti quandoque dicunt aliquod non fuisse, quod Scriptura Veteris Testamenti non dicit fuisse. Unde quia scriptura Geneseos loquens de seductione mulieris, nihil dicit de aliqua seductione viri, edeo Apostolus dicit: *Adam non est seductus, sed mulier.*"

somehow lessens the consequences of the act. Ephrem, in order to forestall any such foolishness, interrupts the third person voice of his commentary and addresses Adam directly in the second person: "But if He gave you a wife, Adam, He gave her as a *helper* and not as a harmer, as someone who receives instructions, rather than as one who gives orders." This rare use of direct address connotes an emphatic act of chastisement. Though Adam did not, in a technical sense, violate the commandment by taking from the tree himself, he is nonetheless just as culpable for what transpired.

C. Ad litteram as contra sensum?

The most radical approach to Timothy is found in the writings of St. Augustine. At first, this may strike one as all the more curious since St. Augustine, in general, strives to be faithful to the literal sense of Scripture. As we will see below, part of the problem lies in the fact that moderns are heirs to a much different sense of the "literal sense" than was prevalent among the ancients. Augustine's interpretation will appear far more sensible if we bear in mind his approach to the Bible's compositional history.

Augustine's interpretation is of even greater moment than that of Origen or Ephrem because of his influence over later Christian thought in the West. His treatment of 1 Timothy was to be quoted approvingly by most after him.[20]

The problem that exercises St. Augustine is the relation of 1 Timothy to Rom 5:12ff., that is, the relation of a text that focuses blame on Eve to a text that pins all the blame on Adam.[21]

> [W]e cannot believe that the man was led astray to transgress God's law because he believed that the woman spoke the truth, but that he fell in with her suggestions because they were so closely bound in partnership. In fact,

---

20. Consider the following passage from Hugh of St. Victor (Patrologia Latina 175:597). Though he does not name Augustine, it is hard to understand this discussion of the matter without knowing Augustine's thought.

> Quaestio XV. *Adam non est seductus, sed mulier.* Quaeritur uter plus peccaverit, an Adam, an Eva? Solutio. Dicunt doctores, quod mulier non solum peccavit; sed etiam virum peccare fecit. Cui solutioni sic objicitur; Adam est seductus, quia non credidit verum esse, quod hostis persuasit; mulier vero est seducta credens verum esse, quod serpens dicebat; et sic consequens est quod ille scienter, et illa per ignorantiam peccavit; sed gravius est scienter peccare, quam per ignorantiam.

21. The text is from *City of God* XIV.11. We have used the translation of Henry Bettenson, *City of God* (New York: Penguin, 1972).

the Apostle was not off the mark when he said, *"It was not Adam, but Eve, who was seduced"* (I Tim 2:14) for what he meant was that Eve accepted the serpent's statement as the truth, while Adam refused to be separated from his only companion, even if it involved sharing her sin. That does not mean that he was less guilty, if he sinned knowingly and deliberately. Hence the Apostle does not say, *"He did not sin,"* but, *"He was not seduced."* For he certainly refers to the man when he says, *"It was through one man that sin came into the world,"* and when he says more explicitly, a little later, *"by reproducing the transgression of Adam"* (Rom 5:12ff).

In brief, Augustine will not allow 1 Timothy to usurp the picture drawn by Romans 5. For St. Augustine believes, not unlike Hays and other moderns, that the affirmations made in Romans 5, like those of 1 Corinthians 15, proceed from the very heart of Paul's theology. If we are forced to read Romans 5 and 1 Timothy as part of the same inspired Bible, then the meaning and force of Romans will trump Timothy.

Hitherto, moderns and St. Augustine are on equal footing: both decenter 1 Timothy in favor of Romans. But things become more difficult and delicate when we consider what Augustine must do with 1 Timothy once he has subordinated it to Romans 5. Unlike Hays and other moderns, Augustine cannot propose that 1 Timothy is a deutero-Pauline letter or that reflection on Adam's sin was inchoate in the first century and therefore allowed for several overlapping if not contradictory positions. Just because Romans has trumped 1 Timothy, this does not mean that 1 Timothy has lost all value. Augustine is bound by his sense of the inspired nature of all Scripture to take every recess and corner of the canon seriously, however obscure and out of the way it may seem. The text of 1 Timothy as it stands must be interpreted, and not in a way that sets it in contradiction to Romans. So, Augustine must reason, if we learn from Romans that Adam sinned and in so doing introduced death into the world, then 1 Timothy must qualify the *nature* of that sin, not the *fact* of sin itself. *"Adam was not deceived"* cannot mean that Adam was innocent; this would contradict the fact of Adam's sin, which is established in Romans 5. It can only mean that Adam's sin differed from Eve's in the *manner* by which it took place. Adam's sin, Augustine is forced to conclude, was possessed of higher volitional content.[22]

To sum up. Augustine does not ignore 1 Timothy; he reconditions it. 1 Timothy, so retrofitted, can now be read smoothly within the larger corpus

---

22. On the position of St. Thomas and his relation to St. Augustine, see K. Børresen, *Subordination and Equivalence: The Nature and Rôle of Women in Augustine and Thomas Aquinas* (Washington, D.C.: University Press of America, 1981) 207.

of the Pauline writings. In a profound, yet somewhat ironic sense, a reading that first appears as *contra sensum* on further reflection can be appreciated as *ad litteram*. Augustine's reading is a canonical one. And this canonical reading was not without significant epigones; to those we now must turn.

II. Milton's *Paradise Lost*

My next source, John Milton's grand poem *Paradise Lost,* will take us some remove from patristic tradition. This influential epic not only became a staple of the poetic canon of English literature in the West, but it also achieved, in a odd way, a limited degree of authoritative religious status. I am thinking here of the peculiar but significant abridgment and annotation of this text done by John Wesley so that his newly minted pastors could have quick and easy access to the basic tenets of the fall and redemption of humankind.[23]

For our purposes what is striking is Milton's strong continuity with patristic tradition, in particular with the figure of St. Augustine. C. S. Lewis has documented very succinctly, yet ably, the contacts with Augustine,[24] and Pelikan has noted, rather wryly, Milton's dependence on the very patristic and quite Catholic notion of Mary as a second Eve.[25] This in spite of Milton's frequent protests against all things Roman. The Catholic influence is particularly evident at the very moment Satan ends his discourse on the virtues of the forbidden fruit. Eve, having stood in rapt attention, drinking in every word and syllable proves an easy target for Satan's guile.

> his words replete with guile
> Into her heart too easy entrance won:

23. F. Baker, ed., *Milton for the Methodists* (London: Epworth, 1988).
24. C. S. Lewis, *A Preface to Paradise Lost* (Oxford: Oxford University Press, 1942). See, especially, the chapter "Milton and St. Augustine," 66-72.
25. Pelikan (*Mary,* 45) writes, "When in *Paradise Lost,* John Milton, who was 'an author unmistakably opposed to Catholicism and its veneration of Mary,' nevertheless described how, in greeting Eve,

> . . . the Angel Haile
> Bestowed, the holy salutation us'd
> Long after to blest Marie, second Eve,

he was quoting the angelic salutation 'Ave Maria' and with it invoking the ancient parallel of [Mary as Second Eve]. But he did so, as a Puritan and Protestant, in a literary and theological context where the counterpoise of the Catholic portrait of Mary had largely been lost."

> Fixed on the fruit she gazed, which to behold
> Might tempt alone, and in her ears the sound
> Yet rung of his persuasive words, *impregned*
> *With reason,* to her seeming, and with truth;   (IX:733-38)

The curious phrase that Satan's words were "impregned With reason" can only suggest our earlier trope of *conceptio per aurem*. But more important than the survival of this Marian idea is Milton's notion of how the guilt for the Fall was shared. And to this let us now turn.

Milton's story of the transgression begins as does the biblical story with the snake approaching Eve alone and engaging her in conversation about the tree. Eve, at first fearful of all things concerning this tree, slowly comes around to seeing the matter from the snake's point of view. The snake has argued that prior to his consuming of the fruit he had been mute like all the other animals. Yet upon eating from this tree not only did he not die, but he was given voice as if by miracle. Convinced of the snake's honesty and moral probity, Eve proceeds to praise this tree,

> Whose taste, too long forborne, at first assay
> Gave elocution to the mute, and taught
> The tongue not made for speech to speak thy praise.   (IX:747-49)

If this tree could bring the dumb to the point of God's own praise, Eve reasons, then how could it be removed from human experience? "In plain then," Eve asserts,

> what forbids he but to know,
> Forbids us good, forbids us to be wise?
> Such prohibitions bind not.   (IX:758-60)

Eve sounds nearly Kantian, claiming that the law is merely posited and as such imposes its duty heteronomously. Human freedom cannot be bound through such arbitrary means.

Eve, now truly deceived and convicted of her own good motives, resolves to consume the fruit:

> So saying, her rash hand in evil hour
> Forth reaching to the fruit, she plucked, she ate:
> Earth felt the wound, and nature from her seat
> Sighing through all her works gave signs of woe,
> That all was lost.   (IX:780-84)

Having eaten of the fruit she turns to seek Adam to tell him of the wondrous tree. Adam will have nothing of this story. Quite the contrary. Adam has recognized from the very start the wrong that has occurred.

> . . . Adam, soon as he heard
> The fatal trespass done by Eve, amazed,
> Astonied stood and blank, while horror chill
> Ran through his veins, and all his joints relaxed;
> From his slack hand the garland wreathed for Eve
> Down dropped and all the faded roses shed:
> Speechless he stood and pale.   (IX:888-94)

Though dumbfounded, Adam turns to consider his desperate state. Eve has eaten of the fruit and so is doomed to die. Adam, if he perseveres in his innocence, will condemn himself to a life alone. Immediately Adam sets to reasoning how this tragic circumstance might be averted.[26] In so doing, he anticipates the very logic that Moses will later use when he surveys the damage wrought by the veneration of the golden calf and hears of God's intention to destroy Israel down to every last woman and child.[27]

---

26. Here, as well, Milton seems to take his lead from Augustine. Augustine believed that Adam knew full well what he was doing when he sinned. But Augustine, aware that if he describes Adam's actions in too pernicious a form he may draw his sin into the rubric of Satan's own sin, a sin which is beyond the pale of forgiveness, modulates his narrative slightly and attempts to explain the motivation behind Adam's volition. Adam is so audacious, Augustine writes (*City of God* XIV.11), "[because] he was unacquainted with the strictness of God, and he might have been mistaken in that he supposed it to be a pardonable offence he had committed." This question about the severity of God's judgment is, of course, the very *modus operandi* of the Mosaic quotation that Milton puts in Adam's mouth. Moses, by his prayerful intervention, was able to bend back the anger and punishment of God toward Israel; Adam, by using a simple tenor of argument, seems to hope for similar success regarding his own sin.

27. God threatens to destroy all Israel to rebuild the nation from the figure of Moses alone, an image that recalls the calamity of the Deluge, when God destroyed the entire world save one man, Noah. Moses, getting word of this intention, vigorously implores: "O LORD, why does your wrath burn hot against your people whom you brought out of the land of Egypt. . . . Why should the Egyptians say, 'It was with evil intent that he brought them out to kill them in the mountains, and to consume them from the face of the earth'" (Exod 33:11-12). The logic of Moses' request is this: Israel, whom you have created and redeemed at great price, will not only come to naught, but Pharaoh and Egypt, before whom you showed your power, will think you fickle and lacking good judgment. Insofar as Pharaoh was typically thought of, in Christian exegesis, as a type of Satan, the analogy of Moses' words to those of Adam is all the closer.

Nor can I think that God, creator wise,
Though threatening, will in earnest so destroy
Us his prime creatures, dignified so high,
Set over all his works, which in our fall,
For us created, needs with us must fail,
Dependent made; so God shall uncreate,
Be frustrate, do, undo, and labour loose,
Not well conceived of God, who though his power
Creation could repeat, yet would be loth
Us to abolish, lest the adversary
Triumph and say; Fickle their state whom God
Most favours, who can please him long; me first
He ruined, now mankind; whom will he next?   (IX:938-50)

Adam, having given vivid expression to the potential predicament God will find himself in, should he be forced to destroy both Adam and Eve, now turns to his real concern: His overflowing passion and ardent love for Eve. Milton nearly becomes maudlin,

So forcible within my heart I feel
The bond of nature draw me to my own,
My own in thee, for what thou art is mine;
Our state cannot be severed, we are one,
One flesh; to lose thee were to lose my self.   (IX:955-959)

Adam's resolve to eat the fruit, whatever its consequences, moves Eve to great joy. She delivers a rather longish hymn of praise to Adam and, having finished, our narrator observes:

So saying, she embraced him, and for joy
Tenderly wept, much won that he his love
Had so ennobled, as of choice to incur
Divine displeasure for her sake, or death.
In recompense (for such compliance bad
Such recompense best merits) from the bough
She gave him of that fair enticing fruit
With liberal hand: he scrupled not to eat
Against his better knowledge, not deceived,
but fondly overcome with female charm.
Earth trembled from her entrails, as again
In pangs, and nature gave a second groan,
Sky loured and muttering thunder, some sad drops

Wept at completing of the mortal sin
Original; while Adam took no thought
Eating his fill, nor Eve to iterate
Her former trespass feared.   (IX:990-1006)

The most striking line is also the most indicting concerning Adam: *"he scru-pled not to eat, Against his better knowledge, not deceived."* In this line, as many commentators have long noted, Milton directly quotes our text from 1 Tim-othy. Yet, and this aspect has rarely if ever been properly grasped, he under-stands this text not in its simple sense.[28] Rather, his understanding is very de-pendent on St. Augustine's daring misconstrual of the passage.

III. The Sistine Ceiling

Michelangelo received his commission to paint the ceiling of the Sistine Cha-pel in the early sixteenth century.[29] This chapel was built on the model of Solomon's temple and had been dedicated to the assumption and coronation of the Virgin on August 15, 1483.[30] Originally, Michelangelo was commis-

28. C. S. Lewis is the best guide on this matter (*Preface*, 68). He notes the connec-tion to Augustine but not the way Augustine has controverted the text from Timothy: "Adam was not deceived. He did not believe what his wife said to him to be true, but yielded because of the social bond *(socialis necessitudo)* between them (*De. Civ. Dei*, xiv, 11). Milton, with a very slightly increased emphasis on the erotic, at the expense of the affectional, element in Adam's motive, almost paraphrases this — 'Against his better knowledge, not deceav'd But fondly overcome with Femal charm' (*P.L.* ix, 998). But we must not exaggerate the difference. Augustine's *ab unico noluit consortio dirimi* is closely echoed in the Miltonic Adam's 'How can I live without thee, how forgoe Thy sweet Con-verse and Love so dearly joyn'd' (ibid. 908)." Note that Lewis has cited Milton according to the original spelling; this is not the convention in most modern editions of *Paradise Lost*.

29. I am, by no means, an art historian. I have depended on reliable guides for all that follows. Among the more important are: E. Dotson, "An Augustinian Interpretation of Michelangelo's Sistine Ceiling," *Art Bulletin* 61 (1979) 223-56, 405-29; Creighton Gilbert, *Michelangelo, On and Off the Sistine Ceiling: Selected Essays.* (New York: Braziller, 1994); R. Kuhn, *Michelangelo. Die Sixtinische Decke. Beiträge über ihre Quellen und ihre Auslegung* (Berlin: De Gruyter, 1975); John O'Malley, "The Theology behind Michelan-gelo's Ceiling," in *The Sistine Chapel: The Art, the History, and the Restoration* (New York: Harmony, 1986) 92-148; L. Partridge, *Michelangelo: The Sistine Chapel Ceiling, Rome* (New York, Braziller, 1996).

30. One of the most striking features of the ceiling is the interest in women. Not only does Michelangelo balance his sequence of biblical prophets with the Sibyls (all of whom, of course, are women), but when he paints the ancestors of Christ — drawn from the geneaology of Matthew — he foregrounds the women. The irony is that Matthew's

sioned to provide a rendering of the twelve apostles. Feeling that this was too insignificant a proposition, Michelangelo requested broader rein for his artistic talents.

Michelangelo, unlike many of his contemporaries, was not a simple, uneducated artisan. Rather he was a deeply religious man who was frequently in attendance at mass, pored over scriptural texts and commentaries, and, in his early years, was deeply moved by the infamous Florentine religious reformer Savonarola. Like many in pre-Reformation Rome, Michelangelo was also deeply impressed with how the beginnings of creation not only were a witness to the glory of the Creator but also pointed, however mysteriously, to our end or *telos* within the cosmos.

It is worth mentioning that Rome during this period was undergoing a massive revival of the study of the church fathers and a return to the scriptural texts in their original languages. Augustine loomed large in this era, for in *City of God* he, like his Renaissance counterparts, spent a good deal of time correlating the message of the Christian gospel to its near analogues in pagan culture.[31] Augustine was also the favored thinker of one of the leading intellectuals present in the papal court, Egidio da Viterbo, who referred to Augustine as "dux meus" and did much to foster a renewed interest and appreciation for this seminal Christian thinker. Modern scholarship has increasingly been of the opinion that Michelangelo was dependent on some form of theological consultation regarding his subject.[32]

The most striking features of the chapel are the Genesis images on the

---

text takes no interest in these women! Significantly these women are all portrayed as caring and doting mothers; as such they anticipate Mary. Also, of the four corner illustrations that allude, allegorically, to the crucifixion and to the despoiling of Hades, two concern female figures, Judith and Esther. On the prominent role of women within the ceiling, see C. Gilbert, *Michelangelo*, 59-150.

31. Mention is frequently made of the striking parallelism between the great prophets of the Old Testament and the pagan Sibyls on the Sistine ceiling. No doubt this interest in a non-Christian witness to the Gospel was influenced by the disovery of "the New World." But it certainly is not accidental that Augustine was also interested in these Sibyls and their relationship to Christ.

32. Dotson, "Augustinian Interpretation," suggests that this consultation was with Egidio, a well-known cleric from an Augustinian order and one of Pope Julius II's favorite preachers. Since he was so prominent at the very time that Michelangelo was working on the Sistine ceiling such a source for the theological inspiration of the paintings would not be unexpected. J. O'Malley does not wish to dare as specific a source as this but he also claims that "[t]he weight of scholarly opinion today favours the hypothesis that some 'learned theologian' or group of theologians planned what Michelangelo executed, or at least that he had some theologian as a fairly regular consultant" ("The Theology Behind Michelangelo's Ceiling," 105).

central axis of the ceiling. The images from Genesis are nine in number and can be broken down into groups of three (see chart 1). The first three detail very enigmatically the creation of the world up through the fifth day. The second three document the events of the sixth day: the *Creation of Adam,* the *Creation of Eve* — which we should emphasize is the fifth of the nine images thus representing the center of the cycle and the focal point of the composition, and the *Temptation and Expulsion.* The last set of three document the life of Noah and take a curious chronological order: first the *Sacrifice of Noah,* then the *Deluge,* and finally the *Drunkenness of Noah.*

Chart 1. Michelangelo: Sistine Ceiling

Altar

Creation:
    I: Separation of Light and Dark
    II: Creation of Sun, Moon, and Plants
    III: Water Brings Forth Life

Adam and Eve:
    IV: Creation of Adam
    V: *Creation of Eve*
    VI: Temptation and Expulsion

Noah:
    VII: Sacrifice of Noah
    VIII: Deluge
    IX: Drunkenness of Noah

Entrance

The set of nine images, if we place ourselves at the entrance of the chapel, unfold in reverse order. They begin with the *Drunkenness of Noah* and work their way back to the *Separation of Light and Dark,* just over the altar.

Taken in their chronological order *(ordo creationis),* these images map out the beginning of the universe through the fall and end quite appropriately with Noah, for he, rather than Adam is responsible for (re-)populating the entire world (see chart 2). But the images can also be read allegorically, or perhaps better, christologically *(ordo salutis),* most profitably as we will see, along the lines delimited by St. Augustine. What is most striking about this christological reading is that it allows one to read the images from the entrance to the altar in a chronological progression, but now, no longer marking out the fall of humankind but humankind's cosmic redemption (see

113

chart 2).[33] Moreover, this striking balance of the literal and the allegorical would certainly have pleased St. Augustine and his epigones in sixteenth-century Rome who claimed time and again that the allegorical sense could only be intelligible and meaningful if it did not do violence to the literal.

Chart 2

ordo creationis	ordo salutis
I: Gen 1:1-5	IX: Incarnation
II: Gen 1:6-19	VIII: Baptism
III: Gen 1:20-23	VII: Crucifixion
IV: Gen 1:26	VI: Reopening of the *porta paradisi*
V: Gen 2:21	V: Creation of Mary/Church
VI: Gen 3:1-24	IV: Re-Creation of Man
VII: Gen 8:20-21	III-I: A New Heaven and Earth
VIII: Gen 7:6-24	
IX: Gen 9:20-23	

The cycle of redemption begins with the *Drunkenness of Noah*.[34] In Christian exegesis it was a commonplace to associate this act of ignominy with the passion of Christ. The cup that Noah drinks is linked to the cup that Christ must consume. It is certainly significant that the cup of Noah lies at his side as he arouses himself from his stupor. Augustine opens his commentary on this section rehearsing this commonplace:

> Now Christ himself planted a vineyard about which the prophet says, "The vineyard of the Lord of Hosts is the house of Israel" (Isa 5:7), and he drinks of its wine. And the wine may be interpreted with reference to that cup which he speaks of when he says, "Are you able to drink the cup which I am going to drink?" (Matt 20:22) and "Father, if it is possible, let this cup pass me by" (Matt 26:39) where it obviously means his passion.[35]

But for St. Augustine, the vineyard had an additional referent. It represented the flesh that Christ assumed for our sake to redeem us:

33. Dotson, "Augustinian Interpretation," has worked this out in exact detail so that each image in this reverse allegorical order conforms to a single moment in the advancement of redemption. I do not think that she is correct in every detail — indeed she tends to want things overly neat and systematic — but her overall thesis can be sustained.

34. Much of the analysis that follows is dependent on the work of Dotson, "Augustinian Interpretation."

35. *City of God* XVI.2.

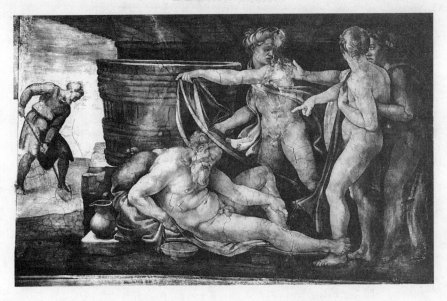

Michelangelo Buonarroti, *The Drunkenness of Noah*.
Sistine Chapel, Vatican Palace, Vatican State.
Alinari / Art Resource, NY.

Or, since wine is the product of the vineyard, we may prefer this meaning, that from the vineyard itself, that is, from the race of the Israelites, was derived the flesh which he assumed for our sake, and the blood, so that he might suffer his passion. *"He was drunk"* — that is, he suffered — and *"he was naked";* for then his weakness was laid bare, that was made evident.[36]

We can see that Augustine's interpretation of the drunkenness of Noah as a type of the incarnation influenced Michelangelo if we compare the posture of Noah, in this miserable state, to the majestic figure of Adam at creation. The postures are strikingly similar, the major difference being that Noah's vision is mournfully cast downward toward earth while Adam looks upward, longingly, toward heaven. Because the creation of Adam could also mirror the re-creation of humankind in the full image and likeness, we can understand the drunkenness of Noah as an act of Christ's self-emptying of his divine form in order to put on a corruptible human body.[37] This rendering of

36. *City of God* XVI.2.
37. This may also explain why the fingers of God and Adam, in the Creation of Adam, do not touch. When we understand this image as pointing to the moment of our re-creation at the end of time — when, as the Father would have said, we will truly become the image — then this spatial gap between the two fingers will achieve closure.

Michelangelo Buonarroti, *Creation of Adam.*
Sistine Chapel, Vatican Palace, Vatican State.
Alinari / Art Resource, NY.

Noah as a type of the incarnate Christ who has come to earth to restore humankind to the divine image also recalls an important patristic (and Renaissance!) notion that the very act and moment of taking on human flesh was perhaps the most important in the soteriological drama.

The next scene, that of the *Deluge,* is a standard Christian *topos* for baptism. According to Dotson, this image represents most specifically the baptism of Christ. In any event it is worth noting a feature of this image that scholars have found difficult to interpret. I refer to the several touching and poignant images of those who have been damned to die in the flood as they seek to save those around them. How could the several individuals in this image who so lovingly respond to those around them not profit from these acts? Are they illicit? Here, we will do well to remember St. Augustine's notion that mere *human* love or desire will not be sufficient to save oneself. Only love directed toward its proper end, that is God himself, will be sufficient. Augustine makes the point time and again that the residents of the two cities are not easily identified by means of human arbitration.[38]

38. Indeed Augustine, on the issue of election, can occcassionally sound more extreme than Calvin. This theme of election shows itself elsewhere in the ceiling, for example, in the portrayal of the brazen serpent lifted up in the desert to save the perishing Israelites, in one of the four pendentives that define the outer four corners of Michelangelo's composition. In this image, some of those Israelites bitten by snakes in the desert are drawn to this salvific image and come near to be healed; yet numerous others are repelled by the image and meet their death amid the harmful snakes. There is no explanation in this image of how the elect are chosen. The image simply draws the starkest form of contrast between the fates of the two groups.

116

Michelangelo Buonarroti, *The Flood.*
Sistine Chapel, Vatican Palace, Vatican State.
Alinari / Art Resource, NY.

The next image is the most difficult because it seems so out of place. In the Bible, the *Sacrifice of Noah* follows the *Deluge,* not following it as in the order of the Sistine paintings. There are two explanations for the order in the chapel that operate in a supporting rather than contradictory fashion. One is that this scene, if understood allegorically, refers to the sacrifice of Christ. As such, this scene neatly follows the *Deluge,* for in Christ's own life, crucifixion followed baptism. On the other hand, taken *ad litteram* the scene would be better attributed to Abel's sacrifice, which not only precedes the flood but also is taken by nearly all Christian commentators as christological in meaning. The work of St. Augustine gives us a way around this problem. Augustine puzzled over how the elect were physically evident to the world at large prior to the age of circumcision. In regard to this, he wrote:

> As for the question whether there was any bodily and visible sign of regeneration before the Flood, like the circumcision which was afterwards demanded of Abraham, and if there was, what form it took, on this the sacred narrative is silent. The account does tell us, however, that those human beings of the earliest times offered sacrifices to God, as is made clear by the story of the first two brothers; and we read that Noah offered victims to God after the Flood, when he had emerged from the ark.[39]

39. *City of God* XV.16.

117

Michelangelo Buonarroti, *The Sacrifice of Noah.*
Sistine Chapel, Vatican Palace, Vatican State.
Alinari / Art Resource, NY.

In Augustine's understanding the act of sacrifice functioned as a sign of the elect. The sacrifices of Cain and Abel at the beginning of Genesis 4 do not mark a unique event but rather illustrate the model that obtained in the pre-Abrahamic era for designating the elect. Augustine infers from all this that Noah must have engaged in the practice of sacrifice before the flood.[40]

The next scene in this sequence is that of the *Temptation and Expulsion of Adam and Eve.* The scene alters the more typical positioning in which either Adam and Eve would flank the tree in a symmetrical fashion, or Eve, being alone beside the tree, takes the fruit and hands it to Adam.[41] The striking

40. According to Dotson ("Augustinian Interpretation," 234, n. 61) it is worth noting that within the frescoes below the ceiling there is mention of the two other scriptural markers of the elect within the City of God. One reads, *observatio antiquae regenerationis a Moise per circoncisionem,* the other, *institutio novae regenerationis a Christo in baptismo.* The addition of the sacrifice of Noah would give us three external markers matching the three periods of biblical history: *ante legem, sub lege,* and *sub gratia.* Also worth noting is the fact that the chapel itself takes its physical dimensions from the temple of Solomon, and so a foregrounding of the role of animal sacrifice in the marking of the elect is hardly surprising.

41. C. Gilbert (*Michelangelo,* 94-95) has underscored how novel Michelangelo is in his depiction of this scene: "Most images naturally follow the account in Genesis 3, where

Michelangelo Buonarroti, *Expulsion from Paradise.*
Sistine Chapel, Vatican Palace, Vatican State.
Alinari / Art Resource, NY.

feature of this depiction is that Adam and Eve both stand to one side of the tree and Adam takes the fruit independent of any assistance from Eve. If we follow our allegorical reading of the ceiling, the placement of this scene after the *Sacrifice of Noah* is altogether fitting since Christ, after his death, proceeds to open the door of paradise for the thief and eventually all the redeemed. The opening of the *porta paradisi* will be followed by the creation of the church through baptism (*Creation of Eve*) and the re-creation of the human form (*Creation of Adam*) in God's image at the end of time.

Let us return to the *Temptation and Expulsion*. A most striking detail for our purposes is the relationship of the snake as tempter to Adam and Eve. A first scan of the image reveals the altogether common parallelism between the snake's visage and that of Eve. Their respective bodily postures also out-

---

the serpent tempts Eve, who eats the fruit, then 'gave also to her husband,' who eats it too. In the Doors of Paradise, a typical representation of the same four events (and only those) as in Michelangelo's three frescoes, Eve hands Adam the apple. Though Ghiberti is always noted as the closest model for Michelangelo's Creation of Adam, as to the interactions of figures, the sin is shown very differently. The other model most often cited for Michelangelo's Temptation, Jacopo della Quercia's marble relief, similarly shows the dialogue of Eve with the serpent while Adam is only an onlooker. In the Sistine Chapel, however, in what seems to be an unprecedented initiative, Adam reaches pressingly to get an apple from the tree. There is no way to see him getting one from Eve or even learning about its delights from her, for she is just now receiving it in her hand. Thus Adam takes a new intiative in sin; when, for once, the male figure is given novel emphasis over the female, it is when he commits original sin."

line strikingly parallel contours. In particular, one should note the lines that define both thigh and torso. Yet this first reading of the image is something of a *trompe de l'oeil*. Because one is so conditioned to expect these similarities, any hint of them conjures up this conventional reading. Michelangelo subjects this conventional image of Eve-as-serpent to a surprising reversal. Far more striking, in principle because they are so unexpected, are the similarities of the snake to Adam. These two figures share similar hair color but most importantly the tense constriction of their musculature is strikingly parallel. Both are straining at the fruit, Adam to wrest it from the tree and the serpent to give it to Eve. Indeed both are so intent on fulfilling their respective intentions that they must grasp and manipulate the tree for leverage as they lunge forward either with or at the fruit. The posture of Eve could hardly be more in contrast. She sits in a reclined position like a matron at a formal Roman dinner and with little observable interest receives the fruit from the aggressive serpent. We might also add that a shadow casts a pall over the face of Adam. This is in strong contrast to the bright and vivifying light that adorns Eve.[42]

This striking portrayal of Adam as an aggressive and active moral agent willfully, if not violently, straining to *seize* the fruit suggests an image of man that Christ decidedly avoided. As Paul so strikingly asserts in the famous lines from the epistle to the Philippians (2:6): *"though being in the form of God, he did not think that equality with God was something to be forcibly seized."* Is it a mere accident that Adam himself, according to the author of Genesis 3, thinks that he is reaching for godliness as he grasps the fruit? In opposition to Adam, we have the serene and nearly angelic posture of Eve who passively receives the fruit. This image, maybe better than any commentary, vividly portrays the relative innocence of Eve in comparison to Adam.

Creighton Gilbert has written quite elegantly on this subject of gender relations in the Sistine ceiling and has noted numerous other features in its artistry that serve to highlight the role of biblical and pagan women. Most strikingly, he also shows that such ideas were not out of the ordinary in Catholic Rome on the eve of the Reformation. Henricus Cornelius Agrippa, in 1509 at the University of Dôle, delivered a declamation on "The Nobility and Preeminence of Women" *(De Nobilitate et Praecellentia Foeminei Sexus).* This essay has been exceedingly popular among feminist scholars and has been hailed as an example of how the humanist movement in the early Renais-

---

42. The shadows on Adam's face suggest the similar effacing of the male faces in favor of the female figures in the illustration of the ancestors of Christ. But putting Adam's face in the shadows could also suggest the more sinister aspect of Adam's desire to sin.

sance period was able to subvert the misogynistic tendencies of earlier medieval Christian culture.[43] As we will see, Agrippa confounds such an evaluation because the exegetical pedigree of his text is not so much Renaissance humanism as it is 1 Tim 2:14 as refracted through St. Augustine.

> Man had been forbidden to eat the fruit, not woman, for she had not yet been created. God wanted her to be free from the start, so it was man, not woman, who commited the sin by eating, man not woman who brought in death *(mortem dedit),* and we have all sinned in Adam *(et nos omnes peccavimus in Adam),* not Eve, and are charged with original sin not through the fault of our mother, a woman, but of our father, a man. . . . God did not punish the woman for eating, but having given man the occasion to eat, which she did from ignorance, tempted by the serpent. Man sinned in full knowledge *(ex certa scientia peccavit),* woman erred through ignorance and deception *(mulier erravit ignorans, et decepta).*[44]

This declamation, which Gilbert rightly believes should be related to the *Temptation and Expulsion,* has drunk deeply from the history of exegesis we have documented. Yet Gilbert, like other feminist scholars working on this remarkable text, haved missed the scriptural texts it depends on.[45] The charge that Adam sinned and "brought in death" and that "we have all sinned in Adam" are clear allusions to Rom 5:12-14. Also, the claim that Eve

---

43. See the fine discussion in A. Rabil's introductory essay to his edition of H. C. Agrippa, *Declamation on the Nobility and Preeminence of the Female Sex* (Chicago: University of Chicago Press) 3-38. Also compare the fine prefatory essay of R. Antonioli found in the French edition of the Latin text cited below (n. 44).

44. H. C. Agrippa, *De Nobilitate et Praecellentia Foeminei Sexus* (Geneva: Librairie Droz, 1990) 65-66.

45. The editors of the series in which Rabil's edition appears describe the intellectual movement into which Agrippa fits as follows: "Misogyny was so long-established in European culture when the modern era opened that to dismantle it was a monumental labor. The process began as part of a larger cultural movement that entailed the critical reexamination of ideas inherited from the ancient and medieval past. The humanists launched that critical reexamination" (*Declamation,* xvi). Rabil himself, in his notes to this particular section, fails to see how Agrippa's ideas were derived from Scripture and from patristic tradition. Instead he quotes one of the more misogynistic writings of Tertullian (*On the Apparel of Women:* "You [Eve or woman in general] are the devil's gateway; you are the first deserter of the divine law; you are she who persuaded him whom the devil was not valiant enough to attack. You destroyed so easily God's image, man. On account of your desert — that is, death — even the Son of God had to die") as an example of the patristic background that Agrippa rejected. No doubt Agrippa was responding to charges like those of Tertullian, but he responded as much within the patristic tradition as without. For Rabil's notes on the matter, see *Declamation,* 62-63, nn. 95-97.

"fell into error through ignorance *and deception*" while Adam violated the command with "full knowledge" is hardly intelligible apart from Augustine's reading of 1 Tim 2:14.

Gilbert's selection of this text from Agrippa as an apt parallel to the *Temptation and Expulsion* is brilliant. What is more, this text represents not a stray and errant opinion in the sixteenth century, but an approach known to many.[46] Yet Gilbert errs in thinking that this insight was somehow privy to the Renaissance intellectuals of early sixteenth-century Rome. This text is not a salvo launched from the front lines of the Renaissance against an earlier, and now antiquated, Christian tradition. To the contrary, these ideas are as old as the patristic period. This particular Renaissance formulation is merely a more eloquent and systematic articulation of their logical tenor.

IV. Conclusion

And where does this leave us? It would seem that two conclusions are suggested. It is frequently stated that Eve, beginning with 1 Timothy, is subject to uninterrupted reproach from churchly elites. As Pelikan puts the matter, "[m]odern polemical writers have combed the works of patristic and Medieval thinkers to find these [negative] stereotypes, and they have amassed a massive catalog that has by now passed from one book and article to another."[47] Clearly the evidence is not as uniform as the massive catalog of secondary literature would suggest. One can hardly deny that these texts exist; this is hardly the point. However we may wish to tell the story, if a complete picture is to be drawn, the data adduced here must be dealt with.

But more important is this question: How, in the end, are we to explain this sympathetic treatment of Eve? As a result of some unnoticed feminist undercurrent in patristic thought? I think not. The theological writers we have cited who picture Eve's guilt in a favorable light would not conform, in other aspects of their thought, to many other concerns of modern feminism. But then, how are we to explain this matter of culpability? Or, to put the matter a different way, why does Romans 5 trump 1 Tim 2:14 in the sources we have examined? I would suggest that these ancient readers came to a position very similar to that of R. Hays or J. Roloff because they were skilled readers of the full canonical form of their Bible. They knew that Romans 5 presented

46. Rabil, *Declamation* 63, nn. 95 and 97, notes several other thinkers of this period who adduce similar arguments.

47. Pelikan, *Mary*, 44.

a picture that cohered more naturally with the other voices of the New Testament. In the face of this strong headwind provided by Romans, the text of 1 Tim 2:14 could do nothing but come about and head for a harbor of rest.

But the pre-Modern sources we have examined were also unique in one small but very important point. It was noted that 1 Timothy was a minority opinion, but it could not be swept aside. Like rabbinic midrash, each verse of scripture pulsated with meaning; if its literal sense proved objectionable because it conflicted with another biblical text, then these two discordant voices would give birth to a third voice, frequently yielding a metanarrative unintended by the biblical author(s). And so it was for Rom 5:12 and 1 Tim 2:14. One verse pins the blame on Adam, the other on Eve. The result: Both Adam and Eve are guilty, but Adam's guilt is greater still. This meaning is found in neither text on its own, but it is for most Christian readers of the pre-Modern era a meaning so obvious that it hardly needed argument.

Toward an Interpretation
of the Shema

R. W. L. Moberly

When first I began the study of theology I was greatly perplexed as to how to understand the relationship between the Bible and contemporary Christian faith. That the Bible and contemporary faith were meant to be related was clear — it is part of the self-definition of Christian faith. But the practice was, to me at least, perplexing; what was one actually meant to do with newly acquired information about, say, the dating, tradition-historical background, and redactional layers within the book of Deuteronomy (other than write essays and answer exam questions about such things)? My attempts to formulate questions about the problem tended to meet with bland reassurances that there wasn't really a problem at all. To this struggling student the writings of Brevard Childs came as a light in the darkness. For I could see that my problem was, *mutatis mutandis*, Childs's problem too, and that to resolve it he was moving beyond familiar and unsatisfactory "conservative" and "liberal" solutions and attempting to reconceptualize as a whole the nature and context of academic study of Scripture.

It took me many years to grasp fully what Childs was proposing, so difficult was it to rethink some of the basic assumptions I already had (a difficulty shared, I suspect, by many others, to judge by the frequency of misrepresentation of Childs by others seeking to expound and either utilize or criticize him). In the course of my learning to rethink the relationship between Bible and contemporary faith, I realized that some of Childs's proposals were better than others (which is presumably an almost inevitable corollary of genuinely pioneering thinking — and Childs himself recognizes that some of his early proposals were inadequate),[1] and I learned also from many other scholars, not least those working in the areas of systematic theology, philosophy, hermeneutics, spirituality, and sociology. Nonetheless, it is a particular pleasure to offer this essay in honor of Brevard Childs, from whom indeed, among biblical scholars, I gratefully acknowledge myself to have learned best and most.

I propose in this essay to offer some reflections on one particular Old Testament text of great importance. I would like to explore some of the interpretive moves that are typically and, I suggest, appropriately made when the biblical text is read as Scripture for today, to illustrate the kind of undertaking that academic biblical study may become in the light of Childs's proposals (though the formulations are, of course, mine rather than his).

I. The Shema: Translation and Significance

The text is Deuteronomy 6:4-5, the Shema:[2] "Hear, Israel: YHWH our God, YHWH is one.[3] So[4] you shall love YHWH your God with all your heart[5] and with all your being[6] and with all your strength."[7]

---

1. *Biblical Theology of the Old and New Testaments* (London: SCM, 1992) 76.

2. I recognize that it is a moot point as to how far just the two verses, Deut. 6:4-5, may appropriately be designated by the traditional Jewish title, "Shema," when Jewish tradition has generally reserved that title for Deut. 6:4-9 (regularly in conjunction with Deut. 11:13-21 and Num. 15:37-41). It is, I suspect, a characteristically Christian usage, based on Mark 12:28-34, which can have the significant hermeneutical effect, evident in Christian tradition and liturgical usage, of separating the content of vv. 4-5 from the instructions concerning it in vv. 6-9.

3. I have argued for this translation of v. 4 in my "'YHWH is One': The Translation of the Shema," in J. A. Emerton, ed., *Studies in the Pentateuch* (Leiden: Brill, 1990), 209-15, reprinted in my *From Eden to Golgotha: Essays in Biblical Theology* (University of South Florida Studies in the History of Judaism 52; Atlanta: Scholars, 1992), 75-81. It has been criticized by T. Veijola, "Höre Israel! Der Sinn und Hintergrund von Deuteronomium VI 4-9," *VT* 42 (1992) 528-41. The main disagreement between Veijola and myself does not concern the primary question of the kind of significance to be ascribed to *'ehad*, but rather the less significant issue of whether *'elohenu* can be predicate to *yhwh* rather than in apposition. Veijola discounts the argument based on consistent usage elsewhere in Deuteronomy on the grounds that later linguistic usage cannot be decisive for the earlier formulation in 6:4b (531). But even if one allows that the words of 6:4b had an earlier existence independent of their present context, this does not mean that they should solely, or even primarily, be interpreted with reference to that earlier context. Or, to put it differently, even if, in another context, *'elohenu* might have been predicate to *yhwh*, its syntactical role changes when it is located in a book with extensive and uniformly consistent us-

The keynote significance of this text is clear for numerous reasons. First there is its intrinsic significance as a statement about God that requires nothing less than the fullest response of which human life is capable. It is a claim of astonishing boldness and scope — without parallel, to the best of my knowledge, in any other religious traditions, other than those which have roots in the Jewish tradition. Second, the history of interpretation has singled this text out. For Jews down the ages, this has been *the* text of Scripture that has defined

---

age of *'elohim* (plus suffixes) in apposition to *yhwh;* in the light of such usage, the syntax of 6:4b, as part of the book of Deuteronomy, is not in doubt.

4. This rendering seeks to capture the nuance of a common deuteronomic idiom, that *waw* consecutive with the second person perfect expresses a linkage of thought that draws out an implication for what Israel must understand and do from what has just been said (e.g., Deut. 7:9, 11; 8:5, 6; 10:19); cf. P. Joüon and T. Muraoka, *A Grammar of Biblical Hebrew* (Subsidia Biblica 14; Rome: Pontifical Biblical Institute, 1991), §119e. I am grateful to Keith Grüneberg for drawing my attention to the significance of the idiom in this context.

5. Arguably one should render *lebab* by "mind," for it is common Hebrew idiom to use *lebab* as the seat of thought (e.g., Isa. 10:7; Ps. 14:1). Most modern translators rightly render Solomon's request for, and God's gift of, a *leb hakam* (1 Kgs. 3:12; cf. 3:9, 11; the sense of *leb* is hardly different from that of *lebab*) as a "wise mind." However, by the time of the New Testament, the introduction into the Shema of *dianoia* ("mind") either as a fourth element (Mark 12:30; Luke 10:27) or as an alternative third element (Matt. 22:37) suggests that "heart" was already understood as in some way distinct from "mind." I think it preferable, therefore, to retain the traditional "heart," and to explain its meaning accordingly.

6. I can think of no modern word that captures the sense of *nepeš,* but regard "being" as slightly less likely to mislead than "soul." However, at a time when there are signs of renewed appreciation of the importance of *enactment* or *performance* as integral to good scriptural interpretation (though as yet within the guild of biblical scholars this is but a cloud no larger than a man's hand), I wish to pay tribute to Rabbi Akiba (as tradition has remembered him) as a supreme interpreter of this word in this context. While being tortured to death, Akiba recited the Shema. When asked by the Roman in charge of the execution why he did so, Akiba replied: "All my life I have been waiting for the moment when I might truly fulfill this commandment. I have always loved the Lord with all my might, and with all my heart; now I know that I love him with all my life *(nepeš)*." And, repeating the verse again, he died as he reached the words, "The Lord is One" (*b. Berakoth* 14b).

7. The sense of *me'od* as a noun is reasonably clear from its usage in 2 Kgs. 23:25, where it depicts Josiah's actions in carrying out his reform as a prime example of obedience to the Shema. Josiah's "strength" in context is the application of his royal power and resources to the implementation of the reform.

The traditional rabbinic interpretation of loving God "with all your might *(me'od)*" as referring to use of money is not, as such, warranted by 2 Kgs. 23:25. Nonetheless, it seems to me a prime example of an interpretation which may be "not original" and "unintended" but is yet a good interpretation, because money so often in practice represents a person's "strength."

their identity and practice as Jews. It is within this tradition that Jesus stands when Mark records him as appealing to this text in answer to a question as to which of God's requirements is the most important of all (Mark 12:28-34). Third, the Old Testament context itself indicates the centrality of the text. Within Deuteronomy, itself a book fundamental to the Old Testament as a whole, these words are the opening, keynote words of Moses' exposition of the covenant between YHWH and Israel; after the Ten Commandments spoken by God (Deut. 5:1-22) and the consequent validation of Moses as the prophet *par excellence,* the one who has unique access to the presence and mind of God and so speaks on God's behalf to Israel (5:23-33),[8] Moses offers a brief preamble to introduce the commandment that he has learned from God (6:1-3)[9] and then speaks the Shema. Fourth, the words immediately following (6:6-9) lay the greatest possible weight on what has just been said:[10] it is constantly to oc-

---

8. Deut. 5:23-33 presents the conceptual understanding of the prophet as one who speaks for God. Although the prime Hebrew word for "prophet," *nabi'*, is not used in this context, it is used in 18:15, where the context (18:16-17) explicitly refers back to ch. 5, thus making Moses the model for prophets.

9. It is notable that Deuteronomy often uses the singular "commandment" *(miṣwâ)* when one might have expected the plural "commandments" *(miṣwot).* It is difficult to be sure of the precise significance of this (one thinks of the puzzling oscillation between "you" singular and "you" plural in Moses' discourse). Nonetheless within Deuteronomy there is an obvious sense for the singular, in that the Shema is precisely that one commandment that in a sense summarizes all the commandments.

10. The precise scope of "these words" (v. 6a) is of course open to debate, but the most natural interpretation of the text as it stands is to take it as referring to what has immediately preceded in vv. 4-5 — as I have already presupposed, by taking vv. 4-5 together as the Shema.

One could make a case that "these words" envisages solely the four Hebrew words of v. 4b. On the one hand, v. 5 may be read in close conjunction with vv. 6, 7, 8, 9 — all these verses begin with *waw* consecutive perfect, and all can be taken as spelling out consequences of v. 4. On the other hand, the public display of a text on armbands, headbands, and the entrances of domestic dwellings and towns (vv. 8-9, cf., e.g., M. Weinfeld, *Deuteronomy 1–11* [Anchor Bible; New York: Doubleday, 1991], 341-43) envisages a text short enough to be readily utilized in such a way — a possible parallel is the succinct *qdš lyhwh* on Aaron's turban (Exod. 28:36; I am indebted here to Veijola [n. 3, 12], many of whose insights may be valid quite independently of his particular reconstruction of the history of the text).

Nonetheless even if such a case were granted (and it remains debatable), Jewish interpretative tradition (as evidenced not least by Mark 12:28-34), in a characteristic and profoundly instructive move, tied v. 5 so closely to v. 4 that one could not speak of God without also speaking of Israel's response to God. So it becomes appropriate to read vv. 6-9 as giving instructions about vv. 4 and 5 together (with, of course, other material also in Jewish tradition).

cupy the attention of Israel through thoroughgoing processes of internalization and appropriation — memorizing, teaching, discussing, reciting, reading, and displaying publicly in places of symbolic significance.[11] The Shema is presented as — to use the wording of Jesus — the pearl of great price, the one thing needful, that which matters more than anything else and will (presumably) make sense of everything else.

If the Shema is so important, what does it actually mean? On the one hand, its wording is so familiar in Jewish and Christian contexts that one can easily forget that the text is in certain ways problematic. On the other hand, the rich history of usage of the Shema, especially in Jewish tradition, gives it a breadth and depth of resonance that in varying degrees may relativize the significance of a discussion of its "original meaning." The purpose of this discussion is not to dull the luster of its resonance and significance for Jews, nor to seek some possible "original meaning" that may lie behind the present wording of the biblical text.[12] Rather, the purpose is to inquire whether a fresh appreciation of the meaning of the text in Deuteronomy and in the wider biblical context may not be able to add to an understanding of its responsible contemporary appropriation for Jews and Christians in their different ways.

II. Approaching the Task of Interpretation

The first question is what it means to say that YHWH is "one" *('ehad)*. This seems to me in many ways an extremely difficult question, not always illuminated by the extensive history of discussion about the "unity" or "oneness" of God.[13] For example, to say that "YHWH is one" may be quite distinct from saying that "there is one God." What does "one" as a predicate of YHWH *mean?*

A characteristic move of biblical scholars at this point is to prescind from theological and philosophical debates and to suggest that the key to un-

11. For some of the possible symbolic resonances of doorposts and city gates, see, e.g., Mircea Eliade, *Patterns in Comparative Religion* (London: Sheed and Ward, 1958), ch. 10.

12. One recent and interesting discussion, which argues that v. 5 and the relative clause in v. 6 are secondary additions and interprets the text without them (and, even with them, solely in the supposed chronological order of addition) is T. Veijola, "Das Bekenntnis Israels. Beobachtungen zur Geschichte und Theologie von Dtn 6,4-9," *Theologische Zeitschrift* 48 (1992) 369-81.

13. See, e.g., E. B. Borowitz, ed., *Ehad: The Many Meanings of "God Is One"* (New York: Tabard, 1988).

derstanding lies within the historical context of seventh-century B.C. Judah, to which the book of Deuteronomy, or at least a significant portion of it, was once directed. The most common form of this suggestion is that Moses' discourse is in one way or other a coded reference to, or program for, Josiah's reform, and that the Shema is part of a program for religious reform on this basis: one God, one people, one cult. Thus, for example, Claus Westermann says:

> This word [Deut. 6:4] brings Yahweh's oneness to consciousness and expresses it conceptually. This confession to the one God grew out of the long and difficult struggle for the independence of the Yahweh-faith in polytheistic surroundings. The centralization of the cult in Jerusalem is commensurate with this: *one* worship for the *one* God.[14]

Or Norman Gottwald says:

> The sonorous, almost mesmerizing, liturgical style of Deuteronomy and DH interpretive passages sets forth a solemn coherent message about the indivisible unity of *one* God for *one people* in *one land* observing *one cult.*[15]

There are undoubted links between the language and concepts of Deuteronomy and of Josiah's reform as told in 2 Kings 23, a point to which we will return. Nonetheless, even on its own terms, there are obvious problems with this kind of interpretation. First, there is the simple difficulty that there is no evidence in either Deuteronomy or 2 Kings for a reform program utilizing the word "one" (*'ehad*) as some kind of slogan or catchword. Where one would most expect it, in the prescriptions for the place of worship in Deuteronomy 12, it is absent; the text speaks not of "one place" (*maqom 'ehad*) but of "the place that YHWH will choose . . ." (*hammaqom 'ašer yibhar yhwh,* 12:5, 11, 14).

Secondly, the intrinsic logic of "one worship for the one God" remains elusive, to me at any rate. That is, I fail to see how it follows that "the one God" (if one allows this to be an adequate representation of *yhwh 'ehad*) cannot be worshiped in more than one place. For example, there are certain obvious senses of this that would be contradicted by the steady emergence and spread of synagogues in the second temple period. If it is argued that "worship" intrinsically means "sacrificial worship," then what is it about sacrifices

---

14. *Elements of Old Testament Theology* (Atlanta: John Knox, 1982; translated from the 1978 German edition), 32. The italics are his.

15. N. K. Gottwald, *The Hebrew Bible: A Socio-Literary Introduction* (Philadelphia: Fortress, 1985), 390. The italics are his.

to YHWH that restricts their offering to one place? Deuteronomy 12 does not address the question as to what it is about the nature of YHWH (as "one") which restricts sacrificial worship to one place. Rather, the text is concerned for the purity of Israel's sacrificial worship, so that Israel may remain faithful to YHWH. This is specified in terms of obedience to divine choice of place of worship. The intrinsically invalid nature of worship in more than one place is not on the agenda.

My concern here, however, is not to argue the merits of particular versions of a well-known religio-historical debate. Rather it is to reflect on the assumptions implicit in posing the problem of interpretation in this form. I suggest that the kind of interpretation offered by the characteristic move to a program of religious reform risks becoming a kind of category mistake. The issue is not the intrinsic usefulness of setting a text in a likely historical context, for the intrinsic value of such an exercise is (or should be) beyond argument (however much one may argue over the details of it). It is rather the assumption that to set the Shema in a context of a specific religious reform says all that really needs to be said about it. The problem is when an issue of theology is not only illumined by a historical background (Josiah's reform, Mesopotamian treaties, epigraphic discoveries, etc.) but is essentially transposed into a question of religious history. Such a transposition is perhaps only possible when "theology" is understood in an attenuated sense as an exercise of the mind on religious texts and topics apart from engagement with fundamental questions of trust, allegiance, prayer, and ways of living — as though "God" were solely a word or concept to discuss and not also the fundamental reality of human existence. The task of interpreting the meaning of YHWH's oneness and Israel's responsibility to love YHWH is thus not completed by hypothesizing a context in which one can explain why, in religio-political terms, such words might have been said, and by proposing an appropriate meaning for the words in that context.

One way of putting this would be to point to the obvious fact that Deuteronomy makes no reference to any specific program of religious reform, Josiah's or anyone else's. As Deuteronomy presents it, the Shema is grounded in the intrinsic logic and implications of YHWH's self-disclosure at Horeb and the contemporary nature of YHWH's covenant with Israel (Deuteronomy 4–5). Moses' discourse climaxes in a challenge to covenant renewal, a choice between life and death (chs. 29–30). To be sure, life is envisaged in terms of obedience to all the stipulations within Deuteronomy. But it is questions of God and Israel, of faithfulness and unfaithfulness, that the book raises. On one level, this is a matter of needing to interpret Deuteronomy as a book. That is, if one accepts conventional accounts of an original legal corpus that has been extensively redacted, one still needs to give an account of the book that is the result of all this, and not just a history of its parts. But it is not just that accounts of religious history need to be extended. The critical questions are those of understanding and evaluation. Is one to understand the language of God and Israel, of faithfulness and unfaithfulness, as solely literary conventions reflective of underlying social, political, economic, and religious practices and conflicts? Or is one also to understand it as representing a discernment of the will of God and of human relationship to God that is of enduring truth?

There are here deep underlying problems with regard to religious language and epistemology and the relationship between religious language and ways of living both in antiquity and today. What is necessary to understand a claim that "YHWH is one" and that Israel should love YHWH without reserve (and what does "understand" mean in this context?)? On what grounds could such a claim be recognized (by whom?) as valid (for whom?) in its ancient context? On what grounds could such a claim be recognized (by whom?) as possessing enduring truth content (for whom?) in subsequent and contemporary contexts? The problem is not primarily that of insufficient historical evidence (meager and difficult to interpret though it is in the case of ancient Israel), nor of maintaining an appropriately dispassionate and objective stance in the evaluation of such evidence (vital and demanding though this is). It is rather that there are dimensions of the interpretative task that do not readily fit within common paradigms of religio-historical inquiry, because they involve the application of criteria which relate to the interpreter's sense of priorities as to what really matters in life (i.e., questions of religious truth). On such matters there is no "right answer" that could even in principle be established that does not also relate to the context and concerns of the interpreter. For the Jew and the Christian the *reception* of the Shema as a scriptural text, definitive of religious understanding and practice, is integral to such context and concerns.

I wish therefore to try afresh to interpret the Shema as a text of Jewish and Christian Scripture. To do this I will utilize various interpretive clues within the biblical text. First is the question as to what "one" means as predicated of YHWH in terms of Hebrew usage. The second question concerns the meaning of "love" within the context of Deuteronomy (and the account of Josiah's reform in 2 Kings 23). Third, I want to reflect on two important differences that a wider canonical context may make to an understanding of YHWH as one and to Israel's love of YHWH. Finally, I will conclude with some reflections on the bearing of such discussion on contemporary life.

III. YHWH Is One

First, the meaning of "one" *('ehad)*. General usage of *'ehad* in the Old Testament is not obviously illuminating with regard to its meaning in Deut 6:4.[16] If other usage is to be genuinely illuminating, it needs to represent the same kind of usage. Initially, therefore, we note that one must seek to understand "YHWH is one" in connection with its immediate sequel; for it is vv. 4 and 5 together that constitute the words to which attention must be paid at all times. That is, what "YHWH is one" means must be something that makes appropriate the total and unreserved response of "love" that is immediately specified. It is an intrinsically religious statement in that it seeks the kind of total response of people that is characteristic of religion as classically understood. The theological affirmation that "YHWH is one" is an affirmation intrinsically related to human response in terms of "love." Language about God belongs in conjunction with a certain kind of human awareness and practice.

The best example of biblical Hebrew usage that illuminates this kind of sense of "one" *('ehad)* is of course already well-known in discussions of the Shema. It is Song of Songs 6:8-9. The man (apparently) is speaking, and he says in praise of the woman:

> There are sixty queens, and eighty concubines, and young women beyond counting. Unique *('ahat)* is she, my dove, my perfect one; unique *('ahat)* is she to her mother, the flawless one is she to her parent. The young women saw her and acclaimed her, the queens and concubines also, and they praised her.

The point is not that the loved woman is an only child, but that she enjoys special favor not only with her lover but also with her mother and that other women who might be rivals for the attentions of the man acknowledge the specialness of this woman. This text interestingly illuminates Israel's confession of YHWH as "one." First, "one" has the sense of "one and only," "unique," not in the sense that there are not in fact other women, but in the sense that this woman matters in a way that other women do not and evokes a uniquely positive response. So the confession of YHWH as "one" is opaque to questions of "monotheism" (a problematic concept whose use is in need of serious reevalua-

16. See, e.g., standard dictionary discussions such as that of Lohfink and Bergman in *TTI*, 193-201, or Sauer in Jenni/Westermann, *THAT* I, 103-7. There is valuable discussion of Hebrew usage in S. David Sperling, "The One We Ought to Love," in *Ehad* (n. 13 above), 83-85. It is sad that he concludes by abandoning the task and suggesting that *'ehad* must be textually corrupt.

tion),[17] for it is concerned to affirm that YHWH must be the recipient of Israel's attentions in a way that no other person or thing can be. The implications for "other gods" are wholly and solely those of displacement, indeed rejection.

Further, the language and conceptuality in Song of Songs is intrinsically personal and relational, as is the religious language of the Shema. What is said about the woman is not separable from the understanding of those who say it. The uniqueness of the woman, in the sense intended, is not something that would in principle be accessible to scientific inspection and examination of the woman, as though it were some kind of empirical datum like other empirical data. The phenomena of relationship, admiration, and love are, to be sure, open to social-scientific and psychological study, insofar as they manifest themselves in characteristic patterns of behavior; but even here there are likely to be dimensions that are important to the participants but elusive in analytical terms — elusive certainly to a nonparticipant and possibly also, though differently, to a participant. The point for our purposes is that religious language shares the characteristics of that kind of human language whose comprehension and appropriate usage is most closely tied to the actual living of certain kinds of human life. To say that YHWH is "one" is not to say something about God that is separable from its human counterpart of "love," but rather designates YHWH as the appropriate recipient of unreserved human "love."

IV. Love of YHWH

What, then, is the specific content given to Israel's "love" within Deuteronomy? A preliminary observation is that "love" in a covenantal context is more about attitude and action than it is about emotion (though emotion could certainly be included within loving "with all your being," *nepeš*). This point, clear already within Deuteronomy (as, for example, in the linkage between "love" and "observing commandments," 5:10), is in some ways under-

---

17. See, e.g., the crisp observations by Christopher Seitz in "The Divine Name in Christian Scripture" in his *Word without End: The Old Testament as Abiding Theological Witness* (Grand Rapids: Eerdmans, 1998) 251-62, esp. 254-57. Seitz observes that in the modern period "we have a theoretical monotheism conjoined to a functionally polymorphous religiosity, summarized nicely by the phrase 'We all worship the same God,'" and that "perhaps the greatest single irony of modern liberal Christianity in the West is that its most self-confident minimal statement (a monotheistic faith) is precisely what has created a functional and widespread polytheism" (256). In other words, "monotheism" in modern parlance has a sharply different significance and dynamic from the Old Testament witness to YHWH as the one God (although arguably it may not be so different from some of the actual religion of ancient Israel).

lined by certain well-known parallels of form with other ancient treaties in which a vassal is obligated to "love," that is, obey,[18] its overlord.[19] Beyond this, however, content is given to "love" by the various emphases of Moses' discourse. Among these, particular attention must be paid to Deuteronomy 7, whose placement so soon after the Shema suggests that it is a primary exposition of the implications of the Shema.

This is something of an embarrassment to the contemporary believer, for Deuteronomy 7 contains the fullest exposition within the Old Testament of what is arguably the single most morally and theologically problematic aspect of the Old Testament, God's command to Israel to practise *herem*. The practice of *herem*, at least as set out in Joshua 1–11 and 1 Samuel 15, envisages the putting to death of an entire population, not only soldiers but also noncombatants, women, children, and livestock, as part of a ritual dedication to YHWH. As a practice of ancient religion, it is on one level fully comprehensible, though it involves some stretch of the imagination for most modern readers (and so the verbal form of *herem* is perhaps best translated by some deliberately archaic and cumbersome term, such as "put to the ban," to give some indication of the problematic nature of conceptualizing what the term means). The practice of *herem* was also apparently shared with at least one of Israel's neighbors (it is attested in the Moabite stone),[20] though it was not characteristic of the civilizations of either Mesopotamia or Egypt. But as something ascribed to the will of God, not merely tolerated but explicitly prescribed with disobedience penalized, it is problematic when it is also proposed that the God who wills *herem* is the God in whom someone

---

18. See W. L. Moran, "The Ancient Near Eastern Background of the Love of God in Deuteronomy," *CBQ* 25 (1963) 77-87; M. Weinfeld, *Deuteronomy and the Deuteronomic School* (Oxford: Clarendon, 1972), 333f.

19. In interpretive terms, this much-vaunted parallel may, I suggest, obscure at least as much as it illuminates. For in the context of treaties between conqueror and conquered, the sense of "love" as obedience is likely to focus maximally on conduct and minimally on intention or motivation (except for fear of reprisal). As such it engenders precisely the kind of obedience that creates cynicism as to whether obedience is a positive and desirable quality for human beings (as opposed to dogs). Deuteronomy, by contrast, insists on the thoroughgoing internalization and appropriation of obedience so that action and intention are in full harmony. In relation to a human overlord, such a total demand would tend toward an obscene and idolatrous totalitarianism (the exceptions being those rulers who may rightly engage the hearts and minds of their people; a response, however, that to be true can only be given, not exacted or manipulated); in relation to the one God it is the condition of life, good, and blessing (Deut. 30:15-20).

20. See, e.g., J. B. Pritchard, ed., *Ancient Near Eastern Texts* (Princeton: Princeton University Press, 1969[3]) 320f.

today might be expected to believe as the one true God. For is not a God who sponsors murder rather the devil, and as such to be shunned at all costs if human well-being is to be promoted?

The issues here are many and complex. One might wish that Kierkegaard, in his critique of rational and moral religion in *Fear and Trembling* and elsewhere, had given some consideration to *ḥerem*, which surely poses problems more formidable even than those of child sacrifice. In the present context, I only offer one observation: Whatever the "literal" implementation of *ḥerem* in certain Old Testament narratives might appear to mean, and whether or not *ḥerem* was ever actually implemented in Israel's warfare,[21] Deuteronomy 7, I suggest, presents *ḥerem* as a metaphor for religious fidelity which has only two primary practical expressions, neither of which involve the taking of life.

Within Deuteronomy 7, the explicit rationale for *ḥerem* is Israel's holiness and election (7:6),[22] which is an essential counterpart to the confession that YHWH is "one" and that Israel is to love him unreservedly. The introduction of the statement in v. 6 with "for" *(ki)* shows that it is being given as the reason for that which immediately precedes, the practice of *ḥerem*. The nature of *ḥerem* is spelled out in 7:1-5. Initially, the scenario of strong opposition within the land YHWH is giving to Israel is evoked, with the requirement that when YHWH gives them into Israel's hands then Israel "shall utterly make them *ḥerem*," making no covenant and showing no mercy (vv. 1-2). What *ḥerem* means is then given content by two stipulations. First, negatively, no intermarriage, for that would lead to religious unfaithfulness (vv. 3-4). Second, positively, religious objects belonging to the cults of other deities are to be thoroughly destroyed and so removed from the sphere of Israel's life (v. 5). These stipulations not only make no mention of the taking of life, but the first of them presupposes that life is not taken (for, to put it crudely, corpses do not raise the temptation of marriage). That which is

21. For a guide to extensive debate on these and related issues, see Gerhard von Rad, *Holy War in Ancient Israel* (Grand Rapids: Eerdmans, 1991). Von Rad's classic modern essay of 1951 has been reissued with an introduction by B. C. Ollenburger, which helpfully situates von Rad's work, and also an annotated bibliography by J. E. Sanderson on issues of war, peace, and justice in the Hebrew Bible. On *ḥerem* specifically there is a useful assemblage of material in P. D. Stern, *The Biblical Herem: A Window on Israel's Religious Experience* (Brown Judaic Studies 211; Atlanta: Scholars, 1991).

22. Deut. 7:6-8 must be a prime candidate for the Old Testament passage most regularly taken out of context by biblical scholars. I have long since lost count of the number of accounts I have read that refer to this passage as a *locus classicus* for election but do not mention that Israel's election is specified in this context to serve as a warrant for the practice of *ḥerem*.

specified for destruction is exclusively religious apparatus. What we have is a retention of the (in all likelihood) traditional language of *herem,* but a shift in the direction of its acquiring significance as a metaphor. Not a "mere" metaphor, for practical action is still envisaged; but it is action of a narrow and specific kind, relating to two issues which become representative of religious fidelity, dedication to God, as a whole. If this understanding is on the right lines, then usage of *herem* terminology elsewhere in Deuteronomy (e.g. 20:16-18) is not a problem. For once it is grasped that the term functions as a metaphor for religious faithfulness, then all injunctions are interpreted accordingly.[23] The practice of *herem,* as a metaphor for religious fidelity, is that which demonstrates and enables Israel's unreserved love for YHWH.

If this is correct, what we can see in Deuteronomy is something deeply characteristic of the biblical tradition and of the Jewish and Christian faiths that are rooted in it. A particular religious practice is not necessarily abandoned when for one reason or other it becomes problematic (though, of course, it may be abandoned) but rather is reinterpreted. In particular, something may cease to be "literally" practiced and yet may retain, or even freshly acquire, considerable significance as a metaphor for religious thought and behavior (as is the case, for example, with sacrifice). Although to the unsympathetic this may seem simply like an attempt to defend the indefensible and a refusal to admit error and break with it (and this may, of course, sometimes be the case), it is at heart a confidence in the intrinsic wealth of resource within the existing tradition that enables renewed vitality through fresh reconfiguration and reappropriation of elements already present. The validity of any such enterprise can hardly be appraised in isolation from the actual practices in life that it encourages and enables.

That *herem* thus understood gives content to love for YHWH is further supported by the biblical text. At the outset of the detailed prescriptions about worship of YHWH in Deuteronomy 12, the stark contrast between worship of YHWH and worship of other gods is again enunciated, with explicit recapitulation of the command to destroy objects representative of the worship of other gods (12:3, cf. 7:5). The one other place in the Old Testament where this language features prominently, apart from a brief usage in the context of Hezekiah (2 Kgs. 18:4; cf. 18:22), is in the account of

---

23. A fuller study of *herem* within Deuteronomy and related literature is of course a necessary test for my proposed interpretation. The present paper is heuristic and exploratory. For a not dissimilar proposal with regard to the interpretation of the book of Joshua, see Lawson G. Stone, "Ethical and Apologetic Tendencies in the Redaction of the Book of Joshua," *CBQ* 53 (1991) 25-36.

Josiah's reform in 2 Kings 23 (esp. vv. 4, 6, 12, 14, 15). This is the more striking in that the concluding comment on Josiah's character and behavior in 2 Kings 23 is that he was a king without parallel in that he "turned to YHWH with all his heart and with all his being and with all his strength, according to all the law of Moses" (v. 25). This is the sole occurrence beyond Deut. 6:5 of the precise wording of the latter part of the Shema. The text uses "turn" *(šub)* rather than "love" *('ahab)* because the context of 2 Kgs. 22:3–23:3 makes such a term of repentance appropriate. But it is clear from the wording that Josiah is portrayed as a prime example of what it means to fulfill the Shema. And if the practice of the Shema involves the practice of *ḥerem*, and *ḥerem* as specified in Deut. 7:5 is precisely what Josiah does, then the portrayal of Josiah's actions as the "love" specified in the Shema is even clearer.

The suggestion that *ḥerem* in Deuteronomy is a metaphor that no longer envisages the taking of life is not necessarily disproved by the reference to Josiah putting to death priests of the high places (23:20). For the overwhelming emphasis in the account of the reform is on the destruction of religious objects and the desecration *(ṭme' piel,* that is, rendering unsuitable for religious practice) of the locations of such objects, and the reference to "sacrificing" the priests is isolated. Moreover, its resonances are not so much with the preceding acts of destruction as with the words of the man of God in 1 Kgs. 13:2, whose strange and symbolic story is referred to at remarkable length at the culmination of Josiah's actions (23:16-18); that is, the act of putting to death may not necessarily be an element of the *ḥerem* that Josiah otherwise practices in his destruction of objects and desecration of places, but may be independently motivated. The important point, however, is not to argue that Josiah's killing of the priests could not have been seen as integral to his religious reform, for it might have been, and reservations (from another age and context) about such killing should not be foisted anachronistically on the Hebrew writer. Rather, even if the killing were integral, it is nonetheless marginal to 2 Kings 23 rather than central. Our concern is to see that in Deuteronomy and the closely related narrative of 2 Kings 22–23, the concept and practice of *ḥerem* is in a process of reinterpretation as a metaphor for fidelity to YHWH in the face of powerful opposition, a process in which the taking of life is being marginalized in favor of other concerns. It is likely that a grasp of the metaphorical nature of *ḥerem* was integral both to the compilation of Deuteronomy in its present form, in which it becomes a primary interpretation of the Shema, and to the preservation and reception of Deuteronomy as Israel's Scripture within the continuing life of Judah.

V. Love of God and Love of Neighbor

In addition to the context for interpreting the Shema provided by Deuteronomy and 2 Kings 22–23, there is, for the Christian, another context, that of the New Testament. Here there is an integral linkage between love of God, as in Deut. 6:4-5, and love of neighbor, as in Lev. 19:18, in the teaching of Jesus (Matt. 22:34-40 par. Mark 12:28-34 and Luke 10:25-28) and elsewhere in the New Testament, implicitly in Paul (Rom. 13:8-10) and explicitly in John (1 John 4:20-21). I offer a few preliminary comments on this.

First, the linkage between love of God and love of neighbor makes explicit one of the most characteristic elements of the biblical witness to God and humanity — not only that loving God and loving one's neighbor are inseparable, but that the latter can be a decisive test of the reality of the former. If one asks how one gives content to claims about invisible spiritual reality, the classic answer is: by considering the publicly accessible moral and relational content of the lives of those who make the claim. A form of this approach is, for example, basic to Jeremiah's critique of King Jehoiakim (Jer. 22:13-19) and of other prophets (Jer. 23:9-32), and it is basic to John's account of the difference between true and false faith (1 John 4).

Second, the New Testament does not present this linkage between love of God and love of neighbor as in any way a novelty, a new quality of insight attained by Jesus. On the contrary, both Mark 12:28-34 and Luke 10:25-28 present the insight as one familiar to, even formulated by, Jesus' interlocutors. That is, it is taken for granted that this linkage had already been made within Jewish tradition.[24] This means that a context of understanding beyond that of Deuteronomy alone had become decisive in that context of Jewish faith in which the Shema had been given prominence.

This is important for interpreting the Shema, because the Shema itself does not make this linkage but it is enriched by it. This is too easily overlooked by Jews and Christians for whom the linkage is taken for granted. Consider, for example, the following statements about the Shema. The first is by a Jew, Gunter Plaut:

> The *Shema* thus came to be like a precious gem, in that the light of faith made its words sparkle with rich brilliance of varied colors. Negatively, it

---

24. Whether or not the linkage of Deut. 6:5 and Lev. 19:18 can be found in Jewish texts that antedate the Gospels, it misrepresents the Gospel portrayal to assert that the linkage is "unique" to Jesus, even though Christians have regularly assumed that such uniqueness must be the case (so, e.g., W. Schrage, *The Ethics of the New Testament* [Edinburgh: Clark, 1988; translated from the German edition of 1982], 71).

underscored the Jew's opposition to polytheism and pagan ethics, to the dualism of the Zoroastrians, the pantheism of the Greeks, and the trinitarianism of the Christians. Positively, the One God was seen to imply one humanity and therefore demanded the brotherhood of all; it spoke of the world as the stage for the ethical life and linked monotheism and morality. It meant that God undergirded all laws for nature and for mankind; hence heaven and earth as well as human history were His domain.[25]

The second is by a Christian, Bruce Birch:

> As a confessing community Israel expresses allegiance to its God as the one true God. This may be seen especially in the *Shema*. . . . This central focus on Israel's God as the one God, and the sole object worthy of full love and loyalty was to be passed on as a precious gift to succeeding generations, and kept constantly before them (Deut. 6:6-9). It was the corrective to all forms of allegiance claimed by the world, for example, idolatry, nationalism. It is this focus on God which is the heart of all commandments and statutes attempting to express the covenant understanding; therefore, it is never the commandment itself which is ultimate but the God to which commandment points as the one to whom obedience is due.[26]

These may perhaps be true of the Shema in its wider biblical context, as construed by Jew and Christian. They are not, I submit, true of the Shema in isolation from that context. The Shema may become compatible with "one humanity and . . . the brotherhood of all" and may become "a corrective to all forms of allegiance claimed by the world . . . nationalism"; but within Deuteronomy it does not signify such things. We should remember that Deuteronomy, among other things, excludes Ammonites and Moabites from the assembly of YHWH in perpetuity and even prohibits Israel from seeking their well-being in perpetuity (23:4-7, ET 3-6); and Israel must not forget to blot out the memory of Amalek from the earth (25:17-19). One suspects that Ammonites, Moabites, and Amalekites might have been less confident than Plaut and Birch about the significance of the Shema. The point is that part of what has enabled the Shema to be of enduring significance is precisely its preservation and interpretation within a canonical context that has given normative guidelines for understanding and use, most of all in the linkage with love of neighbor.

25. *The Torah: A Modern Commentary* (New York: Union of American Hebrew Congregations, 1981), 1369f.
26. *Let Justice Roll Down: The Old Testament, Ethics, and Christian Life* (Louisville: Westminster/John Knox, 1991), 174f.

The injunction "You shall love your neighbor as yourself" is itself not without interpretative problems, one of which is defining who counts as a neighbor. For if, say, an enemy or foreigner does not qualify as "neighbor," then there is no corresponding requirement to love such a person. This is precisely the issue raised by the lawyer in debate with Jesus in Luke's Gospel (10:25-29). Jesus' answer, in the story of the "Good Samaritan," is definitive for a Christian understanding (10:30-37). Jesus entirely rejects the very idea that understanding "neighbor" is a matter of categorization, defining who is "in" and who is "out." Rather, he uses the story to pose the question of what it means to *be* a neighbor, where the generosity of mercy dispenses entirely with the need for categorizing people (and thereby, all too easily, implicitly rationalizing failure to be a neighbor).

There is thus a characteristic logic of engagement in the understanding both of loving God and of loving one's neighbor. In the Shema, the issue is not that of wondering how many beings there are who qualify as deities, deciding that there is only one, and then deciding what an appropriate response might be. To confess that YHWH is "one" is to engage with a divine reality whose very recognition entails a total response of the whole person and an uncompromising rejection of possible rivals or alternatives. Likewise, to "love your neighbor as yourself" is to recognize that one's life is constituted by one's relationship with others and that life is only truly lived in generous self-giving to others. The mutual interplay between these is a major element in both Jewish and Christian faiths.

The recognition that each element (love of God, love of neighbor) on its own could, and historically did, have a narrower significance than in their classic combination can perhaps help that classic combination to be less taken for granted. It can add to one's appreciation of how that combination represents profound penetration into the inmost dynamics of Israel's witness to God and human life, and how the understanding and appropriation of religious faith is not a static or disengaged matter but rather an unending challenge to respond more truly to that which, to him who, is given.

VI. The One God and Jesus

One further issue needs at least to be raised, one that can no longer represent potential common ground between Jew and Christian. It is the Christian reformulation of the nature of God and of humanity in the light of the crucified, risen, and exalted Christ. This reformulation, the history of the early stages of which in the New Testament has received intensive recent study,[27] appears specifically to have involved a reconceptualizing of the meaning and significance of the Shema in a post-Easter context.

A prime text in this regard is 1 Cor. 8:6. On any reckoning, it displays the characteristic early Christian linkage between the person of Jesus and the one God. But a good case can be made for the view that here Paul is deliberately refashioning Israel's historic confession of faith so as to include Jesus within it.[28] The language of a person "loving God" (8:3), far less common in Paul than language of God loving people, may already suggest allusion to Israel's classic formulation of human love for God. The content of the Shema is then explicitly appealed to (v. 4), where the confession of the uniqueness of God as "one" is characteristically combined with denigration of idols. Although the world presents a multiplicity of claimants to people's allegiance (v. 5), there is in fact only one true recipient of that allegiance (v. 6) — which is the concern of the Shema. Yet the way Paul words it is remarkable. As Wright puts it:

> What Paul seems to have done is as follows. He has expanded the formula [of Deut. 6:4], in a way quite unprecedented in any other texts known to us, so as to include a gloss on *theos* and another on *kurios*. . . . Paul, in other words, has glossed "God" with "the Father," and "Lord" with "Jesus Christ," adding in each case an explanatory phrase: "God" is the Father, "from whom are all things and we to him," and the "Lord" is Jesus the Messiah, "through whom are all things and we through him." There can be no mistake: . . . Paul has placed Jesus *within* an explicit statement of the doctrine that Israel's God is the one and only God, the creator of the world. The *Shema* was already, at this stage of Judaism, in widespread use as *the* Jewish daily prayer. Paul has redefined it christologically, producing what we can only call a sort of christological monotheism.[29]

---

27. See, e.g., J. D. G. Dunn, *Christology in the Making: An Inquiry into the Origins of the Doctrine of the Incarnation* (London: SCM, 1980); L. W. Hurtado, *One God, One Lord: Early Christian Devotion and Ancient Jewish Monotheism* (London: SCM, 1988); J. D. G. Dunn, *The Parting of the Ways Between Christianity and Judaism and Their Significance for the Character of Christianity* (London: SCM, 1991); K.-J. Kuschel, *Born before All Time? The Dispute Over Christ's Origin* (London: SCM, 1992; ET by J. Bowden from the German of 1990).

28. See Dunn, *Christology,* 179-83, and esp. N. T. Wright, "Monotheism, Christology and Ethics: 1 Corinthians 8" in his *The Climax of the Covenant: Christ and the Law in Pauline Theology* (Edinburgh: Clark, 1991), 120-36; Wright persuasively relates 8:6 to the wider context of Paul's argument in 1 Corinthians 8–10.

29. Wright, "Monotheism," 129.

What we thus see in 1 Cor. 8:6 is not an isolated phenomenon. Apart from other passages within the Pauline corpus, it bears comparison with the climax of John's Gospel, where Thomas confesses Jesus as "my Lord and my God" *(ho kyrios mou kai ho theos mou,* John 20:28). Although this is clearly not as such an allusion to the Shema, John, through the figure of Thomas, takes the two key terms of the Shema (other than "one"), that is the name of God, rendered in Greek as *kyrios,* and the generic term *theos* "God" and applies both to Jesus (as Paul glosses *theos* and *kyrios).* Precisely what is happening here is difficult to depict adequately. Within the context of the Gospel this is clearly no simple "equation" or "identification" of Jesus with God, for such would not do justice to the predominant language of Father and Son and the depiction of the Son as sent by the Father. Rather, the nature of what it means for a Christian to speak adequately and truly about God is at stake. At least two principles, each developed more fully by subsequent trinitarian theology, appear to be operative. First, there is a principle of language — that language which in Israel's Scripture is predicated of YHWH is appropriately predicated of Jesus (which subsequently becomes the principle that what may be said of God the Father may also be said of God the Son). Second, there is a principle of experience — that the reality of the one God is encountered in and through Jesus Christ. That is, the basic understandings through which Christians recognize human life as genuinely in encounter with the one God are given definitive shape by the New Testament portrayal of Jesus.

For present purposes the significant point is that the God who is "one" and who is to be loved without reserve and to the exclusion of idolatrous alternatives — the Jewish confession — becomes inseparable from Jesus Christ — the Christian confession. If the Christian confession of Jesus is not to succumb to a renewed suspicion of idolatry — that it confuses the creature with the Creator — a robustly trinitarian theology may need to be restored to accounts of Christian interpretation of Scripture.

Another consequence of the Christian construal of God as one in relation to Jesus is that the shape of faithful life can become somewhat different for the Christian, for it is the person of Jesus even more than Torah that gives content to "love" for God. One of the many consequences of this is that the Shema as such loses its primacy as definitive of belief and practice within a Christian context, where the primary symbol becomes the cross and the primary words become the Lord's Prayer. Nonetheless, the principle of unreserved and nonidolatrous love of God, expressed by the Shema, remains as foundational for the Christian as for the Jew, even though its construal may differ.

VII. Conclusion

Three brief concluding reflections, in relation to a context of contemporary understanding and appropriation. First, the way in which Deut. 6:6-9 calls for constant attention to the Shema. Many a reader might initially feel that such a requirement is restrictive and narrowing, indeed (to use popular parlance) oppressive. No doubt it might become so. But the real issue at stake is whether the constant living of that which the Shema represents is a restrictive or enabling way of life. It is a matter of learning what it means to live the whole of life in relation to God. It is all too easy in much contemporary discourse to polarize freedom and faithfulness, and to make them into alternatives. Part of the challenge for Jews and Christians is to demonstrate, conceptually and in practice, that loyalty to God — love — is precisely that which liberates and enables human living to the full.

Second, the requirement to display the words of the Shema publicly. Christian commentators on the passage have a tendency to treat this as a turn of phrase taken with undue literalness by Judaism, or to pose "literal" and "metaphorical" interpretations as alternatives in which actually doing what the text says diminishes its symbolic significance (as with *ḥerem*).[30] In religio-historical terms, however, it is likely that writing and displaying the text was indeed envisaged.[31] Deut. 6:9 envisages a symbolic act, intending that publicly inhabited space (town and home) should be set in the context of a particular allegiance and a particular context of significance, and that this context should be symbolized at the point of transition to or from that place. Historically, the Christian equivalent to displaying the words of the Shema has been to display the cross. Part of the challenge for Jews and Christians today, in their respective contexts, is to reaffirm and develop symbolic acts and practices which appropriately express their fundamental orientation

30. So, for example, von Rad comments: "It is not clear what significance is attached to the tokens which serve as reminders and so forth. Probably we still have to do here with a figurative mode of expression, which was then later understood literally and led to the use of the so-called phylacteries" (*Deuteronomy* [Old Testament Library; London: SCM, 1966; ET from the German of 1964), 64). Or, as D. L. Christensen says, "The injunctions of vv. 8-9 led in turn to specific practices which, at times, caused people to lose sight of the remarkable vision of an 'internalized covenant' suggested in vv. 5-7: namely phylacteries and mezuzoth. Whether or not the words here were intended in a metaphorical sense, they came to be taken literally in subsequent Jewish history" (*Deuteronomy 1–11* [Word Biblical Commentary; Dallas: Word, 1991], 144).

31. See O. Keel, "Zeichen der Verbundenheit. Zur Vorgeschichte und Bedeutung der Forderungen von Deuteronomium 6,8f. und Par.," *Mélanges Dominique Barthélemy,* Orbis Biblicus et Orientalis 38 (1981), 159-240.

in life toward God in an age when traditional symbols are losing their historic resonances and alternative symbolic systems are powerful.[32]

Third, if ḥerem is understood as a metaphor and the proper use of metaphor is grasped, then ḥerem may yet have a role to play in terms of giving content to love of God. This is not a light suggestion, for the killing of people in the name of God is such a recurrent horror within religious practice, common in the past and resurgent today, that it is natural to want utterly to repudiate any text, scriptural or otherwise, that might lend any warrant to such a possibility. Nonetheless, the concept of idolatry as something problematic (of which the destruction of religious objects was a particular expression) may still have a significant role to play. Solomon Schechter, in his memorable exposition of the Shema within the context of rabbinic Judaism, says of "true religion" that "its mission is just as much to teach the world that there are false gods as to bring it nearer to the true one."[33] More recently, Nicholas Lash has proposed an account of Christian theology as "protocols against idolatry" in which the purpose of Christian doctrine is "to help us set our hearts on God (and not on some thing which we mistake for God) and make true mention of him."[34] Idolatry today, if meaningful, has, at least on the surface, a very different significance from that which it had in ancient Israel, and opposition to it would need to take very different forms from those envisaged in Deuteronomy. Jesus' personification of "Mammon" as the idolatrous alternative to God (in essence, a reformulation of the Shema) provides, when understood, a crucial element in envisaging what idolatry might mean to a Christian (Matt. 6:24; Luke 16:13). For if humanity's true nature is realized through love of the one God and of one's neighbor, then there remains a constant need for vigilance and opposition with regard to those ideologies and practices that obscure God and diminish humanity.

---

32. A thoughtful recent reflection on this issue is Deryck Sheriffs, *The Friendship of the Lord: An Old Testament Spirituality* (Carlisle: Paternoster, 1996), ch. 10, esp. 319-25.

33. *Aspects of Rabbinic Theology* (Woodstock: Jewish Lights, 1993; reprint of London: Black, 1909), 77.

34. *The Beginning and the End of "Religion"* (Cambridge: Cambridge University Press, 1996), 89. This is a recurrent theme in Lash's recent writing. Elsewhere in the same book (110) he writes: "The secularity of our culture is an illusion, and a dangerous one at that. Almost all human beings set their hearts on something, have some object of their worship, and if they are distracted or discouraged from that laborious *ascesis* the Christian forms of which make up the costly pedagogy of discipleship, then they will set their hearts on some particular fact or thing, some dream or vision or good feeling, some institution, individual or idea. In other words, the displacement of religion from the realm of truth merely unleashes the horsemen of the Apocalypse, leaves our propensity for idolatry unchecked and unconstrained, with devastating consequences."

The Call of Moses and the "Revelation" of the Divine Name: Source-Critical Logic and Its Legacy

Christopher Seitz

I

No two passages proved more important for emerging source-critical method than Exod 3:1–4:17 and 6:2-9. It is difficult to assign a title to either of these passages without tipping one's hand as to their source-critical significance, but both are frequently referred to as narrating the "call" of Moses. Observations about the phenomenon of doublets elsewhere in the Pentateuch, especially in Genesis, would of necessity come to play a role here as well. Why would Moses be called twice?

But overshadowing this more general problem was the blunt claim in Exod 6:3 that God had not been known by his proper name YHWH until this point in time. Because the name in fact appears in Genesis and in the first five chapters of Exodus, and in the earlier "call" narrative just a few chapters away, a problem was felt for which source criticism had a solution. To a host of compelling literary observations in Genesis could be added a matter of some substance: disagreement as to when the divine name was truly operative in Israel. Now one had some potential purchase on the crazy-quilt alternation of the divine name in Genesis, where YHWH is joined by a host of other appellations (Elohim, El Shaddai, El Elyon, El Olam, etc.).

The results are familiar. The Priestly writer was considered responsible for the second call narrative and those texts that avoid use of the proper name YHWH (at least prior to Exodus 6, if not also problematically after Exodus 6). By contrast, the Yahwist judged the divine name YHWH available and in use in the period of the ancestors and earlier; he gives expression to this belief in Gen 4:26, "At that time people began to invoke the name of YHWH." An Elohist is necessitated to explain non-Priestly texts in Genesis (and beyond) that likewise disagree with the Yahwist about the divine name.

This description of matters should be relatively uncontroversial. There have always been problems with source-critical division at the level of individual texts and in terms of larger conceptuality, and there is a growing literature whose sole purpose is to point out these problems.[1] Nevertheless, one can see from the very terms at work, "Yahwist," "Elohist," "Priestly Writer" (originally called the "later Elohist"), that the criterion of the divine name, based on exegesis of these two texts in Exodus, was central to source-critical logic. This is not to say that other solutions to the plain sense of Exod 6:3 and the problem of the divine name's usage were not available to ancient and modern interpreters — even some who accepted the notion of longitudinal sources. Still, a majority of commentators took the simple existence of these two "call narratives" — and the second's seemingly plain statement regarding the divine name — *as in essential conjunction* with other literary and historical observations. These pointed to the likelihood of continuous sources in the Pentateuch, which saw the matter of the divine name, at least up to Exodus 6, differently. That difference could be interpreted more or less stringently from a theological standpoint, depending on the approach of the individual interpreter.

An extremely thought-provoking alternative to this way of interpreting the two narratives in Exodus and the theological issues surrounding the revelation of the divine name has been put forward by Walter Moberly.[2] Moberly accepts the modern critical judgment that Exod 6:3 does in fact mean to say that the proper name of God, YHWH, was not made known until the time of Moses. He canvasses what he calls "harmonizing efforts," ancient and modern, to correlate divergent perspectives on the divine name, and he rejects these. He then goes further and trumps modern critical thinking and its rough consensus on the notion of sources itself. He argues that Exod 3:1–4:17, the so-called first call narrative, likewise relates the revelation of the divine name to Moses *for the very first time.* The rug is thus pulled out from under source-critical logic from an unexpected angle. Both call narratives,

---

1. R. Rendtorff, *The Problem of the Process of Transmission in the Pentateuch* (*JSOT* Supplement Series 89; Sheffield: JSOT, 1990); H. H. Schmid, *Der Sogennante Yahwist* (Zurich: Theologischer, 1976); R. N. Whybray, *The Making of the Pentateuch: A Methodological Study* (*JSOT* Supplement Series 53; Sheffield: JSOT, 1987).

2. *The Old Testament of the Old Testament* (OBT; Minneapolis: Fortress, 1992).

according to Moberly, are in agreement that the proper name of God was first revealed to Moses and was strictly speaking unknown to the ancestors. Appeal to the divine name as a criterion for source classification in Genesis and elsewhere thus loses its point of departure.

To the obvious question — Then why does the proper name appear in Genesis? — Moberly responds as follows. The narrator of these stories in Genesis — one can no longer call him the Yahwist — operates with full knowledge of the divine name, as do his readers, and therefore is not bothered by what from a historical perspective is the introduction of an anachronism. He merges his perspective with that of the stories and yet assumes that his readers, and also apparently us, will nevertheless catch the full force of the opening chapters of Exodus, which relate as a historical datum God's initial revelation of his name as YHWH. In other words, this would be similar to glossing the Old Testament from the standpoint of the New's plain sense — depicting Abraham as rejoicing at Christ's day — all the while assuming that as a historical reality the birth of Jesus and his significance for Christian faith lie in the future. I choose this illustration with some forethought because Moberly's final purpose is in fact to talk about the relationship between the Christian testaments as analogous to the way Genesis is "the Old Testament of the Old Testament."[3] That is to say, Moberly wishes us to catch the uniform perspective of all biblical narrators that the period of the ancestors is a distinct period, making Genesis an "old testament" prior to Sinai and the revelation of the divine name. Most significantly for source-critical logic, this is not the view of one "Priestly writer" as against one "Yahwistic writer" or of one call narrative of Moses as against another, but of both. Central to his argument, then, is his exegesis of these two Exodus narratives, as was also true for emerging source-critical method.

---

3. I have just, however, shown how this is not altogether true since explicit glossing of the Old did not take place in the manner just mentioned and in the manner Moberly assumes is at subtle work in Genesis, with the divine name YHWH. He recognizes this important distinction (*Old Testament of the Old Testament,* 140):

> . . . the text of the Old Testament was stable by the time of the New Testament. So the rereading from the new perspective could not actually influence the text itself. . . . By contrast, at the time of the Yahwistic storytellers and editors the patriarchal traditions were still being retold in such a way that there was not yet one definitive version of them, and so the new perspective could significantly alter the nature of the text itself.

II

A large percentage of Moberly's exegesis is devoted to a fresh reading of Exod 3:1–4:17. He seeks to establish that the narrative relates a first-time revelation of the divine name and is therefore operating with the same perspective as 6:2-8. In order to do this he focuses on verses 13-15 in a particularly fresh way, due to the thesis he is pursuing. He shows that the logic of the verses is by no means self-evident. As Moberly sees it, these verses introduce a hypothetical situation that is extraneous to a simple divine encounter with the already known YHWH, charging Moses to speak for him on behalf of his people against Pharaoh. They reflect a more mature theological situation.

The scene in which these verses play a role can be easily summarized. Moberly's reading has forced me to reexamine what is being related, by attending to the text in its present form and unfolding logic — rather than assuming from the start a convergence of several sources, which can then be untangled precisely because logical unfolding is absent. This also means setting aside the criterion of the divine name as pointing to sources behind the account.

The narrative relates the following. God makes himself known to Moses as the same One who appeared to the ancestors (v. 6). Though the narrator may use the proper name for the reader (v. 7) it has yet to be revealed to Moses. God then announces his intention to deal with Israel's affliction (vv. 7-9). Moses will be his agent before Pharaoh (v. 10). Moses reacts to this plan of "the God" *(hā 'ĕlōhîm)* who is speaking to him with concern (v. 11). There may be an adumbration of the proper name (YHWH) in verse 12 where God responds to Moses, "I will be with you" *(kî- 'ehyeh 'immāk),* and the status of the sign in the verse has always puzzled interpreters. But as the verse concludes, God still refers to himself in direct speech to Moses as "the God" that Moses is to worship on this mountain.

When the divine name *is* revealed, this happens in the context of a hypothetical situation: Moses is anticipating addressing the people of Israel. Not content with a charge from the God of the ancestors, Moses submits that the Israelites will want to know God's name. In response to these circumstances, not yet unfolded, where the divine name needs to be revealed, Moses asks the God addressing him "what shall I say?" God gives the famous first-person response in the verse that follows, frequently taken as a theologically significant rebuff *('ehyeh 'ăšer 'ehyeh).* Then he even indicates that a first-person form of the name could serve as an answer to the question of the Israelites: "Say to the Israelites 'I am' sent me to you," even though EHYH does not elsewhere serve as God's proper name (so the third person *ho ōn* in the LXX).

Having begun to introduce the proper name (EHYH/YHWH), the narrator now changes his method of procedure and uses the generic "God" for indirect discourse, "And again God *('ĕlōhîm)* said to Moses. . . ." Now follows the full conjunction, a first-time conjunction as Moberly has it, whereby the God of the ancestors is said by God himself to be YHWH. The solemn ending drives home the gravity of the moment: "this is my name forever and my memorial from generation to generation." Moberly concludes thus:

> [T]he most natural explanation is that the writer is depicting the first revelation of the name to Moses and through him to Israel. Both Moses and Israel start by knowing God as "God of the father(s)" (3:6, 13), and the name YHWH is then given and added to the designation "God of your fathers" in a way that makes clear the identity and continuity of YHWH as Israel's God with the God known to the patriarchs. They still know the same God, but now God is to be known in perpetuity by the new name YHWH.[4]

And as for the account in Exodus 6, it "does not portray the revelation of the name YHWH simply because the name has already been revealed in Exodus 3."[5] The accounts cannot only be coordinated, as others have sought to maintain, they are in absolute agreement on this most essential point. The divine name was first revealed to Moses, and through him, to Israel. "Whatever Israel knows about the name of God, it knows only through the mediation of Moses to whom alone a direct self-revelation of God has been given."[6]

One of the most difficult parts of Moberly's argument involves use of the proper name YHWH, especially in direct speech, in the book of Genesis. But I wish to leave that matter to the side for a moment in the interest of pursuing aspects of his stimulating exegesis of Exodus 3 and 6. He has rightly, to my mind, emphasized the signal character of this revelation of the proper name of God to Moses in Exodus 3. And I also believe that the two "calls" are not just coordinatable or compatible, but necessary for the text as a whole to make sense and as such indispensable in the final form of the material. With Moberly I do not think the divine name is a clear arbiter of source division in Genesis. At most it represents an individual narrator's proclivity, and it may have more to do with immediate context than with a consistent theological position maintained throughout longitudinal sources — sources that actually disagree about when the divine name was first known, thus allowing them to be identified in the first place. With him I find the terms "Yahwist"

---

4. *Ibid.,* 24.
5. *Ibid.,* 33.
6. *Ibid.,* 15.

and "Elohist" problematic insofar as they have conflated a question regarding levels of tradition in an aggregate biblical text with a theory about the progressive revelation of the divine name; I would prefer with some recent scholars to speak of early and late traditions or complexes.[7] Even "source" now sounds a bit romantic, and it occasioned an appropriate debate in respect of the priestly level of tradition all along.[8]

Moberly argues that Exodus 3 and 6 both assert that only with Moses is the proper name of God first revealed. Its appearance in Genesis is self-conscious anachronism, which the ancient reader was to recognize as such and to draw neither historical nor theological conclusions from. With Moberly I agree that the reports do not reflect conflicting understandings about when the divine name appeared in Israel. But unlike him I wish to show that both, each in its own distinctive way, presuppose a long-standing use of the proper name for God. The conclusion I will draw from this is that Old Testament texts never concern themselves with a point in historical time before which the name was hypothetically unknown, such that it might then be dramatically "revealed." The appearance of the tetragrammaton (YHWH Elohim) as early as Gen 2:4 comes with no explanation, and the point of its introduction in conjunction with the 'ĕlōhîm of Genesis 1 may well be to ease us toward familiarity with God's personal name, as this was extant even in primeval time. In other words, the Old Testament never takes up the question of how the name as such first came to be uttered by humanity. As many have noted, Gen. 4:26 cannot be pressed into service to depict a first-time revelation of a name for God theretofore unknown.[9]

III

Moberly has rightly seen the signal character of the revelation of the divine name to Moses in Exodus 3. But a central contention here will be that he has gone astray by assuming that that signal character holds true for the Israelites

---

7. My own rough model would involve a priestly editing and supplementing of various earlier traditions, some of them already formed into independent complexes (ancestors, out of Egypt, wilderness journey, Sinai), as Rendtorff urged (see note 1). The much debated problem of deuteronomistic editing remains a point for further work, though even in Rendtorff's model this contribution consists primarily of ligatures at the latest level of redaction.

8. See among others, K. Koch, "P — Kein Redaktor! Erinnerung an zwei Eckdaten der Quellenscheidung," *VT* 37 (1987) 446-67.

9. C. Westermann, *Genesis 1–11* (Minneapolis: Augsburg, 1984) 339-40.

as well as for Moses. My simple thesis is that the question posed by Moses in 3:13ff. has stood at the heart of source-critical discussion, and that the issue there turns on the status of Moses and a correct understanding of his role vis-à-vis Israel in the opening chapters of the book of Exodus.

In these chapters we learn straightforwardly several key facts. The three-month-old child of an anonymous man and woman of the Levite line ends up in the care of the daughter of Pharaoh. She infers that he is a Hebrew, has him nursed, names him, and takes him as her son, "for I drew him out of the water" (2:10), just as YHWH will later draw out his own children. The episode that leads to Moses' flight (2:11-15) reveals his ambiguous relationship to his people. He kills an Egyptian who is beating a Hebrew (v. 12). He "goes out" — it is not clear from where — and, seeing two "Hebrews" fighting, seeks to break it up, only to discover his previous avenging is not a secret. Eventually Pharaoh too hears of it and seeks to kill Moses (2:15). The response of his own people is curious — "Do you mean to kill me as you killed the Egyptian?" — and is best explained as an indication of Moses' liminality. Pharaoh treats him not as Egyptian, the Israelites not as "Hebrew" — or only confusedly so. Moses flees to Midian and helps some shepherds. When they describe him to their priest, he is "an Egyptian" (2:19). He marries the priest's daughter. The son he sires bears a name more than descriptive of his situation: "I have been a sojourner *(gēr)* in a foreign land" (2:22).

What is clear in these chapters is the separation of Moses from his people: raised by Egyptians, married to a Midianite, with a son whose name more than sums up his status. Now at the risk of putting the question too simply: as the narrative is presenting it, with Moses' estrangement the prominent feature, how might we come to think Moses knows of YHWH at all?

When we move to an interpretation of chapter 3 against this backdrop, several features come into prominence. If one tracks the use of the divine name, alert to the difference between Moses' own perspective, that of the narrator, and that of the reader, then verse-by-half-verse source division — here the Elohist, there the Yahwist — proves unnecessary. In vv. 1-5 the narrator tells us something that Moses does not yet know: it is YHWH who is appearing to him in the burning bush. YHWH begins by telling Moses something that will make sense to him: He is the God of his father (singular, though frequently emended). The meaning of this is usually sought in religio-historical reconstructions of ancestral religion or some other such etic analysis. But might the text mean only what it says: the God addressing Moses is the God of his father, that is, the Levite mentioned in 2:1, who is unknown to Moses? This God is the God of his father and his father's fathers before him, the ancestors Abraham, Isaac, and Jacob. This declaration may itself constitute a revelation of something hitherto unknown; that and the simple presence of *hā 'ĕlōhîm* require Moses to hide his face.

In verse 7, YHWH reveals to Moses and to the reader that he has seen quite clearly the affliction of his people: not *your* cry (Moses and the people) but *their* cry has been heard and *their* anguish God knows. This same perspective is maintained through verse 9, where God speaks to Moses about a people *with whom Moses is himself not explicitly identified.* Moses is addressed directly in verse 10: "Look, I am sending you to Pharaoh to bring forth my people, the children of Israel." Moses responds to "the God" from the same perspective of distinguishability: "Who am I that I should go to Pharaoh, that I should bring out the people of Israel?" Only in verse 12 is the mutuality of the people and Moses and God revealed: "when you bring forth *the people,* you shall serve God on this mountain"; *ta'abdun,* a plural form, meaning Moses and the people, is adopted here for the first time in the narrative. The problem of the mysterious sign might consist in this anticipated union. That is, the sign that "I am with you" is not the worship on the mountain as such, but instead that the Moses being charged by God here is assured that he will eventually worship together with the people he is being sent to address. The sentence might be paraphrased: "I will be *('ehyeh)* is with you *('immāk),* and the sign of this is your eventual worship with the people of Israel on this mountain." Moses will not be rejected; God is with him.

This interpretation finds some support as we read on into verses 13ff., so pivotal in Moberly's discussion. Moses anticipates with "the God" this encounter with God's people. Note how the text does not report Moses saying to them, "the God of *our* fathers has sent me to you" but rather "the God of *your* fathers." Now the full force of their hypothetical question is clear. They inquire of Moses what God's name is not because they do not know it. How would his supplying the name either mean anything or be verifiable before those who do not know it to begin with?[10] They ask the name because they do know it and will not be constrained to listen to a spokesman from God who cannot establish that their named God has indeed sent him. Moses knows this too, which is why he asks to know God's name. Only in this way can he verify before the Israelites that their named God has also revealed himself to him and sent him on this bold mission on their behalf.[11]

10. Maimonides' famous treatment was aimed at addressing this conundrum (*The Guide for the Perplexed,* tr. M. Friedlander [London: Routledge, 1951] 93-95).

11. Compare Childs's sophisticated source and form-critical analysis (*The Book of Exodus* [OTL; Philadelphia: Westminster, 1974]). In verse 13 "E" is influenced by the later true-false prophecy discussion and has Moses produce the name to verify his call; "E" also, like "P," thinks the divine name was not revealed until this point. (These two con-

What seems patient of further analysis is the first response God makes to the question of his name, given the mature theological discussion it presupposes. The notion of a careful rebuff or sonorous self-protection, "I am who I am," turns in some measure on the understanding that this is *the* signal revelation of the name.[12] Is Moses being rebuffed, or is the proper name of God, known by the reader and by the Israelites, here being supplied by God with an interpretation of its significance?

That is, this individual revelation of the name to Moses gave the narrator the opportunity to insist that, while Moses was only now coming to knowledge of the name, he was also learning something about it that those who already knew it did not know. This served three purposes: (1) to underscore Moses' special status; even as an outsider he is privy to special knowledge of God, involving attributes to which God's name points; (2) to reveal thereby to the reader something of the meaning of a name with which we are familiar, but only as a proper name as such; (3) to begin to suggest that who God is and has been heretofore is patient of enlargement. God indicates that Moses could just as easily say to the people EHYH as YHWH when speaking of him, even though this never happens and would presumably have had a strange effect. This underscores the significance invested by the narrator in identifying most clearly the known name of God, YHWH, with the verb "to be," whatever the most appropriate translation of *'ehyeh 'ăšer 'ehyeh* might be. The studied adumbration in verse 12 (*'ehyeh 'immāk*) points to an interpretation of the divine name as involving most especially God's presence with Moses and the people *in the events of redemption from bondage,* and as such the account in 6:2-9 is anticipated. More on this below.

The sophistication of the narrative is in full evidence in the unit under discussion (3:13-18). To Moses' question about what name he should give for

---

cerns are somewhat at odds since producing the name for verification and producing it for the first time à la "E/P" makes for complication.) Later, when the identification of the proper name with the God of the ancestors was fully assumed, the question made no sense. Verse 14 therefore interprets the request for the name as a request for its significance. Without all the sense of depth and tradition history, Maimonides comes to something of the same conclusion: "God taught Moses how to teach them [the people], and how to establish amongst them the belief in Himself, namely, by saying Ehyeh asher Eyheh. . . . God thus showed Moses the proofs by which His existence would be firmly established among the wise men of His people" (*Guide for the Perplexed,* 94-95). In both of these cases the question is not Moses' capacity to produce a name others know already, but his capacity to explain a name, maybe even one he and others knew already (something that never happens later in the text).

12. See Childs's brief discussion (*Exodus,* 69).

God when he is questioned, there is a simple answer: "my name is YHWH." But God does not give that simple answer. We are eased toward a direct announcement of the name through a series of explanatory glosses. This protraction has led numerous interpreters to conclude that what we have here is a variety of sources being brought into a conjunction sufficiently clumsy that we can posit their existence to begin with.

God does not give his proper name YHWH in response to Moses' question, but instead speaks in the first person in a terse statement: 'ehyeh 'ăšer 'ehyeh. The *sui generis* "I AM has sent me to you" is only comprehensible as an extrapolation, or parsing, of this first response by God. Its point is to show that the potentially circular "I am as I am" is not a rebuttal (cf. 'ănî 'ăšer 'ănî) but a clue to the meaning of the proper name YHWH. God's name involves something that he will be or become.

But we still have not clarified why this explanation precedes rather than follows the disclosure to Moses of God's name YHWH in verse 15. The answer is that God is truly responding to Moses' request to know his name, but in a way that neither the reader nor Moses is prepared for. God's name is in fact 'ehyeh 'ăšer 'ehyeh. That is, God's name is the most personal revelation of God's own character, and as such is not a proper name in the strict sense (like Jim or Sally), but a name appropriate to God's character as God. In this case, God's "name" consists of a disclosure of purpose; it "means" something approaching "In the manner that I am, or will be, I am who I am." Yet neither we nor Moses is prepared to understand such a "name" yet, because what God will be, and is most essentially, has not as yet been made manifest. Now are we prepared to understand what is at stake in the second "call narrative" in 6:2-9.

IV

The first thing to note about the second "call narrative" is that it does not immediately follow the first. The second thing to consider is why any such narrative might be necessary at all. Source-critical logic supplied one answer to this question: the sources "P" and "J" disagreed about the revelation of the divine name, thus necessitating a second "call narrative." But the same disagreement over the revelation of the divine name is shared by both "P" and "E." "E" is apparently satisfied to gloss the first account, so why is "P" unsatisfied with this procedure? But there are more serious problems with the "two call accounts" theory that have already been alluded to and that form the starting point for this analysis.

The first consideration, however, regarding the present location of the

154

second divine encounter, is worthy of further attention. Do events transpire that make such an encounter pivotal, especially as this involves the revelation of the divine name and its meaning for Moses and the people of Israel? Our procedure will again be to focus on the unfolding of events in narrative sequence.

At the close of chapter 3 God indicates that the trip into the wilderness to worship (commanded earlier at 3:12) will not take place without resistance (3:18-20). In chapter 4, Moses raises a series of concerns about his own capacities. First, while he can state the name of YHWH, there is nothing preventing the people from asking whether or not YHWH has in fact appeared to him, or at least so Moses reckons (v. 1). To meet this objection God provides two signs: a snake becomes a rod, and woe and weal are created, that is, leprosy is caused and removed (4:2-7). A third sign involves water becoming blood (4:8-9). Aaron is then provided as Moses' spokesman to meet the objection that Moses does not speak well (4:14-16). Again God warns Moses about Pharaoh's recalcitrance and indicates that Moses will have to threaten him with death of the firstborn in exchange for deliverance of God's own firstborn son, Israel (4:22-23). The immediately following Zipporah passage (4:24-26) gives Moses a foreshadowing of what is at stake. The One who can make leprous and then heal, who can turn water to blood, who makes "dumb, deaf, seeing, blind" (4:11) is also the One who will slay the firstborn of the Egyptians, all who are not circumcised like Moses' son (and Moses? cf. 12:43-49). The blood that later spares by marking the lintel and the two doorposts, preventing the destroyer from entering (12:23), here also causes God "to leave him alone" (4:26), due to this obscure circumcision ritual, involving son and father. Whatever else the strange night attack means, it sets the proper life-or-death tone and foreshadows future manifestations of God's designs for Israel and Egypt. A distinction will be made (11:7). Not for nothing does Moses describe "YHWH our God" in his very first meeting with Pharaoh as demanding their worship in the wilderness, "lest he fall upon us with pestilence or with the sword" (5:3). Moses has this on firsthand experience. YHWH's intentions for Israel are life-or-death intentions.

What follows is Moses' encounter with Aaron at the conclusion of the chapter (4:27-31). The words of YHWH are communicated to Aaron, and through him, to the people. The signs work. The people believe and worship. No explanation of the name is requested or given. The significance of the *'ehyeh 'ăšer 'ehyeh* and of the name YHWH itself, as this was introduced in 3:13-15, is not referred to here. We will return to this seeming omission in a moment, which might prove very problematic for Moberly's reading, given his theory of the first-time revelation of the name in 3:13ff., whose transmission to the people is here marked by no fanfare whatsoever.

Chapter 5 records the failure of Moses and Aaron's audience with Pharaoh, as God had predicted. Heavier burdens are the consequence of their entreaty, and the people object that Moses and Aaron "have made us offensive in the sight of Pharaoh and his servants" (5:21). As previous commentators have noted, this chapter introduces a concept that functions as a leitmotif until the deliverance in chapter 14. It begins with Pharaoh's declaration, "Who is the YHWH that I should heed his voice and let Israel go? I do not know YHWH and moreover will not let Israel go" (5:2). It culminates in the solemn pronouncement before the Red Sea life-or-death episode, "And the Egyptians shall know that I am YHWH, when I have gotten glory over Pharaoh, his chariots, and his horsemen" (14:18), a recognition that occurs at 14:25: "Let us flee from before Israel, for YHWH fights for them against the Egyptians." We are prepared for this final recognition at numerous points along the way (7:5, 17; 8:10, 22; 9:14, 29; 10:2; 11:7; 14:4) where the key phrase "that you might know that I am YHWH" or some variation appears. The final statement at 14:31 indicates that full knowledge has come to Israel, "And Israel saw the great work which the LORD did against the Egyptians, and the people feared YHWH; and they believed in YHWH and in his servant Moses."

It is from this specific perspective that the so-called second, Priestly "call narrative" in 6:2-9 is to be understood. Note first of all that *in its present context* this unit is neither a call narrative nor even a "seconding" of a first call. It is a solemn response to Moses' complaint in 5:22 that God has not delivered his people as promised; instead the meeting with Pharaoh has exacerbated matters. God's response to the complaint takes the form of a clarification, by which YHWH explains to Moses privately what will take place in the future. God will honor the oath he swore to the ancestors and give them the land he has promised (6:8). Reference to the covenant made with the ancestors occurs twice, in verses 4 and 5. The author of this important unit clearly has Genesis 17 in mind, which tells of the appearance of YHWH to Abram for the purpose of making a covenant — a text reckoned by most to be from the hand of the Priestly writer. Intriguing in that text is the same collocation of terms as in Exodus 6: the divine name YHWH, the verb "appear" *(wayyērā'; wā'ērā')*, and "El Shaddai." The occurrence of the divine name YHWH in a Priestly text required strict source theorists to speak there of a gloss.

Interpretation of this key unit has foundered, in my view, because of the tendency to read verse 3 in isolation, as pointing to a theory about the origin of the divine name and its usage in Israel. The alternative pursued here will focus on the verse (1) within the larger unit in which it appears, especially verse 7, and (2) within the narrative context in which the verb *yd'* and the so-called recognition formula plays an obvious and central role (chs. 5–14).

There is a slight syntactical problem in verse 3 that is frequently glossed over and which cannot be detected — because it is in some sense impossible to replicate — in translations. The first half of the verse is clear: I appeared to Abraham, Isaac, and Jacob in/as El Shaddai *(bĕ'ēl šaddāy)*. This is consistent with Genesis 17, though at least in theory the narrator *could* have said that YHWH appeared to Abram since that is what a putative glossator, later than and familiar with P's divine name theology, was prepared to assert.[13] The second verse-half does not pick up the preposition *(bĕ)*, though many argue it should be supplied under influence of *bĕ'ēl*. The same first-person form of the verb appears, here not *r'h* (see) but *yd'* (know). Both forms of the verb are *niphal*, which can be construed either as passive or middle ("I appeared," "I was seen," "I was [not] known," "I made [not] myself known"). The problem is combining a nominal form *šĕmî* with a first-person verb, *nôda'tî*, without drawing on the preposition in the first half of the verse, producing "my name YHWH I was not known to them." Perhaps for this reason the LXX rendered the verb *edēlōsa,* which matches the *hiphil* of *yd',* producing "my name YHWH I did not make known (reveal) to them."

The verse is generally understood as involving a contrast, concerning whether the name of God was known or not known in the period of the ancestors, as against that of the Mosaic period. If one pays close attention to the larger unit, this does not appear to be the main burden of the text, nor even a

13. It could be argued that the alleged glossator working in Gen 17:1 has introduced YHWH not to Abram but to the reader; to Abram, YHWH is El Shaddai. But is even this distinction consistent with a hard and fast position supposedly held by the Priestly writer about the name YHWH only being first revealed to Moses? Are we approaching the sort of subtlety that such a theory has sought to avoid? Moreover, if such a distinction is at play, it could presumably work within the Priestly "source" itself and should find corroboration elsewhere in Genesis.

It may be true that for the author of Exodus 6 and kindred texts in Genesis, "El Shaddai" was a favorite or distinctive appellation, and that is why it is used here in a description of God's appearance to the ancestors. But what the author wishes to assert is not contrast or discontinuity between names for God (El Shaddai then, YHWH hereafter), but continuity — that is, YHWH and El Shaddai are one and the same. The contrast is between *appearance* to the ancestors and *knowledge* of YHWH as YHWH, which comes about in the events of Exodus 14. It is for this reason that the *hiphil* of *yd'* does not appear in Exod 6:3b, while the divine name YHWH does appear in Genesis texts, including 17:1.

minor theme.[14] The issue is not knowledge of the name *per se* but how God most fully makes himself known as YHWH. "I was not known in respect of my name YHWH" God tells Moses, because this knowledge turns on the events of the exodus, which are as yet unexperienced. The main burden of the unit is revealed in verse 7: "and I will take you for my people, and I will be your God; and you shall know that I am YHWH your God, who has brought you up from the burden of the Egyptians." God has not been truly known as YHWH because this involves the mighty deliverance yet to be accomplished. Such a reading is also consistent with the presentation in chapters 7–14, which center on YHWH making himself known before the Egyptians (7:5), before Pharaoh (7:17), above or beside other gods (8:10), in the midst of the earth (8:22), throughout all the earth (9:16), in all creation (9:29), as distinguisher of Israel (11:7), and before Pharaoh's host (14:4). The recognition formula which appears in 6:7 runs like a red thread through all the subsequent scenes, until the denouement at the sea, when Pharaoh's hosts at last confess, "Let us flee from Israel, for YHWH fights for them" and the Israelites see and fear YHWH and believe in Moses. The author of the unit 6:2-9 knows that YHWH appeared to the ancestors and was sometimes referred to as God Almighty. But God reveals to Moses that he was not known to them as he is about to make himself known.

It is here that the conjunction with the first divine encounter comes into play. Moses was given the divine name in order to appear before the people of Israel as a credible witness. He was also told by God, in response to a request to know God's name, *'ehyeh 'ăšer 'ehyeh,* which we judged to be neither a rebuttal nor a typical proper name, but a statement of God's very self — on the verge of being made manifest. The *hiphil* of *yd'* is not used in the second verse-half of 6:3 precisely to avoid the impression that what is at stake in the contrast between the period of the ancestors and the period at hand is knowledge of the name itself. "I did not make known *(hôda'tî)* my name" might imply that God was known, but simply under another name, like El Shaddai. That is not the contrast the author wishes to make, and therein is a common perspective uniting both accounts. The name YHWH has been known all along, and the first encounter between God and Moses has as one purpose Moses' learning the name so that he might speak in the name of YHWH before those who know the name. What the ancestors failed to know was not the name YHWH, which appears throughout Genesis in direct speech, in indirect narration, on the mouth of foreigner as well as Israelite, or before such distinctions were germane (4:26). Likewise the Israelites in

14. Here I am indebted to an unpublished paper by J. Janzen.

Egypt, Moses, Aaron, Pharaoh, and all his hosts might well know the name of God, but they have yet to know who God wishes to reveal himself as. That will be made manifest in the deliverance of his people and the destruction of those who oppose that deliverance. "He is who he is" in these events and as such makes himself known — fully rather than for the first time — as YHWH.

V

While levels of tradition might prefer to make use of this or that name for God, a comparison of the two calls of Moses in Exodus 3 and 6, and especially verse 3 of the latter, raised to the status of basic criterion a distinction between YHWH and other names for God in pentateuchal texts, at the same time bringing into prominence the notion of a theological disagreement between sources over how and when the personal name of God was revealed to Israel. We have challenged that comparison and its significance for a theory of sources in the Pentateuch. More could be said about the respective functions of Exod 3 and 6. Scolnic's remarks confirm our own, from a different perspective. "Moses, in chapter 6," he notes, "is placed within a genealogy, in the context of his people, which gives a very different impression than the story in Exodus 2–3 of an Egyptian noble who has been disloyal."[15]

We agree and have argued that there is further significance for how and why the personal name of God is used as it is in these two accounts. The first explains how Moses came to privileged knowledge of the name, such that he could state it to the people of Israel. It also indicates that God's "name" involves his freedom to act and be who he most fully is, or *'ehyeh 'ăšer 'ehyeh*. Though God tells Moses to say that this is his name (3:14), we must wait until the second divine encounter to learn just what the name means — or will mean. In this sense, even Exod 6:2-9 does not report the revelation of God as YHWH so much as anticipate it. In the events of the exodus God will be known fully as YHWH. If there is a contrast with the period of the ancestors, so far as God's agency and person is concerned, it would have to involve this full knowledge of God's self. God had appeared, as YHWH and as El Shaddai, to make promises to the ancestors. But in no way did they know him as he would be known in the exodus. A crude distinction may involve

---

15. B. Scolnic, "Strangers in the PaRDeS: Conservative Judaism and the Torah," *Study Guide to the Discovery,* ed. E. S. Schoenberg (New York: Jewish Theological Seminary, n.d.) 8.

not the name under which God is known, but between God's *appearing* — which happens under a variety of names in Genesis — and his *being made known*, which happens in a permanently foundational way in the events of exodus and Sinai. No source, level of tradition, or individual author worked under constraint of a *status confessionis* articulated in Exodus 6 whereby the divine name was not revealed until a second "call narrative" of Moses.[16] What that account seeks to establish is that the God known as YHWH had appeared to the ancestors but was not known as he truly was until Exodus 14 and the victory at the sea. After that the final *'ăšer 'ehyeh* of "I am who I will be" found its proper content: "I am YHWH your God who brought you out of the land of Egypt" (Exod 20:2).

VI

A final note about method. Source-critical method sought to expose two important realities about biblical narrative: (1) that the events reported were not factual in the strict sense but involved sequent, creative authorial voices and (2) that a single point of view could at most be attributed to a final redactor who, unsuccessfully enough for us to appreciate his efforts, sought to wrest a measure of coherence or control out of what lay before him, for a variety of political, theological, moral, or aesthetic reasons, some too obscure or pedestrian for us to recognize at all. The narratives were thought to be about historical events in the first instance, yet critical theory insisted that this reference to history be understood in a very complex way — both views having to do in the first instance with events behind the text to which the text referred and in so doing made its essential point. In this scheme of things, the reader of the material as it existed in its present aggregate form was largely unanticipated, because one audience in history to which one layer of text was directed had been overlaid with new layers and new audiences, the final form proving incapable of completely transcending that complex history of development.

We have returned to the narratives involving the revelation of the divine name and the call of Moses fully aware of this particular history of read-

---

16. As has long been recognized, if such a theological position were indeed pivotal for our interpretation of pre–Exodus 6 texts, it would also follow that after this "revelation" of the divine name, the criterion could need to be abandoned. One might even expect the "priestly" level of tradition to begin only using the divine appellation YHWH, in agreement with other "sources" with which it once took issue. But this simple course is not followed.

ing, now several centuries old. How the text is related to the events it reports we acknowledge to be extraordinarily complex, and in no way do we believe that the narrative is simply reporting what happened to Moses or God in a straightforward sense — how in the light of the reality to which the text is referring could this ever be possible? Instead we have sought to determine if the narratives make sense in their present form and within a set intertextual (emic) world of reference. This has entailed being especially alert to the way the narrator might make key distinctions between the reader's frame of reference, that of Moses, and that of the people of Israel. In coming to terms with this set of distinctions we have tried to understand the logic of what is being narrated as this involves Moses and the revelation of the divine name.

Clearly in the books of Exodus and Genesis we are dealing with a variety of authorial voices, whose characteristics involve matters of style, genre, lexical stock, and distinctive theological proclivity. Whether and to what extent the divine name plays a key role in separating these voices is not as clear as has been maintained. At a minimum, we have questioned whether, in distinguishing a hypothetical "J" from a "P" or an "E," one was misled by the notion of some quite crucial theological disagreement over the actual revelation of the name YHWH.

My remarks do not call for a repudiation of levels of tradition, but a different understanding of their character and relationship to one another. In my judgment these are more synthetically related than the old Priestly versus Yahwist theory held. Perhaps the various hands at work deferred to the literary product on which they labored in such a way that it would both bear witness to but also transcend their various, sometimes discrete efforts. To warn of a "disappearing redactor," as has Barton, is potentially misleading.[17] The question is what sort of criteria truly count for distinguishing levels of tradition. Then the harder task is to come to terms with their relationship to one another in the final form of the text. As long as they were depicted as requiring disentanglement, this question never came into serious play. The point of this essay has been to argue that no level of tradition disagreed with any other over so important an issue as the revelation of God's proper name YHWH. That name was known in primeval time and forever thereafter. But God was not known in his name YHWH fully until the events at the sea. All levels of tradition are in essential agreement here.[18]

17. John Barton, *Reading the Old Testament* (Philadelphia: Westminster, 1984) 56-58.

18. Though we reach different conclusions about when the actual name YHWH was known, I agree with Moberly about a distinction between ancestral and Mosaic period knowledge of God as YHWH.

Sacred Butchery: Exodus 32:25-29

Leslie Brisman

It is not surprising that the terrible violence of Exodus 32:25-29, an episode that might be entitled "the Levites' rampage," should meet a most temperate accommodation in the commentary of Brevard Childs. Professor Childs's lifelong peacemaking between the rival claims of history and canon reached exemplary heights in a few summary sentences:

> The Levites were faithful at an enormous cost. It is likely that the particular formulation of this story reflects a later history of struggle for the priesthood in which Aaron had become a prototype of an unfaithful priest. Particularly in light of Aaron's later prestige, it is all the more remarkable that this story was retained in the tradition.[1]

In what follows, I hope in no way to diminish Childs's wonder at what has been "retained in the tradition," while brooding over the possibility that the real wonder of the literary achievement here is of a different order. There is no doubt that a terrible *historical* irony has overtaken our passage: no one can measure the blood that has been spilled over the ages by "Levites" engaged in self-styled holy war.[2] What I wish to propose, however, is a *textual* irony that can be represented by calling into question the deadly seriousness of Childs's summary statement of the pro-Levite, anti-Aaronite position. What if the point of view of our passage were better represented by adding

---

1. *The Book of Exodus: A Critical, Theological Commentary* (Philadelphia: Westminster, 1974), 571.

2. See Michael Walzer, "Exodus 32 and the Theory of Holy War: The History of a Citation," *Harvard Theological Review* 61 (1968) 1-14.

quotation marks, ironizing Childs's position: "The Levites were 'faithful' at enormous cost."

In unironic tribute to Childs's judicious pairing of "Old Testament Context" and "New Testament Context," I propose a pairing of Jewish and Christian exegesis before turning to what I would polemically call a "New Literary Criticism." By this term I mean to invoke the characteristic emphasis on internal, textual irony in the work of the "New Critics" of literature, and also to challenge the appropriation of "literary" to that mode of rhetorical scriptural criticism that assumes the aesthetic unity of the canonized text. Let us begin by reviewing just how problematic our passage really is and what urges both documentary and ironic solutions to its discontinuities.

I. Problems

It may be difficult, or perhaps arbitrary, to separate the problems with the Levites' action from problems with Aaron's. With Higher Criticism came the question whether Aaron was originally there at all,[3] but readers have always puzzled over his role: The traditional problem, and the subject of endless apologetics, is why Aaron so readily consents to the people's desire for visible representation. One question is whether the action Aaron takes in first calling for gold and then constructing the calf can be described as a stopgap measure rather than itself the major instigation of disaster. The problems associated with Aaron may be represented by the uncertainty or duplication of v. 35: "And Yahweh smote the people because they made the calf that Aaron made." The verse seems to cry out for the sort of fragmentation Higher Criticism indulges: the construction of the calf by the people and by Aaron seem to be different accounts rather than different stages in or perspectives on the same events.

To this we may add the question of how many calves are constructed. The people appeal for more than one: "Up, make us gods, which shall go be-

---

3. Wellhausen supposed an old J strand with no Aaron. From the preeminent work of Lehming, cited below, one might go back to R. H. Kennett, "The Origin of the Aaronite Priesthood," *JTS* 6 (1905) 161-86. Kennett imagines that the golden calf is "an episode which no one in the later period of Israelitish religion would ever have been tempted to invent" (165); but he can imagine (what I would suppose more difficult) that only the negative valuation of the calf episode is belated. A longer critical history of seeing the Aaron material colored by the Jeroboam episode is traced — and significantly supplemented — by Moses Aberbach and Levy Smolar in "Aaron, Jeroboam, and the Golden Calves," *JBL* 86 (1967), 129-40.

fore us" (32:1), making use not only of the plural noun form *Elohim* but the plural verb *yelḥu* — they will go before us. Aaron likewise points in the plural: "These be thy gods, O Israel" (v. 4), with an additional problem in that it is not Aaron, in the singular, but "they" who said, "These be thy gods." Even if one accepts the idea that the text has been influenced by, or written in response to, the construction of the two calves by Jeroboam in 1 Kgs. 12:29, there remains the problem of the inconsistency of the Exodus account. Aaron constructs an altar before a single calf in v. 5. And what Moses sees in 32:19 is the calf, one calf; it is one calf that Moses destroys, one that Aaron claims to have constructed in v. 24. Because of the pointer, "these be thy gods," we cannot say that there was a request for two and a compromise at one; the text just seems inconsistent. And the inconsistency is repeated in God's conversation with Moses before his descent in v. 8.

We may bracket the question of just how the calf or calves are constructed; Aaron's explanation, "I cast it into the fire and there came out this calf" (v. 24) seems too good (too humorous as well as defensive) a reworking of v. 4 ("fashioned it with a graving tool") to warrant a charge of inconsistency. On the other hand, Aaron's relation to the worship of the calf remains more problematic. The RSV translates v. 6, "And they rose up early on the morrow, and offered burnt offerings, and brought peace offerings; and the people sat down to eat and to drink, and rose up to play." Aaron does not specify what he has in mind for the feast day he proclaims, nor does this elusive verse specify what *liṣaḥek* ("to play") involves. The problem is represented, or compounded, by the more unusual verb in v. 25: "Moses saw that the people were broken loose *(para);* for Aaron had let them loose for a derision (*šimṣâ,* another problematic term) among their enemies." The explanatory clause is hardly needed in this place, and seems to have been tacked on by someone wishing to insist on Aaron's culpability for the people's "loose" behavior. The recapitulation of this verse is also difficult to explain in narrative context. Moses seems to see the disarray of the people as though for the first time; if this marks a seam in the text, it seems sloppily sewn.

We come to the problems with the Levite passage proper. These may be said to begin with the general, theological question of what it means to be "for God." It is by no means clear that the people have been clamoring for other gods, rather than a visual representation of Yahweh — a tangible icon of his presence, an assurance of his availability for leadership. Aaron's response seems to imply that there is no change in the object of worship, only in the mode of representation. In v. 5 he proclaims, "Tomorrow shall be a feast to Yahweh." The problem posed by v. 26, Moses' general address to the

Israelites, is that it presupposes not only that worship of Yahweh through the calf is no worship of Yahweh, but also that the people would know this. Or, if we are asked to assume that Moses' destruction of the calf in v. 20 has served its pedagogical purpose, then others besides the Levites should have absorbed the lesson. What purpose, after all, in having the Israelites consume the remnants of their idol if not to disabuse them of its power of representation? And yet Moses' cry is not "All who were faithful to Yahweh rally to me!" but rather "All who [are] faithful" (the Hebrew expressing the present without a present tense verb of being). Either the pedagogy of v. 20 was ineffective, or v. 26 does not know about v. 20.

No sooner does Moses call for those loyal to Yahweh than "All the sons of Levi gathered themselves together unto him" (v. 26). The "all" is unusual and seems to point to a political rather than what we might call a purely narrative purpose. If the purpose of this story is to privilege the Levites, the "all" adds an air of miracle; that may not be out of place in an etiological story, although the effort to counter other tales of the arbitrary privileging of the Levites would seem better served if the story purported to represent historical circumstance (it was the Levites) rather than prevenient, divine intervention (lo, all the Levites!).

Moses' commission of the Levites seems more problematic than anything so far mentioned: "Thus saith Yahweh, the God of Israel: 'Put ye every man his sword upon his thigh, and go to and fro from gate to gate throughout the camp, and slay every man his brother, and every man his companion, and every man his neighbor'" (v. 27). Although we may often pass over, as a matter of indifference, whether a passage that purports to have divine authority specifies, "thus saith Yahweh," Moses' independent action in breaking the tablets (v. 19) and God's apparently independent punishment of the people (v. 35) combine to make us question whether this particular injunction has God's prevenient backing. And then there is the question of just what the Levites are being asked to do. Commentators throughout the centuries specify that the Levites are to slay those "brethren," that is, neighboring Israelites, who participated in (or perhaps those who were most zealous in) the worship of the calf. The problem is that Moses' injunction does not specify this, and a *fatâ*, if *fatâ* there must be, must be specific. A familiar midrash represents this: God calls Abraham to take his son and offer him as a sacrifice, and Abraham feels himself justified in disregarding the command because God has not specified which son; God tells Abraham to take his beloved son, and Abraham still feels reprieved; God tells Abraham to take his only son, and Abraham reasons that Isaac and Ishmael are each the only son of his mother. Only when God specifies Isaac is Abraham obliged. Adding to the problem-

atic lack of specificity in the injunction to the Levites is what we might call
the reverse of specificity in v. 29. Moses tells whom they stood against, but
the list is not identical: "Consecrate yourselves today to Yahweh, yea, every
man against his son, and against his brother; that he may bestow upon you a
blessing this day." Although it is possible to find the second list simply an intensive form of the first, the difference makes one question what, if any, literal component there is supposed to be. "Brothers and neighbors" might be
a figurative way of expressing the element of humanity one sacrifices in the
name of a "higher" cause; but there is at least a question whether "sons and
brothers" is simply a more intense way of envisioning the same obligation. If
intensity is not the only difference — if, for example, one list derives from an
older, independent source, then there is also the possibility that the opposition that the list speaks of is not the opposition of the Levites' murderous as-
sault on idol worshipers. Like the prophets, expected to leave kith and kin,
the Levites might (at least in some prevenient source) be "against" son and
brother in the sense of denying them, turning aside from them, and finding
community instead in the priesthood. This possibility is related to the difficulty attendant upon the injunction in v. 29, "consecrate yourselves today to
Yahweh." Although the Hebrew *milu yedhem* (literally "fill your hands") is
elsewhere used to express consecration, it is at least possible that the phrase
means something else here — given the difference between human blood
shed by the Levites and animal blood elsewhere associated with dedicatory
ritual. There is also a question of how the Hebrew text should be pointed: Is
it *milu* — fill your hands, in the imperative, looking forward from the bloodbath to a second, very different injunction; or is it *mallu* — you have "filled
your hands," already consecrated yourselves in the bloody act you have performed for the glory of God?

The following verses, recounting Moses' intercession to God, seem
oblivious of the slaughter that has just taken place. These verses seem to imply intercession to avert a divine punishment that has not yet taken place.
This may be a punishment in the form of an indiscriminate outbreak, such
as plague. If that is what Moses wishes to avert (or at least contain), then
God's answer in v. 34 would seem to indicate that Moses has been successful:
God would have punished all, but he contains his wrath and restricts punishment to the guilty. All the same, the prophecy of a future, a presumably distant future, as announced in v. 34 ("in the day when I visit . . ."), seems a
thing apart from the visitation of plague in v. 35. It begins to seem that there
are three punishments, that of the Levites "that day," that of God in the form
of a plague, and that foretold for a more distant future.

Last, we may wonder about the relationship between the consequence announced in v. 34, "my angel shall go before you," and the request that began the whole episode. Unlike other rebellion narratives, this one does not present Israelites at fault for wanting a leader to take them back to Egypt (as opposed to one who would take them on to Canaan). Are they then at fault for wanting a leader they could see? One cannot say that the fault lies in the desire for anything tangible, for the text that disapproves of calves allows cherubim — and, more immediately, involves a visible icon in the form of stone tablets. If we stick to the idea of visible leader, is the angel who is now to lead them a concession to their need for mediatory agency, or part of the punishment? In 33:15, Moses seems to imply that a mediatory presence (like a vice president sent on delegation) would not be satisfactory. It is not clear, as ch. 32 closes, whether the angel indicates God's presence or his absence, and whether the Levites' butchery has permitted this much closeness on God's part or contributed to blocking a better arrangement.

II. Rabbinic Solutions

In surveying the precritical literature, I would like to focus not on the way different things seem to be problematic, but on the way literary problems are shared — problems to which commentators operating within and without the tradition of plenary inspiration offer disparate solutions.

Much of rabbinic exegesis of our passage serves to diminish the sense of butchery. In place of indiscriminate slaughter, the rabbis substitute God's discrimination, or even human, judicial process. The Talmud explains that what appear to be two or three punitive responses to the crisis (the imbibing, the Levites' slaughter, the plague) are responses dependent on degrees of guilt.[4] There are two views, curiously associated with two rabbis, but — as if we were dealing with textual burglars wearing gloves — not actually fingerprinted, this view to this thinker. One of them holds that three degrees of culpability in action are reflected in three punishments: Whoever sacrificed and burned incense died by the Levites' swords; whoever embraced and kissed the calf died by plague; and whoever rejoiced in the general worship died from the trial by water. (The general imbibing of water into which the remnants of the calf had been dissolved is understood to be not a general humiliation but a trial by ordeal, a discrimination of the guilty from the innocent on the model of the treatment accorded a woman suspected of adultery in Num. 5:11-31.) The second view discriminates on the basis of mental state

---

4. *Yoma* 66b.

and material witness: he who sinned before witnesses and after receiving warning died by Levite sword; he who sinned before witnesses but without having been warned, by plague; and he who sinned without witnesses to attest and without having been warned was disposed of by God in the trial by water, without further human intervention. Perhaps the very reluctance to say which of these views belongs to Rav, which to Levi, could be said to stand emblematically for the desire to distance human agency from punitive action. Vengeance is the Lord's, and only in that extraordinary case where an individual was specifically warned and doubly witnessed was a punishment at human hands exacted. What is effaced here is not only the sense of indiscriminate slaughter, but in effect the actuality of the three thousand slaughtered. In retrospect, the Levites' slaughter becomes something like a hypothetical possibility, the action that would have had to be taken if, indeed, anyone was witnessed and warned. If this sort of interpretation seems less than candid exegesis, it could also be considered more than mere exegesis; it is "living Bible," old tale adapted to fit the historical circumstances and mental processes of a later civilization.

What the Talmud begins (and Rashi straightforwardly recounts) is handsomely extended by Ramban. Reveling in the anachronism, Ramban supposes that there were just too many sinners to bring to the courthouse. And for preparing all those briefs, we might add in the same spirit, the desert was rather short on photocopy and fax machines. While the Talmud appears to want to bracket the three thousand — as if the mere emphasis on the two modes of God's direct punishment could make this cleanup procedure with the remnant of sinners disappear — Ramban focuses on the size of the bloodbath. By presenting the use of the Levites to administer justice as an emergency procedure, by suggesting the civil procedure that would have obtained under other circumstances, he salvages the account from historical relativism. Moses' judgment, Talmudic standard, and medieval values are all one. The impulse behind such handling of the text is extended by Abravanel, who appears to find in the phrasing about traversing the camp from gate to gate no sign of hasty slaughter but a sense of deliberateness, of meticulous *sifting* of the evidence. "That is to say," he explains, "that they should not proceed in haste. But with due deliberation *(bimtinut hadin)* they are to go from gate to gate and make careful inquiry *(yidrishu hetev)* who sinned in the matter of the calf." Abravanel cannot erase the actual slaying of the guilty, but he can so shift the emphasis that deliberation replaces devastation. The orders are understood to be "slay them — do not show mercy [pervert justice] even if a man finds his brother or relative to be a sinner in this." "Slay them" is still there, but now the reference to relatives and friends is understood as a mark of the unemotional thoroughness and civility of the judicial procedure.

Working to subvert or transform the violence of what we might call the plain sense, rabbinic exegesis is aided in some allied maneuvers. I think it is fair to call "plain sense" the reading that Moses twice acts with haste and anger — first in breaking the tablets (v. 19), second in summoning the Levites to the massacre. Rashi's exegesis of the first verse ignores Moses' anger and supplies this piece of Talmudic reasoning: If, in regard to the Passover sacrifice, which is but one of the six hundred and thirteen precepts, the Torah says, "no alien shall eat of it" (Exod. 12:43), how much more so is it important that they be kept from partaking of the whole Torah, given that all the Israelites are apostates! (*Shabbat* 87a). This piece of reasoning, of clarifying a decision as based on meditation over other prooftexts, is extended in consideration of Moses' second decision, to summon the Levites and to proclaim the massacre as God's will. Moses finds biblical precedent for what he gives as God's word in this case. "Where did He say so? [In the verse:] 'He who sacrifices to [any other] god shall be destroyed'" (Exod. 22:19). If anything, the second argument from prooftext seems less "far-fetched" than the first — not because it comes from a place ten chapters closer, but because the ch. 12 reference involves a metaphor twist: "son of an alien" has to be turned 180 degrees to mean "children of Israel who have 'alienated' themselves," while the reference to ch. 22 seems straightforward: It says that idol worshipers will be exterminated, so let us fulfill the letter of the law. But more important than the comparative "reasonableness" of the second exegetical act is the sense of sharing a worldview, a mode of procedure. Moses is simply assimilated into the circle of rabbinic interpreters of the text; he is not on the scene, issuing orders of destruction, but standing as apart from the scene as the rabbis are.

One curious exception proves the rule. According to *Seder Eliyahu Rabba*, Moses really did act alone, and readers can stand with God, against Moses, in moral condemnation of his Godless violence.[5] The midrashist zealously guards God from imputation that might transfer from what Moses says of God: "I bring to witness heaven and earth that the Holy One, Blessed be he, did not tell Moses to stand in the gate of the camp and to say 'Whoever is on God's side, come to me!' and 'Thus says the Lord, God of Israel. . . .'; rather, Moses the righteous reasoned on his own *[dan kal viḥomer biaṣmo]*.

5. I am much indebted to Professor Marc Brettler of Brandeis University for this reference and for his generous help generally in understanding the literary conventions of the rabbinic exegetes.

He said: 'If I tell Israel to kill, this man his brother, that man his friend, and that man his relative, Israel would say to me, 'That is not what you taught us! The Talmud says, 'A sanhedrin that condemns to death one soul in seven years is called a killer of a sanhedrin' [*Makkot* 7] — and you would kill three thousand in a single day?' Therefore, he made his plea depend on respect for higher authority *[kvod šelimala]*, as it is written: 'Thus says the Lord, God of Israel. . . .' But what do we find after this? 'The Sons of Levi did as Moses bid' [32:28]." The midrash thus explicates the unusual phrase, "as Moses bid," which appears in place of the customary "as the Lord bid." One may argue that such exegesis saves God at Moses' expense (the slaughter of three thousand was Moses' own idea, like the intemperate hitting of the rock in Numbers 20); but the midrash seems more intent on cleverly explaining the disparity between "the Lord said" and "Moses said" than it does in denigrating the injunction given the Levites.

Whether or not this interpretation of the midrash is correct, it seems fair to generalize that rabbinic exegesis assumes the positive valuation of the Levites' zeal. There is some question whether the Levites are sanctified as a result of their carnage or whether they are sanctified *in* their carnage, with human blood substituting for the ritual of sanctification, which ordinarily involves animal blood. But the medieval and Renaissance exegetes assume that in some sense the Levites are rewarded for work well done. The most extreme of these positions may be that of Abravanel, who explains that v. 27, "slay every man his brother, and every man his friend," and v. 29, "[slay] every man his son, and every man his brother" are separate commands. The first command produced admirable zeal on the part of the Levites, who slew three thousand without regard to the fact that the guilty were "brother" Israelites. But then a second command specifies that even if the guilty party is one's own son, no reprieve should be given; and it is in response to this more thorough purge, evincing still purer zeal, that the Levites are rewarded.[6] One notes with relief that Abravanel does not specify whether the second wave of violence he sees in the text produced a greater carnage or a minor, "cleanup" operation. To guard against any such attempt to linger over or multiply the acts of carnage, Ibn Ezra specifies that Moses' restated command, in v. 29, is in the pluperfect. The Levites are rewarded for following Moses' charge to them when he says, "slay every man [the guilty, even if it be] his son or brother." A less literal but more normative reading is offered by Sforno, who wholly separates the sanctification of the Levites from the bloodbath. He explains that the Levites are sanctified because each man was not *against* his

6. *Torah Shlemah*, ed. Menachem M. Kasher (Jerusalem, 1964), 146.

son (bracket the brother) but ready to perform the ritual of circumcision *on* his son. While other tribes suspended this ritual obligation, the Levites carried it out and thus earned the right to the priesthood.[7] This noble effort to tackle the peculiarity of *ish bivno* (every man in regard to [?] his son) in v. 29 further buries or distances the bloodbath of v. 28. That act, perhaps necessary as janitorial work, can be separated from the running of Levitical offices. One might even regard the bloodbath as the last piece of dirty work the Levites perform before their elevation to the office they are to hold because of other, prevenient merit.

III. Protestant Warfare

In his study of Exodus 32 and the idea of holy war, Michael Walzer writes a capsule history of Christianity in which the outbreak of the Levites seems the type for the Protestant Reformation.[8] There always were, he concedes, radical enthusiasts who wanted to model their zeal on the Levites and take arms against those they felt to be their ungodly brethren; but leaders of the church, at least as personified in Augustine and Aquinas, understood the importance of bracketing the Levites' action lest it be taken to license a violent internal housecleaning, a vigilante purging of idolaters. Thus Augustine wrote of Moses' purge as if Moses himself were the agent of destruction, while Aquinas (overlooking not only the Levites' agency but Moses' independent initiative) points to the vengeance against the calf-worshipers as God's own act. Only with Calvin do we get a focus on the Levites as exemplary votaries, models for the community of the elect who, needing no ordination but their own consciences, would be willing to take arms against sinners. In a strange way, the Protestant recovery of the Levites leaps over earlier Christian exegesis to join with something in the rabbinic tradition. Yet if the rabbis overlooked the Levites' violence in describing their acts as though the rabbis' judicial process were in force then, the Calvinist reading reverses the formula. Instead of "they were just like us!" we have, "we could be just like them!"

Calvin himself, as Walzer notes, was not consistent in taking the Levites as a model for the community of saints. In the *Institutes,* he approaches the example of the Levites from the context of a discussion about the magistrate as representative of God on earth, executing God's judgments. To allow "ven-

7. *Sforno: Commentary on the Torah,* tr. and notes by Rabbi Raphael Pelcovitz (Artscroll Mesorah Series; Brooklyn: Mesorah, 1987) I, 406-7.
8. Walzer, 11ff.

geance is mine!" (Deut. 32:35) to mean "vengeance belongs to me — that is, to those who act in my name," Calvin needs to limit the extension to appointed ministers. He has no trouble with his first scriptural citation: Paul says that a civil authority is a minister of God, "a revenger to execute wrath upon him that doeth evil" (Rom 13:4). When he turns to the Pentateuch, however, Calvin has to stretch a point. Moses, in slaying the Egyptian who smites a Hebrew slave (Exod. 2:12), has not been appointed for that office. Calvin licenses Moses by crediting him with prophetic insight into his future appointment: "This motive influenced Moses, when, knowing himself to be destined to become the liberator of his people by the power of the Lord, 'he slew the Egyptian.'"[9] Perhaps to avoid the problems in regarding the Levites as similarly commissioned by prophetic insight into the role they will be given, Calvin treats the slaughter of the three thousand in the *Institutes* as though it were Moses' own doing. He marvels at Moses that "he continued to go through the camp till three thousand were slain." If the plain sense of the text would lead a reader to suppose that the Levites are *sent* through the camp, individually carrying out the rampage, Calvin may find warrant in Moses' call of God's followers "to me" for presenting the vengeance as personally led by Moses. In his *Commentaries,* he similarly speaks of the vengeance "Moses employed" and even separates Moses' will from God's to suggest Moses' role as mediator. "he cleansed the camp of the chief authors of the evil, in order that God might be more inclined to pardon."[10] When he does confront the Levites as ministers themselves of God's vengeance, he interprets Moses' call as a call to "God's servants," a naming that seems to invest them with the ministry yet to come. Calvin is not exactly anticipating the announcement that the Levites will henceforth be servants of God, in the way that commentators like Ibn Ezra assumed that the investiture of v. 29 is in the pluperfect; rather, Calvin imagines that God already "appointed them His ministers for the punishment of a crime." They then can, presumably, be

9. *Institutes of the Christian Religion,* tr. John Allen (Philadelphia: Presbyterian Board of Christian Education, 1936), 783.

10. *Commentaries on the Four Last Books of Moses, Arranged in the Form of a Harmony* (Grand Rapids: Baker, 1843) III, 354. Calvin writes off three thousand as a small percentage, indicative of God's "leniency": "how much milder here is the rate of punishment, when only three thousand perish out of six hundred millions [sic]!" In a slightly different fashion, Wesley picks up the apologetics of the leniency reading: "Yet it should seem they were to slay those only whom they found *abroad in the street* of the camp; for it might be hoped that those who were retired into their tents were ashamed of what they had done." *Explanatory Notes upon the Old Testament* (1765; rep. Salem: Schmul, 1975), 316.

rewarded with the general business of caring for God's tabernacle because they have proven themselves in the hardest part of the "ministry." To ante-date the general appointment, he adds specificity to Moses' call: "The Levites were called out by name, and this we gather from the result; because they all immediately came forward, and not one of any other tribe." If called "by name," they are invested before the slaughter, rather than in recompense for it.

Although Calvin is careful to specify the special, prevenient appointment of the Levites, when focusing on their violence, he might be said to be *separately* interested in using the Levites' zeal as a model for the community of saints. The sermons repeatedly turn "Levites" into a metaphor for the Christian communi-ty: "We be of the order & number of the Levites, that is to say, of them that are dedicated unto God."[11] But the basis for this figurative identification is not a contemporary willingness to take up the sword. On the contrary, it is Christ's peace that has bridged the times: "God hath done us the honor to make us all Levites, according to this saying [Isa. 66:21] that when God shall have restored his people, those which were Levites, before shall then become Priests, & all the common people shall become Levites."[12] The predestinationist Calvin might have emphasized what Isaiah actually says, that *some* of the people will be cho-sen as Levites; but his interest is rather in broadening the category: "nowadays all of us are Levites & a kingly priesthood, as the people of Israel were: let us note that this matter belongeth partly unto us all."[13] It may even be that the "partly" is Calvin's way of separating the Levites' violence from their dedication. It is only in the sense of being willing to set God uppermost that Calvin wishes to take the Levites as a type for the Christian community, and the actual willingness to set aside considerations of kinship in executing idolaters becomes simply a mode of expressing "that God is above all, and ought to bear chiefest sway." In a strange way, Calvin's position is similar to that of the historical critic Gunneweg, who argues that the real meaning (only for him it means the "original" meaning, while for Calvin it is the current meaning) of the Levites' willingness to ignore kinship ties in the slaughter was the individual Levite's willingness to leave kith and kin in taking up the service of God.[14]

11. *The Sermons of M. Iohn Calvin upon the Fifth Booke of Moses Called Deuteronomie,* tr. Arthur Golding (London: Henry Middleton, 1583; Banner of Truth Fac-simile Reprint, 1987) 426b. See also pp. 658b, 1204a.

12. *Sermons,* 658b.

13. *Sermons,* 1203b.

14. A. H. J. Gunneweg, *Leviten und Priester. Hauptlinien der Traditionsbildung und Geschichte des israelitisch-jüdischen Kultpersonals* (Göttingen: Vandenhoeck and Ruprecht, 1965), 29-37. I am indebted to Andrew James Johnston of the Free University

As far as I can tell, then, there is nothing in Calvin's sermons that would clearly support Waltzer's claim that Calvin unleashes the potential for holy war within the Christian community. When discussing the magistrate's right to take judicial action, Calvin either subsumes the Levites under the ministry of Moses or insists on the Levites' prevenient chosenness as God's ministers; when using the Levites as models for "all of us," Calvin extrapolates the willingness to put God over family from the bloody context in which the Levites' example occurs. I pause over Calvin's anxiety concerning the commission of the Levites because I think we can hear a faint rumble of the tidewater of violence that has overwhelmed the history of Christianity from its mythic history in the "Levites of the tabernacle" on. Though Calvin does not proclaim the individual saint's right to assume authority to execute the vengeance of God, there is a glimmer, there has always been a glimmer, of the possibility that something ominous haunts the joyous proclamation of the Levites' "godly" butchery. This shadow is invisible in historical-critical readings of the text, which assume that the episode has been written belatedly for the benefit of the Levites. When I turn to propose a "posthistorical" literary reading, I shall try to recover something of the shadow that haunts both rabbinic and Christian apologetics.

IV. Historical Criticism

Although the slaughter perpetrated by the Levites in vv. 25-29 has been subjected to a remarkable density of critical readings, the variations among these readings might be plotted along a relatively narrow margin of a single axis. At the far end, there is Lehming's carefully reasoned discrimination of no less than eleven layers to the narrative, with multiple Aaron-related additions following the major, post-Jeroboam insertion of the Levite slaughter narrative.[15] I think of this article as the beacon in relation to which others navigate or in relation to which others may be positioned. It is not necessarily that Lehming is more persuasive than anyone else, but that he establishes the most formidable watershed among the critics in proclaiming "Aaron" as

---

of Berlin for help with Gunneweg's German and for suggesting that an anti-Nazi polemic may color the language of the argument about holy war, Levite, and folk.

15. Sigo Lehming, "Versuch zu EX XXXII," *VT* 10 (1960) 1-50. At the other end, we might position R. W. L. Moberly, who simply subordinates the concern over Levite priesthood to a general piety about (Levites') faithfulness unto death (death of others). *At the Mountain of God: Story and Theology in Exodus 32–34* (JSOT Supplement Series 22; Sheffield: JSOT, 1983) 55.

the eponym of the group of priests established by Jeroboam in Dan and Bethel to administer the cult of the calves (1 Kgs. 12:26-33).[16] For Lehming, we must interpret the Levites' slaughter of calf-worshipers in Exod. 32:25-29 as a text invented for the express purpose of supporting the Levite priesthood of Jeroboam's day in its struggle against other, non-Levite priests; this might be called *the* guiding light of historical criticism of the passage. But to this, Lehming adds the voltage of his charged identification of the non-Levite priests as "Aaronide."[17] Thus, anything we see in Exodus 32 that seems to be critical of the character Aaron is to be interpreted as an expression of hostility toward the other priests, to whom the name of Aaron is presumed to have applied.

Cody, who dismisses Lehming's hypothesis of a conflict between Levite and Aaronide priesthood as "not likely," asserts instead that "at the time of the fragment's insertion, Ex. 32 was disparaging the evil of the *cult* itself in Bethel rather than its priesthood."[18] This distinction might be of marginal interest were it not that, in disputing Lehming's insight that "Aaron" is the eponym for a political group, Cody likewise calls into question Lehming's understanding of the dating and the meaning of the verses about Aaron. Cody actually does believe in a later conflict between Levite priests and a group called "sons of Aaron," but he cavils that "in Ex. 32, Aaron's role is not that of a priest." I confess being baffled by this — as though a Republican attempt to denigrate Democratic politics through a character slander on a Democratic president could be waived aside by the specification, "ah, but he wasn't acting *as president* in that adultery!" Indeed, Cody goes on to imagine anyway that the nastiest verses about Aaron were added later, at a time when the "sons of Aaron" was a rival power group; so at most the historical spacing of the additions, though not their order, is altered from Lehming.

Historical criticism cuts a slightly wider swath with Winnett, who does not assume a particular moment of crisis faced by the Levitical priests. Like others, he does believe that the story of the golden calf in Exodus 32 "can only have arisen after the time of Jeroboam."[19] He believes, that is, not only

---

16. The history of the idea of an Aaronide priesthood at Bethel and Dan is reviewed by Marsha White, "The Elohistic Depiction of Aaron: A Study in the Levite-Zadokite Controversy," in *Studies in the Pentateuch*, ed. J. A. Emerton (Leiden: Brill, 1990), 150.

17. *Versuch*, 47.

18. Aelred Cody, O.S.B., *A History of Old Testament Priesthood* (Rome: Pontifical Biblical Institute, 1969) 155.

19. Frederick Victor Winnett, *The Mosaic Tradition* (Toronto: University of Toronto Press, 1949) 49.

that the phrase "these are thy gods" has been borrowed from the Jeroboam story, but that the phrase indicates composition in response to the Jeroboam story, not alteration of an older text (say, one that had "this is thy god") after the Jeroboam incident. But Winnett is concerned to place the story of the selection of the Levites at Sinai in the context of other Pentateuchal accounts of the selection of the Levites. He hypothesizes an original institution of the Levites at Kadesh, after the Korah story in Numbers 17: "But it was intolerable to the levitical priests of Jerusalem that their appointment did not date back to the sacred mountain, and wishful thinking led in time to the rise of a tradition of their mountain origin." The rather strange notion of literary invention "in time" allows Winnett to make sense of two separate references to the institution of the Levites. First, "the assertion in Dt. 10:8f that 'at that time [the time of the provision of a second set of tablets] Yahweh set apart the tribe of Levi to carry the ark of the covenant of Yahweh,' etc., probably represents the first appearance in written form of this claim to a Horeb-Sinai origin." But this explanation is too vague and does not satisfy. So, "in time," the postexilic Levites invented the story we have in Exod. 32:25-29.[20] In a sense, Winnett's understanding of the story in Exod. 32:25-29 is less political, more literary, because he does not imagine a specific historical event (the establishment of the calf images in Dan and Bethel) as the immediate cause for the literary composition of vv. 25-29. And yet the "need" that he imagines giving rise to this composition might just as well be described as a political need — the desire, on the part of the Levites, to give their chosenness the resonance of what, in rabbinic tradition, is known generally as *torah misinai*, quintessentially authentic revelation. The Levites feel the need for a story that has them earn their right to the priesthood at Sinai — and lo, a story is born. Into the furnace of literary inspiration you throw your amorphous need — and out comes this "calf."

A minor but perhaps noteworthy consequence of the "political line" is the way it alters the valuation of redundancy in the text. If we start with a consideration of vv. 25-29 in context, we may be struck by what seems to be an excess of responses to the calf worship. Whether or not one considers Moses' destruction of the calf and the scattering of its dust on waters a separate form of punishment (selective punishment, along the model of the woman suspected of adultery, Numbers 5), there are still the punishment exacted by the Levites and the plague inflicted by God in v. 35. To this list we may add as a separate item the punishment for which Moses' offer of vicarious atonement in vv. 30-34 is denied. Now the explanation that vv. 25-29 respond to

20. Winnett, 146-47.

the Levites' desire for Sinaic authentication allows for the redundancy of v. 35: The plague is what was there in the old text, and it can be understood to have been left there as a way of ratifying the Levites' vengeance with God's own dose of the same. What is interesting, however, is that a later stage of revision, the intercession in vv. 30-34 can be explained by the same politics: Further to represent God's disapproval of the altars still standing at Dan and Bethel, a passage is written in which some future destruction of those directly responsible for the current political apostasy is intimated in the conceit of future destruction to those directly responsible for the calf worship at Sinai. Coats calls this invention of yet more punishment "a concession to the fact that the calves continued to exist, with the thought that the punishment must be eventually executed against the calves' devotees."[21] The irony of "concession" points to the literary achievement of the text itself. It is as though the text had a will of its own, a will to closure, which is thwarted by the continued pressure of history, the continued relevance of passages about divine displeasure.

The historical critic with the most literary reading — or at least the least straightforwardly political reading — may be Gunneweg, who dismisses the rebellion and punishment aspect of the story as all too common and focuses instead on what is unique to this episode, the strange formula in vv. 27 and 29. For Gunneweg, the core material out of which our passage is formed is the initiatory experience of Levites, which he assumes to have been a profession, like that of the prophets, that people of any tribe could enter by renouncing family and inheritance to join the sacred service. Gunneweg interprets the blessing of the Levite tribe in Deuteronomy 33 as capturing, independently of Exodus 32, that pretribal requirement of renunciation: "Who said of his father and mother, 'I regard them not'; he disowned his brothers, and ignored his children" (Deut. 33:9). Literary interpretation: Exod. 32:29 translates or encodes the "historical" fact that Levites renounced their families; "at the price of brother and son" means at the price of renouncing family ties. And more literary interpretation: Exod. 32:27, with its more general terms, "slay every man his brother, and every man his companion," *means* renounce your family. The meaning of v. 27 is to interpret *(zu interpretieren)* v. 29.[22]

If we say of Gunneweg's reading that it is still political — that it still understands the episode as arising from a desire to lend political support to the

---

21. Coats, 187. Noth similarly supposes punishment yet to come on Jeroboam's priests: "This cultic apostasy must still — so the writer gives us to understand — be expiated even if this is not apparent at the time. God has still marked it out for some time" — from the time of Moses to the time of Jeroboam (251).

22. *Leviten und Priester*, 31.

Levites' claim for privilege — we nonetheless need to modify the concept of translation from politics to literature. To quantify it, we might say that the story of vv. 25-29 arises at least as much out of the old proverb about Levites' renunciation as it does out of the general desire for endorsement. Yet the question is not one of quantity, of the relative importance of two causes; it is a matter of priority. If we assume that there is no historical event to which the Levite slaughter refers, but that there is historicity to the Levites' belated need to authenticate themselves, then the old proverb about Levites' renunciation occupies something of the status of a literary *trouvé;* it is that piece of old lore, not originally in any connection with the calf episode, that gives an antique patina to a new etiology. The new story of the Levites' selection at Sinai has a built-in defense against the charge of inauthenticity: throw out the new story, and the old proverb (or what looks like an old proverb) is displayed with greater nakedness as tribute to the Levites' worthiness and antiquity.

V. New Literary Criticism

Gunneweg's work shares with other historical criticism the assumption that the Levites' slaughter is a positive piece of propaganda — that it is written by Levites to promote Levite interests. Suppose, however, that we acknowledge the phrase "written by Levites" to be a figure of speech for "written by some-one who had the Levites' interest in mind." In introducing such a gap in per-sons, we introduce also the difference between political and literary interpre-tation. If we think of an individual author as being "on assignment," whether that assignment is initiated internally or externally, we allow for the possibil-ity that certain features of composition may be related to the writer's sense of the tools of his craft and the writer's idiosyncratic sense of the parameters for his invention. For example, the general assignment, from a political interest group wishing to denigrate the worship at Dan and Bethel, might be "come up with a calf story at Sinai." But this still might leave to the discretion of the writer whether to imagine an original apostasy involving multiple calves, so that the phrase "these are your gods" will seem more easily to fit — or one calf, precisely so that the phrase "these are your gods" will jar and add readerly distaste to theological disapproval. Likewise, the decisions to have the calf be golden, to have gold collected in the form of jewelry, to harken back to a peculiar piece of text about plundering the Egyptians — all such matters may be construed as related to the way the assignment is carried out.

For the episode of the Levites' butchery, the Gunneweg hypothesis broadens and defines the domain of the writer. At the same time, it locates more surely a political signpost — an idea, a word, beyond the manipulation of the writer. That word is *kol* — the strange stipulation that when Moses cried, "whoever is on the Lord's side, rally to me," *all* the sons of Levi gathered themselves to him. The idea that the Levite slaughter reworks old material about Levite renunciation of family intensifies the distinction between the renouncer and the renounced, the slaughterer and the slaughtered. Gunneweg makes it hard to regard "brother and neighbor" as non-Levite idolaters who fall victim to the purge. The rabbinic exegetes, to be sure, did just that, literalizing "brother," for example, as the half-brother of a Levite from the same mother but a different, non-Levitical father. For Gunneweg, on the other hand, the Levites' old renunciation of kin has been reworked into the slaughter of kin, while the slaughter of literal kin has not yet (at the time of composition of vv. 25-29) been reworked into the slaughter of non-Levite Israelites. Gunneweg's reading assumes what Cody, elsewhere, spells out: because of the "act which required the decimation of relatives of the Levites themselves, the *remaining* Levites acquired priestly standing."[23] But if the purpose, the political purpose, of the story is to privilege the Levites, there is something unsavory about the implication that it may have been Levites, though slaughtered Levites, who participated in and perhaps led in the apostasy of calf-worship. The easiest way to counter such a dark thought is to add the specification that all the Levites gathered to Moses. This is to say that the specification of intertribal as opposed to intratribal slaughter is political. We may not be able to surmise with any surety that the specification "*all* the Levites" is the work of a later hand; but we could at least attribute it to the political agenda to which the original compositional idea has been internally or externally subjected.

In the preceding paragraphs, I have followed in Gunneweg's footsteps without questioning the credibility of his hypothesis of a nontribal Levitical brotherhood for which familial renunciation was once required. There are, however, so many points in the Pentateuch where Levi is considered one of the sons of Jacob, where the sons of Levi are treated as a tribe, that it would be unwise to make more than a reading of a passage contingent on so hypothetical a construction. For this reason, I would want to specify that whether or not he is correct, Gunneweg is of great interest, of great heuristic interest, in defining the grounds for a new literary reading. Only admit that there is a

---

23. Cody, 152, italics mine. Cody lets the slaughter of Levites by Levites do double service: "We notice that the story explains not only the priesthood of the Levites but also the partial disappearance of the Levites as a full tribe, for this decimation of kinsmen serves also to explain the reduction of the tribal Levites, who had survived only as *gerim*" (153).

writer behind the text, whatever fragment of text one is considering, and the possibilities for nonpolitical manipulation of material proliferate.

If Gunneweg forces us to reconsider the difference in formulation between vv. 27 and 29, he can also lead us to reconsider the strangeness of a text that preserves an injunction to go out and kill brother and neighbor without specifying something like "kill the apostate, even if he should happen to be brother or neighbor." Gunneweg insists that what grates on the tongue is the residue of old proverb that has not been fully ground down, fully assimilated into the new, political use. Yet once admit the general idea of such residue, and there is no need to limit one's sense of the writer's idiosyncrasy to the interpretation of a particular old proverb. Is it not also possible, for example, that the injunction as we have it indicates something of a sentiment in direct opposition to the political point in which it has been impressed? The irony, the purely, or rather quintessentially, *literary* irony would lie in the injunction to the Levites to butcher people — and the poetic justice that, on the basis of their compliance, they become God's butchers. This *literary* reading does not deny the political motive by which the text may have been solicited or to which the text has been subsumed; but it allows for something other than the political. It is "antihistorical" in the sense that it sees history precisely backward: from the twentieth-century sense of holocaust (the butchery of people) we see an etiology for the priesthood of holocaust (the butchery of endless series of sacrificial animals). And it is "backward" too in the more significant sense of looking back to who Levi was that his sons should be "privileged" with sacred butchery: brother of Dina and Simeon, Levi steals into Shechem and butchers all the men, pillaging all the town.

Once a butcher, always a butcher. The poetic justice of having Levi "disinherited" (given something supposedly greater than a share in the land) for his reward in Exodus 32 fulfills the deeper moral justice of having him disinherited (given something less than a share in the land) for his part in embarrassing Jacob in Genesis 34. Indeed, Jacob's fear of embarrassment *(lihavišeni biyošve ha'areṣ)* seems to haunt the background of the composition of the Exodus passage, for Moses embarrassingly delays *(bošeš)* coming down the mountain,[24] and worries about the dissolute people being (in a difficult, much disputed phrase) *šimṣâ bihamehem*. I propose that "those who stand against them" are not political enemies of Moses' time or the time of the writer but the ghosts of the past who always stand around, in a writer's imag-

24. The peculiarity of the verb *boš* in Exod. 32:1 (but not in Gen. 34:30) is discussed by J. Gerald Janzen, "The Character of the Calf and Its Cult in Exodus 32," *CBQ* 52 (1990) 599.

ination, like the former questers in Browning's *Childe Roland to the Dark Tower Came:* "There they stood, ranged along the hillsides." They are the enemies Jacob worried about, ancestral voices of conscience prophesying war against the corruption of the privileged.

Scholars of the documentary hypothesis have no difficulty attributing the lines of disapprobation over the butchery in Genesis 34 to J; but whether we think of the J author or the voice of Jacob, the perturbed ancestor, it is something of the voice of J that we discern in the narration of the sacred butchery of Exodus 32. I do not mean to tag the verses as belonging to the old J strand, but to pick up, in the controlled silences and ironies of the author of the passage *qua author,* aside from political intent, a voice of moral reservation that comes like the voice of God. The antithetical energy of this voice may be said to be concentrated in the pun on the consecration of the Levites: Moses tells the Levites, *milu yedhem* — literally "fill your hands" (v. 29). They can fill their hands with offerings (being consecrated or initiated thus to the office of those who professionally, repeatedly, fill their hands with offerings) because they have filled their hands with the blood of homicide.[25] The literary irony of holy war or *herem* may be concentrated in the wordplay on the Levites' handiwork, but is not dependent on that particular pun. The irony is implicit in the idea of taking up swords in God's behalf, executing a command understood to have "inhuman" authority.

25. The pun is discussed by Cody, 153-54, though he reads the turn of phrase as redounding only to the Levites' credit. He calls the irony of an etiology based on linguistically and morally questionable wordplay a procedure "splendidly Semitic."

Matters of Space and Time
in Exodus and Numbers

Mark S. Smith

Pentateuchal studies, as with many other areas of biblical research, have been affected profoundly by the work of Brevard S. Childs. Best known of his exegetical works remains *The Book of Exodus*,[1] without a doubt the most important English commentary on this book. Childs's numerous probing works on Scripture have educated and challenged his many readers and students. As a former student and colleague of Childs, I used to sojourn from Yale's campus "downtown" up to *har qōdeš*, "the holy mountain," as my mentor, Marvin Pope, used to call the Divinity School. There I would attend Childs's doctoral seminar and his other courses in Old Testament. Though I labored all my years at Yale in what was then called the Department of Near Eastern Languages and Literatures (now Civilizations), I learned much from Childs, and I benefited from his kindly presence and encouraging advice. In this contribution I wish to pay tribute to, and interact with, Childs's work on the Pentateuch. I am interested specifically in the role that space and time play in the literary arrangement of the priestly redaction of Exodus and Numbers.[2] This essay proceeds in five parts: (1) introduction to current proposals as to the structural relations between Exodus and Numbers and preliminary considerations; (2) analysis of geographical markers in these two books; (3) examination of chronological

---

1. Childs, *The Book of Exodus: A Critical, Theological Commentary* (Old Testament Library; Philadelphia: Westminster, 1974).

2. For further background on this question, see M. S. Smith, "The Literary Arrangement of the Priestly Redaction of Exodus: A Preliminary Proposal," *CBQ* 58 (1996) 25-50.

markers in these books; (4) further reflections on the relationship between Exodus and Numbers; and (5) some broader implications of the markers for the formation and form of the Pentateuch.

I. Current Proposals

The structure of Genesis-Deuteronomy has emerged as a significant line of research after many decades devoted to studying their sources, redactions, and other aspects. Current proposals for the literary structure of the Pentateuch tend to focus on the symmetry displayed especially between Exodus and Numbers.[3] J. Milgrom, for example, argues for the general chiastic arrangement of features in Exodus through Numbers, with the Sinai material of Exodus 19 through Numbers 10 standing as the middle and obviously major element.[4] Similarly, A. Schart has proposed a "Ringstruktur" surrounding the Sinai legislation[5] (see p. 184). The general thrust of this arrangement may be discerned by comparing some of its correspondences. The positive tone of the murmuring stories in Exod. 15:22–17:7 relative to the more negative accents in the murmuring narratives in Numbers 11 and 20 would suggest that the material after Sinai in Numbers is, at least in part, the negative image of the material before Sinai in Exodus.[6] The selection and general tone in the first three stories in Exod. 15:22–17:7 may be due in part to the pur-

3. D. J. A. Clines is to be noted for raising the question of the Pentateuch as a whole in his *The Theme of the Pentateuch* (*JSOT* Supplement Series 10; Sheffield: JSOT, 1978). Clines's agenda is generally synchronic and thematic in its concerns. R. N. Whybray also broaches the issue of synchronic study of the Pentateuch as a whole, but the agenda is pursued only *in nuce* and on the level of theme. Whybray regards the Pentateuch ultimately as the product of a single author who intended it to serve as the preface to the Deuteronomistic History. This view assumes the importance of deuteronomistic material in the Pentateuch, but does not come fully to grips with the final priestly redaction of the Pentateuch. See Whybray, *The Making of the Pentateuch: A Methodological Study* (*JSOT* Supplement Series 53; Sheffield: JSOT, 1987) 221-42; *idem, Introduction to the Pentateuch* (Grand Rapids: Eerdmans, 1995) 133-43.

4. See Milgrom, *Numbers* במדבר (JPS Torah Commentary; Philadelphia/New York: Jewish Publication Society, 1990) xvii-xviii.

5. Schart, *Mose und Israel im Konflikt. Eine Redaktionsgeschichtliche Studie zu den Wüstenerzählung* (Orbis Biblicus et Orientalis 98; Freiburg: Universitätsverlag; Göttingen: Vandenhoeck und Ruprecht, 1990) 52.

6. Milgrom argues that in the Exodus murmuring stories the Israelites had not yet accepted the Sinai revelation and therefore were not yet subject to divine punishment. The degree to which this view is a rabbinically inspired anachronism is debatable. See Milgrom, *Numbers*, xvi.

A	Exod 15:22-25	Wasserumwandlung ("transformation of the water" from bitter to sweet)
B	17:1-7	Wasser aus dem Felsen ("water from the rock")
C	17:8-16	Krieg: Amalek — Israel ("Amalekite-Israelite war")
D	18	Entlastung des Mose (leadership "relief for Moses")
E	18:27	der Midianiter Jitro (חתן משה) ("the Midianite Hobab," who is "Moses' father-in-law")
F	19:1-2	Ankunft am Sinai ("arrival at Sinai")

SINAI

F'	Num 10:11-23	Aufbruch vom Sinai ("departure from Sinai")
E'	10:29-32	der Midianiter Hobab (חתן משה) ("the Midianite Hobab," who is "Moses' father-in-law")
D'	11	Entlastung des Mose (leadership "relief for Moses")
C'	14:39-45	Krieg: Israel — Amalek ("Amalekite-Israelite war")
B'	20:1-13	Wasser aus dem Felsen ("water from the rock")
A'	21:16-18	Brunnen ("the spring")

poses of the priestly redaction. The question is why the priestly redaction left the positive tone relatively intact. It may be suggested tentatively that the priestly redaction may have interpreted the Exodus passages as the people's pilgrimage to the mountain.[7] In contrast, Numbers might be regarded as depicting a pilgrimage journey from the mountain to the sanctuary-land, but not in a manner precisely parallel to Exodus. Numbers manifests a dialectic between the anti-pilgrimage of the older generation, on the one hand, which departs Sinai and sins, and, on the other hand, the pilgrimage of the new generation born in the wilderness and prepared to reach the Promised Land. The water in the wilderness is a source of divine blessing to the people in their pilgrimage journey, but it is a source of testing the people in the book of Numbers. The more positive tone set in Exod. 15:22–16:35 may be attributed to the same cause. The theme of pilgrimage informed the formation of chs. 19–24, and the older traditions of chs. 16 and 17 may have been construed accordingly. The treatment of the Amalekites in Exod. 17:8-16 and

7. For this argument, see M. S. Smith, *The Pilgrimage Pattern in Exodus* (in preparation), chapter eight.

Num. 14:39-43 follows suit: the first passage witnesses the Israelites' utter defeat of the Amalekites while the second mentions the Amalekites as victors over the Israelites. Schart also observes that the Israelites' testing *(*nsh)* Yahweh "these ten times" *(zeh 'eśer pĕ'āmîm)* in Num 14:22 corresponds to the number of the plagues in the priestly redaction of Exodus.[8]

It might be suggested further that these correspondences between the narratives from Egypt to Sinai in Exodus and from Sinai to Moab in Numbers serve a larger thematic purpose. The narrative material in the book of Numbers shows an inverse relationship with the narrative in Exodus, a notion that was not lost on later tradition: ". . . the Lord, who once for all saved a people out of the land of Egypt, afterward destroyed those who did not believe." (Jude 5). Besides the positive-negative mirror images of Israel reflected in the pre- and post-Sinai material, a further notion of import for understanding the priestly redaction of Exodus and Numbers might be suggested: the Egyptians destroyed in the book of Exodus serve both as foil to the saved Israelites in the book of Exodus and perhaps as a foreshadowing to the same generation of Israelites who perish in the wilderness in the book of Numbers.

To the observations of Milgrom and Schart may be added some relevant points made by J. H. Sailhammer.[9] He notes a general correspondence between the figures of Pharaoh and Balak in opposing the Israelites. More specifically, Israel is "a mighty nation" (Exod. 1:9) against whom Pharaoh's heart is "hard" *(*kbd).* Similarly, Israel is called "a mighty nation" (Num. 22:3, 6), and Balaam is "honored" *(*kbd).* In both the plague narratives and the Balaam narratives, the root *kbd* functions as a key word (Exod. 7:14; 8:11, 28; 9:7, 34; 10:1; 14:4; Num. 22:17, 37; 24:11). Sailhammer's analysis also gives some explanation to the placement of the poems of Exodus 15 and Numbers 22–24, which demarcate the books to which they belong and thereby balance one another in function. These insights will play a role in the analysis offered below. Sailhammer's points highlight an overall balance between the first part of Exodus and the final section of Numbers in that both involve holy war.

These studies[10] into the structure of Exodus and Numbers may be ex-

8. Schart, personal communication. Num. 14:14 likewise echoes the dialogue in Exodus 33 and Num. 14:18 echoes (or cites?) Exod. 34:6-8.

9. Sailhammer, *The Pentateuch as Narrative: A Biblical-Theological Commentary* (Grand Rapids: Zondervan, 1992) 42-44.

10. For another proposal for the structure of Numbers, see M. Douglas, *In the Wilderness: The Doctrine of Defilement in the Book of Numbers* (*JSOT* Supplement Series 158; Sheffield: JSOT, 1994). For some trenchant criticisms, see R. Gnuse's review in *CBQ* 57 (1995) 124-25.

tended by examining further the significance of geography and chronology in these books. Indeed, within the geographical and chronological markers of the priestly redaction, Schart's contributions will receive further definition and focus. Two caveats should be noted at the outset. This analysis is premised on the general consensus reached on the priestly material and redaction of Exodus and Numbers. Exodus and Numbers show a number of priestly glosses and compositions, which point to major priestly redactional activity in these books.[11] This redaction is part of a long priestly tradition that made several contributions to the Pentateuch and its formation, including geographical and temporal markers indicating the major blocks of material. Indeed, as commentators have noted, such markers are a staple of the priestly organization of Pentateuchal material.

Furthermore, Leviticus is not examined in this essay because it contains none of these chronological markers. From the chronological discrepancy between Exodus 40 and Numbers 1, it might be inferred that the redaction of Exodus-Leviticus-Numbers allows a few weeks for the events at Mount Sinai recorded in the book of Leviticus. So B. A. Levine comments: "all of the activities prescribed in the Torah between Exodus 40 and Numbers 7 occurred within only a few weeks. Although no dates are given in the book of Leviticus for any events, the entire context of Leviticus belongs, as well, to the beginning of the wilderness period, according to the priestly chronology."[12]

II. Geography in Exodus and Numbers

In the most general terms, Exodus through Numbers exhibit a basic geographical symmetry: Egypt — Sinai — Wilderness/Transjordan. The Israelites travel from Egypt to Sinai, sojourn at Sinai, and then travel from Sinai through the wilderness. The itinerary notices in Exodus and Numbers largely balance one another: six notices chart the Israelites' journey from Egypt to Rephidim, the station before Sinai (Exod 12:37a; 13:20; 14:1-2; 15:22a; 16:1;

11. See F. M. Cross, *Canaanite Myth and Hebrew Epic: Essays in the History of the Religion of Israel* (Cambridge, MA/London: Harvard University, 1973) 315 (esp. n. 77), 325; I. Knohl, *The Sanctuary of Silence: The Priestly Torah and the Holiness School* (Minneapolis: Fortress, 1995). For now, the issue of which material derives from the Holiness redaction proposed by Knohl and which is "priestly" will be set aside. As both are considered priestly by Knohl, this label will be used for both.

12. Levine, *Numbers 1–20* (Anchor Bible; New York: Doubleday, 1993) 253. See also Milgrom, *Numbers*, 4, 364.

17:1) and six notices follow the Israelites from Sinai to the plains of Moab in Numbers (Exod 19:2; Num 10:12; 20:1, 22; 21:10-11; 22:1).[13] "Thus Exodus and Numbers, at least in their wilderness narratives, reveal the same redactional hand."[14] These notices mark not only smaller units; within the priestly redaction they indicate the boundaries of the major middle sections of the two books. Through the notices the priestly redaction indicates balance and correspondence between the two journeys to and from Sinai, as suggested by the following schema:

Exodus	Numbers
1:1–15:21 in Egypt	1:1–10:10 at Mount Sinai
15:22–18:26 in the wilderness	10:11–21:35 in the wilderness
chs. 19–40 at Mount Sinai	chs. 22–36 in Transjordan

In general, the priestly arrangement of Exodus and Numbers presents the geographical progression in the book of Numbers in part as an inversion of the progression in Exodus. The Sinai legislation places Exodus 19–40 and Num. 1:1–10:10 at Mount Sinai. Both sections focus on the tabernacle and the creation of sacred space in and around it. For the final block of Exodus, it is the creation of the tabernacle itself. For the first major block of Numbers, the concern is the arrangement of the camp personnel around the tabernacle and the materials for the tabernacle.

As noted above, Exodus and Numbers use itinerary notices to mark a major middle wilderness section. The itinerary notices demarcate Num. 10:11–21:35 as a major unit. Furthermore, Num. 10:11–21:35 makes frequent mention of the wilderness (by different names) in 10:12, 20:1, 21:11, 13, 18, 23. It is pertinent to note at this point that Schart's observation of a "Ringstruktur" around the Sinai material assumes that chapter 21 ends the second major block in Numbers. The new geographical marker ("in the plains of Moab beyond the Jordan at Jericho") at 22:1 delimits the third major section as chs. 22–36. This division follows B. S. Childs's proposal (following J. de Vaulx) to see 10:11–21:35 as a unit, which is based on the content of Numbers 21, specifically the defeat of the Amorite kings in this chapter, and not on any redactional markers.[15] Childs notes the geographical itinerary for chs. 10–36, but rather than begin with the geographical

---

13. So Cross, *Canaanite Myth,* 310-7; Milgrom, *Numbers,* xvii.

14. Milgrom, *Numbers,* xvii.

15. Childs, *Introduction to the Old Testament as Scripture* (Philadelphia: Fortress, 1979) 194-9.

marker, he surveys the contents and his considerations do not include the schema that the redaction seems to give to the contents of the narrative. To be sure, Childs's reading is not limited to a specific redactional schema, but his view would appear supported by the important geographical marker in 22:1.[16] Finally, Egypt in Exodus 1–15 and Transjordan in Numbers 27–34 correspond in the schema of Exodus and Numbers. Egypt is the beginning point, and Transjordan brings the Israelites to the brink of their final destination.

III. Chronology in Exodus and Numbers

A. Exodus

The chronological markers in Exodus through Numbers have received less attention than geographical markers, in part because they are scattered and the priestly tradition does not provide a helpful summary, as found for the itinerary notices in Numbers 33. Yet given the importance of time exhibited in priestly legislation, the chronological markers in Exodus and Numbers may hold some helpful information for the priestly arrangement of these books.

16. At this juncture it is interesting to note how at odds the suggestions of Childs and Olson are here. Both base their claims on content that both view as important. Without redactional markers to serve as guides, it is difficult, if not impossible, to adjudicate between these claims. See Olson, *The Death of the Old and the Birth of the New: The Framework of the Book of Numbers and the Pentateuch* (Brown Judaic Series 71; Chico: Scholars, 1985) 83. The scholarly discrepancy between Childs and Olson is discussed by R. Knierim in *The Task of Old Testament Theology: Method and Cases* (Grand Rapids/Cambridge: Eerdmans, 1995) 381. Knierim regards Numbers at its highest structural level as the saga of a campaign and therefore as consisting of only two parts, the organization and execution of the campaign (384). This is a valuable insight and is indeed supported by some comparable ancient Near Eastern itineraries (see G. I. Davies, "The Wilderness Itineraries: A Comparative Study," *Tyndale Bulletin* 25 [1974] 46-81, esp. 80; see also Davies, *The Way of the Wilderness: A Geographical Study of the Wilderness Itineraries in the Old Testament* [Society for Old Testament Study Monograph Series 5; Cambridge: Cambridge University Press, 1979]; idem, "The Wilderness Itineraries and Recent Archaeological Research," in *Studies in the Pentateuch*, ed. J. A. Emerton [*VT* Supplements 41; Leiden: Brill, 1990] 161-75). In view of the relation of Numbers to Exodus, this view is not an exhaustive indication of overall structure. To his credit, Knierim recognizes the importance of chronological and geographical markers; for him these stand at a lower structural level. See below for further discussion.

The chronological markers in Exodus present the better part of a year, as indicated in the following list:

Year 1, Month 1, Days 14-21 = Passover/Unleavened Bread
Exod. 12:2: "This month shall mark for you the beginning of the months; it
    shall be the first of the months of the year for you." (see also 12:17-18).
Exod 12:41: "At the end of the four hundred and thirtieth year, to the very
    day, all the ranks of the Lord departed from the land of Egypt." (cf.
    Num 33:3 = exodus from Egypt on the fifteenth day of the first
    month).

Month 3, Day 1 = Weeks
Exod 19:1: "On the third new moon after the Israelites had gone forth from
    the land of Egypt, on that very day, they entered the wilderness of Si-
    nai."
Exod 19:16 (19:11) = day 3 (divine appearance)

Year 2, Month 1, Day 1 = New Year's
Exod 40:17: "On the first month of the second year, on the first of the month,
    the Tabernacle was set up." Cf. 40:2.

The chronological markers in Exodus 12 begin a new temporal reckoning. While time is counted by years from Genesis 1 through Exodus 11, Exodus 12 initiates a counting of time focused on the cycle of the year. This
chapter signals the first pilgrimage feast as the appropriate time for the departure from Egypt. The relationship between the feast of Passover/Unleav-
ened Bread and the exodus story is generally regarded as preexilic. The ancient connection between Passover and the exodus was inherited by the
priestly tradition, which made it the cornerstone of Pentateuchal chronology
in the life of the people of Israel from their departure from Egypt onward.
The chronological scheme was not extended backward. Rather, it was extended only forward.

The chronological marker given in Exod. 19:1 signals the date of the
Feast of Weeks, although the feast is not explicitly celebrated in this context,
unlike Passover in Exodus 12–13. While Exod. 19:1 makes no mention of
Weeks, this verse dates the arrival of the Israelites at Mount Sinai to this holi-
day. The question is whether such a connection is likely to have been accidental or deliberate. Elsewhere the Old Testament does not explicitly connect
Weeks with the giving of the Torah. As the earliest reference for this connection has been thought to be in the Talmud (e.g., *b. Pesahim* 68b), it has been

held that this association is Pharisaic or rabbinic in origin (although allowance is made for an earlier date).[17] A few other pieces of evidence would suggest the late biblical period as the date when this connection was first made.[18] M. Weinfeld notes the association between Weeks and covenant-renewal in 2 Chron. 15:10-14.[19] The placement of the renewal of the Sinai covenant on the feast of Weeks is known in the intertestamental text of *Jubilees* 6:17:

> Therefore, it is ordained and written in the heavenly tablets that they should observe the feast of Shebuot in this month, once per year, in order to renew the covenant in all (respects), year by year.[20]

Jubilees 6:19 likewise assumes the connection between Sinai and the feast: "in your days the children of Israel forgot it until you renewed it for them on this mountain." J. T. Milik argued that the Qumran community likewise com-

17. L. Jacobs, "Shavuot," *Encyclopedia Judaica* XIV, 1320-21; Safrai, "The Temple," *The Jewish People in the First Century: Historical Geography, Political History, Social, Cultural and Religious Life and Institutions* II, ed. S. Safrai and M. Stern (Compendia Rerum Iudaicarum ad Novum Testamentum 1; Assen/Maastricht: Van Gorcum; Philadelphia: Fortress, 1987) 893.

18. M. Weinfeld has made perhaps the boldest claims for the antiquity of this connection. He suggests that Psalms 50 and 81 represent covenant renewal within the context of the pilgrimage feast of Weeks. See M. Weinfeld, "The Uniqueness of the Decalogue and Its Place in Jewish Tradition," in *The Ten Commandments in History and Tradition*, ed. Bren-Zion Segal, tr. G. Levi (Jerusalem: Hebrew University, 1987) 21-27. These psalms are speeches of a cultic mediator who quotes divine speech exhorting the faithful to follow Yahweh's teaching. In Psalm 81 the cultic mediator cites divine words on obedience, citing the past witness of Joseph, the exodus, and the Israelites' experience at the wilderness site of Meribah. (In this connection Psalm 95 should also be mentioned. It, too, quotes divine speech exhorting the congregation not to be stubborn as on the day of Meribah and Massah.) Weinfeld argues that Psalms 50 and 81 quote the Decalogue, and here he follows the work of A. Jepsen, "Beiträge zur Auslegung und Geschichte des Dekalogs," *ZAW* 79 (1967) 303; A. Alt, *Essays on Old Testament History and Religion*, tr. R. A. Wilson (Garden City: Doubleday, 1968) 168; G. von Rad, *The Problem of the Hexateuch and Other Essays*, tr. E. W. Trueman Dicken (Edinburgh/London: Oliver and Boyd, 1966) 22-24; and W. Zimmerli, *I Am Yahweh*, tr. D. W. Stott; ed. and introduction by W. Brueggemann (Atlanta: John Knox, 1982) 23-28. Yet it is difficult to confirm his theory for the festival behind these psalms since other scholars would place these psalms in the context of the Festival of Booths (Sukkot). Therefore Weinfeld's argument for an older date for the connection is not firm. (It is quite possible that such preaching of Torah took place at all the pilgrimage festivals, accented by the Torah narrative celebrated in the feast.)

19. Weinfeld, "The Uniqueness of the Decalogue," 24.

20. O. S. Wintermute, "Jubilees," *The Old Testament Pseudepigrapha*, ed. J. H. Charlesworth (Garden City: Doubleday, 1985) 2:67, cited by R. Hendel, "Sacrifice as a Cultural System," *ZAW* 101 (1989) 373.

memorated their covenant on the feast of Weeks.[21] Here the evidence is less compelling than the references in *Jubilees* 6:17 and 19. As another piece of evidence, Milik cited 4Q267 fragment 18, column 5, lines 16-21 (completed by the parallel material from 4Q270, fragment 11, column 2, lines 11-15): "The sons of Levi and the men of the camps will meet in the third month and will curse whoever tends to the right or to the left of the law."[22] While the character or extent of the communal celebration of the Sinai covenant on Weeks is unclear in the passage, it may be said that it connects the date of Weeks with maintaining the law of the community.

The association between Weeks and the Sinai covenant is paralleled also by the Christian feast of Pentecost, when the divine gift of the Spirit was given to the early Christian community in Jerusalem according to Acts 2.[23] The concept of the giving of the Spirit to the community through the Son at Pentecost seems to parallel the celebration at the Feast of Weeks of the giving of the Sinai covenant through Moses to the Israelite people. F. M. Cross remarks on the significance of Acts 2 for understanding the background of the attachment of the theme of Sinai to the feast of Weeks (Pentecost): "It is intriguing to note that the entry into the new covenant at Qumrân also fell on Pentecost, as does the creation of the church, following old Jewish tradition going back to the priestly chronology [of Exod. 19:1-2]."[24] The prerabbinic evidence for the association of the Sinai covenant with Weeks would suggest a reevaluation of the dating of the arrival at Mount Sinai on Weeks in Exod. 19:1-2. Indeed, the marking of Weeks in Exod. 19:1 is hardly made casually. R. Hendel makes the further point: "In the Priestly chronological framework of Exodus it is clear that the ceremony in Ex 24,3-8 occurs during the spring festival of Shabuot (Ex 19,1)."[25] In short, the connection between Weeks and

21. Milik, *Ten Years of Discovery in the Wilderness of Judaea,* tr. J. Strugnell (Studies in Biblical Theology 26; Naperville: Allenson, 1959) 117; *idem*, "*Milkî-sedeq* et *Milkî-rešaʿ* dans les ancien écrits juifs et chrétiens," *Journal of Jewish Studies* 23 (1972) 135-36. Milik is followed by Hendel, "Sacrifice as a Cultural System," 373. See also J. Tabori, *Jewish Festivals in the Time of the Mishna and Talmud* (Jerusalem: Magnes, 1995) 151 (Hebrew).

22. F. García Martínez, *The Dead Sea Scrolls Translated: The Qumran Texts in English* (Leiden: Brill, 1994) 57, 67.

23. See I. H. Marshall, "The Significance of Pentecost," *Scottish Journal of Theology* 30 (1977) 347-69; M. J. Olson, "Pentecost," *Anchor Bible Dictionary* (New York: Doubleday, 1992) V, 222-23. The Christian imagery of the Holy Spirit as fire may be grounded in the larger Jewish tradition. Olson compares Philo (*De decalogo* 33): "God created a sound on Sinai and changed it into fire." For the comparison of the divine word with fire, see also Jer. 23:29.

24. Cross, *Canaanite Myth and Hebrew Epic,* 312 n. 64.

25. See Hendel, "Sacrifice as a Cultural System," 373.

the giving of the Sinai covenant was known to the postexilic priestly tradition, as reflected by Exod. 19:1. It is difficult to pin down the date for the connection any further, but the evidence of Exod. 19:1 cannot be dismissed out of hand.[26] The marker in Exod. 19:1-2a shows the style of the priestly tradition and should be generally regarded in the same light as the other priestly temporal markers. Priestly chronological notices in Exodus and Numbers reflect a schema correlating the Pentateuchal event with Weeks.[27] In sum, these texts would push back the date of the connection to prerabbinic Judaism. With the description of Passover in Exodus 12–13, the priestly redaction had inherited the connection between pilgrimage feast and Pentateuchal event. This type of connection was extended to the Sinai covenant and the feast of Weeks secondarily by the chronological marker in Exod. 19:1.

The chronological markers in Exod. 40:2, 17 mark the turn of the year. The chronological marker refers to New Year (Rosh Hashanah).[28] Although it might be supposed that the Exod. 40:2, 17 refers to the time of Booths (Sukkot), as this feast occurs at "the end of the year" (Exod. 23:16) or "the turn of the year" (Exod. 34:22), priestly calendars such as Numbers 28–29 distinguish the two feasts and clearly assign the first day of the year to New Year's and not Booths. New Year's in Exod. 40:1 evokes the new creation of Israel's relationship with Yahweh through the creation of the tabernacle and thereby hearkens back to the priestly creation of the world in Genesis 1. Commentators beginning with Martin Buber and Franz Rosenzweig have observed that Exodus 39–40 consciously echoes the end of the priestly creation account (Exod. 39:43a//Gen. 1:31a; Exod. 39:32a//Gen. 2:1; Exod. 40:33b//Gen. 2:2a; and Exod. 39:43b//Gen. 2:3a).[29] Exodus 39–40 is thereby

26. B. Bäntsch and other older commentators regarded this marker as a late redactional means to relate the feast of Weeks with the Sinai covenant. See Bäntsch, *Exodus-Leviticus-Numeri* (Handbuch zum Alten Testament; Göttingen: Vandenhoeck und Ruprecht, 1903) 169-70, 171. Childs rightly criticizes Bäntsch's further supposition that the original date either had fallen out or was probably removed intentionally. See Childs, *The Book of Exodus*, 342.

27. See Hendel, "Sacrifice as a Cultural System," 373. G. von Rad (*The Problem of the Hexateuch*, 34-35) entertains but rejects the theory that Exod. 19:1 reflects a late, priestly dating of Weeks. His alleged counter-evidence of Deut. 31:10-11 may reflect, however, an alternative or earlier tradition. Contrary to the presupposition of von Rad's argument, the priestly tradition may have fixed this chronology in Exod. 19:1 without concern for other reckonings.

28. Milgrom, *Exodus* שמות (The JPS Torah Commentary; Philadelphia/New York: Jewish Publication Society, 1991) 235.

29. For discussion of Buber and Rosenzweig, see E. Blum, *Studien zur Komposition*

connected to the creation story of Genesis: while the account of Genesis marks the creation of the world, the creation language of Exodus 39–40 heralds the new creation of Israel's cultic life with its deity. In sum, the chronological markers in the book of Exodus suggest a year arranged primarily according to the first two of three main pilgrimage feasts: Passover begins the series with the exodus from Egypt, the Israelites arrive at Sinai on the feast of Weeks, and the tabernacle *(miskan)* is completed around the New Year. A full year will not elapse, however, until Numbers 9–10.

B. Numbers

In general, the structure of the book of Numbers is very difficult to gauge. As M. Noth commented, "within these various strata it is difficult to discern any definite lines of continuity."[30] Chronology is hardly exceptional in this regard; it is considerably more complicated in Numbers than in Exodus. The main reason involves the tradition of the forty-year journey in the wilderness. So J. Milgrom comments:

> The tradition that Israel spent forty years in the wilderness following its Exodus from Egypt is demonstrably old (Deut. 1:46; Amos 2:10; 5:25). Yet the chronology within that forty-year period is marred by two major problems. The events of 1:1–10:11 cover nineteen days from the first to the nineteenth of the second month of the second year. Those of the final chapters 21:10–36:13 occur within five months of the fortieth year (see 20:28 = 33:38; 20:29; Deut 1:3). The material in between, 10:12–21:9, is undated but must fall in the intervening thirty-eight years. . . . All that can be

---

des Pentateuch (Beihefte zum *ZAW* 189; Berlin/New York; De Gruyter, 1990), 306-7. See also J. Blenkinsopp, "The Structure of P," *CBQ* 38 (1976) 275-92; *idem, The Pentateuch,* 62, 186, 218; P. J. Kearney, "Creation and Liturgy: The P Redaction of Ex. 25–40," *ZAW* 89 (1977) 375; M. Fishbane, *Text and Texture: Close Readings of Selected Biblical Texts* (New York: Schocken, 1979) 11-13; M. Weinfeld, "Sabbath, Temple and the Enthronement of the Lord — The Problem of the Sitz im Leben of Genesis 1:1–2:3," in *Mélanges bibliques et orientaux en l'honneur de M. Henri Cazelles,* ed. A. Caquot and M. Delcor (Alter Orient und Altes Testament 212; Kevelaer: Butzon & Bercker; Neukirchen-Vluyn: Neukirchener, 1981) 501-12; J. D. Levenson, *Creation and the Persistence of Evil: The Drama of Divine Omnipotence* (San Francisco: Harper and Row, 1988) 78-87; W. W. Hallo, *The Book of the People* (Brown Judaic Stidies 225; Atlanta: Scholars, 1991) 60; B. Batto, *Slaying the Dragon in the Biblical Tradition* (Louisville: Westminster/John Knox, 1992) 120.

30. M. Noth, *Numbers: A Commentary,* tr. J. D. Martin (Old Testament Library; Philadelphia: Westminster, 1968) 4 (see the survey of P material on pp. 4-11).

said is that the wilderness traditions survived, in the main without fixed dates, and they were clustered at the beginning and at the end of the wilderness sojourn.[31]

As summed up by Milgrom's description here, the book of Numbers, like the book of Exodus, contains chronological markers designed to provide some structure to the book:

Year 2, Month 2, Day 1
Num 1:1: "On the first day of second month, in the second year following the exodus from the land of Egypt. . . ."

Year 2, Month 1, Day 1 = Exod 40:9-11 and Lev 8:10 (older chronology?)
Num 7:1: "On the day that Moses finished setting up the Tabernacle. . . ."

Year 2, Month 2, Day 14 = Passover
Num 9:1: "The Lord spoke to Moses in the wilderness of Sinai, on the first month of the second year following the exodus from the land of Egypt."

Year 2, Month 2, Day 20 = end of Passover
Num 10:11-12: "In the second year, on the twentieth day of second month, the cloud lifted from the Tabernacle of the Pact, and the Israelites set out on their journeys from the wilderness of Sinai."

Year 40, Month 1
Num 20:1: "The Israelites arrived in a body at the wilderness of Zin on the first month."

The book of Numbers works with two sets of chronological markers. The first set of markers in 1:1; 7:1; 9:1; and 10:11 relates to the chronology of Exodus and Leviticus. These markers chronologically mirror the beginning of the journey from Egypt. Clearly Num. 9:1 is a problem relative to the chronology of Num. 1:1. B. A. Levine suggests a redactional explanation to the problem with this verse: "There is a simple way of resolving this discrepancy. Most likely the caption of Num 9:1 already appeared in the text of Numbers before the opening caption of the book was added, and may take us back to Exod 40:2."[32] Milgrom prefers a literary solution to the problem; he regards

31. Milgrom, *Numbers*, xi.
32. Levine, *Numbers 1–20*, 295.

the chronological notice as "a flashback."[33] Did the incongruity arise from some redactional reason, but the resultant redactor(s) read the discrepancy in some manner akin to Milgrom's proposal? In any case, the purpose of this notation is to present the beginning of the journey from Sinai in a way that echoes the exodus from Egypt at Passover. With the return to Passover in Numbers 9–10, the cycle of the year, which began with the exodus from Egypt, comes full circle with the departure from Mount Sinai in Numbers 9–10. Prior to and after Exodus 12 through Numbers 10, the time is counted in years, but the special events within these chapters are marked according to the liturgical calendar.[34] These events therefore are placed within the compass of sacred time, unlike the events preceding or following them. In short, the year from departure to departure marks one liturgical year which celebrates Passover at either end.

The second set of markers, specifically Num 20:1, is connected to the forty-year sojourn (cf. Exod 16:35). Yet these two sets of markers are hardly unconnected. For despite the constraints placed on the priestly redaction by the tradition of the forty-year journey, the marker of Num 20:1 returns to the beginning of the year, just like Num 1:1. While the chronological picture presented in the book of Numbers hardly reflects the sort of unified, coherent pattern apparent in the book of Exodus, nonetheless chronological markers provide indicators of structure for the different sections of Numbers. Because of the partial character of the notices in 7:1 and 20:1, Childs claims that "it is highly unlikely that these notices form a structure for the book."[35] However, such formal discrepancies hardly preclude the possibility that these markers have some importance, and indeed the differences in form may not have affected the understanding of the temporal referents in the 7:1 and 20:1. However, in agreement with Childs, chronological markers do not form the only basis for overall structure in Numbers, much less Exodus; rather, geography determines larger units. Geography supersedes chronology as the markers for major sections as shown by 7:1 and 9:11. It would seem that when the two types coincide, for example, Exod. 19:1-2, chronol-

33. Milgrom, *Numbers*, 67.

34. The shift with Exodus 12 was noted by J. Wellhausen, *Prolegomena to the History of Israel* (Gloucester: Peter Smith, 1973), 351. For some of these liturgical connections, see, in a different vein, J. van Goudoever, "The Celebration of the Torah in the Second Isaiah," in *The Book of Isaiah. Le Livre d'Isaïe. Les oracles et leur relectures. Unité et complexité de l'ouvrage* (Bibliotheca ephemeridum theologicarum Lovaniensium 81; Leuven: University Press, 1989) 313-17.

35. Childs, *Introduction to the Old Testament as Scripture* (Philadelphia: Fortress, 1979) 195.

ogy reinforces geography. However, as noted above, the chronological markers serve a variety of other functions, for example, to structure and link the two departures from Egypt and Sinai.

The three sections in Numbers require some elaboration in light of the chronological markers. Apart from 1:1, the first block of material, 1:1–10:10, contains two chronological markers. The chronological marker in 7:1 may have been retained by the redaction in order to mark a transition between 1:1–6:27 to 7:1–10:10. The first section, chs. 1–6, delineates personnel preparations for departure while the second section, 7:1–10:10, describes material preparations. In this case, the poetic priestly blessing may serve as a transition between the two sections. The chronological marker in 9:1 is geared to refer back to the exodus from Egypt and therefore to mark the final block of material in the first major section of Numbers.

The second block of material, 10:11–21:35, is striking for its absence of chronological markers apart from the chronological notice in 10:11. Chronologically, it closes the first part of the book, but the geographical marker of 10:11 serves to delimit the middle section of the book. This section is devoted to two interrelated themes: the sins of the old generation described in chs. 11–16 and the related failure of the leaders to take the land in ch. 13. Chs. 17–19, though largely quite separate originally from chs. 11–16, have been secondarily related by the connections forged between ch. 17 and the rebellion in ch. 16. In their present context, chs. 17–19 serve to make provisions for the kinds of sins experienced in chs. 11–16.[36] Childs rightly observes the lesson to be drawn for future generations in these chapters, but this does not translate into a disregard for the narrative sequence. On the contrary, the successive stories and "priestly concern" (to use Childs's phrase) in 10:11–21:35 set the stage for the separation of the old generation from the emerging one in the third and final section of Numbers. Accordingly, the function of the chronological notice in 20:1 is to mark the narrative as approaching the end of the old generation and entering the final stage in Transjordan. Indeed, the deaths of Miriam and Aaron in Numbers 20 reinforce that this chapter is marking the end of the old generation within the framework of the second major block of material. In sum, the overarching theme of the second major section of Numbers is the sin of the old generation and its failure to enter the land, in contrast with the third block's stress of the emergence of the new generation graced with the prospect of entering the land. The sins described in chs. 11–16 prepare for the passing of the old generation, which begins in ch. 20.

36. See Childs, *Introduction*, 198.

The final block of material, 22:1–36:13, resembles the second in having a geographical notice standing at its head. The third block is devoted to two themes, both of which set it in relation to the second block. The second block begins in ch. 20 the theme of the death of the old generation with the deaths of Miriam and Aaron. The census in the third block, in ch. 26, located now in Transjordan, signals the emergence of the new generation. This conclusion holds major repercussions for Olson's theory regarding the place of the two census lists as the major indicators of structure in the book: "The census lists in Numbers 1 and 26 serve to divide the book of Numbers into two separate generations of God's holy people on the march."[37] Olson highlights the temporal and geographical markers in ch. 26, but their significance in relation to other clearly priestly markers is insufficiently explained. Olson stresses the change in geographical locale in 26:3 ("in the plains of Moab by the Jordan at Jericho") compared to 1:1 ("in the wilderness of Sinai"), but Olson leaves unnoted the geographical change in 20:1 ("at the wilderness of Zin") or the arrival to Transjordan noted in 22:1 ("Then the Israelites set out, and camped in the plains of Moab beyond the Jordan at Jericho."). In contrast, "after the plague" in 26:1 is hardly a significant chronological marker in the priestly style. The chronological marker in 20:1 ("The Israelites arrived in a body at the wilderness of Zin on the first month") refers to year 40[38] and therefore delimits this section from the preceding in a way wholly unlike the chronological marker in 26:1 ("after the plague"), which marks only an immediate transition. It is undoubtedly true, as Olson emphasizes, that the death of the old generation and the birth of the new are central developments in the book of Numbers, but this theme appears already in ch. 20. This chapter, with the geographical and chronological markers mentioned above, begins the passing of the old generation with its description of the deaths of Miriam (v. 1) and Aaron (vv. 28-29).[39] The end of the unit marked by these deaths was at one time — before the inclusion of the book of Deuteronomy — the death of Moses recounted now in Deuteronomy 34. The death of the old and the birth of the new constitutes the major theme of Numbers 20–36.

A further division within the third block can be proposed, one that depends on anticipating the comparison of Exodus with Numbers in the

---

37. Olson, *The Death of the Old and the Birth of the New,* 83. Olson's division is followed by K. D. Sakenfeld, *Numbers: Journeying with God* (International Theological Commentary; Grand Rapids: Eerdmans; Edinburgh: Handsell, 1995) 7-8.

38. So most commentators, including NJPS 241 n. a, citing Num. 33:36-38.

39. So Levine, *Numbers 1–20,* 483.

following section. As Sailhammer observes, the poems in Numbers 22–24 stand at the head of the final block of Numbers just as Exod. 15:1-21 marks the end of the first block in Exodus. The poems have a delimiting function, described in greater detail below. If correct, then Numbers 25–36 requires explanation. Chs. 25 and 31 may constitute a section here. Ch. 31 refers back not only to Balaam (v. 8), but explicitly back to ch. 25 (v. 16). Chs. 25–31 would form a section linked to and following chs. 22–24. While Numbers 25–31 contains a diversity of materials, they mark the final turning point in the death of the old generation in ch. 25, the emergence of the new generation marked by the new census in ch. 26 and the commission of Joshua in 27:12-23. Chs. 32–36 mark a shift to issues that involve preparation for the land: the assignment of Transjordan (ch. 32); Israel's itinerary (ch. 33); the boundaries of the land (ch. 33); the Levitical cities and cities of refuge in the land (ch. 35); and the principle of keeping the family land intact in the land (ch. 36). While these materials are diverse in origin, within the book they stand together as shifting the perspective from the past journeys to the present moment, with the people poised and prepared to enter the land.

IV. Relations in Exodus and Numbers

The preceding discussion makes clear that Num. 1:1–10:10; 10:11–21:35; and 22:1–36:13 are the three main units recognized by the priestly redaction. Furthermore, it is evident that these three sections stand in inverse relationship to the three main sections of Exodus, namely 1:1–15:21; 15:22–18:27; and 19:1–40:38. The inverse relationship between Exodus and Numbers was discussed at the outset of this essay, in noting the proposals of Milgrom and Schart. The question is whether any further specific relations can be proposed on the basis of the books' specific geographical and chronological markers. Despite the apparent lack of "formal literary markers" in Exodus,[40] a careful study of the book suggests the following structure, which may be of use in determining further points of contact between Exodus and Numbers:

---

40. The assessment belongs to Childs, *Introduction*, 170-71. However, the following proposal accounts for the units and themes that Childs deems important to mention. I agree wholeheartedly with Childs's further judgment that "the whole of Exodus is far greater than the sum of its parts" (*Introduction*, 173). For full discussion, see Part Two in Smith, *The Pilgrimage Pattern in Exodus* (in preparation).

Book of Exodus	Book of Numbers
EGYPT: The opposition of Pharaoh 1:1–15:21	TRANSJORDAN: The opposition of Barak and other nations 22:1–36:13
1–2 The emergence of Moses	
Moses' two calls and confrontations:	Preparations for the land:
3:1–6:1 Moses' first call and confrontation with Pharaoh	25–31 Preparation of new generation for the land
6:2–14:31 Moses' second call and Yahweh's confrontation with Pharaoh	32–36 Final preparations for the land
15:1-21 End-poem	22–24 Preface poems
WILDERNESS	WILDERNESS
15:22–18:27 Yahweh's solicitous care	10:11–21:35 Passing of the old, sinning generation
Murmuring stories:	Murmuring stories:
16 Manna and quail	11 Manna and quail
17:1-7 Water at Massah and Meribah	20:1-13 Water at Meribah
17:8-16 Battle with Amalek	14:39-45 Battle with Amalek
18 Help for Moses	11 Help for Moses
18 Moses' father-in-law	10:29-32 Moses' father-in-law
SINAI (and tabernacle)	SINAI (and tabernacle)
19–31 First tablets, tabernacle commanded	1–6 Personnel preparation around the tabernacle: camp arranged around the tabernacle
32–40 Second tablets, tabernacle executed	7:1–10:11 Material preparation for the tabernacle: material contributed for the tabernacle

In the redactional plan of Exodus and Numbers, the blocks of the books stand in inverse relation. Both books divide generally into two major parts according to geography — Egypt and Sinai in Exodus, Sinai and Wilderness-Transjordan in Numbers. Chronology also serves to delimit each book into two major stages. The time in Egypt up to the exodus (Exodus 1–11) runs in the chronology of years until Passover marks its specific ending (Exodus 12–13), and the time at Sinai (Exodus 19–40) runs from Booths through till New Year's. The time at Sinai in Numbers runs up to Passover (Num. 1:1-10), and then the wilderness journey (Num. 10:11–36:13) returns to a schema in terms of years, ending with forty years as the organizational principle.

Exodus and Numbers share some further thematic points. First, as noted above, the Sinai material in both books focuses on the creation of sacred space centered around the tabernacle. For the final block of Exodus, it is the creation of the tabernacle itself. For the first major block of Numbers, the arrangement of the camp personnel around the tabernacle and the materials for the tabernacle are the concern. Therefore, while the Sinai covenant is the subject of the whole section running from Exod. 19:1 through Num. 10:10, it is evident that for the priestly redaction this material was reconfigured and interpreted along the lines that now assume the shape of the five books of the Torah. Second, both books describe how leaders first journey toward the geographical goal, and later accompany the people's movement toward the same goal. In Exodus Moses travels from Egypt to Sinai, only later to move with the whole people to that holy mountain. In the book of Numbers, Joshua, Caleb, and the other leaders travel to the promised land to scout it out, only to accompany the whole people in their progress toward the land through the remainder of the book. Third, both books use poems to signal both the past and the future. While Exod. 15:1-12 refers back to the escape from Egypt, 15:13-18 looks forward to God's holy mountain, which in the priestly redaction signals the journey to Mount Sinai. Similarly, the oracles of Balaam in Numbers 23–24 review Israel's character as a people set apart (Num. 23:9), empowered by God and freed from Egypt (23:21-24), as well as its future conquests (Num. 24:8) and promise in the land (Num. 24:17-19).[41] Although the priestly redaction of the poems was constrained by their traditional positions in the prepriestly narrative, the poems form a transition between major blocks, the first at the end of the first block in Exodus, the second at the beginning of the final block in Numbers. In both books, the poems could still fulfill similar functions for the priestly redaction, namely looking both backward and forward in the narrative. Both sets of poems proclaim God's victory on behalf of Israel and mark the prospects of Israel led under the power of God.

Both books show the priestly redaction's preference for stages occurring in pairs. In the first block in Exodus, the initial audience with Pharaoh fails, only to be followed by the successful confrontation. In the final block of Exodus, the first set of tablets is smashed, only to be replaced by a second set. In the second block of Numbers, the leaders of the new generation try to begin the conquest of the land from the wilderness, unsuccessful due to the old generation's response, then followed by successful campaigns in the Transjordan. The purpose of this redactional strategy is to highlight the fact that Israel's only hope and success lie purely with Yahweh; otherwise, Israel on its own falls into idolatry and failure.

41. Note what Childs (*Introduction*, 200) calls "the strong, eschatological note which was sounded in the final oracle of Balaam."

Finally, both books are infused with "a sacerdotal perspective,"[42] not only in the expressly priestly sections, but also in the arrangement between holy and unholy practices and people. Both books juxtapose incidents of human sin with the descriptions of the tabernacle and its holiness. Both are concerned with the holy tabernacle and the divine presence connected to it and the unholy people, whose behaviors repeatedly threaten the possibility of divine presence among them and therefore any hope for them. Furthermore, Exodus is by comparison the book of divine promise and provision and Numbers the book of human failure. Yet Exodus uses the golden calf story to highlight the people's sinning behavior, which will play itself out more fully in Numbers, and Numbers offers a glimpse of hope in the faithful figures of Joshua, Caleb, and the emerging generation ready to inherit the land. In sum, the chronological and geographical structures of the priestly redaction of Exodus and Numbers bring the two books into relation with one another as studies of sin and sanctity, as Yahweh and Israel live together through the sacred events of Passover and Booths and through the fundamental spaces in Egypt, Sinai, and the wilderness. These would serve as the definitive and defining foundational moments in the religious imagination of ancient Israel and the Jewish people, and in their Christian transformations for the church as well.

V. Toward the Formation and the Form of the Pentateuch

The general importance of the chronological markers is that they mark all five books of the Pentateuch as separate units in the priestly redaction.[43] The disjunction signaled by Exod. 1:1 involves the movement from a family to a new people. As noted above, Exodus 40 concludes with a chronological marker marking the end of the year and a disjunction in the present arrangement of the Pentateuch. Numbers begins with a new chronological marker, which suggests a new beginning. The result is a separate book of Leviticus, although this book is lacking in chronological markers. The materials in Exodus 25–40, Leviticus 8–10, and perhaps Numbers 7 may have originally been all of a piece treating the standard building procedures for a sanctuary,[44] but in their current form these materials have been reordered

42. The expression is Childs's. See Childs, *Introduction*, 198.
43. For a defense of this view, see Knierim, *The Task of Old Testament Theology*, 353.
44. See A. Hurowitz, "The Priestly Account of Building the Tabernacle," *Journal of the Ancient Oriental Society* 105 (1985) 21-30; idem, *I Have Built You an Exalted House: Temple Building in the Bible in Light of Mesopotamian and Northwest Semitic Writings* (*JSOT* Supplement Series 115/ASOR monograph series 5; Sheffield: JSOT, 1992) 267-68.

due to the insertion of additional materials, such as Leviticus 1–7. Although the description of the cloud of the divine presence in Exod. 40:34-37 parallels that of Num. 9:15-23, this parallel no longer functions as a structural indicator due to the insertion of Numbers 1–7 and the chronological markers contained in these chapters. The chronological marker in 1:1 marks the beginning of this book, and the book ends with a summary statement in Num 36:13. As a recapitulation of the events in Exodus through Numbers, the book of Deuteronomy reflects in genre and contents a different sort of unit.[45] From the comparisons drawn above between Exodus and Numbers, a cumulative priestly arrangement for the Pentateuch may be suggested, with the added caveat that this proposal offers only a very broad picture, with little attention devoted to the internal structures of Genesis, Leviticus, and Deuteronomy. The issues pertaining to these books would require full studies of their own, which is beyond the scope of this essay. Despite these limitations, Exodus and Numbers represent a balance of two books, with Leviticus in the middle. J. D. Watts's comments on the arrangement of Exodus through Numbers correctly capture the priestly combination of story and legal material ("list"): "The close relationship between P's narratives and lists suggests that the priestly writers and editors worked with the larger context in mind and intentionally structured the whole to highlight Levitical legislation as the central lists in the Pentateuch's rhetoric."[46]

The book of Genesis seems to divide, minimally speaking, into two blocks of material in Genesis, the primeval history in chs. 1–11 and the patriarchal history in chs. 12–50.[47] In Genesis 1–11, the priestly genealogies reckon ten generations from Adam to Noah and ten more from Noah to Abraham. It would seem, then, that for the priestly redaction, Genesis 1–11 represents a major section with two subunits. In priestly narrative material Noah and Abraham both enter into an "eternal covenant" (*bĕrît ʿôlām*) with

---

45. Dr. Ben Scolnic also points out to me that all the pentateuchal books except Leviticus end on a theme related to the land, which is the goal of the Pentateuch as a whole: Genesis with Joseph's promise to bring the bones of his father back to the land, Exodus with the description of the Israelites' journeys with the tabernacle and the divine presence in its midst, Numbers, in the final verse, placing the Israelites "on the steppes of Moab, at the Jordan near Jericho" (NJPS), and Deuteronomy, in its final chapter, describing Moses' viewing of the land and his burial near Beth-Peor. Leviticus ends with rules on the redemption of land and so is perhaps not exempt from Dr. Scolnic's observation.

46. J. D. Watts, "Rhetorical Strategy in the Composition of the Pentateuch," *JSOT* 68 (1995) 3-22, esp. 21; See further Watts, "Public Readings and Pentateuchal Law," *VT* 45 (1995) 540-57.

47. For a considerably fuller discussion, see Cross, *Canaanite Myth*, 301-7.

God in Genesis 9 and 17 respectively, which are to anticipate and build toward the eternal covenant made at Mount Sinai in the book of Exodus (see Exod. 31:18). Insofar as these priestly covenants anticipate the Sinai covenant,[48] Genesis seems to function in the capacity of prologue for the priestly tradition.[49] Indeed, the life of each patriarch foreshadows the life of his descendants. With slightly different variations echoing one another, Abraham, Jacob-Israel, and Joseph all journey in the land and then to Egypt. For Abraham, Egypt represents only a single incident in his life; for Jacob-Israel, it is the end of a bitter life; and for Joseph it is the salvation of his people thanks to unforeseen divine providence.[50] All three figures are initially subject to the authority of Egypt (for Jacob-Israel, it is because of his own son!), all three are subsequently exalted, and finally all three recognize that Egypt is not the final destination for himself or for the destiny of his family. Abraham travels to Egypt, is exalted by Pharaoh and returns from Egypt in Genesis 12. Jacob-Israel and Joseph both travel to Egypt, and on their deathbeds these two patriarchs instruct their surviving family to bury their bones in the promised land (Gen. 49:29-32; 50:24-25). Encapsulated in the experience of the patriarchs is the experience of the Israelites as a people in Exodus 1–15, who are initially subject to Egyptian authority and later exalted by God, and then they depart for the land promised to their ancestors. This proleptic function is not restricted to the patriarchal narratives for the priestly redaction, however. Genesis 1 serves as prologue[51] in sounding the divine plan of creation, which Israel enters with the book of Exodus.

Deuteronomy was added into the Pentateuch, apparently by the priestly redaction. This was achieved by moving the old story of Moses' death from the end of the old material in Numbers (thereby ending finally the old generation in Numbers) to the end of Deuteronomy.[52] Deuteronomy was basically inherited by the priestly redaction and incorporated into the

48. So many scholars, for example, Cross, *Canaanite Myth*, 295-98.

49. See Wellhausen, *Prolegomena*, 315, 339-40; J. D. Levenson, *The Death and Resurrection of the Beloved Son: The Transformation of Child Sacrifice in Judaism and Christianity* (New Haven/London: Yale University, 1993) 82-86; M. Z. Brettler, *The Creation of History in Israel* (London/New York: Routledge, 1995) 48-61.

50. These comments assume an Abraham cycle (Genesis 12–25), a Jacob-Israel cycle (Genesis 26–36), and a Joseph cycle (Genesis 37–50). There is no longer a separate Isaac cycle; Isaac appears only as Abraham's son and as Jacob's aged father. For specific verbal connections between the Abraham cycle and Exodus, see the links noted very nicely by Levenson, *Death and Resurrection*, 85-88.

51. So J. van Seters, *The Life of Moses: The Yahwist as Historian in Exodus-Numbers* (Louisville: Westminster/John Knox, 1994) 1.

52. So following many commentators, Weinfeld, *Deuteronomy 1–11*, 10.

Pentateuch. While smaller subsections and long additions are apparent in Deuteronomy, overall the book shows three major blocks of material.[53] Two introductions have been detected in 1:1–11:32, namely in 1:1–4:40 and 4:44–11:32. In their present configuration they function as a single introduction. The principle of arrangement of material within the second block in Deuteronomy has been discussed at great length by S. A. Kaufman.[54] Kaufman's basic hypothesis that Deuteronomy 12–26 is arranged according to the order and topics of the Ten Commandments illustrates how principles based on earlier legal material provided order for very diverse materials. Deuteronomy 27–34 covers last things: blessings and curses in 27–30; the commissioning of Joshua, the writing of the Torah, its future use and its deposition in 31:1–32:45-47; and lastly the final episode of Moses' death in 32:48–34:12. It would seem that the book functions within the priestly work as a sort of appendix. If that is correct, then Deuteronomy may function also to balance the book of Genesis.

The book of Leviticus is delimited by the tabernacle in the final block of Exodus and the camp arrangement in the initial block of Numbers. The center of the Pentateuch corresponds to the center of the holy, liturgical life attached to the tabernacle. B. A. Levine suggests the division 1–16 and 17–27 for Leviticus.[55] The priestly redaction incorporated the earlier priestly materials in chs. 1–16 and the Holiness Code in chs. 17–27.[56] No doubt other subdivisions such as 1–9, 10–16, and 17–27 may be proposed,[57] but it is perhaps more important here to stress the central position that the whole book occupies within the Pentateuch.[58]

53. The comments here have little bearing on the historical relations between Deuteronomy and earlier tradition. On this issue, see Weinfeld, *Deuteronomy 1–11*, 19-24. For the historical relations between Deuteronomy and the priestly tradition, see *ibid.*, 25-37.

54. Kaufman, "The Structure of the Deuteronomic Law," *MAARAV* 1/2 (1978-79) 105-58.

55. Levine, *Leviticus* ויקרא (The JPS Torah Commentary; Philadelphia/New York/Jerusalem: The Jewish Publication Society, 1989) xvi.

56. On the Holiness Code and its relations to the priestly tradition, see the important studies of I. Knohl, "The Priestly Torah Versus the Holiness School: Sabbath and the Festivals," *Hebrew Union College Annual* 58 (1987) 65-117; *idem, Silence in the Sanctuary* (Minneapolis: Fortress, 1995); and Milgrom, *Leviticus 1–16*, 13-42. Milgrom holds to a priestly redactor ("P3") who postdates "H."

57. See the discussion in Milgrom, *Leviticus 1–16*, 61-63.

58. For a synchronic reading of the structure of Leviticus, see M. Douglas, "Poetic Structure in Leviticus," in *Pomegranates and Golden Bells: Studies in Biblical, Jewish, and Near Eastern Ritual, Law, and Literature in Honor of Jacob Milgrom*, ed. D. P. Wright, D. N. Freedman, and A. Hurvitz (Winona Lake: Eisenbrauns, 1995) 239-56.

These observations provide some basis for offering a basic proposal for the priestly arrangement of the Torah.[59] The discussion thus far would point to the following chiastic outline:

A. BOOK OF GENESIS as prologue
    1–11 First Things: the Primeval History
    12–50 Patriarchal History

B. BOOK OF EXODUS
    1:1–15:21 EGYPT
        1–2 The emergence of Moses
        3:1–6:1, 6:2–14:31 Moses' two calls and confrontations:
        + 15:1-21 End-poem
    15:22–18:27 WILDERNESS
        solicitous care of Yahweh — murmuring stories:
        16 manna and quail
        17:1-7 water at Massah and Meribah
        17:8-16 battle with Amalek
        18 help for Moses
        18 Moses' father-in-law

    19–40 SINAI (and tabernacle)
    two sets of tablets, tabernacle commanded and constructed

    C. THE BOOK OF LEVITICUS Sanctuary life in the center
        1–16 The manual of practices for the priesthood
        17–27 The manual of practices for the people

B.′ BOOK OF NUMBERS
    1:1–10:10 SINAI (and tabernacle)
        1–6 personnel preparation around the tabernacle
        7:1–10:10 material preparation for tabernacle

    10:11–21:35 WILDERNESS
        passing of the old, sinning generation — murmuring stories:
        11 manna and quail
        20:1-13 water at Meribah
        14:39-45 battle with Amalek
        11 help for Moses
        10:29-32 Moses' father-in-law

59. For a very different view of the arrangement of the Pentateuch that addresses in part the points thus far, see Knierim, *Task of Old Testament Theology*, 351-79. Knierim makes several helpful methodological points. For example, he regards the Pentateuch not simply as Torah in general but as the Torah of Moses and in some sense the biography of Moses.

MARK S. SMITH

22:1–36:13 TRANSJORDAN
   22–24 Preface poems
   25–31, 32–36 Two sets of preparations for the land

A.' BOOK OF DEUTERONOMY as recapitulation
   1:1–11:32 Narrative recapitulated in two introductions
      in 1:1–4:40, 4:44–11:32
   12–26 The Torah recapitulated
   27–34 Last Things

The final product or literary architecture moves slowly toward the mountain of God and sets the norms for life after the mountain, as the people progress toward the land. Mount Sinai is the goal of the book of Exodus and it serves as the defining basis for all following standards in the book of Numbers. It is a gross understatement to say Sinai occupies a central place in the priestly theology of the Pentateuch. Sinai became the Mount Everest of priestly theology and looms larger than subsequent cultic sites such as Jerusalem. For the priestly tradition Sinai would represent the site of the definitive covenant and model for cultic recollection in the land. For the priestly theology, this mountain defines life inside and outside of the land. Sacred space is therefore highlighted in the priestly materials and redaction in Exodus and Numbers.

As for sacred time, time moves in stages, likewise arranged chiastically around the book of Leviticus. Genesis 1 through Exodus 12 and Numbers 10 through Deuteronomy 34 are reckoned by years. Exodus 12–Numbers 10 is counted by months and evokes the liturgical year as a whole. Passover in Exodus 12–13 and Numbers 9, as well as the feast of Weeks in Exod. 19:1, are used to anchor the two great events dominating Exodus through Numbers, namely the exodus and the Sinai covenant.[60] In the book of Leviticus time is hardly reckoned at all, slowing to a virtual standstill. In Lev. 9:1 seven days have lapsed in order for the ritual of priestly consecration to be completed (8:33). Lev. 16:1 assumes some lapse of time when it refers back to ch. 10,

60. In contrast, Booths plays no explicit role in the chronological markers in Exodus or Numbers. The reason for this apparent absence is evident: in the priestly tradition Booths evoked the entire forty-year sojourn in the wilderness, not only the period after the Sinai legislation (Lev. 23:39-43, esp. v. 43). However, while Booths was not immediately malleable to schematization along the lines of Passover and Weeks, it should be noted that the priestly chronological markers caused this sojourn to be weighted heavily to the period after Sinai and not before. The New Year, however, does have a place in the postexilic schema of the year. While it is absent from the pilgrimage cycle of the older calendars in Exod. 23:14-17 and 34:12-13 and Deut. 16:16, it seems to take on sufficient importance for the priestly tradition (Lev. 23:23; Numbers 29) that it is given a place in the plan of sacred events of the year in Exodus 12 through Numbers 10.

206

when Yahweh killed Aaron's sons, Nadab and Abihu, due to their presumed illicit use of "strange fire."[61] Otherwise, the passing of time is hardly noticeable. While the chronology of Num. 1:1 signals that about three weeks have passed in Leviticus, this book provides little or no sense of time, with its virtual absence of time indicators or narrative apart from introductions to divine instructions (and even fewer narrative executions of those commands). Exodus 12–Numbers 10, but especially the book of Leviticus, creates an increasing density of sacred events within an extremely short compass, a kind of compacted time at Mount Sinai, unlike and beyond the normal passage of time. The time at Mount Sinai virtually stops, signaling that the events at the mountain of God are timeless. Those instructions given in that timeless moment were intended to serve for all time.

This study may end where it began. As this study of Exodus and Numbers suggests, the priestly redaction of the Pentateuch shows some liturgical influence in its geographical and chronological markers. It is argued above that Passover and Weeks were evoked in the liturgical year represented by Exodus 12 through Numbers 10. The correlation between pilgrimage feasts and the shape of the Pentateuch did not end with Numbers 10. The final shape of Exodus–Numbers resulted in a broader correlation between the great pilgrimage feasts (and not the other feasts) and the three great themes of Exodus through Numbers. The three feasts taken together recapitulated the central old, foundational events celebrated in postexilic liturgy. In celebrating the exodus from Egypt, Passover begins the chain of events with the departure from Egypt. Weeks continues by celebrating the divine gift of the Torah at Mount Sinai. Booths ends the series by recalling the forty years in the wilderness following the departure from Sinai. Through the use of sacred time and space, the liturgical life of the pilgrimage festivals played a decisive role in the priestly formation of the Pentateuch to which dedicated readers have since returned in the cycles of their years.

61. See Milgrom, *Leviticus 1–16*, 1061.

The Song of Songs, Proverbs, and the Theology of Love

Larry Lyke

From as early as we have evidence, the inclusion of the Song of Songs in the canon of the Hebrew Bible was debated.[1] In particular, over the last two centuries the debate has turned to how the Song was understood by those who placed it in the canon. In general, the consensus is that, given its explicit sexual language, it was likely understood allegorically.[2] Professor Childs, however, has argued that the wisdom context of the Song implies that it was placed in the canon because it was understood to "probe the mystery of human love in the creative order."[3] In the following, I wish to consider the implications of Professor Childs's suggestion that we take seriously the wisdom context of the Song. I shall demonstrate that the metaphors used in the Song for human love can be understood as part of a much larger phenomenon in the Hebrew Bible in which the love of God is consistently described in sexual

1. See for example *Mishnah Yadaim* 3.5, etc.
2. Among the standard commentaries see Robert Gordis, *The Song of Songs and Lamentations: A Study, Modern Translation and Commentary* (New York: Ktav, 1974); Marvin Pope, *Song of Songs* (Anchor Bible; New York: Doubleday, 1977); Roland Murphy, *The Song of Songs: A Commentary on the Book of Canticles or The Song of Songs* (Hermeneia; Minneapolis: Fortress, 1987); and Othmar Keel, *The Song of Songs*, tr. Fredrick J. Gaiser (Minneapolis: Fortress, 1994), originally published as *Das Hohelied* (Zürcher Bibelkommentare; Zurich: Theologischer, 1986). For extended discussion on the history of the interpretation of the Song as well as the question of its place in the canon see esp. Pope, *Song*, 17-229, but also Keel, *Song* 1-37, and Murphy, *Song* 3-105.
3. Brevard Childs, *Introduction to the Old Testament as Scripture* (Philadelphia: Fortress, 1979) 576.

metaphors. More importantly, this suggests that the metaphors for sexuality in the Hebrew Bible are never entirely separable from either their human or divine registers. Therefore, it seems likely that for those responsible for including the Song in the canon, its metaphors were understood in terms of both their human and their divine significance.

I begin with a very small portion of the Song with the goal of using it as a case study for understanding its complex metaphoric language. I shall then consider passages from Proverbs and Ben Sira to locate the use of this language within the wisdom corpus. Finally, I shall consider the use of similar language in the narrative idiom of Genesis and suggest its implications for understanding the Song. The portion of the Song that I have in mind comes in the midst of a larger passage that comprises a lament by the male lover over the inaccessibility of his female counterpart; the whole passage reads as follows:

גן נעול אחתי כלה גל נעול מעין חתום ¹²

שלחיך פרדס רמונים עם פרי מגדים ¹³

כפרים עם־נרדים: ¹⁴נרד וכרכם

קנה וקנמון עם כל־עצי לבונה

מר ואהלות עם כל־ראשי בשמים:

מעין גנים באר מים חיים ונזלים מן־לבנון: ¹⁵

עורי צפון ובואי תימן הפיחי גני יזלו בשמיו ¹⁶

יבא דודי לגנו ויאכל פרי מגדיו:

באתי לגני אחתי כלה אריתי מורי עם־בשמי ¹5

אכלתי יערי עם־דבשי שתיתי ייני עם־חלבי

אכלו רעים שתו ושכרו דודים

¹²A garden locked is my sister and bride, a fountain stopped,
  a spring sealed.
¹³Your limbs are an orchard of pomegranates filled with sweet fruit —
with henna and nard. ¹⁴Nard and saffron,
reeds and cinnamon with all fragrant woods,
myrrh and aloes with all the best perfumes.

¹⁵A garden spring, a well of living water, flowing out of Lebanon.
¹⁶North wind awake, south wind enter, waft over my garden,
  spread its perfume.
Let my love enter his garden, and eat its sweet fruit.
5 ¹I have entered my garden, my sister, bride, have plucked
  my perfumed myrrh.

LARRY LYKE

I have eaten my honey and its comb, drunk my wine with milk.

Eat, lovers — drink, be intoxicated with love.

Amid this verdant and lush imagery I wish to focus on the second half of
v 12, "a fountain stopped, a spring sealed" is my bride. Clearly, this expresses
the male's frustration in being unable to meet his lover, but the language, I
would suggest, is profitably understood in relation to its use in other parts of
the wisdom corpus as well as other parts of the Hebrew Bible. For example,
consider the following from Proverbs 5:15-18:

15שתה־מים מבורך ונזלים מתוך בארך:
16יפוצו מעינתיך חוצה ברחבית פלגי־מים:
17יהיו־לך לבדך ואין לזרים אתך:
18יהי־מקורך ברוך ושמח מאשת נעורך:

15Drink the water of your own cistern, the fresh water of your well.
16Your springs will flow outward, streams of water in the square.
17Let them alone be yours, not some foreign woman.
18Blessed be your fountain, may you rejoice in the wife of your youth.[4]

Here, a young woman is referred to as a cistern, well, spring, stream, and
fountain.[5] Of considerable import is the larger context in which this metaphor takes its meaning. This discussion of the danger of the foreign woman
comes in the part of Proverbs (chs. 1–9) that urges the young man to listen
to his father and to dedicate himself to wisdom, חכמה, a feminine noun.
Moreover, through his dedication to his "bride" wisdom, the young man is
able to maintain and deepen his understanding of, and relationship to, God
(cf. Prov. 2:1-6, etc.). Proverbs' language and complex registers against
which to understand it are too detailed to receive full attention here, but a
few of its implications must be addressed.[6] Note that Proverbs sets up an
equation that can be represented by the following: woman = spring/well =

4. Among the many delights of this passage note the pun in v 18 on the phrase
"from your cistern" in v 15. In v 18 the same consonants בורך (מ) mean "blessed." Here we
see a direct association, in the very language of the passage, between the well (as woman)
and the blessings that come from God.
5. Note that in Prov. 23:27b we are told that "a foreign woman is a narrow well
(ובאר צרה נכריה)."
6. Note that "wisdom" is also associated with creation. Instructive are Prov. 3:19
and 8:22, where wisdom is either the means of creation or the first thing created. These
verses apparently rely on the association of wisdom/woman/water and presume that the
water at the origin of creation is the female principle called wisdom.

210

wisdom. As a result, through his dedication to his own "wife" and to drinking from her "waters" the young man dedicates himself to wisdom, deeper understanding, and to God himself. The spring/well is a trope for his relations with his wife, wisdom, and God. Clearly, the author's reliance on this imagery of woman as spring/well and of it as the crucial link to God's fullness represents a relatively articulate use of the metaphoric language of well and spring, especially within its theological register. A passage from Ben Sira, which is dependent for much of its imagery on various parts of Proverbs, makes another crucial move in this trajectory. In ch. 24 Ben Sira asserts that lady wisdom, the means by which Israel is to relate to God, is none other than the Torah (24:23). Moreover, in 23:13-22 he describes Wisdom (read Torah) in terms remarkably resonant with the passage from Song of Songs above.

The passages from Proverbs and Ben Sira are important for several reasons. First, they represent ways in which the authors of the Second Temple period articulated their theological insights. In particular, in this period the language of love, wells, and fertility, all used to connote human sexuality, are quite naturally used to articulate their theological conceptions. Equally important is that this use is particularly at home in these wisdom texts. In fact, these texts represent two of the crucial elements in understanding how rabbinic Judaism and Christianity became religions of the book. It is easy to see that the sexual metaphor (common in other parts of the Hebrew Bible) has come to be associated with the feminine principle of wisdom (חכמה) and that Israel's loyalty and dedication to its God are now understood properly to be channeled through scripture or Torah, another feminine noun. All of this suggests that the wisdom context was perfectly comfortable with the use of such explicit sexual metaphor for articulating its theology.

In the following I wish to argue, on the basis of the use of similar language and imagery in Genesis and the early part of Exodus, that these metaphors are equally charged with human and divine implications and that within the Hebrew Bible, it is best to understand such language as always connoting a reciprocal benefit from human/divine sexual activity. Put more simply, the Hebrew Bible does not appear to make the distinction, common to most moderns, between erotic and "platonic" love. Within the context of the Hebrew biblical idiom, it appears that the sexual metaphors such as we see in the Song of Songs and our wisdom texts are simultaneously understood as both human and divine. Human love, in other words, is always understood to be part of the larger pro-creative activity of God. All of this, in the end, lends support to Professor Childs's observation that the Song, especially in light of its wisdom context, was not understood merely allegorically but that its complex metaphors contributed to its being understood as an attempt to "probe the mystery of human love in the creative order." Notably, Professor Childs's observations imply what many today would call an "embodied" notion of God.

The task at hand, then, is to conduct a case study using the rather restricted metaphor of the spring that we have culled from Cant. 4:12b, in order to establish its place in the ongoing attempt to articulate the "theology of love" in the Hebrew Bible. As it turns out, the use of the imagery of springs and wells in Genesis provides an excellent background for understanding the subtle and sophisticated theological concepts implied by the use of these two terms in wisdom literature. After our discussion of the import of this language in Genesis, we shall return to what it means for understanding the wisdom context of the Song of Songs.

I. מעין חתום — A Spring Seated

Significantly, the two halves of the passage defined by Cant. 4:12–5:1 begin with the language of springs or wells. After referring to his lover as a "spring sealed" in v. 12, the man again refers to his lover in similar language in v. 15, but with important changes. Here the woman is referred to as a "garden spring" and as a "well of living waters" as well. Of greatest interest is the reinforcing of the notion of the woman as the source of life. In the following discussion we consider the language of wells and springs in Genesis as a means to understand more fully what the notion of a spring sealed connotes in the Song. First, as noted above, we should recognize that it signals the inaccessibility of the woman — at least in v. 12. Our concern, however, is to understand the larger significance of a "spring sealed" in relation to the narrative idiom of Genesis. After doing so, we shall consider the implications of our findings for understanding the phrase in Cant. 4:12.

Perhaps the best place to start in Genesis is with what Robert Alter has called the "betrothal type scene."[7] Alter deals with three texts that are of special interest for our purposes, Gen. 24:10-61; 29:1-20; and Exod. 2:15b-21. One element of this type scene is particularly important for the current discussion. In each of the stories the betrothal begins at the scene of a spring or well. In Genesis 24 it is Abraham's servant, sent to find a mate for Isaac, who meets Rebekah at a spring (עין [המים] in vv. 13, 16, 29, 42, 43, and 45 and באר in v. 29). In Genesis 29 Jacob meets Rachel for the first time at a "well of

---

7. Robert Alter, *The Art of Biblical Narrative* (New York: Basic, 1981) 47-62.

the field" (באר three times in v. 2, twice in v. 3, and once each in vv. 8 and 10). Finally, Moses meets his wife Zipporah and her sisters at a well in Exodus 2 (באר in v. 15b). The alternation between spring (עי[מ]ן) and well (באר) is of little consequence in these stories. Note that in Cant. 4:15 spring and well are placed in apposition and thus understood essentially as synonyms. Without going into detail, we should acknowledge that Alter has pointed out a very useful way of understanding these events in the patriarchal narrative. In fact, Alter also calls attention to an aspect of the language of springs/wells that is central to our discussion. In particular, Alter notes that the "well . . . is obviously a symbol of fertility and, in all likelihood, also a female symbol."[8] In this instance, Alter could have been bolder. It seems indubitable that the imagery of springs/wells in these stories represents not only fertility in general but also women and their wombs. Indeed, it would seem that these texts represent, in inchoate form, much the same theological understanding that we saw above in Prov. 5:15-18, where the equation of women and wells is explicit.[9]

With the preceding in mind, it is necessary to consider, in detail, a number of texts in Genesis that help to give a fuller sense of this idiomatic use of the imagery of wells and springs. We begin with a brief consideration of the "betrothal type scenes" identified by Alter and then turn to a number of other texts that seem to presuppose a similar understanding of this metaphor within the narrative idiom.

The longest of the "betrothal type scenes" in Genesis 24 requires the least of our time. In this story, Abraham's servant travels to Aram-naharaim to find a wife for Isaac. As expected, he meets Rebekah at a spring near the city of Nahor. Again, the alternation in the language referring to the spring is of little consequence. Upon meeting, Rebekah draws water herself from the spring and gives not only Abraham's servant a drink but all ten of his camels as well. This imagery suggests the fertility that is represented by Rebekah: the spring is likely a cipher for her future role as mother of Isaac's children. In

---

8. Alter, *Art,* 52.

9. One could argue that these stories merely represent the reality that wells and springs were a common locus of social intercourse and that they hardly convey the theological import being asserted herein. First, even if these stories do reflect the social realities of ancient Israel, they have undergone a traditionary process that inevitably frames them in the idioms of that culture. To think that this process is entirely independent of the larger processes of articulating theological notions would be naive. Moreover, based on the following argument, the possibility that these stories do reflect the social realities of ancient Israel would strengthen the case that they represent early and tentative attempts at articulating this theological tradition.

the episode of Jacob's meeting with Rachel, the role of the source of water as cipher for the woman is much clearer.

In Gen. 29:1-20 Jacob first encounters Rachel. In vv. 1-3 we learn that in the land where he has arrived there is a well and that when the locals wish to water their sheep, they must roll a stone away from the mouth of the well. In vv. 10-11, when Jacob meets Rachel, he rolls the stone away from the well, waters her flock, and then kisses her. The language in vv. 10b-11a is of interest. Here we read:

ויגש יעקב ויגל את־האבן מעל פי הבאר וישק את־צאן לבן אחי אמו:
¹¹וישק יעקב לרחל . . .

Jacob rolled the stone away from the mouth of the well and *watered* the flock of Laban his uncle, ¹¹then Jacob *kissed* Rachel. . . .

The image of the stone that blocks the well evokes nicely the fact that Rachel is said to be barren (ורחל עקרה [29:31]) and Jacob's rolling of the stone away further brings to mind the time when her womb is opened by God (ויפתח את־רחמה [30:22]).[10] Further, it is tempting to see in the language of these verses another way that the well is equated with Rachel. Note that it is the *mouth* of the well from which Jacob removes the stone to water (וישק) the flock and that he then kisses (וישק) Rachel. Perhaps we make too much of the recurrence of the consonants for "to water" (from the root שקה) and "to kiss" (from the root נשק). In fact, taken literally this pun might even suggest that Jacob kissed the sheep and watered Rachel! Even if the language here is coincidental, the juxtaposition of "well," "mouth," "water," and "kiss" reveals its complex and diffuse nature. Moreover, it is highly suggestive of the association of Rachel with the well and that it is she who will be the source of Jacob's most crucial progeny. Finally, it takes little imagination to see that this well represents not only fertility in general, but also Rachel's womb.

The last of Alter's "betrothal type scenes" also reflects the multi-vocal quality of the language we are tracing. In Exod. 2:15b-22 Moses, fleeing Egypt for the first time, enters Midian and sits by a well. When the daughters of the priest of Midian come to water their sheep, local shepherds try to drive them

10. Alter makes a similar point (*Art* 55). While it is clear that barrenness and a "closed womb" represent considerably different maladies, it seems that the texts focus on the similar consequences of each. Note that Sarah is described as post-menopausal and barren in Genesis. The complex nature of the coalescence of the biblical text complicates interpreting the significance of the difference between the two maladies, but it seems that the focus is on the threat posed to the Israelite lineage by women whose wombs, for whatever reason, are unavailable for the production of offspring.

away. Seeing this, Moses defends the girls, waters their flock, is invited to the house of their father, and is then married to Zipporah. Of significance for this story is Moses' continual association with water in the book of Exodus. In fact, his name means "the one drawn from the water." Furthermore, along with this episode at the well in Midian, we have his parting of the Reed Sea (chs. 14 and 15) and bringing water from the rock in the wilderness (17:1-7). With the story of his betrothal we are more or less in the same conceptual world as the other "betrothal type scenes." Moses' consistent association in the rest of Exodus with water, however, may signal a more complicated understanding of his relation therewith. If we can take into consideration notions such as those found in Proverbs, of wisdom as a fountain that sustains life, etc. (5:15-23), and the equally prevalent association of wisdom with Torah and Mitsvot (Prov 3:1), Exodus seems to represent in very abstract narrative form the association of Moses with the drawer of water, both as life-sustaining moisture and, at a deeper level, as life-giving instruction.

This is all highly speculative, of course, but it is remarkable that Moses' association with water has these consistent and strong resonances with the ideas we are tracing. The resonances between Moses' depiction in Exodus and Proverbs' understanding of wisdom can be explained in a number of ways. One is that Proverbs merely finds the means to articulate explicitly the deep and subtle conceptual word of Exodus that is imbedded in its narrative idiom. Another way of explaining the resonance is to presume that the form of the traditions in Exodus have been shaped by scribal activity in such a way that the narrative reflects later understanding of the relationship between Torah and wisdom.[11] A third way we might explain these resonances is to ascribe them merely to coincidence or the imagination of the reader. On this understanding, the association between Moses' depiction in Exodus and Proverbs is the modern equivalent of midrash. A fourth explanation of the ways in which Proverbs and the depiction of Moses resonate is more complicated and has been implied above. It is likely that neither Proverbs nor Exodus relies directly on the other but, rather, that they each represent, in wisdom and narrative idiom respectively, similar notions about the relationship between women, wells, water, and relations with God.[12] Of interest is that, on

11. This reading presumes that the scribes responsible for the preservation of our text were actively working their material (consciously or not) toward more general and accepted conceptualizations. While this is, to a certain degree, indubitable, we should not discount the subtlety of differences among various idiomatic formulations of the metaphors at hand.

12. Note that the Targum to the Song represents a richly textured, subtle, and keenly insightful interpretation of these and many more parallels between the Song and Exodus.

this reading, the Exodus passage shares with Proverbs this understanding of the subtle interweaving of these literary elements. A sure answer about the relationship between the depiction of Moses in Exodus and the conceptual world of Proverbs is not possible. It is important, however, that we recognize that Exodus manifests the complex and discursive nature of the metaphor represented by the term "spring/well." More importantly, we see in the Proverbs material evidence of the ways wisdom literature and Second Temple texts partake the emergence of a relatively well articulated form of this biblical idiom.

Having considered the category of "betrothal type scene," what can we deduce about the use of the imagery of springs/wells in Genesis and Exodus? First, it is hard to dispute the notion that springs and wells represent fertility. On the one hand, they represent the fertility of the land and on the other, the fertility of the people of God. Of most import for our discussion, the spring in each story is a cipher for the woman, a point made most clearly with the imagery of Jacob removing the stone from the mouth of the spring, which so nicely resonates with the eventual opening of Rachel's womb and subsequent conception of Joseph and Benjamin. Furthermore, our understanding of the significance of Moses' depiction, especially in light of its resonance with Proverbs, suggests that the language of springs has broader, theological, associations. We turn next to a number of texts in Genesis that reinforce the theological significance of the language of "springs."

Under consideration are several texts that have resonance with the "betrothal type scene" but represent significant variations on that form. The first two texts, from Genesis 16 and 38, appear to have some association with the meeting of the patriarch and his mate at a spring or well, although in much less explicit terms than the three texts considered above. In the second set of texts we shall consider, the issue of betrothal is absent but the metaphor of "a woman is a spring" is central.

We begin with a passage in Genesis 16 that, on first glance, may seem unrelated to our discussion but, on reflection, likely relates to it in subtle ways. Genesis 16 tells the story of Sarah's ploy to solve her barrenness by having Abraham engender children with Hagar. Sarah makes Hagar's life miserable once she realizes that Hagar has conceived, and so the maidservant runs away. Of interest is v. 7, where an angel of the Lord finds Hagar at "a spring in the wilderness" (על־עין המים במדבר), "the spring on the way to Shur" (על־העין בדרך שור). The message that the angel of God has for Hagar is that she should go back and submit to Sarah's harsh treatment. The news is not all bad, however, since the angel proceeds to make promises that are quite reminiscent of those given to Abraham (12:2; 13:15; 15:5, etc.). Interestingly, the closeness of these promises to Abraham's suggests that Ishmael might be the promised son. As the narrative continues, however, it becomes clear that this will not be the case (Gen. 17:20-21). More importantly, Hagar, right after we are told that she has conceived and just before she receives the promises for her son, is found next to a spring. It seems that this spring is an analogue to her fertility, especially in contrast to Sarah's barrenness.[13] Hagar's association with a water source is next in evidence in Genesis 21 (considered a second version of the story in ch. 16), where she and Ishmael wander in the wilderness and are saved when God points out a well of water (באר מים). So the stories of Ishmael's birth and subsequent salvation are both located at this symbol of fertility. Ch. 16 vival of the people of Abraham. While Hagar is not the wife through whom Abraham's promises will devolve, she is depicted in ways very similar to, and likely dependent on, the "betrothal type scene." The differences from other examples of the type scene likely signal both the variability of the motif and the fact that Hagar does not have the same status in the Israelite lineage that Rebekah, Rachel, and Zipporah share.

Another text that seems to rely on resonance with the "betrothal type scene," but also diverges significantly from it, is found in Genesis 38. Judah, having sent Tamar away, apparently to preserve his only remaining son, inadvertently propositions her on his way to Timnah. Gen. 38:14 says that Tamar was sitting at the "entrance to Enaim" (בפתח ענים) when Judah encountered and then propositioned her. This Hebrew phrase has always given interpreters difficulty but, in view of the persistent assmakes most explicit the association of Hagar with the well as a symbol of her fertility, but both stories seem to be aware of the role springs play in the surociation of the mothers of Genesis with wells, there is a possibility that we should understand the phrase to mean "at the opening of the two wells."[14] On this reading, we understand the text to signal that this is the woman with whom Judah will have his progeny and, indeed, it is the birth of Perez to Tamar and Judah that maintains the lineage of King David (Ruth 4:18-21). Perhaps we are to take the dual form of ענים to signal that twins will be conceived in the ensuing liaison as well, but this is not entirely clear. What seems certain, however, is that the associa-

---

13. It is of interest that when Sarah finally does conceive it is in a story in which she seems to be associated with a well (Genesis 20 and 21). For details on this association see below.

14. בפתח ענים is quite difficult to decipher. Note that the second term is in the dual. Targum Onqelos and the Syriac and Vulgate versions take it to mean something like "the crossroads to Enaim." Other possibilities include "the opening of the eyes," "the entrance to Enaim," "the opening of the two wells," etc.

tion of the patriarch's mate with a spring, and all the associated resonances, is likely not coincidence.

Genesis 16 and 38 suggest the variability with which the metaphor of "a woman is a spring" could be employed. In reality, it is unlikely that this metaphor is "manipulated" in any purposeful way. It is more likely that the traditionary process, over multiple years and through multiple mouths and hands, slowly forms the stories based on emergent notions of cultural literacy and competence. Significantly, the variations provide differing insights into the value of the language of springs and wells and their association with women. These variations, however, should not obscure the growing evidence for the centrality of the metaphor "a woman is a spring" or its place in articulating the means of divine blessing. We next turn to a set of texts that are less concerned with the issue of betrothal but still rely heavily on the metaphor "a woman is a spring" and share with the Song of Songs the notion of the great threat posed by "a spring sealed."

The first text we need to consider is Genesis 20. This is the story of Abraham's sojourn in Gerar, during which Sarah is taken into King Abimelech's household. This represents the second of what Koch calls the ancestress in danger episodes.[15] There are two elements of particular interest in this text, both of which are found in the last three verses. After returning Sarah to Abraham untouched (vv. 4 and 6), Abimelech says to her:

ולשרה אמר הנה נתתי אלף כסף לאחיך הנה הוא־לך כסות עינים¹⁶
לכל אשר אתך ואת כל ונכחת
ויתפלל אברהם אל־האלהים וירפא אלהים את־אבימלך ואת־אשתו¹⁷
ואמהתיו וילדו
כי־עצר עצר יי בעד כל־רחם לבית אבימלך על־דבר שרח¹⁸
אשת אברהם:

> ¹⁶To Sarah he [Abimelech] said, "Look, I have given a thousand pieces of silver to your brother, let this be a *'covering of the two eyes (springs)'* for all who are with you and with all a vindication." ¹⁷Abraham prayed and God healed Abimelech, his wives, and his slave girls, and they bore children; ¹⁸for YHWH had sealed tight every womb in Abimelech's house on account of Sarah, wife of Abraham.

The first element we must consider is the notice that YHWH had sealed tight the wombs of all the women of Abimelech's house. The language of v. 18 sug-

---

15. Klaus Koch, "The Ancestress of Israel in Danger," in *The Growth of the Biblical Tradition: The Form-Critical Method,* tr. S. M. Cupitt (New York: Scribner, 1969) 111-33.

gests that the closing of the wombs was in some way an appropriate response to Abimelech taking Sarah into his household. We may be meant to understand that Sarah's womb was also "sealed" while there. If this is the case, it represents a redundant element in the story at two levels. First, we are told that Abimelech never approached Sarah while in his house, so her ability to conceive while there is not at issue. Second, we have known since Gen. 11:30 that Sarah is barren.[16] Nevertheless, the fact that YHWH "opens" the wombs at the end of the Abimelech episode may suggest why it is that in the very next chapter, indeed only two verses later, Sarah finally conceives Isaac. We may be meant to understand that Sarah's womb was opened at the same time. More important is the notion that the threat to Abraham and Sarah is perceived to be a threat to their progeny, and the text records the punishment meted out to Abimelech in kind.

The second element of the passage above that is of note is the term Abimelech uses in v. 16 to describe the significance of the silver given to Abraham. He says that it will serve as a "covering of the eyes/springs" for Sarah. This represents a continuing difficulty in the interpretation of v. 16.[17] Many take it to be in parallelism with the last phrase in the verse and therefore understand it to say "let this serve as a clearing" before all. Obscurities like this are difficult in the extreme to resolve, but it is passing strange that this phrase represents nearly the opposite of the phrase in Gen. 38:14 that we have read as "the opening of the two springs." What could be the import of using this phrase, especially in light of the metaphor of "a woman is a spring" found throughout Genesis? If we read the phrase כסות עינים to mean "a covering of the two springs" we might understand it to mean that Abimelech is subtly suggesting that he hopes Sarah's womb (as a spring) will be "covered" like the wombs of the women of his household. This is a possibility only if we presume that Abimelech does not know that Sarah is already barren. On this reading, the phrase "covering of the two eyes/springs" may act as a double entendre. On the one hand, one could understand it, as most translators do,

---

16. Of course, this presumes that the author/redactor/tradent(s) responsible for ch. 20 know Sarah's story. Given that the traditions all seem to understand Sarah as either post-menopausal or barren, it seems likely that whomever we should credit with the story was aware of her inability to have children.

17. Among the difficulties is the fact that the pronoun הוא in "let it (he) be a . . . ." could refer to either the silver or Abraham. If Abraham, the possibilities for interpretation become even more complicated, suggesting that he ought to be a "covering of the spring" for her. In the idioms that we are tracing this presents problems. How would Abraham be a "covering of the spring" unless it is another way in which Abimelech is wishing that the two of them never have children?

to refer to some kind of "vindication." On the other hand, it may well represent Abimelech's wish that Sarah become (remain) barren. This reading must remain speculative since the phrase is so obscure. There is another feature of ch. 20, however, that gives credence to our reading of כסות עינים and continues to help fill in our understanding of the metaphor "a woman is a spring."

We begin by noting that Gen. 21:22 seems to be the logical continuation of the events narrated in ch. 20. Essentially, Gen. 21:1-21 represents an interruption in the narrative of Abraham's dealings with Abimelech. Invariably, there are good reasons for such interruptions, and it is not my purpose to suggest that the narrative as we have it does not make sense. Indeed, there is good narrative logic to have the birth of Isaac and the departure of Hagar and Ishmael where they are.[18] It is important, however, to point out the continuity between the end of ch. 20 and 21:22-34. This continuity includes more than just the continuation of Abraham's dealing with Abimelech. In fact, the language of 21:25 is quite familiar and serves to support the contention that we should read it with ch. 20. In 21:25 Abraham reproaches Abimelech for having seized his "well of water" (באר המים). The result of the ensuing narrative is that Abraham and Abimelech swear an oath by which Abimelech acknowledges that the well, to be known as Beer-sheba, belongs to Abraham. Following the events of ch. 20, it is hard to miss the significance of Abraham's complaint that Abimelech has taken his "well." The juxtaposition of these stories is as close as our texts come to making explicit the association of women and spring/wells in our narratives. There is a final text we need to consider that helps at once to reinforce a number of divergent parts of our argument thus far.

Events narrated in Genesis 26 help to confirm our suggestion that 21:22-34 is profitably read following on ch. 20 as well as support our reading of כסות עינים in 20:16. Moreover, ch. 26 supplies the clearest association in Genesis of the metaphor of "a woman is a spring" with the imagery of a "spring sealed." Gen. 26:1-16 represents the third of the famous "ancestress in danger" episodes, this one about Isaac and Rebekah at Abimelech's court. Significant for our purposes is that vv. 17-22, immediately following the episode, have much in common with 21:22-34. Most important is the notice that Isaac departs from Abimelech and digs the wells of his father that the Philistines had stopped up after Abraham's death (vv. 17-8). Recall that read-

18. Among the reasons for this pericope's location is that once Ishmael and Hagar are officially out of the picture the focus turns to Isaac and the narrative sets up the drama of the Aqedah.

ing Gen. 21:22-34 directly on the heels of Genesis 20 had Abraham depart from Abimelech and immediately get into a dispute over wells that Abimelech had seized. The juxtaposition of the "ancestress in danger" with the "dispute over wells" in Genesis 26 supports the notion that the two elements are profitably read in sequence in Genesis 20 and 21. Interestingly, this juxtaposition in ch. 26 lends support to the claim that the metaphor of "a woman is a spring" is indeed operative in each case. In fact, the "dispute over the well" seems to represent an abstract and symbolic enactment of the events of the "ancestress in danger." The evidence suggests that the juxtaposition of these two literary elements was due to the cultural and literary competence of the tradents of our stories.[19] The two stories were perceived to belong next to each other, likely because each, in its own way, attempts to depict the same threat to the longevity of Israel. Their juxtaposition implies that the survival of Israel hangs in the balance: should Israel lose its "springs" or "wells," the promises of God become irrelevant. This all makes perfect sense when one thinks back to the promises to Abraham and the other patriarchs. The promise is for land and progeny, both of which must continue to be productive if Israel is to survive (Gen. 12:1-3; 13:15, etc.).

Genesis 26 makes an important addition to the "dispute over wells" that makes it especially significant for this study. Note that in Genesis 21 Abraham's complaint was that Abimelech had seized his well. In that instance, we argued, the seizure of the well appears to be the narrative analogue to Abimelech's taking of Sarah into his household. In ch. 26 the complaint is that the wells that Abraham dug have been stopped up by Abimelech. The implication is that a stopped-up well is as much a threat to Israel's survival as one that has been taken. The image of a stopped-up well finds resonance with Abimelech's word to Sarah in 20:16, where he tells her that the money given to Abraham will be a כסות עינים or "covering of the 'springs'" for all around. We suggested above that this phrase may be a double entendre meant to sound like "let this be a vindication" but also connoting "may your womb remain stopped up." This phrase is difficult and we cannot say anything with confidence about how to read it, but its resonance with the events in Gen. 26:17-22 is intriguing. Moreover, in context, Abimelech's words, should we understand them to refer to Sarah's womb/spring, are ironically reversed when only a few verses later we learn that Sarah has conceived and that, like the women of Abimelech's court, her womb has been opened. Fur-

19. Of course it is possible that one or the other instance was purposely manipulated to "look" like the other, but we have insufficient evidence to make such a claim, and the motive for such a move remains obscure.

thermore, Abimelech's words seem to come true only in Genesis 26, where, once Isaac leaves Abimelech's court, Abraham's wells actually turn out to be stopped up. This imagery is strangely resonant with the "stopped-up" wombs of Abimelech's women in ch. 20.

II. Summary

We have seen that the imagery of springs has a currency across much of the Hebrew Bible and is part of a larger phenomenon by which the relationship between Israel and God is depicted in sexual language. In the category of texts that use the language of sexuality for this relationship, the prophets like Hosea provide the broadest background to the ideas we have been tracing. For Hosea (and a number of other prophets) human sexuality is a primary metaphor for the theological concepts he articulates. Central to this notion is the association of human with divine fertility. The book of Proverbs relies on similar conceptions, but has a much more complex metaphoric repertoire, which must be understood against numerous registers. Of most importance for this study is the association of wisdom, women, and springs. Proverbs makes more explicit much of what remains implicit in the texts we have considered in Genesis. In particular, Proverbs, in its equation of women, wells, and wisdom, displays the dual human and theological registers against which the metaphor of "spring/well" must be understood.

In Cant. 4:12–5:1 the language that we have been considering conveys beautifully the depth of the human desire involved. In particular, "a spring sealed" is a metaphor that, while clearly articulating the human sexual "drama," also partakes of a much broader and discursive horizon of possible meanings. In the context of the broader cultural competence as it emerges from the traditions in Genesis (and other parts of the Hebrew Bible), this metaphor has multiple trajectories that are, in all likelihood, "always already" there. That is, the theological and human registers of the metaphor that has provided our focus likely could be read bidirectionally and/or simultaneously from very early in the traditionary process. Indeed, it seems from the standpoint of much of the Hebrew Bible, and especially in the context of wisdom literature, that the human and theological registers of these metaphors are essentially inseparable. This complex dual register of its language must be the origin of any consideration of the Song of Songs, its redaction, or its inclusion in the canon. The Song and its inclusion in the canon cannot be interpreted independently of the cultural and historical processes we have investigated above. Our work implies that the Song likely always was and always should be understood against a full set of metaphoric registers. More importantly, we must keep in mind the degree to which we impoverish our reading of the Song and of the history of its preservation by understanding its metaphors against only one or the other of their registers. All of this becomes doubly important if we take seriously Professor Childs's claim that the wisdom context of the Song is central to determining its meaning. Given the complexity of the notions implied by "spring" and women in Proverbs (5:15-23), the core of the wisdom material in the Hebrew Bible, we need to be attentive to the sophistication of the cross-currents imbedded in its metaphors.

The bidirectionality and simultaneity of the metaphors we have considered have important consequences. First, a result of the complexity of its metaphors is that the theological register of its individual and particular language can be projected to the whole of the Song. Therefore, while always the poetry of human love, it simultaneously can be understood in terms of the ancient idiom that understands humans' relation to God via the same metaphors. It is this expansion of the collective intuitions about its language that leads to the sense that the Song, *as a whole,* can be read allegorically. This allegorical reading, however, is at all times dependent on the prior cultural competence that presumes the "indivisibility" of the human and divine significance of the metaphors on which it relies. This "indivisible" quality of the metaphorical significance of the Song's language is reinforced by a second point.

The second important consequence of the simultaneity of the metaphoric language of the Song is that it would seem to be among the primary vehicles for the sanctifying of human sexuality. More precisely, we would suggest that the influence of the "secondary" theological register on the "primary" human register of the language is to provide one of the means by which it becomes possible to articulate the sanctity of human love. Indeed, perhaps it is better to understand that sanctity as part of the very nature of creation and not secondary. In other words, it may be that it is only from a perspective that presumes a dichotomy between "spirit" and "flesh" that we can even speak of the "secondary" nature of the theological register of the language we have been considering here. Moreover, it is the presumption of this dichotomy that leads to the assumption that the Song must have been read allegorically in order to make it into the canon. At any rate, it is crucial to recognize and acknowledge that human sexuality is at the core of the metaphor and held in very high regard. Professor Childs, it seems, has sensed that those who included the Song in the canon shared this high regard, which is, in part, the result of the simultaneity of the theological and human registers of the metaphors on which we have focused.

"And Pharaoh Will Change His Mind . . ." (Ezekiel 32:31): Dismantling Mythical Discourse

Ellen F. Davis

In his first major publication, *Myth and Reality in the Old Testament* (1960) Brevard Childs addressed the cleavage between the Old Testament concept of reality and the very different view that is expressed in myth. I return to that problem in the present essay, for I believe that it is central to the project that occupies Childs in virtually all his subsequent writings, namely, clarifying the concept of canon: "God had revealed his will, not in timeless universal truths [as myth seeks to assert], but in concrete manifestations of himself, restricted in time and space, and testified to by particular witnesses."[1] The nature of the canon forces us to contend always with the question of how that which is ultimate is related to the concrete experience of historical Israel: "Reality is to be found in Israel and not in an abstraction or restriction of this concrete manifestation."[2] Childs's focus on canonicity as the "rule of faith" means that the church's search for truth excludes two options. First, it excludes the promulgation of "timeless universal truths" abstracted from the ongoing work of exegesis, for exegesis entails openness to new understandings "as the Scripture becomes the bread of life for another generation."[3] On the other hand, it excludes various literary and symbolic approaches that view the text as the only significant reality, from which derives all religious

1. *Biblical Theology in Crisis* (Philadelphia: Westminster, 1970), 105.
2. *Myth and Reality in the Old Testament* (London: SCM, 1960).
3. *Biblical Theology in Crisis*, 107.

224

experience: "A scriptural world is thus able to absorb the universe."[4] In opposite ways, these excluded options would dissolve the dialectical relationship between text and reality, which "are neither to be separated nor fused."[5] The reality outside the text is itself twofold. In Childs's work, the term "reality" refers to both God and to the concrete world of human experience into which God's word enters to transform it.

Childs has consistently maintained that the theological task is to trace with exegetical precision "the relation of extra-Biblical perceptions of reality to the Biblical witnesses."[6] The present essay is a step in that direction. My aim is to explore Ezekiel's oracles against Tyre and Egypt as evidencing a confrontation between two kinds of religious discourse, which I term "mythical" and "metaphorical." They differ essentially in their estimations of the continuity that exists between the divine realm and human experience, and further in their estimation of the potential for human perception and language to approach ultimate realities.

To amplify my terms: *mythical discourse* assumes a fundamental continuity and interpenetration between the divine and the human realms. Accordingly, the "mythic image," that is, the concrete object around which the myth forms, is perceived as absolute, possessed of eternal significance in itself and not in relation to some transcendent reality that differs essentially from the image. The central image of the myths that Ezekiel confronts in these oracles is the nation-state. By contrast, *metaphorical discourse,* as a form of religious speech, is characterized by its recognition of the image *as image,* that is, as a culturally shaped phenomenon that can be understood and properly valued only in the context of history and in relation to the reality that transcends all images, namely God.[7]

The particular usefulness of this contrast with respect to Ezekiel lies in the fact that he is the prophet who works most self-consciously and most impressively with verbal images, as his contemporaries mockingly acknowl-

4. Citing George Lindbeck; see Childs's criticism of his cultural-linguistic approach in *Biblical Theology of the Old and New Testaments* (Minneapolis: Fortress, 1992), 21.

5. *Ibid.,* 22.

6. *Biblical Theology in Crisis,* 118.

7. My understanding of myth is informed by Ernst Cassirer's discussion of mythical consciousness as it confronts (and is transformed by) the religious thinking of the biblical prophets. See his *Philosophy of Symbolic Forms* (New Haven: Yale University Press, 1953-57), II, 235-51. Childs himself identifies mythic thinking as apprehending supreme reality within natural processes (*Myth and Reality,* 20). I believe that Cassirer's focus on the absolute quality of the mythic image allows for a more comprehensive understanding of myth that encompasses political phenomena (e.g., the nation-state) as well as natural processes.

edged with the nickname "Metaphor-Monger" (מֵ לְמ לִים 21:5). Previously I have argued that Ezekiel's use of metaphor is a singularly effective way of engaging his audience in the task of interpreting both current events and the tradition.[8] Here I want to show that it also represents a distinctly theological move. The use of metaphor is Ezekiel's fulfillment of the Second Commandment, the prohibition of images, in the linguistic sphere. E. Cassirer observes:

> The Prophetic world is visible only in the religious idea and can be encompassed in no mere image which is oriented solely toward the sensuous present and remain confined within it. Accordingly, the prohibition of idolatry . . . takes on an entirely new meaning and power in the Prophetic consciousness. It is as though a chasm unknown to the unreflecting, naive mythical consciousness had suddenly been opened.[9]

Arguably, Ezekiel's greatest contribution to Israelite thought is his exploration of the limits of speech about the divine, with full awareness of the dangers such speaking entails in a culture that traffics in myth, magic, and graven images. Therefore his prophecy may shed light on one of the most important questions in contemporary biblical studies: whether and how biblical language bears witness to the transcendent, that is, whether and how biblical language is genuinely revelatory. Childs's work has given impetus to the debate about that question.[10]

The central mythic image that occupies Ezekiel throughout the book is, of course, Jerusalem, with its Temple and monarchy. In confronting the nationalistic absolutism of the foreign nations, Ezekiel is obliquely challenging

8. See my *Swallowing the Scroll: Textuality and the Dynamics of Discourse in Ezekiel's Prophecy* (Sheffield: Almond, 1989) 92-104.

9. *Philosophy of Symbolic Forms* II, 240.

10. See the comment by John J. Collins in a recent review of work by Childs, J. Levenson, and J. Barr: "Childs attempts to justify his confessional stance by claiming that 'the Enlightenment's alternative proposal, which was to confine the Bible solely to the arena of human experience, is just as much a philosophical commitment.' The argument is specious. Liberal biblical scholarship is not based on a dogmatic restriction of the Bible 'solely to the arena of human experience.' The point is that any scholar who wishes to assert more than what is commonly accepted in the community of scholars must assume the burden of proof or provide appropriate arguments. All shades of theological opinion agree that the Bible belongs to the arena of human experience to some degree. Those who wish to assert with Childs that it transcends human experience need to explain how this is so. Confessional assertion is no substitute for reasoned argument" ("Historical Criticism and the State of Biblical Theology," *Christian Century* 110/22 [July 28–August 4, 1993], 745).

Israelite absolutism, which draws absurd confidence from the place which Ezekiel debunkingly calls "the bloody city" (עיר דמים, 22:2; 24:6, 9), using the same phrase by which Nahum once addressed Nineveh (3:1). The resonance between Jerusalem and the foreign nations is evident in the first oracle against Tyre. That city, once God has exposed her to the ravages of "many nations," is twice described as "bare rock" (צחיח סלע, 26:4, 14); the whole scene is a metaphorizing of the name צ ר ("Rock"). The same striking phrase is also twice used in the final denunciation of Jerusalem: God brings down vengeance upon Jerusalem by exposing her shed blood on צחיח סלע (24:7, 8). This oracle, which immediately precedes the oracles against the foreign nations, is dated to the very day that Nebuchadnezzar laid siege to Jerusalem. Doomed Tyre is thus shown to be a mirror image of fallen Jerusalem; it was in fact Nebuchadnezzar's next target after the Jerusalem siege had succeeded.

The fact that Jerusalem's fate is linked to the fates of her enemies is underscored by the dating of the oracles against the nations; most of them cluster in the months immediately before and after Jerusalem's fall in 587. The case has been well made and is increasingly accepted that these oracles are essentially the prophet's own work.[11] Thus they stand in contrast to the oracles against the nations in Isaiah and Jeremiah, which are acknowledged to be largely editorial productions.

There is far less agreement that the placement of Ezekiel's foreign oracles is original. Eichrodt still represents the majority with his view that there is a "ruthless disturbance of the organic arrangement" of the book, in that the foreign oracles separate the warning that Jerusalem's collapse is imminent (24:15:27) from the notice that it has occurred (33:21-22).[12] However, this criticism fails to take note of the pivotal function that the oracles against the nations serve in Ezekiel, a function to which their present placement contributes. They are complementary on one side to the exposure of Israel's own false religiosity, most notably in the Temple vision of chs. 8–11, and its delusory ideology of the nation-state, which Ezekiel mocks in the revisionist histories of chs. 6, 20, and 23. On the other side, they anticipate the reestab-

11. See, for example, Walther Eichrodt's commentary *Ezekiel* (Old Testament Library; Philadelphia: Westminster, 1970). In a recent article, Lawrence Boadt demonstrates the stylistic and theological unity between the oracles against Tyre and Egypt and those against Judah in the preceding chapters ("Rhetorical Strategies in Ezekiel's Oracles Against the Nations," in *Ezekiel and His Book*, ed. J. Lust [Leuven: University Press, 1986], 182-200). Cf. his longer study, *Ezekiel's Oracles against Egypt: A Literary and Philological Study of Ezekiel 29–32* (Rome: Biblical Institute Press, 1980).

12. *Ezekiel*, 352. Similarly Walther Zimmerli, *Ezekiel* (Hermeneia; Philadelphia: Fortress, 1983) II, 3.

lishment of Israel's sacred sphere in the final Temple vision of chs. 40–48. In other words, the oracles against the nations, dated to the year of Jerusalem's fall, mark the transition out of Israel's own idolatrous past into a possible future. Rendering an accurate judgment on the false perception of reality embedded in foreign mythologies is the necessary prerequisite for the renewal of Israel's life (ch. 37) under the dominion of its God.

This paper is then an extension of my earlier argument that the frequently cited "architectonic" structure of this book reflects the design of the prophet himself. Ezekiel is the first writing prophet in the full sense; he created a literary idiom for prophecy and shaped his message as a whole. In other words, he authored a book. For the present argument, the crucial point is that the greater control over material and perspective afforded by written composition enabled the prophet to produce a more thorough ideological critique than had previously been possible, and that Ezekiel's subtle and piercing depictions of Tyre and Egypt demonstrate his mastery of this new medium of prophecy.

The fact that the archenemy Babylon is absent from Ezekiel's roll of seven nations is evidence that this body of foreign oracles serves a different function from those found in Isaiah and Jeremiah. There the prominent denunciations of Babylon (Isaiah 13 and 21, Jeremiah 50–51) indicate that the oracles are intended as an indirect promise of salvation to Israel when the great Destroyer is herself destroyed. But the nations featured in Ezekiel's oracles are not Judah's enemies. On the contrary, Tyre and Egypt were in 587 Judah's fellow rebels, the only other nations still holding out against Nebuchadnezzar. They are presented as object lessons to Judah, just as her "sister" Oholibah-Samaria was previously presented (ch. 23[13]); their fate clarifies her own. Though far more powerful than Judah, these nations, too, will be unable to withstand Nebuchadnezzar's army[14] — and behind that, the will of God. Ezekiel reveals the nationalistic absolutism of the mythmaking kingdoms that would exempt themselves from history. M. Buber's comment aptly expresses what Ezekiel intends Israel to learn from these oracles, which are only nominally addressed to Tyre and Egypt: "The nations can experience the absolute only because of what they are; Israel can experience the absolute only, when, and because that absolute faces it."[15]

13. The treatment of the two sisters, Samaria and Sodom, in 16:44-63 is often considered a later addition.
14. The unsuccessful siege of Tyre forces Ezekiel to revise this judgment in his last-dated oracle, 29:17-20.
15. Martin Buber, "The Gods of the Nations and God," *Israel and the World* (New York: Schocken, 1948), 198.

The foreign oracles show the Israelites where the aspiration to be like the nations has taken them. Taken together, these oracles may be seen as an amplified answer to the longing to which Ezekiel gives ironic expression: "We will be like the nations, like the families of the (foreign) lands, worshiping wood and stone!" (20:32). The echo of Israel's wish in the speech of Edom and Seir, set at the head of the foreign oracles (25:8), confirms the connection. The historical irony is that Judah has in fact partially succeeded in achieving that resemblance and is even now experiencing its consequences: God's devastating judgment on idolatry, executed by means of Babylon.

Yet the ultimate aim of the foreign oracles is to clarify the difference between mythical delusion and the reality that the house of Israel is constrained to observe so that Israel may escape sharing the nations' fate of extinction or — in the case of Egypt — bare survival (29:14-15). That reality is represented by Ezekiel's repeated use of the "recognition formula," וידעתם כי אני/ וידעת/ ידע ("And they/you shall know that I am the Lord," 25:5, 7, 11, 17; 28:24, 26; 29:6, 16, 21; 30:8, 25, 26; 32:15; cf. 38:23). By means of this formula the oracles are directed toward both Israel's and the nations' final acknowledgment of the God who is the sole engineer of world history.

Recognition implies differentiation. In this context, the formula severs the "magical continuum" that myth asserts between the divine sphere and the earthly authorities of state and cult and establishes in its stead "the infinite difference between God and creature, between Lord and servant."[16] The nation that observes the difference can live in security (34:24-31); those who fail to do so are the disposable instruments and casualties of history. The recognition formula, like the Second Commandment, leaves Israel no recourse but to orient itself exclusively to God's singular identity. That God has a coherent identity is signified by God's having a Name to which certain personal attributes regularly attach (כי אנכי יי אלהיך אל קנא, Exod. 20:5b). God's identity, action, and will are discerned not by occult means but rather by consulting the few reliable channels of verbal revelation and, in light of what is said, reflecting on the revelatory pattern of God's action. Steady repetitions of the formula throughout the book reinforce the effect of the stunning *Unheilsgeschichte* in ch. 20. There we learn that God's Name is the one consistent motive force in history. With remarkable lack of sentimentality, God reveals that it is solely "for the sake of my Name" (למען שמי) that God acts, first to spare Israel from extinction in the sight of the nations (20:9, 14, 22)

16. Hans Urs von Balthasar, *Theology: The Old Covenant* (*The Glory of the Lord*, vol. 6; San Francisco: Ignatius, 1991), 225.

and ultimately to restore Israel, beyond all expectation and deserving (20:44). "The bond of the covenant" (מסרת הברית, 20:31) is less a tie of affection for Ezekiel than it is an instrument for maintaining the integrity of God's identity and will within Israel and before the nations.

The connection I have drawn with the image prohibition suggests that Ezekiel's oracles against Tyre and Egypt represent a more ambitious theological project than is undertaken in the foreign oracles of other prophets. I believe it is for this reason that, millenia after passage of the particular political circumstances that inspired them, they remain uniquely powerful within this genre of biblical literature. L. Boadt identifies the "oracle against foreign rulers" (29:1-16, 31:1-18, 32:1-16), a subcategory of the oracles against the nations, as displaying "a moral motive untypical of the more secular and political O.A.N. form."[17] My disagreement would be only in developing the observation further: *throughout* Ezekiel's oracles against Tyre and Egypt there is strongly operative a motive force that is not only moral but distinctly theological. The oracles focus, not on the nations' enmity to Israel (as in the other prophetic books), but rather on how their wildly inflated self-estimations have given offense to God.

In order to show the exact nature of the nations' offense, Ezekiel goes inside the heads of their leaders. Y. Kaufmann's judgment that Ezekiel and Deutero-Isaiah reveal "only knowledge of the externals of paganism and not of its beliefs"[18] is wrong — dramatically so in the former case. He takes insufficient account of the nature of their statements; these are summary representations, heavily tinged with irony, rather than philosophical debates. Their purpose is not to persuade the pagans of the illogic of their views; in Ezekiel's view, not the present oracle but the events of history will eventually change the pagan mind. Rather, they aim to characterize paganism in such a way as to make the exiled Israelites proof against assimilation.

In fact, Ezekiel explores the ideology of paganism in a way unprecedented in previous prophecy, using the same techniques whereby he has already exposed Israel's idolatrous mindset. These are chiefly two, and in my judgment both techniques reflect the greater control over perspective which is made possible by written composition. One is the incorporation within the prophet's oracles of the quoted speech of the opponent, a phenomenon that plays a much greater role in Ezekiel than in earlier prophets.[19] The sec-

17. *Ezekiel's Oracles against Egypt*, 7.

18. Yehezkel Kaufmann, *History of the Religion of Israel: The Babylonian Captivity and Deutero-Isaiah* (New York: Union of American Hebrew Congregations, 1970) 99.

19. The phenomenon of quoting the opponent's speech occurs (also in an oracle against a foreign nation) in Isa. 14:12-14. Although the question of date remains open, it is probable that the oracle against Helel ben Shahar is postexilic and demonstrates a later

ond and related technique is the appropriation of pagan myth, while subordinating it to the pattern and message of Israel's own sacred story.

In my earlier work I have argued that Ezekiel's frequent practice of quoting popular speech is not to be taken at face value; these are not verbatim reports of conversations with his contemporaries.[20] Even more is this true with respect to the citations of foreign potentates. Ezekiel surely never heard Pharaoh say, "My Nile is my own, and I made it for myself" (29:3), and the two boasts of personified Tyre (26:2; 27:3, reading with MT) are even more transparently the prophet's representations, imaginative illustrations of how a pagan thinks. Indeed, the literary structure marks these quotations as far removed from natural conversation; for they are doubly embedded, first in prophetic speech and then again in the divine speech that is the outer frame for all Ezekiel's oracles:

> The word of the Lord came to me, "O mortal, say to the prince of Tyre [*outer frame: God's command to speak, which ostensibly marks the whole oracle as divine dictation*]: Thus says the Lord God [*inner frame, the oracular formula, designating prophetic speech*]: 'Because you have been so haughty and have said [*quoted speech of the opponent*], "I am god/El; a divine habitation I inhabit in the heart of the seas. . . ."'" (28:1-2)

This double-embedding — foreign king's voice within prophet's voice within God's voice — means that Ezekiel has carefully directed the way the audience hears the quoted words. They are part of a complex characterization, and the frame guides the hearer/reader in making an evaluative judgment. For example, in the two verses of divine speech immediately preceding and following Pharaoh's "My Nile is my own, and I made it for myself," the word יְאֹר ("Nile") is repeated four times, always with the personal pronoun suffix: "his/ your Nile." Thus God's diction mimics Pharaoh's, underscoring the absurdity of his proprietary claim. Even if the quote be accurate, it is now, removed from its original context and recontextualized by Ezekiel, subject to a response far different from that which the speaker intended. Ezekiel has created a literary structure admirably suited for directing the battle of opposing ideological forces, and the balance is heavily weighted in God's favor.

The other technique that Ezekiel devised for moving Israel to an accurate judgment on pagan ideology is working from "inside" the myths that attach to the foreign nations, first to expose the truth about what he calls the

---

prophet's awareness of Ezekiel (see Otto Kaiser, *Isaiah 13–39* [Old Testament Library; Philadelphia: Westminster, 1974], 29-32).

20. *Swallowing the Scroll,* 86.

תּוֹךְ ("inmost self," 28:16) of the nation — its motivating force — and then to explode the mythic images. Recalling the contrast between mythical and metaphorical discourse, one might say that by engaging the images of the foreign myths and pushing them to their limits, Ezekiel shows how far they fall short of ultimate realities. Pharaoh is a sea monster lurking in the Nile he claims to have made, and God hauls him out on a fishhook (29:4). Israel's God darkens the sky over Egypt when Pharaoh the sun god is extinguished (32:7). Tyre, which said "I am the perfection of beauty" (accepting MT 27:3), becomes by means of the prophetic imagination a "perfectly beautiful" ship (27:4, 11), loaded with goods, taken out to sea, and sunk by an east wind — the same wind that was instrumental in the crossing of the Sea of Reeds. In the hands of the "Metaphor-Monger," the static and unquestioned myths that sustain national absolutism are revealed for what they are: images rather than eternal verities. As cultural productions, they can be manipulated and their intentions radically changed.

Ezekiel's most sustained and sophisticated theological engagement with the truth claims of myth is found in his answer to the prince of Tyre's claim to be a god (ch. 28). In the two related oracles that compose the bulk of the chapter, Ezekiel establishes clearly, possibly for the first time in the Bible, that economics is a primary arena in which idolatry becomes visible.[21] Tyre has elevated its commercial success to the status of primordial myth. Accordingly, the prophet mixes the languages of cult, commerce, and warfare in order to effect the collapse of that social construct: "Through the greatness of your iniquity, by the dishonesty of your trade, you desecrated your sanctuaries. And I brought forth fire from within you; it consumed you. And I turned you to dust on the earth, before the eyes of all who see you" (28:18). The context of the threat of fire is multivalent: it describes the city under Nebuchadnezzar's (abortive) siege, but the fire brought forth from within also suggests the divine fire that defends God's holiness from incursion (Lev. 10:1-1; Num. 16:35).

The effect of this linguistic admixture is still jarring enough to confound interpreters. Four times Ezekiel speaks of Tyre's "desecration" (חלל III, BDB) at the hands of foreign armies (vv. 7, 9) and God's hands (v. 16), or through her own iniquitous commerce (v. 18). Only the last of these in-

---

21. It is interesting in this connection that the sin of Sodom is identified in this book (Ezek. 16:49-50) not as sexual immorality or even rank inhospitality, but rather "pride engendered by surfeit of food and the luxury of tranquility." Although the passage may be secondary (cf. note 13 above), it seems to accord with Ezekiel's own thought. Moshe Greenberg argues for "a single grand movement from start to finish of this long oracle" (*Ezekiel 1–20* [Anchor Bible; Garden City: Doubleday, 1983], 292-306).

stances — where the object of the verb is "your sanctuaries" (מִקְדָּשׁ) — does the NJPS translate as "desecrate"; elsewhere the verb is translated "strike down" (חלל I, BDB), with a note that the meaning is uncertain.[22] Thus the passage is made to conform to the ordinary language of warfare. But the effect of the fourfold repetition is lost. Ezekiel's point seems to be that Tyre's commercial wealth is her temple, and any attack on her material well-being is a desecration of the sacred sphere.

Ezekiel's consummate skill in manipulating the images that attach to the foreign nations breaks the power of their absolutizing myths. When the stories the nations tell about themselves have been exposed as mere cultural productions, then those who have ears to hear are left with no recourse but to recognize God's imageless identity as the sole foundation of reality: "And they shall know that I am the LORD."

Ezekiel opposes mythic claims with a more truthful form of religious speech, namely metaphor. Metaphor is more truthful just because it is more modest. As J. Soskice has brilliantly shown, a certain vagueness belongs ineluctably to metaphorical speaking; this is in fact one of its advantages, for scientific speech and above all for theology.[23] At the heart of such speech is the recognition that one may refer to phenomena, on earth or in heaven, without defining them. "[T]his separation of referring and defining . . . is what makes it not only possible but necessary that in our stammering after a transcendent God we must speak, for the most part, metaphorically or not at all."[24]

Ezekiel's preference for vagueness in speaking of God is almost painfully evident in the first chapter of his book. The prophet deliberately stammers as he reports what he saw by the River Chebar:

> And above the expanse which was over their heads — the semblance of a throne, something like sapphire; and upon the semblance of the throne, the semblance — something like a human being upon it, above. And I saw what appeared to be *hashmal* — something like fire encased in a frame — from what seemed to be his loins upward. And from what seemed to be his loins downward, I saw something like fire and radiance round about him. Something like the bow that will show in the clouds on a rainy day — such was the appearance of the radiance round about. That was the appearance of the semblance of the glory of the LORD. I saw, and I fell on my face. (1:26-28)

22. Similarly Zimmerli.

23. Janet Martin Soskice, *Metaphor and Religious Language* (Oxford: Clarendon, 1985) 133-34.

24. *Ibid.*, 140.

Palpable here is Ezekiel's anxiety that figurative language about God not be hammered into graven images. He may be the original of what Soskice calls the "critical theological realist," who "can take his talk of God, bound as it is within a wheel of images, as being reality depicting, while at the same time acknowledging its inadequacy as description."[25] The Metaphor-Monger is the staunchest of realists, like the Christian mystics of whom Soskice speaks. Beneath the figures and images in which he is impelled to speak, if he is to be understood at all, is "the bedrock of his experience and it is here that his reference is grounded, and here ultimately that reference is grounded for those who take his account as authoritative."[26]

The final and most surprising point of Ezekiel's instruction to Israel through the oracles against the foreign nations is the ideological conversion of its oldest enemy, Egypt. This point is generally lost through mistranslation of 32:31: אוֹתָם יִרְאֶה פַרְעֹה וְנִחַם עַל־כָּל־הֲמוֹנֹה. The clause is regularly rendered: "These [namely, all the pagan princes and their armies who have gone down to Sheol] Pharaoh shall see, and *he shall be consoled for* all his masses. . . ."[27] Yet this sight gives Pharaoh no reasonable cause for consolation, as Smend notes in treating the verse as "biting mockery."[28] This, however, is not the best solution. The statement makes straightforward sense once one recognizes that the verbal phrase — the *niph'al* verb נחם with the preposition על — has a broad semantic range. The common translation "be consoled" represents one possibility, but in fact it is well-suited to only two occurrences of the phrase (2 Sam. 13:39; Jer. 31:15) in the whole Bible! In each of the many instances where the verb and the preposition occur together (Exod. 32:12; Isa. 57:6; Jer. 8:6, 18:8, 10; Amos 7:3, 6; Job 42:6,[29] etc.), the phrase denotes a profound alteration of feeling, understanding, or intention about something; that is, it denotes a change of mind, either divine or human.

That Ezekiel uses the phrase in this sense is confirmed by 14:22. Surely there will be no reason for consolation when the surviving Israelites see, for the first time clearly, the wicked "ways and deeds" of their sons and daughters. Rather, God anticipates that they will "see and change [their] minds concerning the evil that I have brought upon Jerusalem. . . ." The following

25. *Ibid.*, 141.
26. *Ibid.*, 152.
27. NJPS; similarly RSV, NRSV, NEB.
28. R. Smend, *Der Prophet Ezechiel* (Kurzgefasstes exegetisches Handbuch zum Alten Testament; Leipzig, 1880), ad loc.
29. J. Gerald Janzen correctly translates this crucial passage as "I change my mind concerning dust and ashes," understanding "dust and ashes" as a metaphorical reference to the human condition (*Job* [Interpretation; Atlanta: John Knox, 1985], 251-59).

verse specifies the point on which the change of mind will occur: "that it was not for nothing that I did all I did in her." The point here, as so often in Ezekiel, is theodicy; the survivors in Israel will eventually come to see that God is justified even in executing this terrible judgment.

Similarly in the oracle against Egypt, God anticipates that Pharaoh will eventually come to see things in a truthful light; that is, he will see his own situation as God sees it. When Pharaoh and his mighty army lie in the lowest depths of Sheol, surrounded by all the fallen warriors who once inspired terror on the surface of the earth, then he *"will change his mind concerning* all his masses — those of Pharaoh's men slain by the sword and all his force." When Israel's God "strikes terror in the land of the living, while Pharaoh and all his masses are laid among the uncircumcised" (v. 32), then Egypt's king will have to revise his opinion about the disposition of power in the universe.

L. Boadt comments plausibly that 32:32 has "all the earmarks of a theological addition"[30] — although I believe that the addition reflects Ezekiel's intention. If this is true, however, it means that v. 31 may once have marked the conclusion to Ezekiel's extraordinary oracles against the nations. It is a startling conclusion, for Pharaoh's "conversion" is the last thing that anyone in Israel might have expected at the time of Jerusalem's fall (cf. 20:32). As I have already suggested, the oracles against the foreign nations are far more significant for Israel's self-understanding than for what they indicate about the fate of the other nations. Pharaoh's change of mind will bring some benefit to Egypt; unlike Tyre, it will not be annihilated but rather restored as a "lowly kingdom" (29:14-15), living in humble recognition of Israel's God (29:6, 16). In answer to the question of why Egypt is to be spared complete extinction, Zimmerli observes that Ezekiel, like Jeremiah, recognizes that Egypt is too central to world history simply to be wished away.[31] But one can say more: Egypt is too central to Israel's history. In view of the long historical perspective that informs Ezekiel's prophecy (cf. chs. 16, 20, 23), it seems that the prophet conceives the ideological conversion of Israel's oldest enemy as the final movement of the exodus. This marks an end to Pharaoh's vacillating changes of heart that began when he first encountered the power of Israel's God. More significantly, this marks the end of Israel's vulnerability not only to the armies but also to the religious delusions of its neighbors. Pharaoh's change of mind is the ultimate confirmation of the reality of Israel's God. The conversion of Egypt is a witness even more powerful to compel belief — even Israel's own belief — than would be Egypt's extinction.

30. *Ezekiel's Oracles against Egypt*, 168.
31. *Ezekiel*, II, 115.

At the beginning of this essay, I suggested that Ezekiel's prophecy may shed light on the nature of revelatory language. I turn now to the task of specifying that suggestion, for in my judgment the relation between language and religious truth is the most pressing hermeneutical question in contemporary biblical studies. D. Gunn and D. Fewell have recently pointed to the centrality of this question. Drawing on the work of Stanley Fish, they observe "a major epistemological shift," whereby the "commonsense view" of "self and society as objective realities in a world of ostensible, essential truths and values" is yielding in many quarters to the "rhetorical" view that the human being "fashions the world through language, manipulating reality rather than discovering it, since reality is that which is construed as reality rather than some objective essence." The former view they associate with the purported objectivity of historical criticism. The latter view, to which Gunn and Fewell themselves incline, opens the way for their literary exploration of the inherent slippage of language and the slippery reality that language not only delineates but even constructs. "This world is a carnivalesque one of exuberance and possibility, of enthusiasm and metaphor, of religion, magic and verbal incantation, where [citing Richard Rorty] truth is 'an artifact whose fundamental design we often have to alter.'"[32]

The problem with this bipolar model as a way of evaluating various modes of biblical interpretation (as Gunn and Fewell go on to do) is that neither pole adequately describes the way in which the biblical writers themselves seem to understand the relationship between language and reality. In arguing for a connection between the Second Commandment and Ezekiel's oracles against Tyre and Egypt, I have intended to show that, though this prophet is exceptional in the extreme self-consciousness with which he uses religious language, nonetheless he represents the view that runs throughout the Bible about how human beings may approach and express the deep truths about themselves, this world, and God.

The Bible as a whole may be construed as a massive refutation of the idea that human beings create reality or fundamentally alter the design of the truth. The Psalmists repeatedly appeal to God's truth as the standard and guide for human life. God's counsel (עצה) stands in stark contrast to the deceptive counsel of the nations:

The LORD frustrates the counsel of the nations,
undoes the designs of the peoples.

32. David Gunn and Danna Nolan Fewell, *Narrative in the Hebrew Bible* (Oxford: Oxford University Press, 1993) 10.

The counsel of the LORD stands forever,
the designs of his heart to generation after generation. (Ps. 33:10-11; cf.
Prov. 1:30-31)

The Psalmists are very far from Rorty's "carnivalesque" celebration of human creativity as foundational for reality. Yet their perspective cannot be identified with Gunn and Fewell's "commonsense" understanding that "truth is an eternal object which needs to be discovered."[33] For the structure of reality is not self-evident even to those who wish to know it. It is instructive that the word "truth" (אמת) occurs in the Psalter, the book of prayers, more frequently than in any other book of the Hebrew Scriptures. The Psalmists do not conduct research to discover the truth. They pray for it, recognizing that truth is a gift that God bestows and must perpetually renew:

Lead me in your truth and teach me,
for you are the God of my salvation;
for you I wait all day long. (Ps. 24:4-5; cf. Prov. 22:21)

Do not utterly take true speech out of my mouth
for I have set my hope on your justice (מ׳ פתך). (Ps. 119:43)

Your righteousness is eternal righteousness,
and your instruction (ותורתך) is truth. (Ps. 119:142)

The psalmists, like Ezekiel and all the other biblical writers, display what Soskice calls "a cautious realism." By means of steady, prayerful attention to God, speakers may hope to "mirror the world . . . in the sense of constructing a symbolic representation of that environment."[34] Speakers mirror reality, however imperfectly; they don't invent or revise it. Indeed, the notion of social and political constructions of reality, for which language is the major instrument, is from a biblical perspective delusional and blasphemous. It is exactly this linguistic absolutism that Ezekiel exposes and explodes in the oracles against Tyre and Egypt.

I have already noted that Childs is wary of critical approaches that focus exclusively on the biblical text as constituting the whole world of religious experience. Yet he has pointed to the value of recent literary studies in showing how it is that religious language may have a revelatory aspect:

33. *Ibid.*
34. *Metaphor and Religious Language,* 136, citing Hilary Putnam. Putnam himself is not speaking in a specifically theological context.

Perhaps one of the most important contributions of the focus on text as literature lies in the attempt to explore the nature of the "poetic," that is, non-scientific language in its potential to construct a new vision of reality. Particularly fruitful has been the adaptation of Ricoeur's insight into metaphorical language as a process of creating a new symbolic order which expands the scope of the human experience of the transcendent. . . . The language itself, rather than some form of history, provides the realm in which the events occur through the medium of human experience.[35]

Imaginative or poetic language — a term that fits most of the language of the Bible — has the capacity to disclose the essential features of transcendent reality in a way that overturns our ordinary ways of thinking and presses us to respond, often in uncomfortable ways, to the practical demands of the larger reality that has opened before us, even while its full dimensions remain unknown. I have used the term "metaphorical discourse" to designate the alternative that Ezekiel offers to the mythic discourse of the pagan nations. Just because it is avowedly approximate, metaphorical discourse is the most accurate way of speaking about what God is like and how God operates in the world.

It would be equally apt, within the larger structure of Ezekiel, to term his mode of discourse "visionary." I have argued above that Ezekiel's addresses to Tyre and Egypt play a pivotal role in the book. Dismantling their mythical constructions of reality is the means by which he prepares for the reestablishment of Israel's own sacred sphere in the "blueprint vision" of chs. 40–48.[36] This final vision illustrates a distinction that may be useful to the current discussion about the power of language: namely, the distinction between constructing reality and ordering the world. The first is inadmissible to a discussion of biblical theology; the latter is an important function of religious language. Like his contemporary, the author of the acrostic poems in Lamentations, Ezekiel frames language with extreme precision in order to disclose the unshakable order of a world that ordinary vision would perceive as hopelessly chaotic. Architectural measurements make for dull reading, perhaps, but (contrary to the common critical judgment) these chapters represent no diminution of the prophet's inspiration.[37] For after the Temple court and its storerooms have all been measured, the "man" in the vision moves on to show Ezekiel that God's (re)ordering of the world finally escapes all reckoning. In what some believe to be the last words Ezekiel himself

---

35. *Biblical Theology of the Old and New Testaments,* 19-20.

36. See my discussion in *Swallowing the Scroll,* 120-25.

37. In a brief but helpful comment, Walter Wink speaks of "numbering" as an aspect of revelation (*Unmasking the Powers* [Philadelphia: Fortress, 1986], 138).

wrote (47:1-12),[38] the vision culminates with the river that gushes out from the south wall of the Temple and quickly swells beyond measuring, tumbling into the "eastern region," where it miraculously fills the Dead Sea with life in a way beyond comprehending.

38. Walther Eichrodt comments that 47:1-12 "agrees . . . strikingly with the former description given by the prophet of the miraculous change in Israel's fortunes, and brings it to a conclusion . . . characteristic of him" (*Ezekiel*, 582). By contrast, he considers 47:13–48:35 loosely linked with the preceding sections (591). Georg Fohrer likewise assigns this section to the original "account of an ecstatic experience" and sees 47:12b, 14, 21-23 and 48:1-35 as coming from another hand (*Die Hauptprobleme des Buches Ezechiel* [Berlin: Töpelmann, 1952], 97-100). Zimmerli reads 47:12b as the "resounding conclusion" of an early version of the visionary description, possibly originating with the prophet himself (*Ezekiel*, II, 549).

Swimming with the Divine Tide:
An Ignatian Reading of 1 Samuel

Claire Mathews McGinnis

I. Introduction

In his *Introduction to the Old Testament as Scripture* Brevard Childs notes that his approach to the canon of the Old Testament is wrongly conceived of as simply "another historical critical technique" (and hence, as "canonical criticism"). "Rather," he observes, "the issue at stake in relation to the canon turns on establishing a stance from which the Bible can be read as sacred scripture."[1] While by no means ignoring the gains of the various forms of historical criticism — indeed, a recognition of "the depth dimension" of the biblical texts seems integral to his approach — Childs observes that his concern with canon relativizes "the claims to priority of the historical critical method." He continues, "It strongly resists the assumption that every biblical text has first to be filtered through a set historical critical mesh before one can even start the task of interpretation."[2] In this regard, Childs's approach in his *Introduction* exhibits passing similarities with literary-critical approaches. These generally also focus on the text as presented to us, rather than on the text's literary prehistory, although, as Childs notes, there are also significant differences. He argues, for instance, that "the canonical approach differs from a strictly literary approach by in-

---

1. Brevard S. Childs, *Introduction to the Old Testament as Scripture* (Philadelphia: Fortress, 1979) 82.
2. *Introduction*, 83.

terpreting the biblical text in relation to a community of faith and practice for whom it served a particular theological role as possessing divine authority." The "community of faith and practice" referred to seems primarily to be that of the historical Israel responsible for shaping the biblical texts in the light of her own experiences.[3] It might also be extended, however, in some sense to include the Christian community, for "by accepting the scriptures as normative for the obedient life of the church," Childs acknowledges, "the Old Testament theologian takes his stance within the circle of tradition, and thus identifies himself with Israel as the community of faith. Moreover, he shares in that hermeneutical process of which the canon is a testimony, as the people of God struggle to discern the will of God in all its historical particularity."[4] In further discussion of the relationship of his project to that of the literary critic, Childs suggests that theological, rather than literary, objectives often took primacy in the shaping of biblical texts, such that in some cases "the original poetic forms were lost, or a unified narrative badly shattered." Such a judgment about the process of the text's formation finds its correlate at the interpretive end of his undertaking: the canonical approach, as opposed to the literary one, "is concerned to understand the nature of the theological shape of the text rather than to recover an original literary or aesthetic unity."[5]

In *Reading in Communion* Stephen E. Fowl and L. Gregory Jones address the variety of approaches toward biblical interpretation in terms of *communities of interpretation* and of *interpretive interests*.[6] Such an approach acknowledges the existence of multiple approaches, but avoids the error of having to claim that one, and only one, of those approaches is "correct." Fowl and Jones observe that the interpretive interest that one pursues is largely determined by one's particular social context (a community of interpretation). Thus, they argue,

> ... the question of which interpretive interest to adopt in any specific situation is quite different when asked about a Christian community's interpretation of its Scriptures than of a university department's or professional

---

3. See, for instance, his discussion in *Old Testament Theology in a Canonical Context* (Philadelphia: Fortress, 1986), 11.

4. *Old Testament Theology,* 15.

5. *Introduction,* 74.

6. Stephen E. Fowl and L. Gregory Jones, *Reading in Communion: Scripture and Ethics in Christian Life* (Grand Rapids: Eerdmans, 1991) 4-21. The authors note that the expression "interpretive interests" is borrowed from Jeffrey Stout's essay, "What Is the Meaning of a Text?" *New Literary History* 14 (1982) 1-11.

society's interpretation of the Bible. This is primarily because Christian communities already stand in a particular relationship to the Bible. For the university department or the professional society, the Bible is simply one of the texts on which scholars might exercise their interpretive interests. But the Bible constitutes the authoritative Scripture of Christian communities, and this makes a decisive difference. The life of Christian communities is to be formed and regulated by the interpretation of Scriptures. . . .[7]

Later they continue,

> Scripture not only shapes the political contexts of faithful interpretation, it also tells us who God is and how we ought to live in relation to that God. *Christian communities interpret Scripture, then, so that believers might live faithfully before God in the light of Jesus Christ. The aim of faithful living before the Triune God becomes the standard to which all interpretive interests must measure up.*[8]

Although Childs does not speak specifically of *communities of interpretation* or of *interpretive interests,* the stance of Fowl and Jones — that "Christian communities interpret Scripture . . . so that believers might live faithfully before God in the light of Jesus Christ" — is present at least implicitly in both of Childs's works cited above. For while, again, he neither abandons nor decries historical-critical methodologies, Childs acknowledges that the primacy of such approaches is in large part responsible for "the failure of biblical specialists to render [the Old Testament] in such a way which is not theologically mute."[9] In other words, while critical approaches are instrumental in revealing the complex history of the biblical texts' formation, Christian interpretation cannot be satisfied with an interpretive approach that only asks the questions, and achieves the results, of such critical methodology but fails to engage the texts theologically.

One thing that literary-critical approaches to the Bible have helped recover for us is a sensitivity to its literature characteristic of those so-called "precritical" readers. The acuity — and cleverness — of those engaged in literary readings have helped unearth the complexity of the texts as communicative documents, a feature obscured by other modern approaches. And yet many of these readings seem to go self-consciously against the grain of the literature, refusing, as a matter of principle, to be

7. *Reading in Communion,* 19.
8. *Reading in Communion,* 20, emphasis added.
9. *Old Testament Theology,* 17.

persuaded by the perspective of the text.[10] Granted, all reading is a form of dialogue, of give and take. As Childs has observed, "the theological enterprise" (like any reading of an ancient text) "involves a construal by the modern interpreter, whose stance to the text affects its meaning." But as Childs also observes, the appropriate stance for a Christian engaged in a theological reading is the "faithful disposition" of one "who await[s] the illumination of God's Spirit."[11] The illumination of God's Spirit will certainly lead one to insights about the text deeper than, and could conceivably lead one to a reading that seems contrary to, that which is on the surface. Yet if one places oneself within a community that claims the Bible as sacred Scripture, as Scripture by which one's character and life are to be shaped, then it would seem that an appropriate reading stance would be one that takes seriously the theocentric perspective that the text seeks to inculcate and so to be willingly seduced, through the text as a vehicle of revelation, by the loving and mysterious Holy One of Israel.

The present study is a theological exegesis of 1 Samuel that takes seriously Fowl and Jones's claim that the standard for interpretive interests in the context, and in the service of, Christian communities, is "the aim of

---

10. A good example of this phenomenon is David J. A. Clines, "Metacommentating Amos" in *Of Prophets' Visions and the Wisdom of Sages: Essays in Honour of R. Norman Whybray on his Seventieth Birthday,* ed. Heather A. McKay and David J. A. Clines (*JSOT* Supplement Series 162; Sheffield: JSOT, 1993) 142-60. In "metacommentating" Amos, Clines observes "some of the things commentators do." "First, they adopt the view of the text regarding the social and economic situation in ancient Israel. Secondly, they adopt the ideology of the text regarding the existence of God and the authenticity of the prophetic vocation." In contrast, after reading Amos's indictment against the rich in 6:4-7 Clines asks, "What exactly is the crime of these Samaritans for which they are being threatened with exile? Is there some sin in having expensive ivory inlays on your bedframe? . . . And as for singing idle songs, who among the readers of Amos can cast a stone? Has karaoke suddenly become a sin, as well as a social disease? . . . Does being wealthy and conspicuously consuming renewable natural resources (wine, oil, mutton and elephant tusks) put you in line for exile, by any reasonable standards? What are the rich supposed to have been doing? If expensive oil is on sale in the market and you have the money in your pocket to buy it, where is the sin?" (144-46).

Just as one might question whether a text can have an ideology or even a meaning (see Stephen Fowl, "Texts Don't Have Ideologies," *Biblical Interpretation* 3 [1995] 15-34) so one might also ask whether texts can rightly be said to have perspectives. That they can, I think, is well illustrated by the example from Amos given above. Few would disagree that the reader is meant to identify with Amos's perspective regarding the Israelites' actions and that Clines's questions constitute a reading that decidedly — and self-consciously — goes against the grain.

11. *Old Testament Theology,* 12.

faithful living before the Triune God." In one sense, my reading of Samuel is akin to works like Gregory of Nyssa's *Life of Moses* that see in biblical characters models for our own "spiritual ascent."[12] But while Gregory in his day could freely move between the historical and spiritual senses of the text, my approach is much more modern (and perhaps mundane). It might best be described as a cross between literary and canonical approaches, one that is concerned with character-building in both its literary and its moral senses. I am not as interested in analyzing the admittedly many layers of this complex text as in letting the story in its present, or final, form communicate something of and about Israel's God, whom Christians also worship, and, more particularly, about how one might draw near to that Holy One.

I have described the present study as an "Ignatian reading" of the book of 1 Samuel because it grows out of an insight that arose while working through Ignatius of Loyola's *Spiritual Exercises* and teaching the books of Samuel in the same semester. It builds on Childs's delineation of the canonical shape of 1 and 2 Samuel, but also uses Ignatius's observations about discernment as its starting point. As Childs himself has acknowledged, "By placing the canonical text within the context of the community of faith and practice a variety of different exegetical models are freed to engage the text."[13]

In writing this piece I recalled one of Childs's lines famous among the students in his Introduction to Old Testament class at Yale Divinity School: "If you want to become a better exegete, become a deeper person." This line always brought a spontaneous laughter of recognition. The statement seemed so characteristic of the teacher we had come to know and love: deceptively simple, behind it a staggering grasp of the complexity of the issues, inspiring us toward excellence and awakening humility, all at the same time. While this work will undoubtedly fall short of the depth worthy of our illustrious teacher, I hope that at the very least it will serve as an example of how a potentially mute text might be made to speak when read within the context of a particular community of faith and practice; at most, I hope that it might inspire readers toward patient discernment of God's will in their own lives.

12. Gregory uses Moses' ascent of Mount Sinai as a starting point for discussing the Christian's eternal progress toward God. See Gregory of Nyssa, *The Life of Moses*, tr. Abraham J. Malherbe and Everett Ferguson (New York: Paulist, 1978).
13. *Introduction*, 83.

II. Indifference and Discernment

In *The Spiritual Exercises,* Ignatius of Loyola promotes a certain "indifference" to the things of this world. Such a stance might suggest a negative evaluation of the created order, or a position of neutrality at best. But for Ignatius, it is the contrary. Indifference does not stem from ambivalence toward creation; rather, the very goodness of creation requires it. Humankind is created "to praise, reverence, and serve God our Lord." The "other things on the face of the earth" are intended to help us toward this end. Inasmuch as they do so, they are to be embraced. Inasmuch as they hinder us, they are to be cast off. Indifference is to be cultivated in order to determine when the former is the case, and when the latter. Writes Ignatius:

> God freely created us so that we might know, love, and serve him in this life and be happy with him forever. God's purpose in creating us is to draw forth from us a response of love and service here on earth, so that we may attain our goal of everlasting happiness with him in heaven.
>
> All the things in this world are gifts of God, created for us, to be the means by which we can come to know him better, love him more surely, and serve him more faithfully.
>
> As a result, we ought to appreciate and use these gifts of God insofar as they help us toward our goal of loving service and union with God. But *insofar as any created things hinder our progress toward our goal, we ought to let them go* [emphasis added].

Ignatius recognizes that, when faced with a choice, it may not immediately be clear whether an option will help or hinder progress toward our goal. It is in such a situation that he counsels indifference.

> In everyday life, then, we should keep ourselves indifferent or undecided in the face of all created gifts when we have an option and we do not have the clarity of what would be a better choice. We ought not to be led on by our natural likes and dislikes even in matters such as health or sickness, wealth or poverty, between living in the east or in the west, becoming an accountant or a lawyer.
>
> Rather, our only desire and our one choice should be that option which better leads us to the goal for which God created us.[14]

14. David L. Fleming, S.J., *The Spiritual Exercises of Saint Ignatius: A Literal Translation and a Contemporary Reading* (Saint Louis: Institute of Jesuit Sources, 1978) 23. This quotation offers Fleming's contemporary reading of the Principle and Foundation. The original text (as translated from the Spanish by Elder Mullen, S.J.) reads (p. 22):

It is clear from this passage that when Ignatius speaks of the ". . . things on the face of this earth" he is referring not only to material possessions that one might have and hold, but to one's commitments as well. Further, he is quite plainly not seeking to cultivate in his students an attitude of perpetual indifference, or of freedom from engagement in an active life. Indifference is beneficial only for the purposes of discernment, the clarification of choices. It is a guard against confusing our "natural likes and dislikes" with the purposes of God.

Nowhere is the complex entanglement of divine and human intention to which the *Spiritual Exercises* alludes more vividly portrayed than in the books of Samuel. The narrative is uncompromising in its calibration of events according to the unbending measures of human devotion or disobedience on the one hand, and of divine providence and punishment on the other. At the same time, however, one encounters here the fullest exploration of human psychology in all of biblical literature. The convergence of what Robert Alter calls the "theological" and the "psychological" axes of the story is especially noteworthy in the portrayal of David and Saul.[15]

In 1 Samuel 8 Israel's request for a king is portrayed as a rejection of God's leadership over them. This perspective is made plain by YHWH's direct statement to that effect:

> And the LORD said to Samuel, "Listen to the voice of the people in all that they say to you. . . . It is not you that they have rejected; they have rejected me as king over them. They are acting just as they have from the day I brought them up out of Egypt to this day . . ." (1 Sam 8:7-8).

It is also intimated by the people's own insistence that they "are determined to have a king over us, *so that we may also be like other nations . . .*" (8:19-20 NRSV, emphasis added). As a people bound by covenant to YHWH, "like

---

Man is created to praise, reverence, and serve God our Lord, and by this means to save his soul.

And the other things on the face of the earth are created for man and that they may help in him prosecuting the end for which he is created.

From this it follows that man is to use them as much as they help him on to his end, and ought to rid himself of them so far as they hinder him as to it.

For this it is necessary to make ourselves indifferent to all created things in all that is allowed to the choice of our free will and is not prohibited to it; so that, on our part, we want not health rather than sickness, riches rather than poverty, honor rather than dishonor, long rather than short life, and so in all the rest; desiring and choosing only what is most conducive for us to the end for which we are created.

15. Robert Alter, *The Art of Biblical Narrative* (New York: Basic, 1981) 140.

other nations" is something Israel is decidedly not — or ought not be. Thus, from the perspective of 1 Samuel 8, the people's request for a king and YHWH's concession to that demand can come to no good. Or so it would seem. In chs. 9–10 however, a combination of "coincidence" and prophetic inspiration bring Samuel and Saul together for Saul's anointing. It is clear that YHWH has both handpicked Saul for the task and ensured his selection. Saul's description in the beginning of ch. 9 is auspicious: "There was not a man among the people of Israel more handsome than he; he stood head and shoulders above everyone else" (9:2 NRSV). And later, after Samuel anoints Saul in private, the prophet describes to him the three signs that will befall him on the way home, instructing, "when these signs happen to you, do whatever you see fit, for God is with you" (10:7). Saul's selection as king is confirmed by lot in the presence of all the tribes of Israel (10:20-24), and in ch. 11 he proves himself a fit military leader by rallying the Israelites to the defense of Jabesh-Gilead against the Ammonites.

No sooner is Saul's kingship established, however, than he is rejected by God in favor of a man whom the Lord has sought "after his own heart" (13:14), one who is also described as a man "better than" Saul (15:28). From the moment of this judgment, the comparison between Saul and David and the bestowal, or withholding, of God's favor on the men are central to the narrative in numerous ways. They are, in fact, the driving force of the plot from ch. 16 to Saul's death in ch. 31, reinforced in both conversation and episodic contrast. The transference of the kingdom from Saul to David, though inevitable, does not come easily. The tortured trail of their interaction crosses a literary expanse proportionate to the amount of actual physical territory covered in Saul's relentless pursuit of his rival. The portrait of David that emerges in these narratives in many respects shows him, indeed, to be "a better man than his neighbor," Saul.

The issue at stake in both stories recounting Saul's rejection as king is Saul's disobedience. David, for his part, is also not without sin. Indeed, the account of David's reign in 2 Samuel is organized into two major sections: "David under the Blessing" (chs. 2–5) and "David under the Curse" (chs. 9–24).[16] But while in the latter section David's sins do not go unpunished, "in the end the messianic promise to his house remains unchanged in force."[17] Indeed, the election of David's house, alluded to in Hannah's song (1 Samuel

---

16. This division, adopted by Childs, is originally that of R. A. Carlson, *David, the Chosen King: A Traditio-Historical Approach to the Second Book of Samuel*, tr. Eric J. Sharpe and Stanley Rudman (Stockholm: Almqvist & Wiksell, 1964).

17. Childs, *Introduction*, 276.

2) and reaffirmed in David's (2 Samuel 22), is one of the wonderful divine mysteries celebrated by the books.

Unlike David's, Saul's reign is seen as a false start.[18] Saul is not rejected by God as king for naught, and as for David, God will have mercy on whom he has mercy. Nonetheless, the reader may be troubled by God's differing response to the two men, which, if not arbitrary, may seem at least inconsistent. That such a reaction might not be inappropriate is affirmed, it would seem, by the fact that even Samuel, twice having pronounced the sentence, grieves over Saul (1 Sam. 16:1). And notwithstanding God's freedom to act in history according to divine, and not human, purposes and ways, that God's differing response to the men's transgressions may have something to do with their character is hinted at in the description of David as "better" than Saul. I contend that Ignatius's perception about the relationship between indifference and discernment helps illuminate a feature of the portrayal of Saul and David in 1 Samuel and offers insight into the ways in which David, but not Saul, is portrayed as a man after God's own heart (13:14).

Discernment of God's will is a central issue in 1-2 Samuel, both for the individual and Israel as a people. While the Israelites had access to a variety of means for discernment not ordinarily available to the modern devotee — for example the urim and thummim, the lot, and the prophet — this does not mean that discernment of the divine will was any less problematic. The variety of channels for divine-human communication illustrate just how much this was a concern and a problem for our predecessors. However, the main actors in the story of 1-2 Samuel are portrayed at times as having to make choices — often in crisis situations — without the assistance or luxury of these formal means of discernment. Furthermore, knowing the divine will is not always tantamount to choosing it. Indifference not only plays a role in discerning the good, but in choosing it as well. An inordinate attachment to one option over another may cloud one's judgment and influence one's action. In what follows I will argue that one feature of the comparison between Saul and David realized by the first book of Samuel involves the characters' ability to achieve indifference with regard to their own aspirations and fears, in order to discern the direction of divine activity.[19] I will show that, while

18. Childs, *Introduction*, 277.
19. I focus primarily on 1 Samuel because it is here that the contrast between Saul and David is an explicit concern. I will point, however, to episodes in 2 Samuel that confirm the aspect of David's characterization under discussion. Admittedly, the characterization of David is complicated by episodes recounted in the second book. I would argue, however, that this further unfolding of David's character does not negate the portrait in

Saul, from the beginning, seems to be perpetually swimming counter to the divine tide, David, especially in 1 Samuel, exhibits an adeptness at discerning the direction of God's movement in history. This quality not only keeps him from sin on several occasions, but also enables him to place himself in the stream of divine activity in such a way that he is carried along by it.

III. Saul's Misstep at Gilgal

1 Samuel offers two accounts of Saul's rejection as king by YHWH (chs. 13 and 15). In both cases Saul's disobedience is the focus of, and grounds for, his rejection. Yet the stories also reveal other aspects of Saul's character, his fears and attachments, for instance, which contribute to his failure to understand and perform the divine will. During Saul's initial encounter with Samuel, he receives instructions to go ahead of Samuel to Gilgal, where the prophet will meet him and will offer burnt offerings and sacrifices of well-being. Samuel impresses upon Saul, "Seven days you shall wait, until I come to you and make known to you what you should do" (10:8). However in ch. 13 Saul takes it upon himself to make the offerings when he finds that Samuel does not show. In the text's present arrangement, much intervenes between this episode in ch. 13 and Samuel's original instructions at 10:8, including a trip by Samuel, Saul, and all the people to Gilgal to renew the kingship (11:14-15). Thus, it is not wholly clear that Saul and Samuel's rendezvous at Gilgal in ch. 13 is that to which Samuel alluded at 10:8. The mention of Saul's having waited "seven days, the time appointed by Samuel" suggests, however, that this is the case.

The account opens with the narrator's simple statement of facts:

> [Saul] waited seven days, the time appointed by Samuel,[20] but Samuel did not come to Gilgal, and the people slipped away from him. Saul said, "Bring the burnt offering and the offerings of well-being to me," and he offered the burnt offering. As soon as he had finished offering the burnt offering, Samuel arrived, and Saul went out to meet him and salute him. (13:8-11 NRSV)

Samuel's immediate question, "What have you done?" provides an opportunity for Saul's re-presentation of events. Saul's answer begins with his obser-

---

1 Samuel, which, I am arguing, seems to be addressing in part the reasons for the election of David's house over that of Saul.

20. Or "until the time Samuel had stipulated." So, P. Kyle McCarter, Jr., *1 Samuel* (Anchor Bible Commentary; Garden City: Doubleday, 1980) 224.

vation of the circumstances: ". . . I saw that the people were slipping away from me, and that you did not come within the days appointed, and that the Philistines were gathered at Michmash . . ." (13:11). After describing the circumstances, Saul explains his thought process: "I said to myself, 'Now the Philistines will come down upon me at Gilgal, and I have not entreated the favor of the Lord'; so I forced myself, and offered the burnt offering" (13:12 NRSV). Saul's account reverses the order of the narrator's chronological description of events, placing first, rather than last, the observation that the people were "slipping away" from him, and thereby confirming what the chronological account had suggested in its own way: that the people were slipping away from Saul was one of the factors, if not the most determining factor, that drove him to the first of his "rash" acts.[21] Yet Saul offers a seemingly pious account of his actions. He recognizes his need for the Lord's favor to gain victory over the Philistines, and presents himself as concerned about properly complying with the requirements of devotion.

Samuel's interpretation of Saul's actions, on the other hand, paints quite a different picture of Saul. His prophetic pronouncement emphasizes Saul's disobedience, and its consequences:

> You have done foolishly; you have not kept the commandment of the LORD your God, which he commanded you. The LORD would have established your kingdom over Israel forever, but now your kingdom will not continue; the LORD has sought out a man after his own heart; and the LORD has appointed him to be ruler over his people, because you have not kept what the LORD commanded you (13:13-14 NRSV).[22]

The severity of the military threat confronting the Israelites in this episode, the chaos of the moment and the Israelites' panic help set the stage for Saul's actions. The suspense is tangible, and the reader, who feels Saul's predicament intuitively, is tempted to empathize with Saul's decision to proceed with the offerings sans Samuel. But Samuel's evaluation of the situation admits of no sympathy. And however much the reader may be tempted to view Saul's transgression sympathetically in light of the mitigating circumstances, Samuel's evaluation of Saul's action is to be seen as the most authentic, for, as

21. See discussion of 1 Samuel 14, with its mention of Saul's "rash act," below.
22. McCarter translates, "If you were careful of the appointment that Yahweh, your God, gave you, then [he] would have established your kingship over Israel forever" noting that the charge against Saul ". . . delicately balances the two ideas: Saul did not keep the appointment (with Samuel), and so also he did not carefully execute his appointment (as king) (1 Samuel, 224-25 and notes, p. 228).

the Lord's prophet, his voice has proven itself trustworthy. "Not a word of his falls to the ground" (3:19).[23]

In *The Fate of King Saul,* David Gunn discusses at some length the nature of Saul's transgression. As he observes, the history of exegesis exhibits some debate among interpreters over whether "the command of the Lord" referred to in Samuel's judgment refers to Samuel's instructions in ch. 10 or "to some *general* law which Saul has broken by himself offering the sacrifice, the most likely being a law which prohibited any but a priest from officiating at the sacrifice."[24] Since no such law is clearly attested in biblical literature (other than in 2 Chron. 26:16-21, a much later source) Gunn concludes, rightly in my opinion, that "the command of the Lord" must refer to that given through the prophet. The problem with this, Gunn notes, is that Saul is said to have waited the requisite seven days (13:8) as Saul's protestation in v. 11 also attests. Yet Samuel accuses him of *not* having kept the command. Gunn proposes the following solution. The heart of Samuel's instruction is not the seven days, which is itself "merely an approximate indication of time that Saul should allow to elapse before expecting Samuel," but that Saul should wait (about seven days) *until Samuel comes* (39). In other words, "the instruction 'to wait' is ambiguous with regard to time" (39). While Saul sees himself as having dutifully waited the requisite number of days, according to Samuel's interpretation of the commandment Saul "should have waited [longer than seven days if necessary] until the prophet came and issued further instructions" (39). In other words, "the instruction can be seen both ways, but Yahweh, through Samuel, requires of Saul 'this' rather than 'that' interpretation" (40).

Gunn's solution is undeniably clever. He does not attempt to diffuse the quite troubling nature of Saul's predicament and of Yahweh's judgment. In fact, his larger argument magnifies it. For, he contends, God *chooses* to find Saul guilty when such an outcome is not necessarily inevitable. God is initially openly hostile or at least reluctantly acquiescent toward the people's request for a king, Gunn asserts. Saul is kingship's scapegoat, and therefore, Yahweh is predisposed to reject him as king (115-25). For this reason he "requires of Saul 'this' rather than 'that' interpretation" of the command.

Without denying the presence of a "dark side" to God, which Gunn defends, I do take issue with his conclusions concerning 1 Samuel 13's depic-

23. For a very different view of Samuel and of Saul, see Robert Polzin, *Samuel and the Deuteronomist: A Literary Study of the Deuteronomic History: 1 Samuel* (San Francisco: Harper and Row, 1989) 127-31.

24. David M. Gunn, *The Fate of King Saul: An Interpretation of a Biblical Story* (*JSOT* Supplement Series 14; Sheffield: JSOT, 1980) 34.

tion of God. The prophet's command to Saul is not in itself ambiguous, or would not have been had Samuel appeared on the seventh day. The ambiguity arises only when the seven days stipulated pass and the prophet does not appear. Saul's dilemma in such a circumstance is precisely the kind that requires a special kind of discernment — a moment of crisis when one's usual guides and landmarks fail, when one does not know whether to turn to the left or the right, to act, or to refrain from acting. According to Gunn's reasoning, had Saul refrained from acting, Yahweh and Samuel would have opted for precisely the opposite interpretation of the command. At the end of his study Gunn guards against reading the Bible in terms of an "optimistic God," a God who is the embodiment of the all-good, the all-just (131). But is viewing God's rejection of Saul as justifiable necessarily to take such an optimistic view? Is finding fault in Saul to be untrue to the text, as Gunn implies? On the contrary, I would argue that to read the Bible *as scripture,* that is, as literature shaped and received as an authoritative witness to a living God by a community of faith and practice, is to affirm the reliability of the character of God (in both senses) in spite of that which remains mysterious or dark. Perhaps that we as readers find ourselves so sympathetic to Saul here serves as commentary on our own capacity for patient obedience in the face of overwhelming insecurity.

If one assumes the reliability of the character of God, then one must do likewise for the prophet who speaks God's word. Given Samuel's incontrovertible analysis of Saul's transgression at 13:13-14, Saul shows himself to be a man who does not fully grasp what it is that the Lord requires of him. What was called for was strict obedience — to wait the seven days *and* for Samuel to come. And in such a situation, obedience required of him a deep trust, trust in the face of the mounting threat of the Philistines and the rapid unraveling of his own forces. Instead of an obedience founded on trust, Saul operates with an almost magical view of divine response: "the Philistines will come to me at Gilgal and I have not entreated the favor of the Lord (13:12)."[25]

---

25. Peter Miscall takes a very different approach to this passage, one which, nonetheless, is consistent with my argument concerning the problem of discernment. In *1 Samuel: A Literary Reading* (Indiana Studies in Biblical Literature; Bloomington: Indiana University Press, 1986) 87, Miscall argues that

Saul's foolhardiness . . . has nothing to do with sacrificing, since it is the product of his overall understanding of the situation and how he should respond to it. The commandment is not in Samuel's assertion in 1 Sam. 10:8, but in his statement in 1 Sam. 10:7 — "When these signs come true, do whatever your hand finds to do,

IV. Saul's Rejection Confirmed

Saul's misguided predilection for sacrifice over obedience is revealed much less ambiguously in the second account of his rejection as king. Indeed, while this second account seems superfluous, even jarring, to the modern reader, who will wonder how and why God would reject Saul's kingship a second time, as we shall see, the second account actually serves to resolve and clarify ambiguities of the first.

In contrast to the first story of Saul's rejection, with its tenuous relationship to the earlier command in 10:8, the account of Saul's rejection in ch. 15 opens with an explicit command to Saul to attack and utterly destroy the Amalekites and all that belong to them (ארנ־עמלק והחרמתם אנ־כלא רלו לך והכיתח, 15:3). These instructions are reinforced and clarified with the attendant warning, "Do not spare them." The totality of the destruction enjoined is further reinforced by a series of merisms: "You shall kill man and woman, child and infant, ox and sheep, camel and donkey" (15:3). The narrator's account of Saul's actions in v. 8 observes that Saul seizes Agag, king of the Amalekites, alive, although he utterly destroys the rest of the Amalekites by sword. While it is clear that Saul has at least partially fulfilled the mission, his ultimate intentions concerning the fate of Agag are unclear. The narrator's subsequent statements cast further doubt on Saul's motivations.

> Saul and the people spared Agag and the best of the sheep and of the cattle — the fat ones and the young — all that was of value.[26] *They were not willing to destroy them. But all that was despised and worthless, those things they destroyed.* (15:9, emphasis added)

Although in later conversation Saul will attempt to lay blame solely on the people, the narrator's account identifies Saul as the primary subject in the act of sparing. Further, the emphatic construction of the narration with its isolation of what Saul and the people were, and were not, willing to spare ("But

---

for God is with you" — and in the Lord's commission to Samuel in 1 Sam. 9:16 — "He will save my people from the hand of the Philistines. . . ."

Samuel simply cannot believe that Saul is still at Gilgal preparing burnt offerings rather than engaging in full battle with the Philistines. Saul had blundered and revealed himself as unfit, because he does not act on his own as king (1 Sam. 10:17); he assumes that Samuel has told him exactly what to do and that he must do it without question. He arrives at the wrong word of the Lord in his interpretation . . .

26. " — the fat ones and the young — " (so McCarter, *1 Samuel*, 258).

all that was despised and worthless, those things they destroyed") suggests that their transgression has been motivated by greed.

Saul's guilt, suggested in the contrasting accounts of the command (ולא תחמל, v. 3) and event (ויחמל אול v. 9), is confirmed by God's change of heart and description of Saul's actions in his address to Samuel: "I regret that I made Saul king, for he has turned back from following me, and has not carried out my commands" (15:11 NRSV). But when Samuel comes to meet Saul, Saul greets him with a self-evaluation directly counter to YHWH's evaluation of Saul: "I have carried out the Lord's command" (15:13). Samuel protests: "What then is this bleating of sheep in my ears, and the lowing of cattle that I hear?" (15:4 RSV). In his response to Samuel's question, Saul's account differs from the earlier account of the narrator in that he ascribes sole responsibility to the people for sparing the animals, albeit for pious reasons: "They have brought from the Amalekites that which the people spared from among the best of the sheep and cattle in order to sacrifice to the Lord your God" (15:15). Saul does include himself, however, in recounting the actions that did fulfill the Lord's command: "*They* have brought . . . that which the people spared . . . but the remainder *we* destroyed" (15:15, emphasis added). Further contrasting evaluations of Saul's behavior are presented in the ensuing dialogue. Samuel asks, "Why did you not obey the voice of YHWH?" (15:19). Saul replies: "I did heed the voice of YHWH" (15:20). He continues,

> I have gone on the mission on which the Lord sent me, I brought Agag the king of Amalek and I have utterly destroyed the Amalekites. But from the spoil the people took sheep and cattle, the best of the things devoted to destruction, to sacrifice to the LORD your God at Gilgal (15:20-21 NRSV).

Saul's insistence that he has obeyed the command of YHWH need not be taken as disingenuous. Samuel points to the presence of sheep and cattle, which, as we have seen, have at least a plausibly pious explanation. But it is Saul who mentions Agag. If Saul were genuinely attempting to deceive Samuel, it is unlikely he would have lain on the table the less controversial piece of evidence (although there is a certain rationale to lying boldly). Rather, it seems that at this point Saul genuinely persists in the belief in his own innocence. Not until Samuel's prophetic and poetic decree does the intent of the divine command begin to dawn on him. Samuel states, "Has the LORD as great delight in burnt offerings and sacrifices as in obeying the voice of the LORD? Surely to obey is better than sacrifice, and to heed than the fat of rams" (15:22 NRSV). This speech brings Saul to a confession. "I have sinned;

for I have transgressed the commandment of the LORD and your words, because I feared the people and obeyed their voice" (15:24 NRSV).[27] One reading of Saul's intentions would be that, while he is aware of the ways in which he has deviated from the divine command, he attempts to convince Samuel otherwise, confessing the truth only after he sees that Samuel will not be fooled. But does Saul really think he can fool the prophet? A more plausible reading is that Saul really thinks he has fulfilled the spirit, if not the letter, of YHWH's command. It is not until confronted with Samuel's prophetic indictment that Saul becomes aware that he has failed to keep God's command, and that he becomes conscious of his own motivation.

"I have transgressed the commandment of the Lord and your words, *because I feared the people and obeyed their voice*" (15:24, emphasis added). As in the story recounted in ch. 13, here execution of the divine decree requires of Saul a deep trust in YHWH in the face of pressures to act otherwise from the very people he has been anointed to lead. Required of him is a trust that all will be well with him if he fulfills the Lord's command. And even more is demanded; obedience requires a willingness to fulfill God's command even if the results are contrary to Saul's own desires. While Saul's kingship is appointed by YHWH, the people's confidence and assent is necessary for the effective exercise of the office. Given that in ch. 15 Saul has no reason to fear for his life, his self-professed fear must have more to do with his concern that the people will "slip away" from him than anything else. In other words, Saul's fear of the people reflects his own attachment to the office of kingship, despite his initial ambivalence toward the role.

27. Continuing the argument begun in his analysis of ch. 13, Gunn argues that in this case as well Saul's disobedience is merely a matter of competing interpretations. Nothing in Saul's instructions, he argues, details the circumstances of the destruction enjoined. Thus Saul and the people consider bringing the best animals back to sacrifice (זבח) them as one way of devoting them to destruction (חרם). Yahweh and the prophet, Gunn argues, choose to interpret the instructions otherwise; Saul should have killed Agag and all living things on the spot (41-56). Gunn tries to mitigate the effect of Saul's confession by stressing the fact that in this instance "fear" probably means "respect" or "honor" rather than "terror." His paraphrase of Saul's confession reads as such: "my action in going along with the people's wish has turned out to be tantamount to honoring *them* instead of Yahweh, obeying *their* voice instead of his commandments" (53). Saul's statement of "fear" is probably intended to include both honor and fear in the more normal sense. At any rate, it is unclear how Gunn's paraphrase of Saul's confession makes his offense any less an offense.

Interestingly, Gunn does not discuss the wording of 15:9, "they were not willing to destroy them" (ולא אבו החרימם) which seems to suggest that Saul's motives were not as pure as Gunn would have us believe.

Put differently, in 1 Samuel 15 we are confronted with the portrait of a Saul who lacks the most basic discernment of YHWH's will. A command that, to the reader, is lacking in all ambiguity — "Go and attack Amalek, and utterly destroy all that they have; do not spare them, but kill both man and woman, child and infant, ox and sheep, camel and donkey" — is less than clear to the king of Israel. Saul, on whose ears fall the same words as those on the readers', hears them differently. If Saul's confession is to be trusted, his failure to perceive God's clearly-stated will results from his lack of indifference, to use Ignatius's word, toward the pressures of the people he rules and ultimately, toward the kingship — his inability, again to use Ignatius's words, to "let them go."

V. Saul's Failings Confirmed

As noted earlier, that 1 Samuel contains two stories of Saul's rejection as king appears, initially, as curiously redundant. In fact ch. 15 addresses and resolves several of the problematic aspects of ch. 13's account. The command that Saul fails to keep in ch. 13 is apparently that given through Samuel in 10:8. That several episodes intervene between the command and Saul's transgression of it at Gilgal, including an episode that also takes place in Gilgal, creates some ambiguity. Further, Samuel's command is that Saul wait for him in Gilgal seven days. 18:8 notes that Saul "waited seven days, the time appointed by Samuel"; it does not say however, whether Saul takes it upon himself to make the offerings at the beginning or the end of, or even after, the seventh day. Thus it is unclear to the reader whether, in Saul's mind, and in fact, Saul has fulfilled the minimum requirement of the command, or whether, on the contrary, he has waited the full seven days and experiences what would appear to be legitimate confusion over how to proceed. If he had taken upon himself Samuel's prerogative to offer the offering *early* in the seventh day, then the fact that the people were slipping away from him would seem to be a much greater factor in influencing Saul's action than mere confusion over how to act when Samuel fails to show. It is precisely this ambiguity about whether Saul was acting from fear, or in good faith, that gives a reader the impression that it is not so much Saul's action as God's rejection of him that is premature in ch. 13.

Ch. 15's story, on the other hand, admits of no such ambiguity. The command given to Saul, and his failure to keep this command, are both incontrovertible. Another point clarified by the second of the two accounts is the nature of Saul's misstep. That which was implicit in ch. 13 is made explicit in Samuel's prophetic decree, namely, that Saul has mistakenly considered the offerings more important from the divine perspective than his obedience to YHWH's command ("Surely to obey is better than sacrifice, and to heed than the fat of rams," 15:22). Finally, while in ch. 13 it is clear that Saul has chosen the wrong path, his motivation is in question. As noted above, his decision to go ahead with the offerings before Samuel arrives might seem like an honest mistake, especially if one concludes that he has waited for Samuel the full seven days. But given that in his explanation of his actions, Saul reversed the narrator's chronological account of events and makes the people's slipping away primary on his list, one may conclude that Saul's real motive is his fear of losing the people, the battle, and his kingship. Fear is precisely the motive that Saul confesses to Samuel in 15:24. In this way ch. 15 not only clarifies and resolves the problematic issues of ch. 13, it also confirms our analysis of Saul's characterization in the earlier story, that his attachment to the kingship interferes with his ability to discern the divine will.

VI. Saul Misses the Mark Again

The placement of 1 Samuel 14 between the two rejection stories conveys a sense of the passage of time from one to the other, which helps mitigate the sense of redundancy produced by the doublet. At the same time, this passage contributes in important ways to the emerging portrait of Saul. Jonathan serves as a foil to Saul in this intervening account. His critique of Saul's oath and the contrast between Jonathan's willingness to follow YHWH's lead and his resultant success on the one hand and Saul's attempts to secure success through an oath and his impetuous decision to further pursue the Philistines on the other contribute to the portrait of Saul as a man who acts when he should refrain and who fails to act when commanded otherwise. A portrait, in short, of one who finds himself perpetually swimming against the divine tide.

In this story Saul "[lays] an oath on the troops" that they not eat before evening and before he has been avenged on his enemies. While taking an oath is not necessarily inadvisable, a carelessly formulated oath may inadvertently put others at risk, a fact to which Jephtha's daughter could also well testify (Judg. 11:34-40). Jonathan is off slaughtering the Philistines when Saul makes the oath. Indeed, it is Jonathan's initial success that initiates the momentum for Saul's subsequent victory (14:1-23). Following the account of Jonathan's victory, the narrator turns our attention back to Saul and the rest of the troops. The Israelite army comes upon a honeycomb dripping its sweet nectar on the ground and Jonathan, now reunited with the troops, takes a taste. When his transgression of the oath is made known to him, Jonathan voices his judgment of Saul's oath:

My father has troubled the land! See how my eyes brightened because I tasted a little of this honey. How much better if today the troops had eaten of their enemies' spoil which they found; for now the slaughter of the Philistines has not been great. (14:29-30)

In the Masoretic Text this account of events opens with the observation that "the men of Israel were hard pressed that day, for Saul had laid an oath on the people" (14:24). As an interpretive statement, this evaluation of Saul's action is only mildly negative and leaves room for interpreting Jonathan's assessment. When Jonathan declares that his father has "troubled the land," is he simply taking a defensive posture because of his own inadvertent transgression, or are we to grant some weight to his evaluation of his father's action? As the story unfolds, it is actually not the troops' hunger as much as Jonathan's transgression of the oath that keeps Saul from a relentless pursuit of the Philistines (14:36-46). And yet, Jonathan is not wholly off the mark in his negative evaluation. If not for the oath, Saul's pursuit of the Philistines might not have been aborted, and his victory would have been greater. Furthermore, it is because the troops are faint with hunger that they later slaughter animals from the spoil on the ground and eat them with the blood (14:31-35). In this way, Saul's oath leads the people to sin.

The Septuagint renders the opening line of this episode with an unmitigated critique of the oath: "Now Saul committed a rash act on that day." This states openly that which would otherwise only be implied in the story: the special measure Saul takes to ensure victory over the Philistines ultimately works against him; Saul's oath was a foolish undertaking.[28] When one approaches the story from this initially supplied perspective — that Saul committed a rash act on that day — then Jonathan's judgment of his father's oath is heard much less ambiguously. Indeed, his analysis concurs with the narrator. And that Jonathan has already been portrayed as responsible for setting in motion, with God's help, the day's victory offers further warrant for trusting the rightness of his view. While Jonathan describes his father as having troubled the land, by way of contrast, the people later proclaim Jonathan to have "worked with God today" (14:45 NRSV).

---

28. Even here, the description of Saul's action as rash leaves ambiguity, as the reader is left to wonder whether the rash act consists of the oath itself, Saul's willingness to kill Jonathan, his decision to pursue the Philistines without inquiring of God, or all of the above.

When Jonathan initially sets out against the Philistines, he expresses a confidence that the Lord will fight for him. "Come, let us go over to the garrison of these uncircumcised" he says to his armor-bearer. "It may be that the Lord will act for us; for nothing can hinder the Lord from gaining victory, whether by many or by few" (14:6). But his trust is tempered with humility. In his openness to the Lord's lead Jonathan devises the following scheme:

> Now we will cross over to those men and will show ourselves to them. If they say to us, "Wait until we come to you," then we will stand still in our place and we will not go up to them. But if they say, "come up to us," then we will go up; for the LORD has given them into our hand. That will be the sign for us. (14:8-10 NRSV)[29]

In this case also Jonathan's approach serves as a contrast to that of his father Saul, for later in the episode Saul would have pursued the Philistines headlong into the night — to disastrous effect — had the priest not restrained him with an insistence that they first inquire of the Lord concerning their plan. Thus one other thing that this mediating account suggests, consistent with the portrayal of Saul in the two rejection stories that surround it, is that while Saul is quick to make deals with God at the hardship of his troops and even, as it almost turned out, at the cost of his son's life, he is neither diligent nor adept at discerning what God would have him do.

VII. A Man Better Than Saul

In the two accounts of Saul's rejection Samuel describes Saul's successor as "a man after [the Lord's] own heart" (כלבבו א, 13:14) and as "your neighbor, who is better than you" (הטוב ממך, 15:28). As it quickly becomes clear that David is the one referred to, the reader is invited to consider in what way David is a man after the Lord's heart and is better than Saul. As we shall see, the narrator's repeated observations that the Lord is with David suggest that we are to understand David's success as YHWH's doing, and not his own. And yet, the unfolding characterization of David also suggests that the favor David finds in YHWH's eyes is not wholly undeserved.

Although David is given no lines and remains offstage for most of his anointing story, the narrative achieves several subtle contrasts between him

---

29. Miscall raises the possibility that Jonathan's sign is simply "a ploy to bolster his armor-bearer." But Miscall does not want to claim either the positive or more cynical view of Jonathan's action as definitive (*1 Samuel*, 91-92).

and Saul. The earlier introduction of Saul had described him as "a handsome young man." Indeed, the description continues, "there was not a man among the people of Israel more handsome than he; he stood head and shoulders above everyone else" (9:2). The introduction of David at his anointing echoes these initial impressions of Saul, but points reader and prophet in a different direction. When Samuel comes to Bethlehem to find Saul's successor among the sons of Jesse and lays eyes on Eliab, he is immediately taken by him. But the Lord instructs Samuel, "Do not look on his appearance or on the height of his stature . . . ; for the LORD does not see as mortals see; they look on the outward appearance, but the LORD looks on the heart" (16:7 NRSV).[30] Not only do these instructions pick up on the reference to David as a man "after his own heart," but they suggest that somehow the criteria for, or the qualities that result in, David's election are fundamentally different than for that of Saul. Whereas Saul's stature suggested, at 9:2, that he was fit to be king, David's fitness runs deeper than appearances. (Curiously, David is soon after described as "ruddy, with attractive eyes, and good looking" [16:12], observations that may partially explain the people's — and Michal's — fondness for him.)

A similarly subtle contrast between David and Saul is achieved in their shared absence at the time for public, or semi-public, anointing. In ch. 10, when Saul emerges as the king-elect through casting of the lot, he is hiding among the baggage. Here, again, it is observed that "when he took his stand among the people, he was head and shoulders taller than any of them" (10:23 NRSV). Whether Saul's decision to hide himself among the baggage, like his earlier decision not to tell his uncle about "the matter of the kingship of which Samuel had spoken" (10:16), arose out of a diplomatic humility or out of a real reluctance to assume his role is unclear. The latter would be consistent with the reader's earliest impressions of Saul: Saul's initial hesitancy to inquire of the seer Samuel early in ch. 9 nearly resulted in his turning back from the divinely appointed destiny awaiting him. Only at the urging of his servant does he stumble into it, as the end of his search for lost asses.

Although David's absence at the time of his would-be election evokes a comparison between the two anointing stories, his absence achieves a different effect. Since his election has not been made known to him beforehand, no motive can be attributed to David's absence. After the seventh of Jesse's sons has passed before Samuel, the prophet and reader alike discover that

---

30. Or "do not look upon his appearance or his stature. . . . For it is not as a man sees that God sees: a man looks into the face, but God looks into the heart" (McCarter, *1 Samuel,* 273 and 274, note).

David, the last and youngest, is off keeping the sheep. This revelation of David's whereabouts is auspicious; tending the sheep is precisely where the future shepherd of Israel ought to be. Given that David's introduction is so favorable, the narrator's subsequent statements that the Lord is with David come as no surprise. Saul observes this success, as does Jonathan, and their differing responses to David are illuminating.

Chapter 18 traces a kind of evolution in Saul's increasingly hostile response to David and to his success. When the people ascribe to Saul his thousands but to David his ten thousands, Saul "eyes" David from that day on (18:9). He tries twice to pin David to the wall. When David twice eludes him, Saul "fears David, because the Lord was with him but had departed from Saul" (18:12).[31] Saul removes David from his presence and makes him a commander of a thousand. Here, too, David is successful, and "when Saul saw that he had great success, he stood in awe of him" (18:15 NRSV). Saul plans to make David fall at the hand of the Philistines (18:25), but when this attempt fails and, in fact, the requested bride price of a hundred Philistine foreskins increases David's fame, "Saul feared David even more" (18:28). By the end of this quick account of events it is clear that Saul now knows what the reader knows — "Saul knew that the Lord was with David" (18:28). But clarity does not bring for Saul a change in heart. Instead, "Saul was David's enemy continually" (18:29). On one hand, Saul's animosity toward the successful David is understandable. He rightly perceives David as a threat to the throne. (How far Saul seems to have come from his initial reluctance!) On the other hand, it is a further act of madness for Saul to make as his enemy one with whom the Lord is. At the very least, as Jonathan observes, David's "deeds have been of good service" to the king (19:4 NRSV).

David also would seem to be a threat to Jonathan as well, as the king points out to his son, observing, "as long as the son of Jesse lives upon the earth, neither you nor your kingdom shall be established" (20:31 NRSV). But Jonathan does not see it this way. After David's defeat of Goliath, Jonathan "loved him as his own soul," giving over his robe, armor, sword, bow, and belt as gifts (18:3-4 NRSV).[32] Here again, Jonathan serves as a favorable contrast to his father, in that he has "chosen" the Lord's chosen. While from

31. Whether Saul is yet cognizant of what the narrator has just observed — that the Lord was with David but had departed from Saul — is unclear, perhaps intentionally so. After the series of events that follow, though, Saul is left without doubt.

32. The proximity of this observation to the description of David putting Goliath's armor in his tent is suggestive. It is not only the giant Philistine who has been smitten by the heroic, faith-filled David. "All the people of Israel and Judah" are "smitten" by David as well (cf. 18:16).

Saul's perspective Jonathan chooses against his own self-interest, in doing so Jonathan places himself squarely in the center of God's movement in Israel's history. This does not save him from an untimely death, but it does, at least, ensure the survival of his descendants when David takes the throne (cf. 2 Sam. 21:7).

VIII. David's Mettle Tested

Just as the narrative contains two accounts of Saul's rejection, so David has two introductions to Saul. In the first, the newly inspirited David is brought to soothe the tormented Saul (1 Sam. 16:14-23). This account heightens the contrast between the descent of YHWH's spirit on David and its departure from Saul. Since the reader is privy to the knowledge of David's anointing as Israel's future king, this initial story of their meeting evokes the sense of "providential coincidence" present also in Saul's original encounter with Samuel, suggestive of the divine plan working its way out in the contingencies of human agency. The second account, in ch. 17, serves more as an introduction of David to the reading audience than to Saul himself. And it is here that the reader gets the first real glimpse of those character traits that make David fit to be king. In this, the story of David and Goliath, the heavily armed and armored Philistine giant finds a formidable foe in the young and ruddy slingshot-toting shepherd. The contrast between combatants underscores the assertion that David himself voices in the story, that the battle belongs to the Lord, who "does not save by sword or spear" (17:47). But the story is not so much about YHWH's character as it is about David's. The reader is to be impressed by David's courage, courage that depends on a profound and tested faith in God. As David explains to Saul, "The Lord, who delivered me from the paw of the lion and from the paw of the bear, will deliver me from the hand of this Philistine" (17:37). Despite the menacing appearance and threats of the Philistine, David does not fear for his own life. The threefold reference to Goliath's "defiant" words reveals that this confrontation is as much a physical as a theological one for David. The Philistine baits the Israelites, shouting, "Today I defy the ranks of Israel" (17:10). David responds with a rhetorical question, ". . . who is this uncircumcised Philistine that he should defy the ranks of the living God?" (17:26; cf. 17:36). David's alteration of the Philistine's challenge is illuminating. What Goliath describes as "the ranks of Israel," David more rightly refers to as "the ranks of the living God." In this subtle modification David shows that he sees the affront as one to God, and not to man, and that, although victory may accrue to his own benefit, its primary aim is that "all this assembly may know . . . the Lord . . ." (17:47).

While the story of David and Goliath illustrates David's deep trust in God's power, nowhere are David's ability to separate God's will from his own desires and his patience to wait for God's vindication more starkly illustrated than in 1 Samuel 24, the story of Saul and David's encounter at the cave in the wilderness of the En-Gedi. The immediate context for this account contributes to the story's impact as much as the telling of the tale itself. Ch. 23 recounts two specific episodes in Saul's pursuit of David that are illustrative of an ongoing process, to which 23:14 testifies: "Saul sought him continually, but God did not give him into his hand." That David and his men are left to wander "wherever they might" (23:16),[33] and, in the second episode, only very narrowly escape from Saul and his men closing in on them (23:26-38) contributes to the overall portrayal of the relentlessness of Saul's pursuit and the tenuousness of David's existence and that of his men. As a result, in ch. 24 when David finds Saul in *his* hand yet spares him, David's restraint is perceived as all the more remarkable.

Ch. 23 sets the stage for the episode in ch. 24 in another way, through its depiction of David's repeated attempts to inquire of God and his accompanying access to divine knowledge, which is contrasted with Saul's misreading of the way God is, or is not, acting on each man's behalf. David inquires of the Lord twice concerning whether he should go attack the Philistines fighting against Keilah — once on his own initiative and once in response to his men's concerns about the danger involved (23:2-4). Later he inquires whether the inhabitants of Keilah will give him up to Saul, receiving an affirmative answer enabling him to flee in time. Curiously, however, while David is first portrayed as inquiring of God in ch 23. at vv. 2-4, that Abiathar had fled to David from Nob with the ephod, facilitating such inquiry, is not revealed until v. 6. This delayed disclosure concerning the ephod is not then followed directly by David's request that the ephod be brought near for his third inquiry, however, as one might expect. Instead, the mention of the ephod's presence, and of David's consultation through it, are separated by pertinent information concerning the occasion of the consultation: "When Saul was told that David had come to Keilah, Saul said, 'God has given him into my hand; for he has shut himself in by entering a town that has gates and a bar'" (23:7-8).[34] Saul jumps quickly to this conclusion on the basis of visible circumstances and not through a process of discernment. That Saul's

---

33. So McCarter, *1 Samuel*, 368.
34. McCarter, *1 Samuel*, 369, note to v. 7.

reading of God's initiative is completely wrong becomes evident as the story plays itself out, and David escapes capture — with divine aid.

The problem of discerning the direction of the divine tide, thus introduced in ch. 23, resurfaces in ch. 24's episode at the cave. Saul's incorrect interpretation of events in 23:7 is echoed at 24:4, although in this instance it is David's men who wrongly interpret the situation. David and his men are hiding deep in the cave when Saul comes in to relieve himself. David's men say to him "Here is the day of which the Lord said to you, 'I am giving your enemy into your hand, and you shall do to him whatever seems good to you'" (24:5). On one level the men are correct; Saul has indeed been given into David's hand and there is nothing to stop him from doing "what seems good." However, David's men who, like Saul, make their assumption about God's design solely on the basis of circumstance, assume that what seems good will be to kill Saul, who has been seeking David's life. This is not, ultimately, what seems good to David. And here, David's actions reveal his attachments. His heart stricken for having impulsively cut the corner of Saul's cloak, David says to the men, "The Lord forbid that I should do this thing to my Lord, the Lord's anointed, to raise my hand against him; for he is the Lord's anointed" (24:6 NRSV).[35] David is not grasping at the kingship as Saul is grasping to hold on to it. In his restraint David shows himself to be more devoted to YHWH than to attaining the kingship or even to preserving his own life. He is not willing to raise his hand against the Lord's anointed — because he is the Lord's anointed — even if that one is seeking his life without cause. Having recently only narrowly escaped capture and a sure death, he is willing to risk finding himself in such a position again. David himself is aware that this moment of decision reveals something of his character. He quotes for Saul an ancient proverb, "Out of the wicked comes forth wickedness." "But," he continues, "my hand shall not be against you" (24:13 NRSV). In David's mind the choice is more than a question of character; the road he takes is one that depends on being mindful of what God has chosen, on putting this above one's own immediate advantage, and on trusting YHWH for vindication. "May the Lord . . . be judge, and give sentence between me and you" he calls out to Saul. "May he see to it, and plead my cause, and vindicate me against you" (24:15 NRSV).[36]

---

35. See Alter's helpful discussion of characterization through dialogue in this episode in *The Art of Biblical Narrative*, 36-37, 67.

36. In his exegesis of 2 Samuel David Gunn offers an interpretation of David's reign in terms of giving and grasping. His assertion that David's grasping results in disastrous effects while his actions attuned to giving lead to success is somewhat similar to my comparison of Saul and David's behavior in 1 Samuel. See David M. Gunn, *The Story of King David: Genre and Interpretation* (*JSOT* Supplement Series 6; Sheffield: JSOT, 1978) 94-111.

IX. Complications in the Portrayal of David

In characteristic fashion, 1 Samuel contains a duplicate account of David sparing Saul's life (ch. 26). In this account David does not come upon Saul by accident, but has gone down into Saul's camp intentionally. Again, one of his cohort interprets the circumstance for David, saying, "Today God has shut your enemy up in your hand; let me pin him to the ground with one thrust of the spear" (26:8), and again David resists the temptation to dispose of Saul easily. The rationale for his restraint, though similar to that in the earlier episode, is also more explicit: "Do not destroy him; for who can raise his hand against the Lord's anointed, and be guiltless?" (26:9). And although he again strongly protests, "The Lord forbid that I should raise my hand against the Lord's anointed," these reservations do not keep him from stealing Saul's spear and water jar as a visible sign of his having spared Saul's life. In this episode, David's expression of his earlier hope that "the Lord vindicate me against [Saul]" (24:12) is less articulate (26:10), and on the whole the element of surprise responsible for creating David's critical moment of discernment and decision is removed. Nothing in the entire encounter seems left to chance. Not only has David gone down into Saul's camp intentionally, neither Saul nor his guard awaken "because a deep sleep from the Lord had fallen upon them" (26:12). As a result, the overall effect of this account is less powerful than the earlier one.

What is intriguing, however, is that nestled between these two accounts is one that describes an occasion when the good sense and quick action of a woman are almost all that stand between David and a senseless, vengeful slaughter. In that episode David requests provisions for a feast from the aptly named Nabal, whose flocks and shepherds David's entourage had "guarded" in the wilderness.[37] Nabal refuses. David's murderous reaction to Nabal's insult seems disproportionate when considered against the considerable restraint exercised with regard to his pursuer Saul. This dissonance only serves to emphasize the respect, or at least the care, David reserves for his treatment of Saul *because* Saul is the Lord's anointed. What does seem consistent about ch. 25's portrayal of David, however, is his own willingness to listen to good sense when confronted with it. When Abigail assuages David's fury with a generous peace-offering, David proclaims,

> Blessed be the Lord, the God of Israel, who sent you this day to meet me!
> Blessed be your good sense, and blessed be you, who kept me today from

---

37. Nabal means "fool," in the sense of one who acts inappropriately or impiously.

bloodguilt and from gaining victory by my own hand. Surely as the Lord the God of Israel lives, who has restrained me from hurting you, unless you had hurried and come to meet me, truly by morning there would not have been left to Nabal a single male (25:32-34).

While David is plainly indebted to Abigail for her initiative, he also recognizes God's hand in these events. "Blessed be the Lord, the God of Israel," he proclaims, for it was he "who sent you this day to meet me!" (25:32). As when confronted later by Nathan, and even later by Gad, David is not reluctant to admit his own guilt. He continues, ". . . blessed be you, who have kept me today from bloodguilt and from gaining victory by my own hand!" (25:33). In sum, the portrayal of David in ch. 25 does not undo the characterization of David in chs. 24 and 26, but it does complicate it. While the story of Saul in 1 Samuel has primarily been a depiction of human resistance to divine initiative, that of David has largely been a depiction of synergy between human and divine action. David's impulsive reaction to Nabal appears as an aberration, particularly in comparison to the two episodes surrounding the tale. But here even an aberration may be telling. As David proclaims after sparing Saul,

> The Lord rewards each man for his righteousness and his faithfulness; . . .
> As your life was valuable today in my sight, so may my life be valued in the
> sight of the Lord, and may he rescue me from all distress (26:23-24).

The placement of this episode between the two accounts of David's sparing Saul suggests that YHWH has shown mercy in keeping David from bloodguilt through Abigail's agency *because* of the faithfulness David has shown to the Lord and to his anointed, Saul. In other words, while David's success is attributable to the divine favor he receives, David's general willingness to place YHWH's interests above his own, his desire to discern the direction of God's activity and to act in accordance with it, play an integral role in the favorable outcome of events.

X. David's Patient "Indifference" to an Unfolding Fate

Despite Saul's violent reaction to David, David has not made an explicit move for Saul's throne. He has simply acquired fame, albeit more fame than Saul, through his deeds "in service of the king." A comparison of Saul's reaction to this threat to a later incident recounted concerning David, when Absalom usurps the throne, perhaps best exemplifies the manner in which Saul swims counter to the divine tide, to his own detriment, while David is willing to be carried by it, even when it may require "letting go." In 2 Samuel 15, as David flees Jerusalem, Shimei, of the house of Saul, comes out cursing and throwing stones at David and his entourage. When it is suggested that Shimei be killed, David's response is one of restraint and acceptance of his fate — if this, indeed, is to be his fate:

> The king said . . . "If he is cursing because the Lord has said to him, 'Curse David,' who then shall say, 'Why have you done so?' . . . My own son seeks my life; how much more now may this Benjaminite! Let him alone, and let him curse; for the LORD has bidden him. It may be that the LORD will look on my distress, and the LORD will repay me with good for this cursing of me today." (16:10-12 NRSV)[38]

In his response David exhibits a recognition that things are not always as they seem, and that patience is required in discerning God's will as it unfolds. He also indicates his willingness to accept humiliation and defeat, if the Lord so bids. Of course, this acceptance of the Lord's hand does not mean that David himself sits on his own hands, as the handling of the Absalom affair makes plain; David is also one to take action, when there is hope the Lord might be swayed by one's appeal, or when the divine will is made plain.

David exhibits a similar stance in his response to the illness of Bathsheba's child. Admittedly, David's taking of Bathsheba and the murder of her husband Uriah would seem to undermine any claim that David is adept at discerning and acting on that which is pleasing to the Lord. Yet David's response to Nathan's confrontation differs sharply from that of Saul when confronted by Samuel in a comparable situation. On the whole, David is more quick to repent and to hope in God's mercy. David responds immediately to Nathan's parable and oracle of judgment with his confession, "I have sinned against the Lord" (2 Sam. 12:13). This is unlike Saul, who, in 1 Samuel 15, attempts to justify his actions to Samuel and only reluctantly admits wrongdoing. Whereas Saul takes hold of Samuel, imploring him to "pardon my sin, and return with me, so that I may worship the Lord" (1 Sam. 15:25, 30), David fasts and pleads with God directly, hoping that God will turn back his judgment that the child born of his adultery will die. David's servants are puzzled by his actions, which to them seem counter-intuitive; he fasts and weeps while the child is alive, but when the child dies David rises and eats. David explains himself, saying,

38. McCarter translates, "If someone curses that way, it's because Yahweh has said, 'Curse David!' to him" (P. Kyle McCarter, Jr., *2 Samuel* [Anchor Bible; Garden City: Doubleday, 1984] 362).

While the child was still alive, I fasted and wept; for I said, "Who knows? The Lord may be gracious to me, and the child may live." But now he is dead; why should I fast? Can I bring him back again? I shall go to him, but he will not return to me. (2 Sam. 12:22-23 NRSV)

David does not contest the judgment Nathan has proclaimed over his house (12:11-13). He does hope, however, that God, in his mercy, will pity his new-born son. That David readily accepts it when God does not pity the child, need not indicate callousness on David's part, or that his fasting and prayer were coolly calculated; on the contrary, having admitted his sin, David is willing to accept the punishment, as his response to Shimei has also shown. David's multifaceted response in this situation again differs from that of Saul, who seems unable ever fully to accept the judgment declared by Samuel (cf. 1 Sam. 28:3-25).

A third event, at the end of David's life, likewise illustrates his acceptance of God's judgment coupled with an abiding trust in God's mercy. Having been incited to take a census of the people, David is confronted with a trinity of choices: three years of famine on the land, fleeing for three months before his foes, or three days' pestilence. David's response: "Let us fall into the hand of the Lord, for his mercy is great; but into human hands let me not fall" (2 Sam. 24:14). As in the episode discussed above, David's response can be read in more than one way. One might want to emphasize the us/me distinction in David's answer and argue that the more fitting response would have been the choice of a judgment to fall on David alone.[39] (David himself defends the people's innocence at 2 Sam. 24:17.) Yet one must also not overlook the rationale for his choice, that God's mercy is greater than humans'. This rationale reflects the same confidence in God's mercy and power that David exhibits in 1 Samuel's stories about him, a trust that inspires him to act courageously, as against Goliath, with restraint, as with Saul, and that shapes his ability to accept God's determinations, even when against him.

XI. Conclusion

In introducing this reading of 1 Samuel, I stated that my interest was in "character building" in both its literary and moral sense. On the one hand, my concern has been with the development of the characters Saul and David

39. "Let *us* fall into the hand of the Lord . . . but into human hands let *me* not fall" (2 Sam. 24:14, emphasis added).

as the reader moves from the beginning to the end of the book. On the other, I have also been interested in the nature of each one's character, as it emerges through characterization. Literary characterization is indeterminate in that a reader's perception shifts as he or she moves through the text and weighs present information with what came previously, reassessing earlier understandings on the basis of new information. At the same time, any such material may be open to multiple interpretations. In this essay I have sought to highlight one particular aspect of the characterizations of Saul and of David and of the contrast between the two. Of course, there are many aspects of their characterizations that have been neglected in favor of this particular one, just as there are competing ways of interpreting the episodes I have discussed. Not all readings serve the same interpretive interests however. I affirmed earlier Fowl and Jones's claim that for Christian interpreters "the aim of faithful living before the Triune God becomes the standard to which all interpretive interests must measure up." Biblical narratives not only testify to how an earlier community perceived God acting in the past, but serve as analogues for God's action in our own communities and lives. Biblical stories capture our imaginations, shaping the way we interpret our own lives, and, in many instances, providing models for right living. I have argued that Ignatius's insights about the process of discernment illuminate some aspects of Saul and David's portrayal and, conversely, that 1 Samuel serves to illustrate the stance that Ignatius seeks to inculcate in his readers. I have argued that Saul, on his part, is shown to be neither diligent nor adept at seeking the direction of God's movement. His inability to distance himself from his own attachments, concerns, and interests in order to perceive God's will — his inability to achieve indifference, to use Ignatius's term — contribute to this failure. Saul acts when he should be still and fails to act when action is commanded. Since Saul's very introduction in 1 Samuel 9 shows him ready to turn back, nearly missing his divinely appointed meeting with the prophet, it is hardly surprising that later episodes show him perpetually swimming against the divine tide.

David, on the other hand, is depicted from the beginning as acting courageously in the name of YHWH, without fear for his life, just as he later shows considerable restraint with regard to Saul's life, even when this is apparently not in David's own interest. In spite of David's later transgressions recounted in the second book of Samuel, David shows himself willing to accept humiliation and defeat if that be God's will, all the while hoping in God's abundant mercy. As a result of the indifference that David is able to achieve with regard to his own interests, he, in contrast to Saul, is able to place himself in the direction of the divine tide and to be carried along by it.

269

This is not to argue that Saul's and David's fates are determined solely by their own choice and action. The mystery of God's election is by far a more prominent element in the story than the mystery of human freedom. Neither Saul nor David is without sin. Even so, the one receives God's unchanging promise to his house, the other's reign is shown to be a false start. Yet even those who argue that the transgressions behind Saul's rejection are mere technicalities justifying an already determined outcome concede that the relationship between "causality and (moral) responsibility" in the story is a complex web; that, in other words, Saul, and David for that matter, contribute to their own fate.[40] Ultimately, God remains a mystery, who acts in mysterious ways. The lifelong process of discernment is no guarantee that we will be successful or that things will always go our way. But the indifference that leads to effective discernment enables us, like David, to position ourselves rightly in relation to a merciful God who has given the world as a gift, "created for us, to be the means by which we can come to know him better, love him more surely, and serve him more faithfully."[41]

40. So Gunn, *The Fate of King Saul*, 116.

41. I am indebted to my colleagues Angel Russell Christman and L. Gregory Jones for their comments on an earlier draft of this paper.

III. CANONICAL READINGS AND
THE NEW TESTAMENT

Dogs at the Foot of the Cross and the Jesus Who Never Tires of Meeting Us

Kathryn Greene-McCreight

Focusing on the theological problem of the Quest of the Historical Jesus may seem an unlikely way to contribute to a volume in honor of the life and work of Brevard Springs Childs. Indeed, while Childs does include in his latest book a section on the Quest, he evidently does not consider worth mentioning at all the work of the so-called Third Quest.[1] Any scholar of the stature of Childs is certainly not unfamiliar with the work of Ben Witherington, N. T. Wright, John Meier, Marcus Borg, John Dominic Crossan, and others. And most who read the daily news will not be ignorant of the work of the Jesus Seminar. So why contribute an essay devoted to the hermeneutical issues around the Third Quest in such a volume as this? The answer is simply that the topic is apparently of great interest to the church, much more now even than when Mr. Childs wrote his *Biblical Theology* six years ago. Scholars such as Borg and Crossan are invited to speak at ministerial gatherings and conferences and are well-received.[2] Many laypeople are familiar with and convinced by Crossan's fanciful suggestion that the reason the tomb was empty

---

1. "The Hermeneutical Problem of Critical Reconstructions," in *Biblical Theology of the Old and New Testaments* (Minneapolis: Fortress, 1993) 212-16.
2. At a recent meeting of the Massachusetts Conference of the United Church of Christ, Borg's address was greeted enthusiastically, with at least one of the attendees declaring that his scholarship signaled the new Pentecost of the church.

The research for this paper was underwritten by a grant from the Pew Evangelical Scholars Foundation.

was that it was never full, for the wild dogs that gathered around the typical cross in the first century would have devoured the body before it could be buried. This essay will be an attempt to assess the current revival of interest in the topic in hopes of offering a new perspective on these matters informed by the work of Brevard Childs.

The two polar opposite positions between which Christian theology has ranged over the last two hundred years in responding to the question "Who was the historical Jesus?" are that, on the one hand, the truth of Christianity entails the factual and demonstrable accuracy of the biblical record in its entirety and, on the other, that the truth of Christianity does not rest on the historical reliability of the biblical record in whole or even in part. An early representative of the first option was H. S. Reimarus, who assumed that the truth of Christianity depended on the demonstrable factual accuracy of the Gospel accounts, but thought he had demonstrated that they were a "tissue of lies." He therefore concluded that he had debunked Christianity as a viable option in the religious marketplace. Another example of the first option is represented by the Rationalists of the nineteenth century and by fundamentalist Christianity of the twentieth, both of which assume that the truth of Christianity depends on the Bible's demonstrable factual accuracy, but also assume that they are able to demonstrate that accuracy successfully. The second option is represented by David Friedrich Strauss, Rudolf Bultmann, Paul Ricoeur, and Luke Johnson. They assume that the truth of Christianity does not rest on facts to be proven or gleaned from the biblical record but on ideas, consciousness, experience, or existence presented within and mediated by the biblical record. Schleiermacher is an interesting case of this second option; he believed, for instance, that the resurrection was an "event" in the life of Jesus himself, but that it bore no theological significance. For him, the truth of Christianity rested on the God-consciousness mediated by Jesus, and therefore Jesus' death and resurrection were beside the point theologically.

In keeping with Brevard Childs's "canonical" hermeneutics, I want instead to claim that Christianity stands or falls with the truth of key propositions embedded within the canonical narrative of the life of Israel before God, and with the life, death, and resurrection of Jesus of Nazareth as it mirrors, culminates, sums up, stands in for, and thus transforms the life of Israel before God. That faith cannot be proven by historical inquiry, but it can in principle be falsified.[3] The notion that Christian theological claims are

3. See Hugo A. Meynell, "Faith, Objectivity and Historical Falsifiability," in *Language, Meaning and God: Essays in Honour of Herbert McCabe OP*, ed. Brian Davies (London: Chapman, 1987).

falsifiable is the corollary of the "life-and-death" meaningfulness of those claims. Our access to the "real Jesus" is in part through the canonical Gospels' witness, but also through the biblical witness as a whole, a claim that most "historical Jesus" researchers would surely reject out of hand. Choosing to trust the biblical witness is a matter not only of assent of the intellect but also of the will. It therefore involves not only a reasoned and critical reading of the accounts, but also a self-conscious turning and commitment, which Christians understand to be possible only in the power of the Holy Spirit. This indicates yet another avenue of access to "the real Jesus": there is an extent to which the "historical Jesus," if he is to be found apart from the biblical witness at all, enters history and meets us yet again as we are conformed to his likeness. We who are the "earthly historical representation and form of the presence and action of Jesus Christ" exist in an earthly-historical correspondence to his life, his afflictions, and his passion, and his resurrection.[4] This "experiential" element is the goal of the biblical witness, but it is only secondary to the grounding in the prior and primary avenue of access of the biblical witness itself.

While the phenomenon of research on the Historical Jesus is itself a fascinating topic in the history of ideas,[5] the recent expansion of literature on the Historical Jesus does give one the sense of "dejà-vu all over again."[6] The many branches of such research have seen much critique over the last century. The "Old Quest" was axed by Kähler, Schweitzer, and Wrede; the Second Quest withered along with the decline in popularity of Existentialist philosophy; and most recently Luke Timothy Johnson has attempted to saw off the stump's sucker known as the Jesus Seminar. But by far the most astute

4. Karl Barth, *Church Dogmatics* 4/2, tr. G. Bromiley (Edinburgh: Clark, 1958) 601 = *Kirchliche Dogmatik* 4/2 (Zurich: Zollikon, 1955) 680: *"irdisch-geschichtliche Darstellung."*

5. See Dieter Georgi's essay in *Harvard Theological Review* 85 (1992) 51-83.

6. It will not be within the scope of this essay to outline the history of the question of the "historical Jesus." Those unfamiliar with the literature will want to consult Albert Schweitzer, *The Quest of the Historical Jesus: A Critical Study of Its Progress from Reimarus to Wrede* (New York: Macmillan, 1957); James Robinson, *A New Quest of the Historical Jesus and Other Essays* (Philadelphia: Fortress, 1983); Ben Witherington, *The Jesus Quest: The Third Search for the Jew of Nazareth* (Downers Grove: InterVarsity, 1995); Luke Timothy Johnson, *The Real Jesus: The Misguided Quest for the Historical Jesus and the Truth of the Traditional Gospels* (San Francisco: HarperSanFrancisco, 1996); Marcus Borg, *Jesus in Contemporary Scholarship* (Valley Forge: Trinity, 1994); Bruce Chilton and Craig A. Evans, eds., *Studying the Historical Jesus: Evaluations of the State of Current Research* (Leiden: Brill, 1994); C. Stephen Evans, *The Historical Christ and the Jesus of Faith* (Oxford: Clarendon, 1996).

theological critique was that by Martin Kähler, who exposed the problem of our sources for historical Jesus research. First published in 1892, his lectures on the topic appear in English under the title *The So-called Historical Jesus and the Historic Biblical Christ.* One of Kähler's contentions is that we do not possess adequate sources to reconstruct the life and teachings of Jesus because the Gospels are not intentionally objective reports. The confessional nature of the sources makes it impossible to cull the Jesus-as-he-actually-was from the reports about the Christ of faith. The Gospels are not reliable sources for historical reconstruction, they cannot be traced in entirety to eyewitnesses, and they are isolated reports with little external corroborating evidence. They tell mainly of the shortest and latest period of Jesus' life, and in fact, according to Kähler, the Gospels are Passion narratives with extended introductions. While Kähler can understand the interest in the person of Jesus, such research reads the Bible against the grain.

> I regard the entire Life of Jesus Movement as a blind alley. A blind alley usually has something alluring about it, or no one would enter it in the first place. It usually appears to be a section of the right road, or no one would hit upon it at all. In other words, we cannot reject this movement without understanding what is legitimate in it. The Life-of-Jesus movement is completely in the right insofar as it sets the Bible over against an abstract dogmatism. It becomes illegitimate as soon as it begins to rend and dissect the Bible without having acquired a clear understanding of the special nature of the problem and the peculiar significance of scripture for such understanding. . . . The justification for the movement can be expressed in Luther's statement that we can never draw God's Son deep enough into our flesh, into our humanity. . . . But Luther's statement makes sense only if Christ is more than a mere man. It has no meaning at all for those who wish to maintain and demonstrate that he is of no more importance to us than any other significant figure of the past. This was not Luther's view, nor can it be ours. . . . Every detail that we can learn about [Jesus] becomes precious and meaningful for us. The tradition about him cannot be studied diligently and faithfully enough.[7]

Yet the quest continues as though Kähler and those who followed him in critique of Historical Jesus research never made a contribution to the debate.[8] Kähler's objections were not so much on theological grounds, as is evi-

7. Martin Kähler, *The So-Called Historical Jesus and the Historic Biblical Christ* (Philadelphia: Fortress, 1988): 46-47.

8. Perhaps part of the reason Kähler is generally ignored is that he is largely misread by those who engage in Jesus research. He is often understood as *creating* the distinc-

dent from the above quote. The quest is theologically valid, for Jesus was a person within time and space and not simply a character in a novel. Even the Gospel accounts care enough to point out that his resurrection appearances "happened," whatever "happened" might mean in the case of Jesus' resurrection, within the time-space continuum: "See my hands and my feet, that it is I myself; handle me, and see; for a spirit has not flesh and bones as you see that I have. And while they disbelieved for joy, and wondered, he said to them 'Have you anything here to eat?' They gave him a piece of broiled fish, and he took it and ate before them" (Luke 24:38). And again: "Then he said to Thomas, 'Put your finger here, and see my hands; and put out your hand, and place it in my side; do not be faithless but believing'" (John 20:27). We might do well to distinguish between the two "Quests" operative here. The first is possible because Jesus was a person within the time-space continuum: this is the Quest for Jesus' historical context, the social, cultural, political, and religious milieu of the first century of the common era. The second, however, is historically *and* theologically impossible because of the nature of the sources: this is the Quest for Jesus "as he actually was," as though this character could be culled from the witness of the Gospels.

Mounting a search for the "Historical Jesus" thus begs the prior question: what is meant by the phrase itself, "the Historical Jesus"? Whom or what are we seeking? Where do we look, and what goes into such historical research? The elusive phrase, "the Historical Jesus," is used in many different ways by those who work on this topic, indeed, sometimes in different ways in different contexts by the same scholar.[9] The slipperiness of the term "history" and its ambiguous relationship to a nest of concepts such as memory, story, description, fiction, and belief is seldom acknowledged in such research.[10] "History" can indicate many layers of witness to something that happened in the past. It can refer not only to an event in the past, but also to the experience or perception of an event by those who witness it, or to a de-

---

tion between the Jesus of history and the Christ of faith, when he seemed rather to be *commenting* that this distinction, assumed valid by those before him from Reimarus to Strauss, was not reflected in the canonical Gospels. Therefore, according to Kähler, inquiry into the historical Jesus reads the Gospels against the grain. Some Jesus scholars seem to think that this leaves one in the position of having no option but Bultmannian myth, hence the justification for "historical Jesus" research.

9. E.g., see John Meier, *A Marginal Jew: Rethinking the Historical Jesus* (New York: Doubleday, 1991) vol. 1, *The Roots of the Problem and the Person*, 25-31. Here Meier confuses the different uses of the phrase "historical Jesus" and also muddies the distinction between *Historie* and *Geschichte*.

10. See the interesting study by Robert Frykenberg, *History and Belief: The Foundations of Historical Understanding* (Grand Rapids: Eerdmans, 1996).

scription or narrative account of the event, or additionally to an explanation or analysis of an event, and even to beliefs about the significance of the event. In the mix of these competing uses of the term "history," the historian must acknowledge that whatever "events" may have occurred, the evidence that remains of it in the descriptions or analysis or narrative, etc., have already filtered out a myriad of detail and culled only that which is deemed "significant." In other words, "history" as a discipline is from the outset a fabric woven of the objective and the subjective. Thus, one can untangle from the mass of publication on the "Historical Jesus" at least seven distinct uses of this phrase:

1. *"Jesus as he actually was."* This refers to the raw, uninterpreted "event" or "events" of the life of Jesus, the "video camera Jesus," which is of course itself a chimera. Marcus Borg is typical of Historical Jesus research over the past two hundred years in splitting the "Jesus-as-he-actually-was" (Borg calls this the "pre-Easter Jesus") from the "Christ of faith," which the church supposedly has embroidered over this more "historical" pre-Easter Jesus.

2. *The historian's reconstructed Jesus.* This refers to the portrait of Jesus offered by the scholar of this genre of research. The historian who offers a reconstruction will often claim that the reconstruction is, indeed, Jesus "as he actually was," but as Schweitzer brilliantly pointed out, reconstructions are more often mirror images of the reconstructers, or, I would add, images of what the historian wishes Jesus had been or could be, than they are accurate representations of the character himself.

3. *The memory impression of Jesus.* This use of the phrase refers to the perspectival image of Jesus as preserved and transmitted by his first eyewitnesses. This is more or less what Bultmann sought to unfold in *Jesus and the Word,* that is, the earliest witness to Jesus.

4. *The canonical Jesus.* This image is that of Jesus as molded by the views of the particular communities that wrote the canonical Gospels. Whereas the previous category is chronologically the first layer or witness to Jesus as the Christ, this category is the second or even third layer. While some may object that the canonical Jesus is not what anyone means by the phrase, "the Historical Jesus," it seems certain that the Gospel writers were interested in passing on what they deemed was significant about the Jesus who existed in time and space. In this sense, the canonical Christ is a "historical Jesus."

5. *The historic Jesus.* The phrase "the Historical Jesus" sometimes refers in fact to "the historic Jesus," that is, to the portrait of Jesus that influ-

enced his followers. This use of the phrase is less interested in the portrait itself of Jesus than in the portrait's effects. An example of this might be Jaroslav Pelikan's work, *Jesus through the Ages.* This "historical Jesus" was a decisive event on the scene of world history, both for those who believe and for those who do not believe. Note that the claim of decisiveness here is not a religious or theological claim, but can be a purely secular one: evidence that Jesus is "historical" or an historic character in this sense can be seen in the way Western culture reckons this to be the year 1998, or in such cultural artifacts as a gothic cathedral or "A Miracle on 34th Street."

6. *The earthly Jesus.* This use of the phrase dovetails with some aspects of other uses of the phrase, in particular the canonical Jesus, but refers to Jesus' life up to the episode of his Ascension. Often this use of the phrase appears alongside the claim that the historical Jesus is crucial because the Gospels refer to things that the authors and original readers believed occurred in time and space, or the claim that the Historical Jesus is necessary for us to avoid a Docetic christology.[11] Those who want to take the Chalcedonian confession seriously can be swept into the debate over the historical Jesus in this use of the phrase, since this tends to conflate the humanity of Jesus with his historical reconstructibility. Nevertheless, there remains and will remain an unbridgeable gulf between Jesus' humanity and his historical reconstructability. My great-great grandmother was a historical human being, and my confidence in this will not be shaken by the fact that I have very few historically provable details of her life and sayings.

7. *The actual Jesus.* The "actual Jesus" is the intersection between categories one, four, and six above. The "actual Jesus," as the area of overlap between the sets represented by the categories of the canonical Jesus, the earthly Jesus, and the video camera Jesus, is the Jesus that interests and compels the church. But can that Jesus be "found" via the methods of historical investigation? We have no first-century video camera, and Historical Jesus research usually as a methodological presupposition proceeds on the basis of mistrust of the canonical witnesses. And while there are indeed "historical" elements in the canonical and the earthly Jesus, they cannot be "scientifically" verified. "The historical Jesus" as sought by the likes of the Jesus Seminar is a flight from the "actual Jesus," and is in fact not very "historical" at all, for it separates the empir-

11. So Stephen Patterson of the Jesus Seminar, in conversation, March 1996, and Richard Hays, "Faith and History," *First Things* 64 (1996) 44-46.

ical data (the Gospel accounts) from its narrative framework (the biblical story).

This last category then begs a prior question: how is the "historical Jesus" to be sought? By what criteria, methods, and goals, and using which sources, do we determine what the Historical Jesus is, assuming we could come to a consensus on what the phrase "the Historical Jesus" meant? The general methodology followed and the assumptions made in the process of the search for "historically verifiable" data about Jesus are fascinating and complex.[12] Insofar as historical-critical methodology was at its inception fueled by a passion to liberate the truth of the biblical texts from the distortions of tradition accreted to them (Schweitzer acclaimed historical criticism as the "struggle against the tyranny of dogma"), Historical Jesus research is a quintessentially Protestant undertaking, even though Roman Catholics now take part in such research. Historical-critical methodology tends to assume (self-consciously since Troeltsch) that:

1. the Bible can and must be read like any other book;
2. in giving a scientifically based account of the past, one may rely only on what is knowable within the canons of reason and the laws of nature;
3. historical method seeks genetic relationships and antecedents that can be connected in a chain of events; and
4. the burden of proof rests on the evidence, in this case, the data of the biblical text. In "legalese," the text is guilty until proven innocent, and skepticism is a matter of principle. This is what is known as "the hermeneutic of suspicion."

Since determining the teachings of the reconstructed Jesus relies on the assumption of cause and effect, and we must extrapolate from what we know to what we do not know, this necessarily and categorically excludes the "unique." We cannot investigate historically the accounts of Jesus' miracles or his resurrection because these phenomena are beyond the bounds of normal

---

12. This will be a broad sketch with little reference to specific scholars. This discussion is not intended to be read as lumping all Jesus scholars together under one umbrella, for they are a diverse lot indeed. Compare, for instance, the methodology of John Dominic Crossan as outlined in his Prologue to *The Historical Jesus: The Life of a Mediterranean Jewish Peasant* (San Francisco: HarperSanFrancisco, 1991), and that of Martin Hengel in his Schaffer Lectures, Yale Divinity School, 1993. Nevertheless, both of them, with only a few exceptions, follow many of the assumptions outlined in the following sketch.

cause and effect.[13] Here we begin to see the foundation of Historical Jesus research crumbling, for the demand to read the Bible like any other book is in effect undercut by the three assumptions that follow it. That is, no other book is truly read the way New Testament critics read the New Testament. The work of the historian is always conducted on the basis of testimony, and the New Testament writers claim to be presenting testimony to the character of Jesus of Nazareth. They all agree that there were multiple witnesses to the empty tomb and to the risen Jesus. Simply because these witnesses claim that something out of the ordinary "happened," whatever "happened" might mean in the case of the resurrection of Jesus, is not grounds for dismissing the witnesses themselves as historical evidence. We may come to the conclusion that the witnesses were deluded fools. However, the canons of historical research do not allow us to assume from the outset what we may eventually conclude.

The methods used to determine what Jesus really did and said conceal unexamined assumptions about what counts for "evidence" and "proof" that would astound any historian from outside the scope of the guild of New Testament studies. While the following "methods" are derivative of the First and Second Quests, and while the Jesus Seminar branch of the Third Quest advertises its own work as discontinuous with the first two Quests, indeed as discontinuous with other elements of the Third Quest, nevertheless one finds that they all operate on the basis either of some or all of the following criteria, or versions thereof, or on the assumptions on which the criteria rest:[14]

13. Martin Hengel and N. T. Wright are for the most part in the minority in questioning the validity of this assumption. They see a methodological problem here that most Jesus scholars do not see: that which is being investigated is the accounts of Jesus' miracles, not the miracles themselves. The accounts, as accounts, are as such not beyond the bounds of investigation. This becomes clear when the same scholars who choose on methodological grounds not to include miraculous accounts as data for "historical Jesus" reconstruction do use them to point out the many parallel accounts in the ancient world, with the effect of discrediting the witness to Jesus' miracles.

14. For a classic critique, see Morna Hooker, "On Using the Wrong Tool," *Theology* 75 (1972) 570-81. My remarks are informed also by D. Calvert, "An Examination of the Criteria for Distinguishing the Authentic Words of Jesus," *New Testament Studies* 18 (1972) 209-18, and John Gager, "The Gospels and Jesus: Some Doubts about Method," *Journal of Religion* 54 (1974) 244-72. Cf. "The Limitations of History," ch. 4 of Luke Timothy Johnson, *The Real Jesus* as well as his "Epilogue: Critical Scholarship and the Church" in the same volume and Austin Farrer's classic attack, "On Dispensing with Q" in *Studies in the Gospels*, ed. D. E. Nineham (Oxford: Blackwell, 1955) 55-88. Despite Crossan's protestations to the contrary, he is indeed working with assumptions similar to those underlying these criteria, even if not actually with every last criterion here listed. He purported-

1. *The Criterion of Dissimilarity.* "The earliest form of a saying we can reach may be regarded as authentic if it can be shown to be dissimilar to characteristic emphases both of ancient Judaism and of the early Church . . . [and] . . . the nature of the synoptic tradition is such that the burden of proof will be upon the claim to authenticity. . . . This seems to many to be too much to ask, but . . . there is no other way to reasonable certainty that we have reached the historical Jesus."[15] In other words, if we can show that the earliest form of a saying is unlike anything we know from Judaism and unlike anything we think that the church may have added, it is claimed according to this criterion that we have reached "reasonable certainty" that the saying came from the lips of Jesus himself.

For example, Jesus' threefold Passion prediction in Mark's Gospel: The criterion of dissimilarity does not allow us to argue that Jesus did not predict his own passion, but it would press us to say that the Passion predictions are too similar to the church's faith to have a strong chance of historical probability. Conversely, regarding Jesus' preaching of imminent arrival of the kingdom: by the time the Gospels were written, it was becoming increasingly clear that the kingdom was delayed. The criterion of dissimilarity would therefore allow us to argue with confidence that Jesus did indeed announce the imminent arrival of the kingdom.

Note that this criterion relies on the assumption that Jesus was a self-determining subject, uninfluenced by his environment. To presuppose no connection between Jesus and the Judaism of his day is historically, philosophically, theologically, and ethically suspect. It fails to block the possibility of repeating such tragic errors from the church's past from those of Marcion to the German Christians. Also, this criterion presupposes what it seeks to discover, namely that Jesus' teachings were distinct from those of the church that followed him. However, it would not be odd for the church to have pre-

---

ly adds other criteria, but when one tries critically to assess them, they show themselves to be closer to values or interests rather than methodological criteria. *Pace* Crossan, "Responses and Reflections," in *Jesus and Faith: A Conversation with the Work of John Dominic Crossan,* ed. Jeffrey Carlson and Robert A. Ludwig (Maryknoll: Orbis, 1993) 158-61. For a different view of the criteria from that presented in this essay, especially the criteria used by the Jesus Seminar, see Stephen J. Patterson, "Sources for a Life of Jesus," in *The Search for Jesus: Modern Scholarship Looks at the Gospels* (Washington: Biblical Archaeology Society, 1994) 9-36. See also M. Eugene Boring, "The Historical-Critical Method's 'Criteria of Authenticity': The Beatitudes in Q and Thomas as a Test Case," *Semeia* 44 (1988) 9-44. On the "Criterion of Embarassment," see Meier, *A Marginal Jew* II, 9-233.

15. Norman Perrin, *Rediscovering the Teaching of Jesus* (New York: Harper and Row, 1967) 39.

served in its own teachings something of the teachings of its master. It would indeed be strange if Jesus' teaching had been so unique and yet had no influence on the church.

2. *The Criterion of Multiple Attestation.* "This is a proposal to accept, as authentic, material which is attested in all, or most of the sources . . . behind the synoptic gospels."[16] This criterion often determines the authenticity of themes rather than individual sayings or events, although John Dominic Crossan uses it at great length and with some degree of refinement to inventory Jesus sayings in minute detail.[17] Since Jesus' repeated dealings with tax collectors, sinners, and outcasts, his use of parables, and his distinctive eschatology are multiply attested, according to this criterion they are likely to have historical reliability. (However, it should be noted that the Jesus Seminar rejects the historicity of Jesus' eschatological teaching, presumably because it does not fit the socio-political image of the Jesus whom they want to portray.)

Here, again, we must be realistic and admit that even if a theme appears in several early traditions, this proves nothing about the facticity of its appearance on the lips of Jesus himself. Rather, it may prove only that these traditions have an early date, or possibly only that they simply agree with one another.

3. *The criterion of coherence.* Material can, according to this criterion, be accepted as authentic if it can be shown to cohere with material established as authentic via the criterion of dissimilarity. In other words, if a saying is consistent with something previously judged authentic by criterion 1 above, it would have equal chance of historical probability. This criterion is based on a criterion that itself was only dubiously useful at best.

4. *The criterion of linguistic and environmental tests* rejects as authentic sayings or events that are incompatible with the world of Jesus' ministry. For example, the teaching on divorce in Matt. 5:31-32 is more likely to be authentic than that in Mark 10:10. Mark mentions the case of a woman divorcing her husband, which was a possibility under Roman law but not under Jewish law. According to this criterion, we can say that this appears to be Mark's accommodation of Jesus' teaching to his own situation. This criterion cannot work in reverse; just because something is consistent with Jesus' environment does not mean that it is therefore historically probable. A variation of this criterion is the criterion of Aramaisms, which would have us accept as authentic those sayings that make best sense when they are "retro-translated" from Greek into Aramaic, or those sayings that appear in our Greek text as

16. *Ibid.*
17. See his Appendix 1 to *The Historical Jesus*, 427-50.

Aramaic transliterations, such as *Talitha cumi,* or the *Amen* sayings.[18] The assumption behind this criterion, of course, is that Jesus spoke Aramaic, which seems to be a sound assumption. However, our knowledge of first-century Palestinian Aramaic is limited, and there is not widespread agreement as to what can be counted as Aramaisms in the text. In addition, we must remember that not only Jesus but also his first followers probably spoke Aramaic, and presumably Palestinian Christianity in general. Again, this criterion may only indicate a saying's early date or Palestinian origin.

We see, then, that objectivity of research with such tools is elusive at best, and that the very conclusion that a saying is or is not "authentic" is problematic. "Authenticity" is supposed to indicate those sayings of Jesus that are, according to these criteria, traceable to Jesus himself. It does not follow, however, that sayings judged to be inauthentic are *not* traceable to Jesus, as is implied by the black-print sayings in Robert Funk's *The Five Gospels.* Simply because a saying was elaborated on or a tradition shaped by the early church does not mean that it does not reflect the teachings of Jesus. Jesus may have indeed said something quite similar, but our criteria do not allow us to "prove" that such is the case. The Jesus Seminar in particular takes up the fundamental problem, as did the New Quest, raised by form criticism's recognition that the New Testament traditions about Jesus were influenced by the function or role they played in the life of the transmitting community. Both conservatives and their mirror-image twins in the Jesus Seminar tend to assume that the conclusion to be drawn is that the traditions were made up out of whole cloth by the transmitters. While conservatives will often therefore reject out of hand the methods and conclusions of, for example, form critics, the Jesus Seminar assumes that they can with confidence conclude that Jesus did not say such and such a thing.

In addition, the assumption that "earliest is best" is problematic. For example, if, indeed, Q did exist as a text independently of its instantiation in Matthew and Luke, it apparently had no Passion account, among other things. In comparison to the picture presented by the canonical Gospels, Q's portrait of Jesus is therefore incomplete. If Q is indeed earliest, it would be best only if we take the Passion stories of the canonical Gospels to be either fictions or irrelevant, or both. Indeed, the Jesus Seminar's reliance on a calcified notion of Q, as is illustrated in Burton Mack's *The Lost Gospel of Q,* is highly suspect. Q is a concept, a heuristic device, and a useful one at that, when used within the bounds of its definition as that which denotes material

18. Joachim Jeremias, *The Eucharistic Words of Jesus,* tr. Norman Perrin (Philadelphia: Fortress, 1977) 118 ff.

appearing in Matthew and Luke but not in Mark. There is no independent evidence for Q, no text, no papyri. Yet scholars speak of Q as though copies of it had been unearthed in the Judean desert, and they claim to find redactional layers of Q and to posit "communities" behind Q. However, Q is simply the alternative to the hypothesis that Luke read Matthew or vice versa, and its refutation is that the alternative is possible.[19]

These are just some of the hidden assumptions that muddle the historical task in much of Historical Jesus research, with the result that many theological statements and conclusions are couched as "historical fact." To state the obvious, the real question at issue in Historical Jesus research is the relation between faith and history. While the New Testament writers were not historians in the modern sense, we must not make the conceptual error that they were therefore uninterested in the time-space continuum. Indeed, they are preeminently interested in things that they claim happened in the public realm. One can reasonably say that the Gospels present a multiply attested and coherent picture of Jesus, which in fact can be called after a fashion "historical" and which does indeed agree with instead of subverting Christian confession. The picture they present of Jesus can be called "historical" insofar as the basic outlines of the sketch are attested outside the canonical Gospels, in both evidence external to the Bible[20] and internal in the non-narrative New Testament material.[21] It is not necessary to prove the thoroughgoing veracity of the texts in order to take them as historical evidence, but the claims about Jesus made in the Gospels are themselves indeed well attested outside the canonical Gospels. The historical evidence they present, however, does not point to Jesus himself but to the claims made about Jesus, the testimony to him. And the testimony to him presents him as Lord and Messiah. *It is the specific nature of the New Testament's "double vision" in its dual witness, both historical and theological, that renders problematic any investigation into what Jesus "really said and did." Any such investigation that refuses to read the Gospels as they present themselves to the reader necessarily harmonizes this dual witness, distorting the vision presented in the texts themselves.*[22]

19. See Austin Farrer, "On Dispensing with Q"; Michael D. Goulder, "Is Q a Juggernaut?" *JBL* 115 (1996) 667-81.

20. Josephus, *Antiquities* 18.3.3; 18.5.2; 20.9.1; Tacitus, *Annals* 15.44.2-8; Suetonius, *Life of Claudius* 25.4; Pliny, *Letters* 10.96; *Babylonian Talmud Sanhedrin* 43a, 106a. See Johnson, *The Real Jesus*, 112-22.

21. Gal. 4:4, 6; Rom. 1:3; 8:15-16; 15:8; 1 Cor. 2:8; 5:7; 7:10; 9:14; 11:23-25; 1 Tim. 5:17; 6:13; 2 Tim 2:8, etc.

22. One example of the harmonizing of this dual witness is the distinction between "the historical Jesus" and "the Christ of faith."

Of course, this poses the obvious question of exactly how the Gospels present themselves. What are the Gospels? This question itself is related to the question of the relationship between faith and history. One way the question of what the Gospels are has typically been posed in contemporary scholarship in terms of their genre: what is the Gospel's genre and how do we determine it? Do the Gospels present themselves as biography? If so, how? This question has been addressed in a "one-more-time-around-the-mulberry-bush" frolic from Schmidt to Burridge. Karl Ludwig Schmidt and Julius Schniewind saw the four canonical Gospels to be *sui generis,* neither representative of any literary genre nor related to developments of genre in the history of ancient literature.[23] Contemporary scholarship has for the most part questioned this assumption to varying degrees, claiming instead that the Gospels do indeed resemble ancient biography. Some understand the canonical Gospels to be a distinctive type of ancient biography combining Hellenistic form and function with Jewish content, however reflecting the popular literary culture of the lower classes.[24] Some want to claim that the similarities between the Gospels and ancient biography allow and impel the Quest for the Historical Jesus.[25] Helmut Koester has proposed a minimalist working definition for "Gospel" on the basis of content. His definition includes literature across a spectrum of genres and theological perspective: Gospels are "all those writings which are constituted by the transmission, use and interpretation of materials and traditions from and about Jesus of Nazareth."[26]

Unfortunately, these observations about the nature of Gospel literature do not help us to read or interpret the Gospels themselves. How else might we approach the question of the nature of the Gospels? If we were to compare them, particularly their content, with other New Testament material,

23. See Helmut Koester, *Ancient Christian Gospels: Their History and Development* (Philadelphia: Trinity, 1990) 24.

24. E.g., David Aune, *The New Testament in Its Literary Environment* (Philadelphia: Westminster, 1987). Charles Talbert argues that the Gospels are biography insofar as they present the "essence of Jesus' character." See *Semeia* 43 (1988) 53-73. In the same volume, David Moessner responds that the Gospels seem less interested in what sort of a person Jesus is than in who Jesus is in the light of God's dealings with Israel. Adela Yarbro Collins also responds there that Mark's intention was to write history, a narration of the course of eschatological events yet to be completed (hence the open ending).

25. E.g. Richard A. Burridge: "The emphasis on the centrality of the person of Jesus is an hermeneutical consequence of the gospels being βιοι. . . . Similarly, the βιος genre of the gospels affects the 'Quest for the Historical Jesus' . . . [since] this is a life of an historical person written within the lifetime of his contemporaries, there are limits on free composition." *What Are the Gospels?* (Cambridge: Cambridge University Press, 1992) 257-58.

26. Koester, *op. cit.,* 46.

what would we find?[27] Most of the non-Gospel literature is non-narrative, so it is not surprising to find that there is little reference to the Jesus narratives and sayings at all outside the narrative material of the New Testament. There is debate over the extent to which echoes of or allusions and parallels to Jesus' teachings appear in Paul's own correspondence.[28] The point here, however, is not to assess how much Paul knew about the Jesus traditions or how he knew it, but to note that even his sparse use of it is so completely different from the Gospel genre as to provoke serious theological questions. Unlike Dio Chrysostom's interest in the biographical details of Diogenes or Jeremiah's disciples' inscribing his words in the canonical book of Jeremiah, the New Testament non-narrative literature bears little apparent interest in the life of Jesus. Instead, we have for the most part ad hoc addressing of community crises. Apart from 1 Cor. 7:10-11; 9:14; and 11:23-25, Paul for the most part does not refer to Jesus' teaching or life to back up his own argumentation.[29] To be sure, Jesus is referred to time and again (e.g., 1 Thess. 4:1; 2 Thess. 3:6; Col. 2:6; Rom. 14:14); traditions about Jesus are passed on (e.g., 1 Cor. 15:3ff.); teachings that parallel Jesus' sayings appear (e.g., Rom. 13:9; 16:19); Jesus is alluded to as an example (e.g., 2 Cor. 8:9; Rom. 15:1-5; the *imitatio Christi/Pauli* theme). The hypothesis that the Jesus traditions were in the hands of Paul's enemies[30] does not adequately explain the lack of di-

27. Jesus tradition in Paul is sketchy at best. S. G. Wilson, "From Jesus to Paul: Contours and Consequences," in P. Richardson, et al., eds., *From Jesus to Paul: Studies in Honor of F. W. Beare* (Waterloo: Wilfrid Laurier University, 1984) 6-7: "Few would now deny that Paul's interest in the person and teaching of Jesus is minimal." But see James D. G. Dunn, "Jesus Tradition in Paul," in Chilton and Evans, edd., *Studying the Historical Jesus,* 155-78.

28. D. C. Allison, "The Pauline Epistles and the Synoptic Gospels: The Patterns of the Parallels," *New Testament Studies* 28 (1982) 1-32; F. Neirynck, "Paul and the Sayings of Jesus" in *L'Apôtre Paul,* ed. A. Vanhoye (Bibliotheca ephemeridum theologicarum Lovaniensium 73; Leuven: Peeters, 1986): 265-321; J. Piper, *"Love Your Enemies": Jesus' Love Command in the Synoptic Gospels and the Early Christian Parenesis* (SNTS Monograph Series 38; Cambridge: Cambridge University Press, 1971): 102-19; Peter Stuhlmacher, "Jesustradition im Römerbrief. Eine Skizze," *Theologische Beiträge* 14 (1983) 24-50; D. Wenham, "Paul's Use of the Jesus Tradition: Three Samples" in *The Jesus Tradition outside the Gospels* (Gospel Perspectives 5; Sheffield: JSOT, 1985) 7-37; A. J. M. Wedderburn, *Paul and Jesus: Collected Essays* (JSNT Supplement Series 37; Sheffield: JSOT, 1989); M. Thompson, *Clothed with Christ: The Example and Teaching of Jesus in Romans 12:1–15:13* (JSNT Supplement Series 59; Sheffield: JSOT, 1991); T. Holtz, "Paul and the Oral Gospel Tradition," in *Jesus and the Oral Gospel Tradition,* ed. H. Wansbrough (JSNT Supplement Series; Sheffield: JSOT, 1991) 380-93. See in particular James D. G. Dunn, "Jesus Tradition in Paul."

29. Dunn, *op. cit.,* 155.

30. So Wedderburn, *op. cit.,* 100-101.

rect early literary interest in the traditions of the pre-Ascension Jesus. There is a deeper theological force at work here: even in the Gospels Jesus is presented not as an ideal personality to be emulated, the focal point of the biographer, but as the Lord of Life and thus the object of the community's worship. This points again to the "double vision" of the gospel's theological and historical witness. Thus, we come back around to where Schmidt and Schniewind started: the Gospels are *sui generis*.

But this statement is made not on the basis of observations about the nature of ancient biography per se. Rather, if the Gospels are *sui generis*, it is because of the One to whom they witness. In the words of Karl Barth, "It may well be asked whether also the whole of the miracles of Jesus are not to be regarded, so to speak, as backward-striking rays of the glory of the Risen One, in fact whether in short the entire life of Jesus is not meant to be considered in this retrospective illumination."[31] The gospel's stance of "retrospective illumination" is evident most clearly in the fact that they were written for the converted, for those who already believed. If the entire life of Jesus, which is the miracle in and of itself, is meant to be considered in retrospect, as "backward-striking rays of the glory of the Risen One," then to expect the Gospels or their interpretation to reverse the direction of these rays' striking is indeed to undo the specific witness of the Gospels themselves. This is what Historical Jesus research in effect attempts to do.

Another way to approach the question of what the Gospels are such that their own scope and orientation is highlighted is to ask: How do we read them? What are we looking for, and what are our interests?[32] The question here is not "what is the meaning of the Gospels?" as though one could pinpoint a single specifiable or even a discreet set of "meanings," presuming indeed that we could settle the question of what "meaning" is in the first place.[33] The question, rather, has to do with the relationship between how we understand the task of reading the Gospels and what we understand the Gospels to be saying and doing. To be sure, the Gospel accounts of Jesus have been read in many different ways in the history of their interpretation, especially in the modern period, and the answer to this question will vary with the identification of the referent of the pronoun "we" in it. Historical Jesus

31. Karl Barth, *Church Dogmatics* I/1 (Edinburgh: Clark, 1936) 452, 518.

32. See Stephen Fowl, "The Ethics of Interpretation, or, What's Left Over after the Elimination of Meaning?" in *The Bible in Three Dimensions: Essays in Celebration of Forty Years of Biblical Studies in the University of Sheffield*, ed. David J. A. Clines, Stephen E. Fowl, and Stanley E. Porter (Sheffield: Sheffield University Press, 1990) 379-98.

33. See the now classic essay by Jeffrey Stout, "What Is the Meaning of a Text?" *New Literary History* 14 (1982) 1-12.

research in its own right reads the Gospels in many varied ways, but for the most part excludes the one category that takes seriously the Gospels' dual vision and therefore their function as Scripture within the Christian canon.[34] Some of the ways the Gospels have been read are sketched out as follows:

1. *Gospels as historical journalism.* Under this category, the Gospels are read as a collection of material ranging from historically verifiable and therefore useful accounts to historically unverifiable and therefore useless accounts. The material deemed useful is seen as a data mine for the historian's reconstruction of Jesus. The historian's reconstruction is then passed on to the theologian, who constructs theology for the church based on the findings of the historians. The Jesus Seminar operates in some respects with this model when they suggest that the church will need to change its confession based on their "findings." This is most obvious in the now classic remark of John Dominic Crossan that "If you cannot believe in something produced by reconstruction, you may have nothing left to believe in."[35] The first "quester," H. S. Reimarus, also worked with this understanding of the Gospels. However, he came to the conclusion that all the material was not only useless, but indeed that it was intentionally deceitful. Interestingly enough, many evangelicals and fundamentalists tend to read the Gospels under this category as well. Carl Henry, for example, assumes that the Gospels must be objectively and systematically verified in their entirety, but, unlike Reimarus, Henry is confident that all the material of the Gospels will fall into the "useable" category.[36] Ultimately, this category imports an understanding of the text's reference that the text shares only in part, that is, ostensive referentiality,[37] or its referentiality to the time-space continuum. However, this view then subsumes the text's referentiality in entirety under the larger framework of modern notions of objectivity and verifiability and conflates the text's dual witness to the historical alone. Here, the engine that makes the machine of interpretation run is derived externally from the text and from the world depicted by the text: in this sense it is anachronistic.

---

34. The two notable exceptions to this general rule that I have come across are found in the work of N. T. Wright and to a lesser degree in that of Martin Hengel. In fact, it is this that makes their work appear quite unlike other historical Jesus research.

35. *The Historical Jesus,* 426.

36. For this reading of Carl Henry, see George Hunsinger, "What Can Evangelicals and Postliberals Learn From Each Other? The Carl Henry/Hans Frei Exchange Reconsidered," *Pro Ecclesia* 5 (1996) 161-82.

37. This phrase is used by Hans Frei in *The Eclipse of Biblical Narrative* (New Haven: Yale University Press, 1974) to describe how the rationalists of the eighteenth and nineteenth centuries understood the meaning of the biblical text to be located.

2. *Gospels as mythic representations of existential realities.* This category also imports an understanding of the text's reference that the text shares only in part, that is, ideal referentiality,[38] its reference to nonmaterial or psychological reality. This was in part because those who adopted this view tended no longer to assume that the text could refer to the time-space continuum in any straightforward way, hence it must instead "be about" the inner life of the soul or the existential realities of consciousness. As in the previous category, the biblical narrative is then subsumed under an extratextual explanatory framework, this time the larger rubric of modern philosophical categories. The ties to the "historical" elements of the narrative are loosened, and the text's dual witness is conflated to the theological alone. D. F. Strauss fell into this category of reading, and for him the larger framework with which he read the Gospels was German Idealistic philosophy. Rudolf Bultmann later championed this way of reading the Gospels, but for him the larger framework into which the Gospel accounts were made to fit was Existentialist philosophy. In both cases, the engine that made the whole machine of interpretation run was derived in great measure, again, externally to the text itself. In a sense, Luke Johnson also reads the Gospels in this fashion, for what ultimately "matters" for him in reading the Gospels is the immediate experience of Jesus in the ecclesial community.[39] This may be philosophically lower flying, and certainly more appropriate to Catholic theological sensibilities, but nevertheless bears striking resemblance to Strauss and Bultmann in its focus on the theological witness of the Gospels to the exclusion of the historical. The most influential example of this type of reading in our own day is Paul Ricoeur.[40]

3. *Gospels as Literature.* This category reads the Gospels not for their reference to an external world, whether ostensive as in the first category or ideal as in the second, but as containers of their own world. For someone such as Northrop Frye, this world created by the biblical text forms the framework or "mythological universe" for Western literature. As in the previous two categories, this view of the Gospels as creating literary worlds does not adequately convey their own self-presentation. Instead of applying

38. This is the term used by Frei to describe how Strauss and others of the German Idealist philosophical tradition understood the location of the meaning of the biblical text.

39. Luke Johnson, *The Real Jesus.*

40. See Hans Frei's comments on this in "The Literal Reading of Biblical Narrative in the Christian Tradition: Does it Stretch or Will It Break?" in *The Bible and the Narrative Tradition,* ed. Frank McConnell (New York: Oxford, 1986).

(narratively-)externally derived categories to run the machine of interpretation, however, the engine is reduced in size from either the grandiose "objectivity" of the first category or the "idealism" of the second. Here the engine is limited to handling questions of genre and narratology, authorship and reader's location, etc. This means that the machine of interpretation does not cover as much ground as in the two previous categories and does not even attempt to explain the world of the text either in historical or theological terms. The project is purposefully less ambitious philosophically, for the goal is to allow the literary qualities of the biblical text to emerge in the reader's aesthetic experience. It is also in many cases self-consciously as nontheological as many of the approaches in the first category, for in limiting itself to the world created by the text it does not seek to investigate the possibility that the text may speak of a divine reality beyond the narrative itself.

4. *Gospels as Realistic Narrative.*[41] This category consciously attempts to correct the errors of the first two categories, and only thus, as if backing into the position, incorporates elements from them both, and indeed from the third as well. That is, the narratives of the Gospels are read as "history-like" depictions of the identity of Jesus. They are like history insofar as they make claims about the appearance of Jesus within the time-space continuum, but only *like* history insofar as they demand and can tolerate a much lower-flying epistemology.[42] They are narratives more than historical journalistic reports because an essential element of their depiction of Jesus is the flow and fit between his intention and action, between narrative development and character disclosure. This category, represented by Hans Frei, shares some of the features of the third category in having a similarly "limited engine." Like the third category, no external conceptual engine is supplied to run the machine of interpretation. It is not surprising, therefore, that this category is often taken to be identical to the third one, but this is only partially true. The Gospel texts are indeed read here as literature, but as literature of a specific genre. The genre itself, "realistic narrative," impinges on our reading, and the text itself holds sway over the classification of genre, not vice-versa. But as "realistic narrative," the Gospels are allowed to mean what they say and to

41. "Realistic narrative" is the term used by Hans Frei to describe the genre of the Gospels. See his *Eclipse of Biblical Narrative* and *The Identity of Jesus Christ: The Hermeneutical Bases of Dogmatic Theology* (Philadelphia: Fortress, 1975).

42. See Hans Frei, "Literal Reading." The epistemology would not involve a self-contained theory of how we know, but would draw the understanding of how we know from the biblical narrative itself in an ad hoc, "as-needed" manner.

present to the reader the identity in all its unsurpassability and non-negotiability of the central character depicted. The non-negotiability of the identity of the central character, namely Jesus, is not a factor in the investigation of the meaning of the text, but is a factor indeed in its theological use and significance. Unlike the previous category, this reading of the Gospels therefore takes seriously the "totalitarian" or world-absorbing quality of the narrative.[43]

5. *Gospels as canonical witness to Jesus Christ.* This category, like the one before it, attempts to draw on the Gospel texts' own self-presentation, this time keeping an eye not only on the texts but also on how they appear in their canonical placement between the Old Testament prophets and the New Testament epistles. In a sense, this category wants to extend the consideration of the narratival depiction of the character of Jesus back into the narratival depiction of the God of Israel in the Old Testament. This does not entail "finding the cross of Jesus in every tree of the Old Testament," but means that in order to understand the narratives about Jesus, their setting within the narratives of Israel becomes crucial. In addition, this category wants to extend consideration of the narratival depiction of the character of the God of Israel forward into the New Testament's depiction of Jesus. In other words, it is not simply to insist that the Old Testament "leans" into the New, or necessarily flows and culminates there, without a reverse hermeneutical move. This is because the Gospels are read as instances of the *canonical witness* to Jesus, and not under the more restrictive category of "realistic narrative," which has the potential to allow the isolation of the narratives about Jesus from the larger story of Israel, not to mention the other (non-Gospel) writings of the New Testament.

Representing this category is, of course, Brevard Childs, and to some extent other "canonical critics" such as James Sanders. Like the previous category, no textually external engine is supplied to run the interpretive machine, but the field of material considered as "text" is broadened to cover the entire canon, even when it is only the Gospels that are under immediate investigation. The "canon" is generally loosely defined in this schema. That is, it does not seem to be a matter of ultimate significance for this category whether the Christian canon is based on the Vulgate or the Masoretic text, or how one handles textual variants such as would be supplied within *Biblia*

---

43. Frei described premodern appreciation of the text's totalitarian nature as its ability to allow the text to "absorb the world," rather than the world to absorb the text. That is, the "real world" is taken to be the world depicted by and in the text, which then interprets the phenomenal world of the reader, not vice versa.

Hebraica Stuttgartensia or by Nestle-Aland.[44] It is the phenomenon of canon rather than its more precise details that power this machine.[45]

One may argue, and many have, that to use the canon as interpretive device is unjustifiably artificial, a theological layering on the pure bedrock of historical data, not withstanding Wrede's remarks almost a century ago about the irreducibly theological witness of even the more "historical" Gospel of Mark. The canon is indeed now and was, among other things, an interpretive device. There are grounds for the claim that the canon is not an extratextual interpretive framework such as those that dominate the first two categories, since it is in fact not extratextual at all. In other words, the canon is not a list of rules appended to the Gospels as to which one to prioritize, nor is it an independent ontology or epistemology by which the Gospels are to be interpreted. It is rather the sum and shape of the identity of Jesus portrayed in the canonical Gospels in the form of narratival shaping of Scripture as a whole. In a sense, this category takes the classical bidirectional hermeneutical flow of Old Testment to New and New to Old and makes an analogous move in negotiating the relationship between canon and gospel story. That is, the gospel story generates the shaping of the canon, which in turn shapes the reading of that story. Which comes first, the chicken or the egg? Neither: both canon and gospel story bear witness to the reality of Jesus of Nazareth, who is the image of the otherwise invisible God. This is probably the most promising implication of reading the Gospels as canonical witness for the muddled question of Historical Jesus research. It reads the Gospels for what they are: witness, both historical and theological. This in turn helps us to understand what is at issue in the vexing but prevalent distinction between the "Jesus of History" and the

44. Some have indeed taken Childs to say that the canon to be used in canonical interpretation is the Masoretic Text alone. "The term canonical text denotes that official Hebrew text of the Jewish community which had reached a point of stabilization in the first century AD" (e.g., J. M. M. Roberts, "Historical-Critical Method, Theology, and Contemporary Exegesis," in *Biblical Theology: Problems and Perspectives,* ed. Steven J. Kraftchick, et al. [Nashville: Abingdon, 1995] 133). Cf. Childs, *Introduction*, 100. However, the discussion in the first two opening sections of Childs's latest book, *Biblical Theology of the Old and New Testaments* (Minneapolis: Fortress, 1992) indicate a fit between what Childs means by "canon" as interpretive norm and the Rule of Faith. It would seem that urging the interpretation of one text in light of the other texts of the canon points not to the issue of canon-as-a-list-of-books but to the deeper question of the overall content or subject matter of Scripture.

45. E.g., "The very phenomenon of a canon provides a basic warrant for inferring that the material of the New Testament was shaped toward engendering faith and did not lie inert as a deposit of uninterpreted data from a past age." Childs, *The New Testament as Canon* (Philadelphia: Fortress, 1985) 51.

"Christ of Faith," the phantom figures that Jesus research in effect creates by extracting them from the canonical Gospel presentation of Jesus of Nazareth.

While the first category above presumes to offer us a portrait of the "Jesus of History," the second category presumes to offer a portrait of the "Christ of Faith." The third category makes no pretense at doing either, while the fourth and fifth assume that the very distinction between the Jesus of History and the Christ of Faith is faulty. The distinction between the Jesus of History and the Christ of Faith assumes falsely that the only access we have to Jesus of Nazareth is through historical research according to the methods of modern historiography. To accept the distinction is therefore either implicitly or explicitly to accept the notion that the church's faith is either in part or completely discontinuous with this Jesus. As I have attempted to point out in my earlier remarks about Historical Jesus research, this is to assume that one already knows the phenomenon that one is purportedly investigating.[46]

The distinction between the Jesus of History and the Christ of Faith therefore assumes that the categories of "history" and "faith" are for the most part separate and unrelated one to the other. This, however, flies in the face of the Gospels' dual witness, theological and historical. It is indeed the logical analogue to the rejection of the doctrine of the incarnation. Christian confession has insisted that the ineffable God of Abraham enters our time-space continuum fully in Jesus of Nazareth, without compromising the divine transcendent ineffability and without subsuming or erasing the full humanity of that Jesus. The assumption on the part of modern biblical scholarship of the separability and indeed the separation of the categories of faith and history rests on a prior negative appraisal of the relationship between the New Testament narratives about Jesus and what actually "happened" in the life of this otherwise obscure rabbi from Galilee.

More significantly, the distinction between the Jesus of History and the Christ of Faith is not a construal appropriate for use in the interpretation of the Gospels because it is not reflective of them nor organic to them. That is, it involves introducing categories or conceptual structures external to the biblical narrative to explain the text. This itself is a typical hermeneutical strategy of the modern period, but one that is logically similar to ancient and medieval allegorical interpretation in its importation of external explanatory categories in the act of biblical interpretation.[47] While the likes of Bultmann, Strauss, and

---

46. This is, of course, where both Martin Hengel and N. T. Wright diverge significantly from the bulk of historical Jesus research.

47. See James Barr, "The Literal, the Allegorical, and Modern Biblical Scholarship," *JSOT* 44 (1989) 3-17.

Johnson would object strenuously as historical critics to allegorical reading, there remains little self-conscious reflection on the conceptual similarity between their projects and medieval allegorical readings of Scripture.

The New Testament in fact intermingles the two categories of the "Jesus of History" and the "Christ of Faith" so thoroughly that they cannot be separated. This is what Kähler was saying, and it is why Frei speaks of the Gospel narratives as "history-like." Since the New Testament witness is a postresurrection phenomenon, there is no getting behind its faith or "bias" back to Jesus as he actually was. Jesus as he was is portrayed as the Christ and therefore as the object of faith. This does not mean we must accept him as the object of *our* faith in order to *understand* the New Testament narratives. We may justifiably choose to reject acting on the New Testament's portrayal of Jesus as the Christ, and we still may indeed have grasped the meaning of the text aright. But the fact that the Gospel texts function as thoroughly integrated historical and theological witness is undeniable.

We must therefore acknowledge that the work of the Jesus Seminar (or any other such research that refuses to read the New Testament accounts on their own terms) can lead only toward negative proof of Christian faith, and not positive proof. Such negative proof may indeed demolish the ground for our belief and religious practice.[48] Most Jesus researchers know this instinctively but tend to be reticent to admit it openly. No positive proof regarding what Jesus said or did can be offered *beyond what the New Testament witness offers.*

The lack of positive proof, of course, is of little consequence to the life of the faithful. Since faith is by definition a trust in the not-yet-verified, lack of positive proof is to be expected. Not only is it of little consequence in shaking people's faith, it is also of little consequence in establishing faith. In other words, if we could prove without a doubt that Jesus in fact did say and do what the Gospels record, it would most probably have little effect if any on the rate

48. Here I part ways with Luke Timothy Johnson, *The Real Jesus* 141-42: "although the Christian creed contains a number of historical assertions about Jesus, Christian faith is directed to a living person. The 'real Jesus' for Christian faith is the resurrected Jesus, him 'whom God has made both Lord and Christ' (Acts 2:36) . . . the *real* Jesus for Christian faith is not simply a figure of the past but very much and above all a figure of the present, a figure, indeed, who defines believers' present by his presence." The "real Jesus," I would argue, is indeed equally a figure from the past and a figure of the believing community's present, equally and inseparably. Yet I would disagree also with Richard Hays, who, in his review of both Johnson and Ben Witherington's *The Jesus Quest,* says that an important control for experiential knowledge must be "a careful and reverent examination of the evidence concerning the Jesus of history." See *First Things* 64 (1996) 46. I hope it is clear by now that my point here is that neither of these point to adequate readings of the Gospels.

of adult baptisms. This simply underscores the extent to which the life of faith involves not only cognitive assent but also deliberate turning from a former life and commitment to a new life, which Christians understand to be possible only in the power of the Holy Spirit. For example, in the covenant of marriage, we pledge our whole life, trusting that our spouse will put up with us until we die, trusting that we will find the resources to love our spouse unconditionally, trusting that no matter the hand life deals us, God in his mercy will make of our life together a witness to his redeeming love and grace. Such audacious claims can be made only with great risk, and an equal amount of trust. If we insisted on guarantees and verifiability, we would never get or stay married. The biblical writers link the covenant of marriage analogically with the covenant between God and Israel, Jesus and the church: giving oneself to God in faith, and God giving himself to us, is more like living out the marriage vows on a day-to-day basis than it is like drawing up a prenuptial agreement that protects both parties from financial or other material risk.

While the impossibility of positive proof may be ambiguously related to the life of faith, the possibility of negative proof is indeed of great significance. The only "proof" or "evidence" to be offered by Historical Jesus research, if it can even offer that, would be indeed such negative proof. This is not because of the methodology of any of the Quests, but because of the specific nature of the relationship between Christian faith claims and the time-space continuum that becomes clear when we recognize the Gospels to be both historical and theological witness. If, for instance, it could be proven without substantial doubt that Jesus did not say on the night before he was betrayed, "This is my body, broken for you . . . this is my blood of the New Covenant, shed for you and for many," or something quite like it, we would have to rewrite our central liturgies, prayers, confessions, etc. Likewise, if bones were found that could be undeniably, scientifically proven to be Jesus' very bones (a complete impossibility, to be sure), buried around AD 80, the bones of an old man, it would no longer be justifiable for the church to claim that Jesus was crucified under Pontius Pilate as a young man, or that the tomb was empty and that he rose from the dead.[49] The church's celebration of the Eucharist and of Easter would still be meaningful, but it would be a meaningful deceit.

This all goes to point out something very important that has largely been ignored in the debate over the Historical Jesus, but is in fact the most signifi-

49. See N. T. Wright's work on the meaning of resurrection in first-century Judaisms and the significance of the empty tomb in the Gospels in *Jesus and the Victory of God* (Minneapolis: Fortress, 1996).

cant lesson we may draw from the over 200 years of the hermeneutical gaffes and blunders on this topic. Unless and until historical research can persuade us beyond reasonable doubt that the New Testament's witness to who Jesus was and to what Jesus said and did is fundamentally false, we have no grounds as Christians to speak of the Christ of faith as though this were separable from Jesus as he was. The Christ of faith is an "idea," a concept, but Jesus is a character depicted within a narrative, a narrative that makes totalitarian claims about his significance for human life and death. Not only do we have no grounds to speak of a Jesus of History versus a Christ of Faith, we have no place speaking of Jesus as a "concept" or "idea" or "consciousness" or "metaphor" as though he represented something other than or apart from himself like some allegorical pointer. Indeed, when Jesus points to the God of Israel, he does so by pointing to his hands and his side. This is another way of recognizing that the New Testament narratival witness to Jesus, whose identity is portrayed in the fit between his intention and action, follows closely the Old Testament rendering of the identity of the God of Israel in its fit between character disclosure and plot. This is the literary observation that undergirds the Christian theological claim that Jesus is "God incarnate."

Ultimately, the Quest for the Historical Jesus stumbles over the same rock as did Reimarus and many others in his tracks: the presence of four distinct witnesses within the canon to the one gospel. This is a modern problem, even if the observation itself is not by any stretch of the imagination distinctly modern.[50] That such pluriformity and diversity was not a problem for faith before the modern period points out for us that the Quest for the Historical Jesus operates on distinct assumptions about what one is looking for and about what counts as important when reading the Gospels. Even though the Jesus Seminar claims to be comfortable presenting any number of different portraits of Jesus, and although the members of the Seminar would object strenuously to pious harmonies of the Gospels, the underlying assumptions about the nature and goals of their research are similar to the attempts throughout the history of biblical interpretation to come up with a "harmony" of the Gospels, to reduce the pluriformity.

Yet pluriformity is what the canon preserves for us. This means that Jesus will necessarily elude being defined as the Quest seeks to do. Of course, the question "Who was Jesus?" is entirely reasonable to ask, for Christianity is "basically a vigorous appeal to history, a witness of faith to certain particu-

---

50. See H. Merkel, *Die Widersprüche zwischen den Evangelien. Ihre polemische und apologetische Behandlung in der alten Kirche bis zu Augustin* (Wissenschaftliche Untersuchungen zum Neuen Testament 13; Tübingen: Mohr, 1972).

lar events in the past, to certain particular data of history."[51] From Kähler's first observations about how the Quest reads the Gospels against the grain to the work of Childs on the theological and hermeneutical importance of canon, it has become increasingly clear that the Historical Jesus research is a protracted attempt to isolate and scrupulously disregard what is most significant about the biblical texts that bear most of the historian's data about Jesus: that these texts are woven of the warp of historical witness and the woof of theological witness. One cannot be unraveled from the other without entirely disfiguring and misshaping the garment of the biblical narrative. This is apparently preferred, however, judging from the record sales of the Jesus Seminar books, to the actual reading of the Gospels on their own terms. This may be because reading the Gospels as theological and historical witness would confront us unequivocally and uncomfortably with the claims made there about the totalizing significance of Jesus' life and death.

There is in fact great advantage in our having access to Jesus only through the witness of others, through the texts that preserve what they deemed important about Jesus. We should not sing too easily the words of the old pious hymn, "I wish that his hand had been placed on my head, that his arm had been thrown around me. . . . I would like to have been with him then." Our historical setting may put us at the mercy of someone else's testimony, but we should be glad that we were not there with Jesus. If we had been, we more likely would have found ourselves in the crowd shouting for Barabbas's release and Jesus' crucifixion rather than among those weeping in hiding. This could, of course, put us in the inconvenient position of risking our lives on the testimony of those who believed it to be true that Jesus died for the sins of the world. After all, more Christians have been martyred in the twentieth century than in all the rest of Christian history. While many of us are happily unscathed by our confession, the stakes are still quite high in some areas of the world. The amazing thing, of course, is that where Christian confession can indeed result in martyrdom, people are usually not bothered at all by hypotheses of Jesus research that would overturn the New Testament witness. But where Christian confession apparently costs us little, where we do not pay the price for our confession with our lives, we seem to prefer to paint and gaze at portrait after portrait of who Jesus "really" was. Instead of coming up with zany thought-experiments about why the tomb was empty, we might do better to imagine ourselves as those dogs gathered around the cross, remembering that Jesus never tires of meeting even us, even there.

51. Georges Florovsky, "The Predicament of the Christian Historian," *Christianity and Culture* (Belmont: Nordland, 1974) 31.

The Text of John 1:34

Peter R. Rodgers

When I came to New Haven in 1979 to be the pastor of St. John's Church, I was honored to have Professor Childs attend my service of institution. I had met him previously in Cambridge, England, and his lecture there on the church's use of the Psalms had opened my eyes to the history of biblical interpretation. During my first year in New Haven Professor Childs delivered lectures on the New Testament as Canon, which later became his book under that title. Having worked with G. D. Kilpatrick in Oxford, I was especially interested in New Testament textual criticism and had learned through the eclectic method, which he championed, a nonconventional and refreshing approach to the discipline. I found Professor Childs's lecture on the subject especially engaging, and it was one of the factors that led to my beginning to publish my views on textual problems in the New Testament. The invitation to contribute to this volume honoring Brevard Childs offers me the opportunity to thank him for his encouragement and contribution and to engage with his insights on New Testament textual studies.

In "Excursus 1" of *The New Testament as Canon, an Introduction,* Professor Childs speaks of two principles at work in the study of the New Testament text: the critical principle and the inclusive principle. The critical principle represents "the constant effort to preserve the 'best,' 'purest,' and 'oldest' text of the Gospels, a concern which was reflected in the various revisions and recensions of the Greek text." This discipline was best represented by the Alexandrian school. The inclusive principle, on the other hand, "sought to include the widest possible number of variant traditions actually in use by the Christian communities through conflation and harmonization." This effort was represented by the Byzantine tradition. Childs referred to these two principles as "two seemingly contradictory principles, both de-rivative of canon."[1] How we seek to recover the apostolic witness, which be-came canonical, while also appreciating the text that functioned as canon in the church, remains a lively issue. Witness the debate over the choice of the *textus receptus* as the collation base for the International Greek New Testa-ment Project for Luke and John.[2]

I offer here a study of the well-known textual problem of John 1:34. It is a singularly interesting problem from the standpoint of text, canon, his-tory of interpretation, and early Christian social history and theology. It also bears on contemporary issues of hermeneutics and translation. Further-more, I believe that, in a curious way, thorough study of this text and its problems demonstrates that the two principles outlined by Childs are not al-ways as contradictory as they may seem.

At the end of the testimony of John the Baptist to Jesus at John 1:34, the KJV, RSV, NRSV, and other translations, following the *textus receptus* read, "This is the Son of God." The NJB and REV, however, following their predecessors, read "this is the elect of God." The *apparatus criticus* for UBS[4] sets out the full supports for the variants, and conflated readings.

The vast majority of manuscripts read "Son" (ο υιος). These include the early papyri 𝔓66 and 𝔓75, as well as the great uncials A and B. Those who defend this reading as original point to the age and diversity of the witnesses supporting it and the importance of the Son in the Gospel of John. "Elect" or "Chosen One" is never used elsewhere in John.[3] Those who argue in favor of "Chosen" (ο εκλεκτος) point to the tendency of scribes to alter "Chosen" to "Son" and not vice-versa.[4] The echoes of Isa. 42:1 and other parallel passages in the Synoptic accounts of the baptism of Jesus and other hints of the "Servant of the Lord" in John are offered as arguments favoring the reading.

This century has witnessed the steady growth in the fortunes of the reading "Chosen" (ο εκλεκτος) in John 1:34. Since Wescott and Hort placed it in their margin as the reading of the original hand of Codex Sinaiticus (א) in 1881, more testimony has come to light favoring the reading. In their edi-tion of papyrus 𝔓5 in 1899, Grenfell and Hunt conjectured that the lacuna at

1. Brevard S. Childs, *The New Testament as Canon: An Introduction* (Philadelphia: Fortress, 1984) 527.

2. D. C. Parker, "The International Greek New Testament Project: The Gospel of John," *NTS* 36 (1990) 157-60.

3. B. M. Metzger, *A Textual Commentary on the New Testament* (New York: United Bible Societies, 1975) 200.

4. R. E. Brown, *The Gospel According to John* 1 (New York: Doubleday, 1966) 57.

John 1:34 is only filled by the reading ο εκλεκτος. The abbreviation ΥΣ would be too short for the space on the line.[5]

F. C. Burkitt, in his edition of the Curetonian Syriac Gospels in 1904, cited the agreement of Syr[c] and Syr[s] with the comment, "The accession of s [Syr[s]] to the list of authorities for ο εκλεκτος ought, I think, to incline us to accept it."[6] Moreover, Burkitt referred to an evident dislike on the part of later scribes and editors for words that seemed to imply choice or approval of Jesus Christ by the Father and an unwillingness to call Jesus "the Chosen of God" because of adoptionist overtones or the implication of a time or state in which he existed before God chose him.[7]

Alexander Souter published his edition of the Greek New Testament in 1911. It cited the old Latin Codex b (Veronensis) from the fourth century as an authority for the conflated reading ο εκλεκτος υιος, "chosen Son." This reading was followed by the British and Foreign Bible Society's 1958 edition, edited by G. D. Kilpatrick. It is the reading given in Bianchini's edition of 1749, reprinted by Migne.[8] In that same year, 1911, E. S. Buchanan brought out his edition of the old Latin Codex b, in which he rejected all but the work of the original copyist ". . . my object being to give to the reader the Manuscript as it left his hands." He stated that *filius,* "Son," was the addition of "a cursive corrector using brown ink in the twelfth century."[9]

We have already noted that the reading ο υιος has had its gains, too. In this century it has found the weighty support of the papyri 𝔓66 and 𝔓75. But "Chosen" or "Elect" increasingly commends itself to commentators and translators. Nor can one imagine that the situation will improve for the reading "Son" in an age of inclusive language.

Gordon Fee is among those who favor ο εκλεκτος. Whether or not Fee's argument that "Elect" fits the context of John is convincing, he offers in his discussion what may be a clue for deciding on the text of this *crux interpretum.* Fee

5. B. P. Grenfell and A. S. Hunt, *The Oxyrhynchus Papyri Part 2* (London: Egypt Exploration Fund, 1899) 7. Modern commentators supporting "elect" include Spitta, Zahn, von Harnack, Lagrange, Loisy, Windisch, Cullman, Jeremias, Mollet, den Bussche, Boismard, Barrett, Lightfoot, and Schnackenburg. We may now add P. Oxy. 65-4445 (London, 1998), which reads εκλεκτος. This third-century papyrus of John is 𝔓[106] on the international list.

6. F. C. Burkitt, *Evangelion da Mapharreshe* 2 (Cambridge: Cambridge University Press, 1904) 309.

7. *Ibid.,* 308. Now see the thorough study by Bart D. Ehrman, *The Orthodox Corruption of Scripture* (Oxford: Oxford University Press, 1993), which investigates the influence of doctrinal debates on the text, especially pp. 69-70 on John 1:34.

8. Patrologia Latina 12:359.

9. E. S. Buchanan, *The Four Gospels from Codex Veronesis* (Old Latin Biblical Texts 4; Oxford: Clarendon, 1911) xi-xii.

asserts, "The question is whether it reflects the Messianism of such a passage as Psalm 2:7 or that of Isaiah 42:1."[10] The question, then, is whether John 1:34 is alluding to the "Son" text of Ps. 2:7 or to the "Servant" text of Isa. 42:1. Fee opts for the latter. I believe that when the question is put this way, focusing on the allusions to the Old Testament in the voice at the baptism of Jesus, we may want to reconsider the conflated reading "elect Son," ο εκλεκτος υιος. Although it has slender support, I am increasingly convinced that it may point to the original reading. On the surface it looks like a conflation of the kind common in the Byzantine and later church text, but given the combined allusion to Ps. 2:7 and Isa. 42:1 in the three Synoptic accounts of the voice at the baptism, this succinct phrase in John may be a true parallel and not a later conflation.

I am especially attracted to the reading "Elect Son" for several reasons. The first is that I believe that the Old Testament allusions or echoes in the voice at the baptism are conscious on the part of the evangelists and provide a clue to their christology. Now the voice at the baptism is clearly quoted in the Synoptics, but only alluded to in John. However, if we look more closely at John's treatment of the Old Testament, we find that he often alludes to a text or theme without citing it as such (e.g. chs. 4 and 7, living water; ch. 15, the vine). The slightest allusion or echo of a word or phrase seems to be enough for his readers to catch the reference. So what I believe John is doing here is saying in shorthand form, to those very familiar with the Old Testament, that this is the Son of Ps. 2:7 and the Servant of Isa. 42:1.

But there is more data to be considered, if we are to apply the inclusive principle and survey the broadest range of textual variants considered canonical in the history of the church. The fourth edition of UBS notes that the reading of some manuscripts of the Palestinian Syriac Lectionary represents the Greek as ο μονογενης υιος (only begotten son).[11] That the Syriac *(yhidh)* represents the Greek μονογενης is a conjecture, and we have no Greek manuscript that gives this reading. We know that μονογενης ("only begotten") is an important word for John, and we are safe in assuming that if this late lectionary preserves what John wrote, then the word μονογενης would have been found in this place. On this reading of the matter, we have a third allusion in John 1:34 corresponding to the third Old Testament echo in the Synoptics. Of course, the word is αγαπητος, usually translated "beloved." Now what intrigues me is that the words αγαπητος and μονογενης were frequently found together as synonyms. This is already the

10. G. D. Fee, "The Textual Criticism of the New Testament" in *The Expositors Bible Commentary,* ed. Frank E. Gaebelein, 1 (Grand Rapids: Zondervan, 1979) 432.

11. Agnes Smith Lewis and Margaret Dunlop Gibson, *The Palestinian Syriac Lectionary of the Gospels* (London: Clay, 1899) liii. Ms C adds ο μονογενης αυτου. A and B add ο εκλεκτος αυτου. See p. 4.

case in the LXX, where they appear together in Judg. 11:34 and Baruch 4:16. Furthermore, we notice that in Gen. 22:2 Aquila reads μονογενης instead of αγαπητος, and this is the case for Symmachus in Gen. 22:12, where μονογενης is also a variant in several LXX manuscripts. We note as an example in early Christian literature of the use of the words as synonyms Irenaeus, *Against Heresies* 4.5.4 (του ιδιον μονογενη και αγαπετον υιον) in relation to the sacrifice of Isaac. Now it is generally agreed that the term αγαπητος in the Synoptic accounts of the voice at the baptism is an allusion to Gen. 22:2, "Take your son, your only son, whom you love . . ." (λαβε του υιον σου του αγαπητου ηγαπητας). Here I believe we are right in following the seventeenth-century Dutch scholar D. Heinsius and the twentieth-century British scholar C. H. Turner in arguing that in Mark 1:11 αγαπητος meant "only" rather than "beloved." Under the powerful influence of αγαπη, the word quickly begins to mean "beloved" in Christian circles, but the older meaning is not lost and we find Athanasius appealing to it as he argues against the Arians that Jesus is God's only Son. "From Homer to Athanasius the history of the Greek language bears out . . . that αγαπητος υιος is rightly rendered 'only son.'"[12]

Recently Gerard Pendrick has pointed to a similar development with regard to μονογενης. Whereas in Johannine usage the word meant "only," later generations began to take its meaning as "only begotten."[13] If the arguments of Turner and Pendrick are plausible, as I think, then here is another exact correspondence between the Synoptic and Johannine accounts in their allusion to Gen. 22:2.

Few will allow, of course, that a reading supported only by late lectionaries should have a claim to originality. Yet the inclusive canonical principle calls us to take all readings seriously, and in this case with surprising results. Here is what happened, as I read the matter: all three Synoptists were influenced by Gen. 22:2, and the word αγαπητος/μονογενης in the voice at the baptism reflects that influence. There, as in classical, LXX, and Hellenistic usage, the word meant "only" but quickly came to mean "beloved" under the pervasive influence of αγαπη. This seems to be the case already by the time Paul writes to the Romans and he uses του ιδιου υιου ("his own son"), rather than του υιου σου του αγαπητου, in 8:32 to echo Gen. 22:2. All the more this must be the case when John represents the witness at the baptism of Jesus and chooses μονογενης rather than αγαπητος to affirm that Jesus is the "only" Son. This is John's special word and is his distinct contribution. So

12. D. Heinsius, *Exercitationes ad Novum Testamentum* (Leiden, 1639). C. H. Turner, *JTS* 27 (1926) 113-29.
13. G. Pendrick, "ΜΟΝΟΓΕΝΗΣ" *NTS* 41 (1995) 587-600.

then John's use of μονογενης at 1:34 is his allusive way of affirming that Jesus is the only Son, in conscious echo of Gen. 22:2.

Then came the second century and the harmonizing tendency exemplified in Tatian's *Diatessaron*. Since John's μονογενης seems to have no discernible parallel in the Synoptics (from the view of some mid-second-century copyists) it drops out of many copies and survives only in that tradition represented by the Palestinian Syriac lectionaries, of which our extant copies are from the eleventh century.

One problem remains with the view that all the readings are original. We must still explain the omission of ο υιος from the few manuscripts that do not have it in John 1:34. One possible explanation suggests itself. υιος appeared in the early manuscripts in abbreviated form *(ΥΣ)*, and coming just before θεου *(ΘΥ)*, it is possible that *ΥΣ* could have slipped out through accidental omission due to similarity. Word order, a factor in the versional evidence, may have played a part too.

So then, I am arguing, as a debtor to Professor Childs, that the canonical approach to the text calls us to apply the inclusive principle and accept the widest range of variants as original. I believe that John wrote something like ουτος εστιν ο μονογενης ο εκλεκτος υιος θεου, "This is the only, the chosen Son of God." In a curious way, because the key to understanding the voice at the baptism of Jesus lies in the allusions to three Old Testament texts, the rigorous application of the inclusive principle causes us to do justice to the critical principle. So my view on the variants at John 1:34 is that all win and all must have prizes.

*   *   *

My usual custom with textual notes is to make the text-critical observations and leave the matter there, only venturing a hint with regard to theological or ethical implications.[14] But in an essay honoring Brevard Childs it would be inappropriate and perhaps irresponsible to stop there. As Professor Childs reminds us, "The discipline of text criticism is not a strictly objective, or non-theological activity, but is an integral part of the same interpretive enterprise which comprises the church's life with its scriptures."[15] There can be no isolating of text from history or theology or ethics. So here are some observations of a student of the text, in fellowship with the church, emboldened and encouraged by Professor Childs's teaching.

14. See *Journal of Theological Studies* 41 (1990) 92-94.
15. Childs, *op. cit.*, 529.

One major issue raised by the unearthing of the Old Testament echoes in the account of the baptism of Jesus in all four canonical Gospels is that the texts thus echoed bespeak a very high christology. If in fact the use of the Old Testament in the New may constitute what C. H. Dodd called "the substructure of New Testament theology,"[16] then we may be confident in finding in the voice at the baptism, if anywhere in the Gospels, a clue to the christology of the apostolic church. And a christology that affirms Jesus as the "Son," the "Servant," and the "Sacrifice" is a very high christology indeed. It is worth reflecting on the curious phenomenon that the highest christology may be the earliest! Standard and fashionable theories of developing christology may have to be revised.

Another issue is addressed by my observations on the textual complexities of John 1:34. There is something to be learned by both the interpreter and the preacher. The way in which John especially echoes the Old Testament here and elsewhere should provide a model for all who take the church's engagement with its Scripture seriously. The interpreter is on solid ground the more closely he or she engages with the text of Scripture and allows it to be formative for both thought and phraseology. As their engagement with the Old Testament was formative for the theology of the first Christians, so our engagement with our canonical Scriptures should be formative for our own theology and method.

The preacher will seek always to encounter the Scripture and to grapple with it on its own terms, and in its long-term life and growth in the church, and to enter into that rich fellowship. He or she brings the scriptural witness to Christ, in the life of the church, to bear upon the contemporary world. As a preacher I have pondered the voice at the baptism in all its canonical (and original!) richness in all four Gospels. The increasing conviction that John offers an exact parallel, albeit in allusive form, to the Synoptics has caused me to see the baptism of Jesus with the three Old Testament texts at center stage. So in preaching I come to affirm the meaning of baptism for Jesus, and for us, as suggested by the three foundational texts:

Baptism means sonship (Psalm 2).
Baptism means service (Isaiah 42).
Baptism means sacrifice (Genesis 22).

I suspect that Professor Childs will be pleased that on this occasion the text critic, interpreter, theologian, and preacher are the same person.[17]

---

16. C. H. Dodd, *According to the Scriptures* (New York: Scribner, 1953) 127.
17. I am grateful to John Savoie for his help on this article.

The Good Shepherd: Canonical Interpretations in the Early Church?

Rowan A. Greer

Childs's work can be regarded as having initiated a multifaceted conversation, and one can pay tribute to the contribution he has made in many different ways. Those who have entered directly into the conversation underline its significance not only by agreement but also by attempts to deepen or qualify Mr. Childs's proposals and even by disagreement with them. For those of us who are not competent to enter the discussion in so direct a fashion there may be another way of paying tribute. There seems to me a sense in which "canonical criticism" is more than a methodological or hermeneutical proposal. It is also and at a deeper level an appeal to read Scripture faithfully and theologically without abandoning the insights of the historical-critical method. If this be true, we are invited to explore the way in which "canonical criticism" correlates with other theological readings of Scripture.

My own tribute to Childs's work, then, will take the form of reflection upon correlations between his proposals and the patristic exegesis of the Good Shepherd. I shall wish to include as broad a range of evidence as possible, but my focus will be upon the interpretations of John 10 found in the commentaries of Theodore of Mopsuestia and Cyril of Alexandria and the homilies of John Chrysostom and Augustine, all of which may be dated some time in the half century preceding the outbreak of the Nestorian controversy in 428.[1] With the possible exception of Origen's commentary on John

---

1. Theodore's commentary, which exists only in a Syriac translation, is probably the earliest, but there is no way of establishing a precise date. Theodore died in 428. John

(which, of course, is fragmentary and does not include a treatment of the tenth chapter), these writings are the only extended discussions of the Fourth Gospel surviving from the early church.

I. Three Characteristics of "Canonical Criticism"

At the risk of oversimplifying the issues involved, let me suggest that Mr. Childs's proposals involve three interrelated claims. The first is, at least implicitly, that there can be no such thing as a correct interpretation of Scripture; rather, we must speak of valid interpretations and raise the question of the limits of validity:[2]

> The canon therefore provided a context for the gospel, but did not attempt a final formulation of its message. It marked the arena in which each new generation of believers stood and sought to understand afresh the nature of the faith. It did not establish one doctrinal position, but often balanced several or fixed the limits within which Christians might rightly disagree.

This claim insists upon diversity of interpretation and refuses to equate unity with uniformity. But, of course, it also argues that there are limits to diversity and a point beyond which diversity can compromise unity.

A second claim is that the meaning of the biblical text is not confined to its historical setting. Mr. Childs wishes to insist that "the function of canonical shaping was often precisely to loosen the text from any one given historical setting, and to transcend the original addressee."[3] It is clear enough

---

Chrysostom's homilies were delivered in Antioch, possibly in 391. Cyril's commentary is to be dated before the outbreak of the Nestorian controversy. Augustine's homilies fall into two groups (1-54 and 55-124) and have been assigned differing dates by scholars. All appear to agree, however, that they belong at some point between 411 and 420.

2. Brevard S. Childs, *The New Testament as Canon: An Introduction* (Philadelphia: Fortress, 1985) 29. Cf. his *Introduction to the Old Testament as Scripture* (Philadelphia: Fortress, 1979) 83: "In one sense the canonical method sets limits on the exegetical task by taking seriously the traditional parameters. In another sense the method liberates from the stifling effect of academic scholasticism. . . . By placing the canonical text within the context of the community of faith and practice a variety of different exegetical models are freed to engage the text, such as the liturgical or the dramatic. In sum, the canon establishes a platform from which exegesis is launched rather than a barrier by which creative activity is restrained."

3. *The New Testament as Canon*, 23. Cf. *Introduction to the Old Testament as Scripture*, 42, where Childs argues that the strengths of the early Christian understanding of canon included receiving the texts "as a divine word which claimed an immediate author-

that he does not mean by this claim that we can dismiss or ignore the original setting. Rather, the point is that Scripture is always capable of speaking anew. Not only should we refuse to repudiate the historical-critical method, we can also find its insights sometimes helpful in enabling the text to speak to us. Loosening the text from its historical setting need not mean reducing the Bible to a set of timeless truths.

The third claim is implicit in the first two. The emphasis upon diversity and flexibility, as well as the conviction that Scripture is not chained to its historical meaning, suggest that the chief aim of interpretation involves appropriating the scriptural message for a community of faith and practice:[4]

> The critic presumes to stand above the text. . . . In contrast, the canonical interpreter stands within the received tradition, and, fully conscious of his own time-conditionality as well as that of the scriptures, strives critically to discern from its kerygmatic witness a way to God which overcomes the historical moorings of both text and reader.

There may be some ambiguity as to whether we are speaking of the faithful person or of the faithful community, but the main point is clear. Scripture is not a relic of the past to be preserved in a museum but is a living message to be appropriated ever anew by Christians in their own time.

I shall wish to keep these three claims in mind as I turn to the Good Shepherd in the ancient church and to the patristic interpretations of John 10. They will not, however, supply the structure for my discussion, since I wish to begin by seeking to describe and interpret the early Christian texts as much as possible in their own terms. Nevertheless, I shall return to them in my concluding reflections upon the correlation between patristic exegesis and canonical criticism.

---

ity," accepting diversity, and establishing "a dynamic relationship, testified to in the church's liturgy, . . . between scripture, its author (God), and its addressee (the church)." He goes on to describe the weaknesses of the early church as an inability to hear the Old Testament in its own terms, the subjection of the text "to the dominance of ecclesiastical tradition," the claim that the New Testament superseded the Old Testament, and the tendency to deny the Jews a right to their own Scripture.

4. *The New Testament as Canon*, 51f.

II. The Good Shepherd in the Early Church: General Observations

One of the problems involved in studying Mithraism in the early centuries of this era is that very little literary evidence survives. Imagining what the cult was like depends largely upon reading the iconographic and architectural evidence. Suppose that we were obliged to understand early Christianity in the same way. What conclusions might we draw? There can be little doubt that one deduction would revolve around the frequency with which Christ, as the focus of the Christian cult, was portrayed as the Good Shepherd. The image of the shepherd carrying the sheep on his shoulders appears in the catacomb frescoes and on the sarcophagi; statues also survive. The image, of course, is not necessarily a Christian one, since it was commonly used by pagans to symbolize *humanitas*.[5] But in Christian contexts it is associated with other images — Jonah, Daniel, Noah, the raising of Lazarus. The Good Shepherd is clearly the Savior, who effects the deliverance implied in the other images.

According to Tertullian the cup (used in the Eucharist?) often had the Good Shepherd depicted on it.[6] The fresco over the baptismal pool in the house church at Dura Europos (third century) depicts the Good Shepherd. Eusebius in his *Life of Constantine* tells us that Constantine in building his new capital excluded pagan idolatry:[7]

> On the other hand one might see the fountains in the midst of the market place graced with figures representing the good Shepherd, well known to those who study the sacred oracles, and that of Daniel also with the lions, forged in brass, and resplendent with plates of gold.

It may not be going too far to suggest that the Good Shepherd occupies the central iconographic place for the early church that the crucifix does for the West in the Middle Ages. In any case, the association of the image with funerary and baptismal art means that we can conclude that the Good Shepherd brings a double deliverance — from alienation in this world and from death in the age to come.

The literary evidence helps confirm this conclusion. For example, *The Martyrdom of Perpetua and Felicitas* incorporates the diary kept by Perpetua before her martyrdom, in which she reports her dreams. In one dream she

---

5. See A. Grabar, *Early Christian Art* (New York: Odyssey, 1968) 11, 36.

6. Tertullian, *On Modesty* 7, 10 (ANF IV, 80, 85). No examples of such cups survive. See Sister Charles Murray, "Art and the Early Church," *JTS* 28 (1977) 322.

7. Eusebius, *Life of Constantine* 3.49 (NPNF 2/I, 532).

climbs a ladder and sees "an immense extent of garden and . . . a white-haired man sitting in the dress of a shepherd, of a large stature, milking sheep."[8] The shepherd welcomes her, gives her a little cake of cheese, and so assures her that her hope lies in the sweetness of the life to come. It is difficult not to conclude that Perpetua's dream is informed by the images in the church with which she was familiar. The Good Shepherd is Christ, welcoming his martyr to the bliss of the resurrection life. Perpetua's contemporary, Clement of Alexandria (ca. 200), cites what is apparently an early Christian hymn, which treats the resurrection life as a present hope:[9]

> Bridle of colts untamed . . . Shepherd, with wisdom tending Lambs of the royal flock: Thy simple children bring in one, that they may sing in solemn lays their hymns of praise with guileless lips to Christ their King. . . . Jesus, Saviour of our race; Shepherd, who dost us keep. . . . Lead us, Shepherd of the sheep, Reason-gifted, holy one. . . .

We could add many other examples, but the point I wish to make seems obvious enough. The Good Shepherd is a central image for early Christianity and depicts Christ as the Savior.

This conclusion is by no means unrelated to the question of how the early church understood Scripture. We have already seen Eusebius's observation, in passing, that those familiar with Scripture will understand the significance of the Good Shepherd. When we examine the literary evidence, what we often find is the weaving together of scriptural citations and allusions. For example, in one of his homilies Gregory Nazianzen says:[10]

> . . . He [God the Word] humbled Himself for thee; because the Good Shepherd (John 10:11), He who lays down His life for His sheep, came to seek for that which had strayed upon the mountains and hills, on which thou wast then sacrificing, and found the wanderer; and having found it (Luke 15:4ff.), took it upon His shoulders — on which He also took the Wood of the Cross; and having taken it, brought it back to the higher life; and having carried it back, numbered it amongst those who had never strayed. Because He lighted a candle — His own flesh — and swept the house, cleansing the world from sin; and sought the piece of money, the Royal Image that was covered up with passions. And He calls together His Angel friends on the finding of the coin, and makes them sharers in His joy, whom He had made to share also the secret of the Incarnation.

8. *The Passion of Perpetua and Felicitas* 1 (ANF III, 700).
9. Clement of Alexandria, *The Instructor* 3.12 (ANF II, 295-96).
10. *Oration on the Theophany* 38.14 (NPNF 2/VII, 349).

Luke's parables of the lost sheep and the lost coin dominate Gregory's exhortation, but he identifies Luke's shepherd with the Good Shepherd of John 10. He also locates his interpretation in an incarnational view couched in narrative terms and building upon what modern scholars call the Redeemer myth.[11]

We find a similar interpretation in Augustine's *Confessions:*[12]

> O God, who are so good, what is it that makes men rejoice more for the salvation of a soul for which all had despaired, or one that is delivered from great danger, than for one for which hope has never been lost or one which has been in less peril? You too, merciful Father, *rejoice more over one sinner who repents than over ninety-nine souls that are justified and have no need of repentance.* (Luke 15:7) We also are overjoyed when we hear that the sheep that was lost is carried home on the happy shepherd's shoulders and that the coin is returned to your treasury. . . .

Augustine writes these words on the eve of his conversion. Like Justin Martyr he thinks of himself as the lost sheep, and it can be fairly argued that his search for the lost coin is his quest for the lost image of God.[13] At one level Gregory and Augustine articulate the same view. God through His incarnate Son has brought humanity redemption. On the other hand, were we to explore their views of God, the incarnation, and redemption, we should find significant differences. We shall be able to see this in more detail when we turn to the patristic interpretations of John 10. Suffice it to say at this point in the argument that the identification of the Good Shepherd with the incarnate Lord dominates the patristic understanding of the biblical passages involved, chief of which are Luke 15 (and the parallel in Matthew 18) and John 10.[14]

---

11. It is worth noting that Irenaeus, Tertullian, and Hippolytus speak of the Gnostic and Marcionite use of the Good Shepherd theme (Irenaeus, *Against Heresies* 1.8.4; 1.16.1; 1.23.2; 2.5.2; 2.24.6; Tertullian, *On the Flesh of Christ* 8; Hippolytus, *Refutation* 6.47). Related to this may be a Christian gem, dated by Reitzenstein to the third century, which depicts a shepherd carrying one lamb with six others at his feet and seven stars in the sky. The point may be that the Good Shepherd preserves his flock from the evil planetary powers. See Alan Scott, *Origen and the Life of the Stars* (Oxford: Clarendon, 1991) 102-3.

12. *Confessions* 8.3.6 (NPNF 1/I, 119); cf. 1.18.28 and 10.18.27.

13. Justin Martyr, *Dialogue* 3. Cf. Augustine's use of the parable of the lost coin in *Confessions* 10.18-20.

14. Other biblical passages, of course, enter the picture, for example the sheep and goats of Matthew 25 (Clement of Alexandria, *Instructor* 1.5; Origen, *Homily on Song of Songs* 1.9; Gregory of Nyssa, *Homily Two on Song of Songs, Gregorii Nysseni Opera*, ed. W. Jaeger, vol. 6 [Leiden: Brill, 1960], 65), the lost sheep of Israel in Matt. 15:24 (Origen, *Homilies on Luke* 34.4); 1 Pet. 5:4 (Origen, *Homilies on Luke*, fragment 38); Zech. 13:7 (= Matt. 26:31 par. Mark 14:27) (*Barnabas* 5; Justin, *Dialogue* 53; Irenaeus, *Demonstration*

Several subordinate themes are common in filling out the meaning of the Good Shepherd. He gives his life for the sheep (John 10:11) and by doing so becomes himself a sheep, the lamb that takes away the sin of the world (John 1:29).[15] This theme takes us to the heart of the Christian liturgy, the Pascha. John 19:36 makes it clear that Jesus is identified with the paschal lamb (John 1:29, 36), and the irony implied by John 19:14 is that at the very hour the lambs were being slaughtered in the Temple the true paschal lamb was sacrificed on Golgotha. Melito of Sardis echoes these themes in his *Paschal Homily:*[16]

> Come, then, all human families, defiled with sin; receive the forgiveness of your sins. For I am your forgiveness, I am the Passover of salvation, I am the lamb slaughtered for you, I am your ransom, I am your life, I am your resurrection, I am your light, I am your salvation, I am your king.

The shepherd, then, effects redemption by his death and resurrection as the paschal lamb; and redemption means the abolition of sin and death.[17] Redemption also involves bringing Christ's "other sheep" into the one fold

76; Tertullian, *De fuga* 11; Origen, *Homilies on Exodus* 11.2; John Chrysostom, *Homilies on Matthew* 82.2); Isa. 40:11 (Clement of Alexandria, *Instructor* 1.5); Ezekiel 34 (*Instructor* 1.9; Cyprian, *Letter* 2.1; pseudo-Cyprian, *Against Novatian* 14); Psalm 23 (Origen, *Commentary on Song of Songs* 2.4; Paulinus of Nola, *Letter* 42.2).

15. See, for example, Cyril of Jerusalem, *Catechetical Lectures* 10.3 (NPNF 2/VII, 57): "He is called a Sheep [John 1:29; Isa. 53:7-8; Acts 8:32], not an irrational one, but the one which through its precious blood cleanses the world from its sins, which is led before the shearers, and knows when to be silent. This Sheep again is called a Shepherd, who says, *I am the Good Shepherd* [John 10:11]: a Sheep because of His manhood, a Shepherd because of the loving-kindness of His Godhead." Cf. also Paulinus of Nola, *Letter* 11.8, where Christ is described as the priest, victim, lamb, and shepherd and where Paulinus cites Isa. 53:7 and John 10:17f. and alludes to Heb. 10:10f. and Luke 15.

16. *Paschal Homily* 103 (Sources chrétiennes 123:122).

17. Of course, this general view implies a number of problems. In general, the early church does not sever Christ's death from his resurrection. Moreover, there is a tendency to regard redemption primarily as the abolition of mortality. Christ is the victor over death more than he is the victim atoning for sin. With Augustine these emphases begin to shift. The sacrifice of the paschal lamb is usually understood as an aversion sacrifice, turning away death, sin, and Satan. (See Frances M. Young, *The Use of Sacrificial Ideas in Greek Christian Writers from the New Testament to John Chrysostom* (Cambridge: Philadelphia Patristics Foundation, 1979). For examples of discussion of Christ as the paschal lamb see Gregory Nazianzen, *Oration* 12 (NPNF 2/VII, 246); Gregory of Nyssa, *Life of Moses* 126 and *Inscription of Psalm 58* (*Gregorii Nysseni Opera*, ed. W. Jaeger, vol. 7/1 [Leiden: Brill, 1964], 72f; vol. 5 [Leiden: Brill, 1962], 171); Chrysostom, *Homily 27 on Hebrews* (NPNF 1/XIV, 487); Cyril of Alexandria, *Commentary on John* ad loc. 1:29 and *Quod Unus Sit Christus* 774 (Sources chrétiennes 97:498-99).

(John 10:16); Jews and Gentiles are, in principle, united.[18] Finally, the leaders of the church are also to be regarded as good shepherds.[19]

I cannot argue that my discussion has been complete, but I hope that it will suffice to show that the Good Shepherd touches upon central aspects of the life of the early church. The image, drawn from Scripture, articulated in terms of iconographic conventions familiar in the Roman world, and explained by the church's understanding of the Savior and his work, has a central place in the church's liturgy. We may readily suppose that these associations are in the minds of the exegetes to whom we must now turn. Rather than treating Theodore, John Chrysostom, Cyril, and Augustine one by one, I wish to discuss their interpretations under the following rubrics: the setting of John 10, the wicked characters in Jesus' parable, the positive details in the parable, Christ, and redemption. My consideration will move from the setting of the passage in its literary context, which the church Fathers will identify with the historical setting in Jesus' ministry, to the church's larger vision of Christ's person and work.

III. The Setting of John 10

All the interpreters agree that Jesus' discourse and the narrative in ch. 10 belong in the context of his controversy with the scribes and Pharisees. Theodore begins his explanation by treating Jesus' word as a figurative response to them, claiming that "the office of teacher belongs more to him than to them" and that their expulsion of the blind man (ch. 9) was unjust because "the power of rejecting and accepting belongs to him and not at all to them."[20] Thus, the Good Shepherd discourse is both a particular response to the way the scribes and Pharisees have treated the blind man and a general rejection of their au-

---

18. See Origen, *Homilies on Numbers* 6.4; *Homilies on Joshua* 26.3; Augustine, *Harmony of the Gospels* 3.4.14; *Sermons on New Testament Lessons* 38.10; *On the Gospel of John* 49.27; *On the Psalms* 72.9; 78.3; and 115.10; Leo the Great, *Sermon* 67.6. The verse from John can, of course, also be used to refer to the unity of the church without reference to Jews and Gentiles.

19. See, for example, Clement of Alexandria, *Instructor* 1.6; Tertullian, *De fuga* 11; Origen, *Homilies on Joshua* 7.6; *Homilies on Luke,* fragment 38; Cyprian, *Letter* 2.1; Gregory Nazianzen, *Oration* 1.7; John Chrysostom, *Homily on Ignatius* 1; *Homilies on the Statues* 3.1; *Homilies on 1 Timothy* 10 and 15; Jerome, *Letter* 16.1; Paulinus of Nola, *Letter* 42.2; Augustine, *On the Gospel of John* 123.5.

20. J.-M. Vosté, *Theodori Mopsuestini Commentarius in Evangelium Iohannis Apostoli* (Corpus scriptorum Christianorum orientalium, Scriptores Syrii 4/3 [Paris: Typographeo Reipublicae, 1940] 139).

thority. Chrysostom takes a similar approach. Jesus' words in John 9:41 ("If you were blind, you would have no guilt; but now that you say, 'We see,' your guilt remains.") are directed both to the blind man and to the Pharisees:[21]

> He showeth that what they deemed a great matter for praise, brought punishment upon them. He also comforted him who was blind from his birth . . . and then speaketh concerning their blindness. For He directeth His whole speech to this end, that they may not say, "we did not refuse to come to thee owing to our blindness, but we turn away and avoid thee as a deceiver."

More broadly, however, the incident of the blind man's healing and Jesus' response in ch. 10 is part of the larger controversy. Chrysostom refers to ch. 8, to the Jews' attempt to stone Jesus (8:59) and to their calling him a demoniac (7:20, 8:48, 8:52, 10:19).[22] Cyril and Augustine do not significantly differ in their interpretations.[23]

The interpreters do differ, however, in the degree to which they feel able to move away from the narrative setting to more general issues. Both Chrysostom and Augustine, as we shall see, turn rather quickly to the concerns of their own time — the problem of heresy and schism and the "hireling" teachers in the church. In contrast, Theodore maintains the reference of the text to its original setting. The parable is restricted to the Law. The sheepfold is its teaching; the sheep, those who obey the Law. Christ is true to the Law, while the scribes and Pharisees are not.[24] It is possible we can explain this by appealing to the distinction Theodore makes in his introduction to the commentary between the interpreter and the preacher. Cyril also keeps his attention fixed upon the narrative, and we might argue that the commentators feel less able to move beyond it than the homilists do. The contrast Theodore makes, however, revolves around the interpreter's focus upon difficulties in the text as opposed to the homilist's concern to explain even what is quite clear.[25] It is, then, more likely that Theodore's insistence upon the narrative meaning is a factor of his basic approach and his horror of allegorism.[26] In any case, what we can con-

---

21. John Chrysostom. *Homilies on John* 59.1 (NPNF 1/XIV, 213).

22. *Homilies on John* 59.1-2 and 60.3 (NPNF 1/XIV, 213 and 218-19).

23. See P. E. Pusey, *Cyrilli Archiepiscopi Alexandrini in D. Joannis Evangelium* (Impression Anastaltique; Brussels: Culture et Civilisation, 1965) II, 207-8; Augustine, *On the Gospel of John* 45.1 (NPNF 1/VII, 249-50).

24. Vosté, 140, 141, 144.

25. Vosté, 2.

26. Here, of course, I am interested in the content of Theodore's exegesis rather than with his theory and method. For an excellent discussion of views of the latter see

clude is that all the interpreters take the *historia* seriously and that they make no distinction (as we should) between the biblical narrative and the historical conflict between Jesus and the Jewish leaders.

The four interpreters, however, characterize this conflict in somewhat differing ways. For Theodore, as we have seen, the issue is Jesus' authority and his loyalty to the Law. Chrysostom understands the controversy as one in which Jesus shows that he "is not a deceiver, but a Shepherd."[27] Both Cyril and Augustine shift the understanding of the controversy to the more general question of accepting or rejecting Christ. For Cyril the Pharisees "supposed him to be a false shepherd and a false leader, approved by his own purpose and not because he was God made human according to the most ancient preaching of the inspired Scripture."[28] Their rejection of the incarnate Word is also a rejection of God's monarchy, and that is why they say "We have no king but Caesar."[29] Augustine faults the Pharisees for refusing to become "the sheep of Christ," disowning him and not entering by the door.[30]

One other point in the setting of John 10 attracts the attention of the Greek interpreters. Why does Jesus speak figuratively and enigmatically? One reason for this question is that in 10:6 we find the word *paroimia* (RSV "figure") rather than *parabolē*. Cyril explicitly identifies the two terms.[31] The deeper issue, however, is why Jesus uses figurative language. Theodore answers the question by arguing that Jesus wishes to make his claim indirectly so as to avoid pride.[32] Chrysostom thinks that Jesus spoke "obscurely" to "make them more attentive." V. 9, in his view, removes the obscurity.[33] Later, when Jesus says they are not his sheep (10:26), he does so "that they might strive to become sheep."[34] Thus, Chrysostom shifts attention to those whom Jesus addresses and treats Jesus' speech as one designed to convert the Pharisees.

In contrast, Cyril understands Jesus' parable as an enigmatic rejection of the Jews. As is his custom, Jesus does not answer the words addressed to

---

Bradley Nassif, "The 'Spiritual Exegesis' of Scripture: The School of Antioch Revisited," *Anglican Theological Review* 75 (1993) 437-70.

27. *Homilies on John* 59.2 (NPNF 1/XIV, 213).

28. Pusey, 218.

29. John 19:15; Pusey, 225-26.

30. *On the Gospel of John* 45.2-4 (NPNF 1/VII, 250).

31. Pusey, 210. Cf. Apollinaris of Laodicea in J. Reuss, *Johannes-Kommentare aus der Griechischen Kirche* (Berlin: Akademie, 1966) 23.

32. Vosté, 140 and 141. Chrysostom also speaks of Christ's humility but does not connect the virtue to his use of figurative language (NPNF 1/XIV, 219).

33. *Homilies on John* 59.3 (NPNF 1/XIV, 214).

34. *Homilies on John* 61.2 (NPNF 1/XIV, 223).

him but the secrets of the heart that lie behind those words. His answer is simple, but the Pharisees are incapable of understanding it.[35] We find, then, considerable differences in the way the interpreters understand the narrative, however much they agree it must be the point of departure for exegesis. It is difficult to see that the text rules out any of the three explanations given for Jesus' use of figurative speech. The difference between Chrysostom and Cyril seems to be a difference in their understanding of Jesus' attitude toward the Jews. Yet both agree in their hostility toward Judaism. We might, then, argue that Chrysostom's view is not so very different from Cyril's after all. Jesus may have sought to convert the Pharisees, but he obviously failed. And his benevolence toward them might simply underline their hardheartedness.

IV. The Wicked Characters in Jesus' Parable

By locating John 10 in Jesus' conflict with the scribes and Pharisees the commentators imply that the parable (whether it is identified with vv. 1-5 or with the whole of Jesus' speech) has a polemical purpose. The objects of the polemic are described as "thieves and robbers" and the "hireling." The "wolf" is also an enemy. All four interpreters distinguish the "thieves and robbers" from the "hireling." According to Theodore, the first are to be understood as anyone who "does not first display a diligence for the precepts of the Law and then go on to teach the others entrusted to him."[36] Such a person does not enter by the proper door. Theudas and Judas the Galilean (Acts 5:34-37) are examples of "thieves and robbers."[37] Chrysostom uses the same examples and characterizes them as "false Christs" and "exciters of sedition."[38] They differ in three respects from the Good Shepherd. Their teaching is not "from the Scriptures"; the sheep do not obey them; and they "did all as rebels, and to cause revolts. . . ."[39] Cyril agrees, but he treats Theudas and Judas the Galilean also as false prophets.[40] Augustine's interpretation is somewhat more vague. The "thieves and robbers" are by implication the blind Pharisees, who stand for good pagans, philosophers "with rattling jaws," and heretics —

35. Pusey, 208-10.
36. Vosté, 141.
37. Vosté, 142.
38. *Homilies on John* 59.3 (NPNF 1/XIV, 214).
39. *Ibid.*
40. Pusey, 219, where Cyril cites Acts 5:37 and Jer. 23:16. Cf., however, p. 209, where the "thieves and robbers" are false rulers and where Cyril cites Hos. 8:4 and Isa. 30:1.

none of whom enter by the door. Augustine omits the reference to Acts 5 and moves quickly away from a setting in Jesus' ministry. He can identify the thieves and robbers with the Donatists.[41]

Both Theodore and Chrysostom sharply distinguish the "thieves and robbers" from "the hireling." The scribes and Pharisees are the hirelings, since they have official status as leaders of the people.[42] Chrysostom makes the distinction more clearly by speaking of "two kinds of spoilers; one, the thief who kills and steals; the other, one who doth not these things, but who when they are done doth not give heed nor hinder them."[43] The false leaders like Theudas are distinguished from "the teachers of the Jews," whom Ezekiel foretold (Ezek. 34:2). Implied by the distinction is a view that Jesus' enemies are a conspiracy devised by false leaders and false teachers, and we might think of an alliance of Zealots and Pharisees. But Chrysostom immediately moves beyond the historical setting and includes as "hirelings" the teachers Paul rebukes in Phil. 2:21 and 1 Cor. 10:24. Cyril also sees the difference between thieves and hirelings and identifies the Pharisees with the latter. But he makes very little of the distinction and shifts his attention to the Good Shepherd, who contrasts with both.[44]

Augustine is least concerned with the narrative setting of the parable and immediately equates the hireling with those holding office in the church, of whom Paul (in the verse Chrysostom also cites) says "who seek their own, not the things that are Jesus Christ's."[45] This identification introduces a somewhat extended exhortation to listen to the Shepherd's voice in the hireling but to refuse to follow the hireling's example. Jesus' advice regarding the Pharisees ("do what they say; but do not do what they do" (Matt. 23:2-3) supplies a warrant for the exhortation. In this way one can gather the grapes

41. *Sermons on New Testament Lessons* 87.12 (NPNF 1/VI, 521); cf. 88.9 (NPNF 1/VI, 526).

42. Vosté, 144.

43. *Homilies on John* 60.1 (NPNF 1/XIV, 216f.). Chrysostom, however, introduces the scribes earlier in his discussion when he identifies them with those who climb in by another way. "He alluded to the Scribes, because they taught for commandments the doctrines of men, and transgressed the Law." The allusion is to Matt. 15:9 and possibly Matthew 23; and Chrysostom also cites John 7:19. *Homilies on John* 59.2 (NPNF 1/XIV, 213).

44. Pusey, 223.

45. Phil. 2:21. *On the Gospel of John* 46.5 (NPNF 1/VII, 257). Cf. *Sermons on New Testament Lessons* 87.9 (NPNF 1/VI, 520): "But attend to a more clear proof that the Church hath such as these [hirelings]. Lest any one should say to us, 'He spake entirely of the Pharisees, He spake of the Scribes, He spake of the Jews; for the Church hath none such.' Who then are they of whom the Lord saith, 'Not every one that saith unto me, Lord, Lord, shall enter into the kingdom of heaven.'?" (Matt. 7:21)

of true doctrine from the thorns of wicked examples.[46] Thus, while we must beware the wolf, the thieves, and the robbers, we must bear with the hirelings.[47]

Two minor points deserve brief attention. All but Theodore identify the wolf with Satan.[48] But they do not elaborate. More interesting, all but Theodore are aware of the danger of equating "all who came before me" (v. 8) with the prophets. Chrysostom simply denies this heretical opinion on the grounds that Christ and the prophets are in accord.[49] Cyril agrees, but discusses the point at some length. His text omits "before me," but his interpretation contrasts the prophets who were *sent* and the others who *came*. His argument appeals to a number of prophetic texts.[50] Augustine, whose text also lacks "before me," excludes the reference to the prophets because they did not "come" apart from Christ:[51]

> Before the advent of our Lord Jesus Christ, when He came in humility in the flesh, righteous men preceded, believing in the same way in Him who was to come, as we believe in Him who has come. Times vary, but not faith.

Augustine's interpretation not only rejects the heretical view and understands John 10:8 to mean "all who came apart from me are thieves and robbers," but also adds the positive point that those who foresaw Christ were proleptically his sheep and citizens of the City of God. Augustine's tendency is to move away from the historical setting of the text.[52]

---

46. Augustine refers to Matt. 7:16. Cf. the parallel passage in *Sermons on New Testament Lessons* 87.13 (NPNF 1/VI, 521f.).

47. *On the Gospel of John* 47.1 (NPNF 1/VII, 260). Cf. *Sermons on New Testament Lessons* 87.5 (NPNF 1/VI, 519): ". . . ye have found, holy brethren, both those whom ye should love, and those whom ye should tolerate, and those of whom ye must beware. The Shepherd is to be loved, the hireling is to be tolerated, of the robber must we beware."

48. Chrysostom, *Homilies on John* 59.3 (NPNF 1/XIV, 215); Cyril (Pusey, 223); Augustine, *On the Gospel of John* 46.7 (NPNF 1/VII, 258).

49. *Homilies on John* 59.3 (NPNF 1/XIV, 214). The heretical opinion could be Gnostic or Marcionite. Hippolytus says that the Valentinians used John 10:8 and Col. 1:26 in this way. See *Refutation of All Heresies* 6.30 (ANF V, 89). Cf. Clement of Alexandria, *Stromateis* 1.17 (ANF II, 318-19).

50. Pusey, 213f. The biblical texts are Hos. 12:10; Jer. 1:7; Ezek. 2:3; Jer. 23:21; 14:14; 34:15; and 23:28. Cf. Theodore of Heraclea (Reuss, 91-95).

51. *On the Gospel of John* 45.8-9 (NPNF 1/VII, 251f.)

52. Augustine's reputation as a theologian of history may well be undeserved. One can argue that for him only sacred history counts, and even here everything points forward or back to Christ. See R. A. Markus, *Saeculum: History and Society in the Theology of St Augustine* (Cambridge: Cambridge University Press, 1970) 17, 18, 20f.: "The significant

V. The Positive Details in the Parable

The sheepfold, the shepherd, the door, and the doorkeeper all function positively in John 10, and I shall want to say more about Christ as the Good Shepherd and about his redemption of the sheep in what follows this section. Nevertheless, let me make some preliminary observations about the four interpretations of these positive aspects of the text. Theodore and Chrysostom tie their exegesis to Scripture. For Theodore the sheepfold stands for "the teaching of the Law." The sheep are those dedicated to this teaching and introduced to it by the legitimate teacher, the Good Shepherd. Moses is the doorkeeper.[53] These identifications suggest that true religion is the true understanding of the Old Testament and that Christ alone, witnessed by Moses, supplies the authentic key. Theodore's understanding enables him to keep his exegesis closely bound to the narrative setting and to Jesus's ministry.

In a similar way Chrysostom implies that true religion and Scripture belong together:[54]

> Observe the marks of a robber; first, that he doth not enter openly; secondly, not according to the Scriptures, for this is the, "not by the door." . . . And with good cause He calleth the Scriptures "a door," for they bring us to God, and open to us the knowledge of God, they make the sheep, they guard them, and suffer not the wolves to come in after them. For Scripture, like some sure door, barreth the passage against the heretics. . . .

The door is also Christ, and so we may presume that since Christ's teaching is that of Scripture, to follow Scripture is to follow Christ. Moses is the doorkeeper, "for to him were entrusted the oracles of God."[55] Chrysostom sees no problem in identifying Christ with both the door and the shepherd, since the terms simply refer to differing "dispensations." As the door he brings us to the Father; as the shepherd he cares for us. And his care is paradoxical because unlike ordinary shepherds he leads the sheep instead of following them

---

divisions in human history are, for Augustine, the turning points in the sacred history. . . . The landmarks of the sacred history are the fixed points in universal history; universal history is articulated in a meaningful structure in so far as its course is projected on to a map defined by the coordinates of the sacred history. . . . The decisive event of the Incarnation tends to eclipse the sixfold division by casting its shadow backwards. . . . since the coming of Christ, until the end of the world, all history is homogeneous, . . . it cannot be mapped out in terms of a pattern drawn from sacred history."

53. Vosté, 140-41.
54. *Homilies on John* 59.2 (NPNF 1/XIV, 213).
55. *Homilies on John* 59.3 (NPNF 1/XIV, 214).

and sends them toward rather than away from wolves.[56] By extension "shepherd" can also refer to those who preside over churches.[57]

The ecclesiastical theme predominates over the scriptural one in the interpretations of Cyril and Augustine. Cyril preserves the scriptural allusion by saying that the food preached in the church is Scripture.[58] But the main line of his interpretation reveals itself by his double interpretation of Christ as the door. He is the door because through him we have "familiarity with God, as he himself testifies when he says: 'no one comes to the Father, but by me'" (John 14:6). Or he is the door because through him "we come to the leadership and governance of spiritual flocks in accordance with Paul's words: 'one does not take the honor upon himself, but he is called by God'" (Heb. 5:4).[59] Correlative with this interpretation is Cyril's suggestion that the doorkeeper is either Christ or the "angel appointed to preside over the churches."[60] A soteriological meaning coheres with an ecclesiastical one.

With Augustine the ecclesiastical interpretation becomes dominant:[61]

> Christ's sheepfold is the Catholic Church. Whoever would enter the sheepfold, let him enter by the door, let him preach the true Christ.

We must knock on this door, believing in order to understand. As we shall see, what Augustine means by this is that there is no salvation outside the Catholic Church; and the only Catholic Christians to be saved are those predestinated by God. Perhaps for this reason, if the doorkeeper is not to be identified with Christ, we may think of the Holy Spirit, who will guide his sheep to the truth, which is Christ.[62] In a similar way Christ is both the door as "the one Mediator between God and humans" (1 Tim. 2:5) and the shepherd because he enters in by himself. What Augustine appears to mean is that the incarnate Lord is both the link between God and those who will be saved and the first principle of this new humanity. The idea is that we can think of Christ as the head of the body or as the body. In his second aspect we can share with him in his functions. Thus, "Peter, and Paul, and the other apostles were, as all good bishops are, shepherds."

56. *Ibid.* The second paradox is a reference to Matt. 10:16.
57. *Homilies on John* 60.1 (NPNF 1/XIV, 216).
58. Pusey, 210.
59. Pusey, 212.
60. Pusey, 209.
61. *On the Gospel of John* 45.5 (NPNF 1/VII, 250).
62. *On the Gospel of John* 46.4 (NPNF 1/VII, 257).

But they cannot be the door, since this term refers to Christ as the head of the body.[63] There are many shepherds in the church; but since they are members of Christ's body, there is still but one shepherd. Augustine's train of thought will find its term in his predestinarian theology. For the moment it will suffice to conclude that, whereas Theodore and Chrysostom relate the positive elements of Jesus' parable to Scripture, Cyril and Augustine tend to drive them toward an ecclesiastical interpretation.

VI. Christ, the Good Shepherd

Of all the interpreters Theodore is the most concerned with christology, and his commentary focuses upon what he regards as a proper understanding of the Good Shepherd. He refers the reader to his dogmatic writings, and he regards the texts that speak of Christ laying down his soul (life: vv. 11 and 17) as a refutation of Apollinaris's denial of a human soul in Christ.[64] As we should expect, Theodore's concern to maintain the distinction between God and the created order even at the level of the incarnation leads him to his customary distinction between God the Word and the assumed Man and to an identification of the Good Shepherd with the Man. Theodore paraphrases the first five verses of John 10 by having Christ speak to his opponents:[65]

> Therefore, if Moses in his book praises the one who fulfills the precepts of the Law, certainly the fulfilment of the precepts is found within me and not within you. . . . It is I who am truly of right and merit named shepherd, because I have first observed the Law exactly and have used the proper entrance shown to me by the doorkeeper and because then I have diligently done everything that had to be done for the benefit of the sheep.

Theodore is making two points about Christ as human. First, he is the perfect moral exemplar; second, he is the proximate agent of redemption.

Theodore's emphasis is characteristically upon the second of these themes. Christ is the door "because he is for all the first principle of entrance into truth . . . and the cause that all may know the Father." The only way to

63. *On the Gospel of John* 47.3 (NPNF 1/VII, 261). Cf. *Sermons on New Testament Lessons* 88.5 (NPNF 1/VI, 524), where he makes explicit reference to the *totus Christus caput et corpus* theme.
64. Vosté, 150 ("If anyone wishes to know how this must be understood . . . let him examine the book I have written about the humanity of our Lord . . .") and 149 ("For it was not the divine nature that spoke of his soul, but the human nature.")
65. Vosté, 141.

attain truth is to believe in our Lord and through his precepts attain entrance to the truth and enjoyment of the good things we possess by access to the Father through him.[66] Christ is also the first principle of the resurrection, and so he effects redemption in both its spiritual and moral dimensions.[67] Even though the passages to which I have referred do not speak explicitly of the human nature, there can be little doubt that Theodore intends that reference.

This conclusion finds confirmation in his interpretation of the mutual knowledge of shepherd and sheep (vv. 14-15). It is as though Christ said "I have assumed them into familiarity with me as my own possession because of their good will, and they receive special care from me as their reward." Theodore goes on to say that Christ speaks of his human nature, as the context makes clear:[68]

> . . . that is, just as I have unceasing familiarity with the Father and cannot ever be separated from him because I am his Son through my union with God the Word, so too I have taken my sheep as my own into familiarity with me. They likewise know me as their shepherd and cannot renounce my lordship. . . .

Christ's human nature, then, supplies the mediating link between God and those who are redeemed. At the same time, the human nature has this power only because of the Man's union with God the Word. It is this union that gives the Man the power not to die, and we can think of the examples of Enoch and Elijah.[69] Theodore treats Christ's special powers as belonging to the Man but explained by the gracious union he has with the Word. The Word, then, remains the prime mover in the incarnation. For that reason Theodore attributes John 10:30 ("I and the Father are one") to the Word of God. Christ in his divine nature argues that if Scripture can call humans "gods," how much more must the term apply to the one who is Son of God by nature.[70]

If Theodore's commentary betrays his characteristic christology, Chrysostom's interpretation reflects his tendency to avoid theological controversy. To be sure, Chrysostom can appeal to Christ's human example. His

66. Vosté, 142.
67. Vosté, 147.
68. Vosté, 145.
69. Vosté, 148. The comment refers to Christ's power to lay down his life and take it again (John 10:17-18).
70. Vosté, 152-55.

silence and refusal to respond to the accusation in v. 20 ("He has a demon") was in part "to teach us all meekness and long-suffering."[71] Moreover, the death and resurrection of Christ are clearly human. On the other hand, Chrysostom treats Christ's knowledge as divine rather than human, and the "charge" Christ has received from the Father (v. 18) is a way of speaking of his "unanimity" with the Father as the one equal with God who emptied himself in the incarnation.[72] Moreover, John 10:30 ("I and the Father are one") refers to the consubstantiality of the Father and the Son.[73] Chrysostom clearly has an understanding of Christ as God incarnate, fully divine and fully human. But he refuses to enter into the mystery and shifts attention from the person of Christ to the response his sheep ought to make.

Cyril's interpretation reflects his christology more clearly than is the case for Chrysostom, but we find little polemic and no hint of the Nestorian controversy. Cyril locates his christology in the context of the story of redemption. "The Good Shepherd lays down his life for the sheep" (v. 11) refers to what was accomplished by Christ. Humanity had "bounded away from love towards God" and so had become "exiled from the sacred and divine fold," expelled from paradise. But Christ "endured the cross for our sake that he might slay death by death." This is why "he says to us: 'Fear not, little flock, for it is your Father's good pleasure to give you the kingdom.'"[74] Christ's death and resurrection overcomes death, the penalty we have inherited from Adam, thereby freeing us also from sin. And Christ is the Word of God incarnate.

Cyril at numerous points in his commentary reflects both the trinitarian solution achieved at Constantinople in 381 and the Alexandrian christology that had been most clearly articulated by Athanasius during the Arian controversy. As we should expect, John 10:30 prompts Cyril to state his Nicene orthodoxy:[75]

> We say that the Son and the Father are one, not by numerically combining the monads as those do who say that the Father and the Son are the same, but by believing that the Father exists in his own way and the Son in his own way and by bringing the two into a single sameness of essence and by

71. *Homilies on John* 60.3 (NPNF 1/XIV, 219).

72. *Homilies on John* 60.1 (NPNF 1/XIV, 217), where he cites Rom. 11:2; 2 Tim 2:19; and Luke 10:22, and *Homilies on John* 60.3 (NPNF 1/XIV, 218), where he cites Phil. 2:7.

73. *Homilies on John* 61.2 (NPNF 1/XIV, 224).

74. Pusey, 223-24. The citation is Luke 12:32. Cf. Pusey, 241: Christ lays down his life and takes it again "so that he might slay death. . . ."

75. Pusey, 254.

knowing that they have a single power, since the one is seen in the other without deviation.

The Word, then, consubstantial with the Father, is one of the three divine *hypostaseis*. His consubstantiality means that Christ's knowledge is divine.[76] The divine Word, then, empties himself to become incarnate and takes the form of a servant. Cyril characteristically employs Philippians 2 as a way of speaking of the incarnation.[77] We should, then, not be troubled if Christ is called a servant or a prophet. These terms do not affect his nature as the consubstantial Son of God, but instead refer to the time when he became human and are used "economically." Similarly, Christ's statement that "the Father is greater than I" (John 14:28) must be understood "economically."[78] What Cyril means is that the double judgment of Scripture about Christ can be explained by distinguishing what pertains to Christ by nature as God and what pertains to him in virtue of the "economy" of the incarnation. "Economic" predication is real, but does not affect the nature of the Word. When the prince becomes a pauper, he truly adopts a pauper's condition; but this does not affect his status as the prince. Examples could be multiplied from Cyril's commentary, but it is sufficient to point out that his christology differs from Theodore's, which handles the double judgment about Christ in Scripture by distinguishing two subjects rather than two modes of attribution.

While Theodore and Cyril articulate a clear christology, Chrysostom and Augustine both tend to avoid the problem. One looks in vain in Augustine's writings for any extended treatment of christology. On the other hand, Augustine clearly intends to repeat the orthodoxy of his day. The parallel between vv. 28 and 29 ("no one shall snatch them out of my hand/the Father's hand") means that "the power of Father and Son is one; for their Godhead is one." The point is clinched by v. 30, which affirms the unity of Father and Son; and Arius finds his refutation.[79] The same view informs Augustine's interpretation of the incarnation. Christ is many things metaphorically — rock, door, cornerstone, shepherd, lamb, lion:[80]

> But what is He properly? "In the beginning was the Word, and the Word was with God, and the Word was God." And what, as He appeared in hu-

76. Pusey, 230-31.
77. Pusey, 228-29.
78. Pusey, 244-46.
79. *On the Gospel of John* 48.7-8 (NPNF 1/VII, 268).
80. *On the Gospel of John* 47.6 (NPNF 1/VII, 262).

man nature? "And the Word was made flesh and dwelt among us." (John 1:1, 14)

The divine Son of God remains the subject in the incarnation, and the purpose of the incarnation is that he may lay down his life and take it again, that is, he dies that he may rise again. The reference to Christ's soul (life: v. 17) shows that his is a "complete humanity," thus refuting the Apollinarians.[81] Augustine also uses the body-soul analogy to explain the unity of God and humanity in Christ.[82]

So far none of the themes Augustine articulates are at all surprising. He simply repeats the orthodoxy of his day. In two respects, however, his homilies reflect his own emphases. First, as we have seen, he can treat the incarnate Lord as "head" and as "body." Though Christ is the one mediator as head of the body, he is also to be identified with those who are members of his body.[83] Second, he underlines the sacrificial character of Christ's death, setting the stage for the later Latin doctrine of the atonement:[84]

> . . . you are the sheep of Christ, purchased with the blood of Christ. You acknowledge your own price. . . . He, and only He, was the buyer, who shed precious blood — the precious blood of Him who was without sin.

This theme may show that Augustine's attention has shifted from Christ to his work and from death to sin as the fundamental human problem.

VII. Redemption

It is easy to summarize in general terms the way the four interpreters understand redemption. All agree that it involves both spiritual union with God and the resurrection of the body.[85] Cyril elaborates the spiritual dimension by explaining the knowledge the sheep have of the shepherd as a "partaking of the divine nature" (2 Pet. 1:4). Redemption is *theosis.* All the interpreters

---

81. *On the Gospel of John* 47.9 (NPNF 1/VII, 263).
82. *On the Gospel of John* 47.12 (NPNF 1/VII, 264-65).
83. *On the Gospel of John* 47.3 (NPNF 1/VII, 261).
84. *On the Gospel of John* 47.2 (NPNF 1/VII, 260).
85. For the spiritual dimension see, e.g., Theodore (Vosté, 142); Chrysostom, *Homilies on John* 59.3 (NPNF 1/XIV, 214); Cyril (Pusey, 232); Augustine, *On the Gospel of John* 48.6 (NPNF 1/VII, 267). For the physical dimension see, e.g., Theodore (Vosté, 143); Chrysostom, *Homilies on John* 60.1 (NPNF 1/XIV, 217); Cyril (Pusey, 224); Augustine, *On the Gospel of John* 45.15 (NPNF 1/VII, 255).

also raise the question of the limits of redemption. Theodore restricts redemption to those who obey Christ.[86] Chrysostom agrees, and indeed concludes each of his three homilies with an exhortation to such obedience. The Christian cannot serve two masters (Matt. 6:24), and the service of Christ involves caring for the poor. We must imitate Christ's humility the way the sheep in Matthew 25 do by visiting prisoners and caring for others. Jesus' retirement at the end of ch. 10 supplies us with an example followed best by the pious women who use the power of their retirement for good.[87] Cyril agrees that only the obedient receive the benefits of the resurrection and have true fellowship with the incarnate Lord.[88]

Augustine differs from the others by arguing that the limits of redemption are established by God's predestination of the elect. The fact that the Good Shepherd "calls his own sheep by name" (v. 3) means that "The Lord knows those who are his" (2 Tim. 2:19). And, as Rom. 8:29ff. demonstrates, these are the saints predestined for salvation:[89]

> Such sometimes do not know themselves, but the Shepherd knoweth them, according to this predestination, this foreknowledge of God, according to the election of the sheep before the foundation of the world: for so saith also the apostle, "According as He hath chosen us in Him before the foundation of the world." (Eph 1:4)

Christ's words in v. 26 ("you do not belong to my sheep") teach the same lesson. Christ saw that the Pharisees were "predestined to everlasting destruction, not won to eternal life by the price of His own blood."[90] The wheat and the chaff are kept together on the threshing floor of the Catholic Church until the harvest at the end of the world.[91] Then the elect will be separated from the reprobate and the two cities constituted for eternal bliss and damnation.

VIII. Concluding Reflections

Let me return to the three claims it seems to me Mr. Childs is making and raise the question how far the interpretations that have been examined co-

---

86. Vosté, 143, 145.

87. See the concluding sections of *Homilies* 59-61.

88. Pusey, 220 and 252.

89. *On the Gospel of John* 45.6, 12 (NPNF 1/VII, 251, 253-54).

90. *On the Gospel of John* 48.4 (NPNF 1/VII, 267).

91. *Sermons on New Testament Lessons* 87.7 (NPNF 1/VI, 520).

here with them. There can be little doubt we have seen diversity of interpretation at a number of levels. The setting of John 10 in Jesus' controversy with the Pharisees sometimes involves the authority of the teacher, sometimes that of the leader of the people. Jesus' aim for Chrysostom is to convert his enemies; for Cyril, it is to demonstrate their incapacity to hear. The parable as a whole is closely tied to Scripture for Theodore and Chrysostom, but has a more ecclesiastical meaning for Cyril and Augustine. Theologically, for Theodore the Good Shepherd is the assumed Man, whereas for Cyril he is the Word incarnate. One could add the Cappadocian interpretation, which treats the Good Shepherd as the Word of God and the lost sheep as human nature. Still more striking is Augustine's definition of the sheep as those predestined to salvation rather than those who have sought to obey Christ.

At the same time, these differences, as well as differences of detail, need not necessarily be regarded as contradictory interpretations. All four interpreters treat John 10 as a way of speaking of the incarnate Lord and the redemption he has brought. To be sure, the christological differences to be found in Cyril and Theodore are precisely the differences that later led to the Nestorian controversy. Yet if my understanding of Chalcedon is correct, the Definition recognized moderate forms of the Antiochene and the Alexandrian christologies as legitimate, though differing, expressions of the same faith.[92] Augustine's doctrine of predestination poses a more difficult problem. The Greek Fathers would surely agree with his insistence upon grace, but they would as surely disagree with the notion that grace overrules our capacity for good by acting in a sovereign fashion. Even here, however, there might be a way to insist that God's grace and human obedience need not cancel one another out. At least up to a point we can argue that diversity of interpretation need not mean a breach of union. And certainly Augustine himself would recognize that there can be no certainty about *the* correct meaning of Scripture. For him any interpretation that does not violate the rules of faith and of charity has validity.

The second claim I have seen Mr. Childs making is that the meaning of

---

92. Cf. A. Grillmeier, *Christ in Christian Tradition* II/1: *From Chalcedon to Justinian* (Atlanta: John Knox, 1987) 4: "The formula and teaching of Chalcedon absorbed the attention of the old imperial Church, whether we look at Emperors, Popes, bishops, the monks or the theologians, or finally the mass of church people. Yet both before and after the Council, there was a life inspired by faith in Christ which neither needed the formula of Chalcedon for its existence, nor was directly enriched by it. This was because the Church possessed and lived the *content* or the *matter* of this teaching, namely, faith in the one Christ, true God and true man, even though it was not expressed in more advanced philosophical terms."

Scripture can be loosened from its historical context. While the church Fathers make no clear distinction between the historical and the narrative setting of the text, it is certainly clear that they would heartily approve letting the text speak anew to the contemporary situation. All the interpreters think of the heretics of their day, and Augustine keeps the Donatists in mind. The homilists, in particular, are concerned with how the text addresses the demands of the Christian life. At the same time, none of them are prepared to sacrifice what they regard as the historical setting, the controversy between Jesus and the Pharisees reported by John.

There is also a correlation between the interpretations examined and the third claim, that Scripture must be appropriated by the community of faith. As we have seen, that appropriation for the early church involves iconography as well as the interpretation of Scripture by commentators and homilists. This appropriation keeps one eye trained on what will benefit those who read the commentaries or hear the sermons and one eye trained upon the way the church has sought to distinguish right belief from the heresies of, say, Arius and Apollinaris.

If there are clear correlations between patristic exegsis and "canonical criticism," we must also admit that there are also some important differences. One of these involves the appeal to the rule of faith. For Irenaeus basic authority lies not so much in Scripture itself as in the Apostolic Faith expressed both in the Bible and in the rule. At one level, of course, the rule is to be equated with what I think Irenaeus would be comfortable in calling the canonical meaning of Scripture. At another level, however, the rule tends to become a principle external to Scripture capable of being employed as a hermeneutical key. Augustine takes a slightly different line. He appears to think of the rule of faith as not in all respects equatable with the creed. One thinks of "the mind of the church," which would include the creed and represent the church's way of understanding Scripture, but would in the long run be identified with "the Catholic faith." Augustine also appeals to the rule of charity and argues that any interpretation that fails to build up the love of God and neighbor must be pronounced invalid. I have entered into complex problems, but one conclusion seems clear to me. The early church would not be comfortable with any view that insisted upon Scripture alone as the authority for Christian belief and practice.

A second difference, as it seems to me, revolves around what might be meant by "the community of faith." This expression seems to me vague and seems to beg the question as to what we might mean by the church. In much of Protestantism there is a tendency to think of the church as a voluntary association of believers. On this view, what really counts is the belief of the individual. One can understand why Cardinal Newman denied that Protestantism had any claim to be "historic Christianity." The early church would think of itself as a community established by the divine will of Christ and not as one constituted by the faith of its members.[93] For this reason the primary function of interpretation must not be to make an innovative or individual contribution but to articulate the community's belief in such a way that individuals may be shaped and benefited by it.

A third difference has to do with the contrast between ancient and modern understandings of history. To be sure, the exegetes of the early church were concerned with the *historia* of Scripture, but by the term they did not mean history in our sense so much as the obvious narrative meaning of the text. At the same time, they were concerned to use the technical tools of their time in order to understand the *historia* and to establish the basic facts of the Christian story. Indeed, Theodore's antipathy to allegorism springs largely from his conviction that the allegorists do away with what actually happened. And, if we move away from an Enlightenment view of what historians can accomplish, we may find an understanding of history in our time that takes account of the role of imagination and interpretation.[94] Once again I have raised massive philosophical and theological problems without being able to solve them.

What, then, can we conclude? One possibility is to argue that the differences outweigh the correlations and that we cannot learn very much from patristic exegesis. On the other hand, I am tempted to conclude that there may be a way of defining "canonical interpretation" that would benefit from correlations with the ancient church. Surely we can argue that no one would any longer oppose Scripture to the creeds or the theological tradition in precisely the way that characterized the debates of the sixteenth and seventeenth centuries. Moreover, I should hope there is some room left for those who think of the church as more than a voluntary association and of theological

93. Cf. Robert N. Bellah, et al., *Habits of the Heart* (New York: Harper and Row, 1985) 227: "The very freedom, openness, and pluralism of American religious life makes this traditional pattern hard for Americans to understand. For one thing, the traditional pattern assumes a certain priority of the religious community over the individual. The community exists before the individual is born and will continue after his or her death. The relationship of the individual to God is ultimately personal, but it is mediated by the whole pattern of community life. There is a givenness about the community and the tradition. They are not normally a matter of individual choice."

94. Here, of course, I am thinking of the work of Collingwood and Carr. Carr seeks to find a way of blocking a subjective understanding of Collingwood's definition of history as "the imaginative reconstruction of the past."

traditions as living and organic. And finally, as we leave the Enlightenment behind and take more seriously the imaginative and interpretive role of the historian, we can see more clearly that the early church was not without a concern for history. The distinction between precritical and postcritical interpretation will, of course, not disappear. But the distinction need not be seen as an opposition, and the dialectic established between our study of Scripture and a precritical study may be treated as a dialectic that can inform us.

The Council of Jerusalem in Acts 15 and Paul's Letter to the Galatians

David Trobisch

I. Introduction

In ch. 15 the book of Acts reports that Paul and Barnabas traveled from Antioch to Jerusalem to discuss with Peter and James whether it is true that *"unless you are circumcised according to the custom of Moses, you cannot be saved"* (Acts 15:1). The meeting was successful. The participants formulated a written agreement, which was sent as a letter to the Gentile Christians in Antioch, Syria, and Cilicia. The text of this agreement is quoted in full (Acts 15:23-29).

In ch. 2 of his letter to the Galatians, Paul refers to a visit to Jerusalem, where he and Barnabas met with James, Peter, and John. They came to an agreement and gave each other the right hand of fellowship.

At first glance both passages seem to refer to the same event. The main characters of the stories — Peter, James, Paul, Barnabas — and the location Jerusalem appear in both accounts.[1] However, several inconsistencies have caused confusion during the eighteen centuries of documented Christian exegesis and have led to apparent disagreement among biblical scholars to this very day.[2]

---

1. Irenaeus, *Adversus Haereses* 3.13.3. Cf. Wayne A. Meeks, *The First Urban Christians: The Social World of the Apostle Paul* (New Haven: Yale University Press, 1983) 111-13.

2. For bibliography and discussion see Ernst Haenchen, *The Acts of the Apostles: A Commentary* (Philadelphia: Westminster, 1971); Alfons Weiser, "Das 'Apostelkonzil' (Apg

II. The Problem

One of the more obvious difficulties is caused by the observation that the agreement in Acts does not touch either of the two issues Paul refers to in his letter to the Galatians: *"James, Cephas, and John gave to me and Barnabas the right hand of fellowship, that (a) we should go to the Gentiles and they to the circumcised; the only other issue being (b) that we should remember the poor, which of course I am eager to do"* (Gal. 2:9-10). Instead, the official document of Acts 15 asks Gentile Christians that they *"abstain from what has been sacrificed to idols and from blood and from what is strangled and from unchastity"* (Acts 15:29).

Martin Hengel tries to alleviate the tension between these two accounts in the following way: *"For Luke . . . James is the decisive authority who ends the dispute with a compromise. . . . However, Paul knows nothing of legal concessions of this kind; indeed he asserts that no obligations were laid on Barnabas and himself (Gal. 2.6). Here we may trust him* [Paul], *rather than Luke's account."*[3]

But why should we trust Paul more than Luke, and why should we trust him in this specific case but not in other cases? Hengel suggests: *"In reality," "the resolute and unyielding approach of Paul and Barnabas to the 'pillars' had met with success."*[4] This is, of course, only one of several possibilities.

Nevertheless, critical scholarship through the centuries proved that the historical events behind Acts 15 and Paul's letter to the Galatians cannot be reconstructed in a manner that would convince the guild.

In his article in the *Anchor Bible Dictionary,* Charles Cousar lists several alternative attempts to link Paul's report in Galatians with passages from Acts.[5] Instead of connecting Paul's remarks to Acts 15:4-29, which according to Acts would have been Paul's third visit to Jerusalem, scholars have proposed to see his second visit (Acts 11:30; 12:25) or his fourth visit (Acts

15,1-35). Ereignis, Überlieferung, lukanische Deutung," *Biblische Zeitschrift* 28 (1984) 145-67, here 147-49; Gerd Lüdemann, *Early Christianity according to the Traditions in Acts* (Minneapolis: Fortress, 1989) 1-9; A. J. M. Wedderburn, "The 'Apostolic Decree': Tradition and Redaction," *Novum Testamentum* 35 (1993) 362-89, here 362. For a comparison of the book of Acts to literature of the time see Richard I. Pervo, *Profit with Delight: The Literary Genre of the Acts of the Apostles* (Philadelphia: Fortress, 1987).

3. Martin Hengel, *Acts and the History of Earliest Christianity* (Philadelphia: Fortress, 1980) 116.

4. Hengel, *Acts,* 116.

5. Charles B. Cousar, "Jerusalem, Council of," *Anchor Bible Dictionary* (1992) 3:766-68; cf. Stephen G. Wilson, *The Gentiles and Gentile Mission in Luke-Acts* (Cambridge: Cambridge University Press, 1973) 178-91.

18:22) reflected in Galatians. Others have considered the possibility that Paul refers to a conference but, unfortunately, Acts does not mention Paul's presence. Such a conference is reported in Acts 11:1-18. And, in theory at least, Galatians could refer to a conference not reported at all.

Many interpreters seem comfortable with the answer that there is no answer. Consequently, they either do not address the problem[6] or they confront their readers with a whole set of alternatives.[7]

The objective of this short study is to demonstrate that the solution supported by the editors of the New Testament is that the letter to the Galatians was written shortly before Paul left for his visit with the apostles in Jerusalem (Acts 15:4-29).

III. Authorship and Sources

Much of the confusion is caused by two major difficulties. First, there are good reasons to think that Luke, the companion of Paul, did not author the book of Acts.[8] Second, it is not clear which sources the author used.[9] Whether the author knew Paul's letter to the Galatians or whether *"Acts refers to events told of also in Galatians but without knowledge of the letter"*[10] is of particular interest.

From a canonical perspective both questions may be answered with a high degree of certainty.

When looking at the book of Acts and the letter to the Galatians as parts of the same larger publication, the New Testament, it is important to keep one obvious reading instruction in mind: information referring to the same event but being recorded in two separate books is not presented to prove to the readers of the collection that one account is correct and the other false.

By arranging the writings and adding titles, the editors of the New Tes-

---

6. Hans Hübner, "Paulus, Apostel: I: Neues Testament" *Theologische Realenzyklopädie* (Berlin: de Gruyter, 1996) 26:133-53.

7. Wedderburn, "Apostolic Decree," 370-74.

8. For an extensive bibliography and discussion see Claus-Jürgen Thornton, *Der Zeuge des Zeugen: Lukas als Historiker der Paulusreisen* (Wissenschaftliche Untersuchungen zum Neuen Testament 56; Tübingen: Mohr, 1991).

9. For a brief history of the debate see Lüdemann, *Early Christianity*, 1-9.

10. Hans Dieter Betz, "Galatians, Epistle to," *Anchor Bible Dictionary* (New York: Doubleday, 1992) 2:875. Cf. John Knox, *Chapters in a Life of Paul*, revised edition with introduction by Douglas Hare (Macon: Mercer University Press, 1987).

tament provided information which is not easily accessible from a close reading of the texts alone. Most of this information concerns authorship and literary genre of the writings, and it was obviously intended to guide the readers through the seemingly disparate material of the collection.[11]

Only a few sections of the book of Acts are written in first person plural. Therefore, not all events are presented as if they were experienced by the author himself.[12] On the other hand, the redactional title of Galatians describes the genre of this writing as being a "letter of Paul" to the Galatians.[13]

The editors are thus telling their readers that Galatians is not based on secondhand information, as opposed to much of the book of Acts. On the contrary, every word was written and experienced by the letter writer himself.

The consideration that both writings refer to the same events leads to the insight that Galatians was written before Luke finished the book of Acts.

There are three editorial suggestions: (a) the insight that Acts and Galatians are not included in the same collection to prove that one of the accounts is wrong, (b) the presentation of Galatians as the authentic voice of Paul, and (c) the earlier date of Galatians in relation to Acts. These suggestions instruct the reader to rely on the letters of Paul as the primary source and to read Luke's book of Acts as a trustworthy narrative, which might shed some light on the events preceding and following this letter. Or — in reference to Hengel's words — Acts describes the "reality" behind the text, which led Paul to formulate his letter to the Galatians.

The other question, whether Luke knew and used the canonical letters of Paul, is also clearly answered by reading the texts from a canonical perspective. For the editors of the New Testament and for their readers, Galatians and Acts formed two parts of the same publication. This observation alone dismisses any reading that will separate the testimony of Galatians from the testimony of Acts.

11. Concerning the theory of a final redaction of the New Testament, see David Trobisch, *Die Endredaktion des Neuen Testaments. Eine Untersuchung zur Entstehung der christlichen Bibel* (Novum testamentum et orbis antiquus 31; Göttingen: Vandenhoeck; Freiburg: Universitätsverlag, 1996).

12. For a thorough discussion of the evidence and its interpretation see Jürgen Wehnert, *Die Wir-Passagen der Apostelgeschichten. Ein lukanisches Stilmittel aus jüdischer Tradition* (GTA 40; Göttingen: Vandenhoeck, 1989).

13. David Trobisch, *Paul's Letter Collection: Tracing the Origins* (Minneapolis: Fortress, 1994) 24.

IV. Canonical Reading

Let me now demonstrate what the events behind Acts 15 and Paul's letter to the Galatians look like, when reading the texts from a canonical perspective.[14]

After introducing the main theme of his report, that is, that he received his gospel not from a human source but through a revelation of Jesus Christ (Gal. 1:12), Paul writes about his trips to Jerusalem, demonstrating that he did not receive his gospel from any apostle in Jerusalem. Paul's comment that he was persecuting the church in his former days is related to the readers of the book of Acts at the first introduction of Paul (Acts 7:58–8:3).

Gal. 1:13-14 You have heard, no doubt, of my earlier life in Judaism. I was violently persecuting the church of God① and was trying to destroy it. I advanced in Judaism beyond many among my people of the same age, for I was far more zealous for the traditions of my ancestors.②	Acts 7:58–8:3 Then they dragged him [Stephen] out of the city and began to stone him; and the witnesses laid their coats at the feet of a young man named Saul. (. . .) And Saul approved their killing him.② (. . .) But Saul was ravaging the church① by entering house after house; dragging off both men and women, he committed them to prison.

As Paul continues, he insists that it was God who revealed his son to him (Gal. 1:15-16). Luke explains the comment *"afterward I returned to Damascus"* by adding the information that Paul experienced this revelation close to Damascus (Acts 9:3).

Gal. 1:15-17 But when God, who had set me apart before I was born and called me through his grace, was pleased to reveal his Son to me,① so that I might proclaim him among the Gentiles, I did not confer with any human being, nor did I go up to Jerusalem to those who were already apostles before me, but I went away at once into Arabia, and afterward I returned to Damascus.②	Acts 9:3-5 Now as he was going along and approaching Damascus,② suddenly a light from heaven flashed around him. He fell to the ground and heard a voice saying to him, "Saul, Saul, why do you persecute me?" He asked, "Who are you, Lord?" The reply came, "I am Jesus, whom you are persecuting."①

14. The English text of the following tables is quoted from the New Revised Standard Version (1989) to demonstrate that the crosslinks between Galatians and Acts are very apparent and do not require a close reading of the Greek text.

DAVID TROBISCH

Next, Paul writes about his first visit to Jerusalem after his conversion (Gal. 1:18-19). And in the continuation of his story of Paul, Luke gives an account of a visit in Jerusalem, corroborating that Paul met with the apostles at that occasion (Acts 9:27). Luke specifies Paul's vague remark that he *"went into the regions of Syria and Cilicia"* (Gal. 1:21) by mentioning the name of the Cilician city, Tarsus (Acts 9:30), and the name of the Syrian city, Antioch (Acts 11:26).

Gal. 1:18-24 Then after three years① I did go up to Jerusalem② to visit Cephas and stayed with him fifteen days; but I did not see any other apostle③ except James the Lord's brother. In what I am writing to you before God, I do not lie! Then I went into the regions of Syria→⓪ and Cilicia,④ and I was still unknown by sight to the churches of Judea that are in Christ; they only heard it said, "The one who formerly was persecuting us is now proclaiming the faith he once tried to destroy."⑤ And they glorified God because of me.

Acts 9:23-30 After some time had passed,① the Jews plotted to kill him, but their plot became known to Saul. (. . .) When he had come to Jerusalem,② he attempted to join the disciples; and they were all afraid of him⑤ for they did not believe that he was a disciple. But Barnabas took him, brought him to the apostles③ (. . .) He [Paul] spoke and argued with the Hellenists; but they were attempting to kill him. When the believers learned of it, they brought him down to Caesarea and sent him off to Tarsus.③

Acts 11:25-26 Then Barnabas went to Tarsus to look for Saul, and when he had found him, he brought him to Antioch.⓪←

The next trip to Jerusalem described in Galatians is difficult to relate to the book of Acts for many interpreters. However, a plausible reading does not seem very difficult from a canonical perspective. Paul's comment that he left for Jerusalem *"in response to a revelation"* (Gal. 2:2) is explained by Luke as a reference to the prophet Agabus (Acts 11:28), who had predicted a famine. The Christians of Antioch had organized a collection and they sent it with Paul and Barnabas to Jerusalem, thus representing Paul's visit as a response to Agabus's revelation. Paul's dating of the trip, *"after fourteen years"* (Gal. 2:1), is specified by Luke to have ocurred *"during the reign of Claudius"* (Acts 11:28). The request of the apostles to *"remember the poor"* and the comment of Paul that this *"was actually what I was eager to do"* (Gal. 2:10), are interpreted by Luke as referring to the collection he and Barnabas had just delivered to Jerusalem (Acts 11:30).

336

Gal. 2:1-10 Then after fourteen years① I went up again to Jerusalem② with Barnabas,③ taking Titus along with me. I went up in response to a revelation.④ (. . .) They gave to Barnabas and me the right hand of fellowship, agreeing that we should go to the Gentiles and they to the circumcised. They asked only one thing, that we remember the poor,⑤ which was actually what I was eager to do.⑥

Acts 11:27-30 At that time prophets came down from Jerusalem to Antioch. One of them named Agabus stood up and predicted by the Spirit④ that there would be a severe famine over all the world; and this took place during the reign of Claudius.① The disciples determined that according to their ability, each would send relief⑤ to the believers living in Judea; this they did, sending it to the elders② by Barnabas③ and Saul.⑥

Paul then addresses the event for which he probably prepared his readers from the very beginning of the letter: his clash with Peter in Antioch (Gal. 2:11-14). Luke translates Paul's reference to *"certain people from James," "the circumcision faction"* (Gal. 2:12) into *"certain individuals from Judea teaching that 'you cannot be saved unless you are circumcised'"* (Acts 15:1), Luke not mentioning the apostle Peter. Among other details, both accounts agree in the events taking place in Antioch while Paul and Barnabas were present and in the fact that there was *"no small dissension"* (Acts 15:2).

Gal. 2:11-14 But when Cephas came to Antioch,① I opposed him to his face, because he stood self-condemned; for until certain people② came from James he used to eat with the Gentiles. But after they came he drew back and kept himself separate for fear of the circumcision③ faction.④ And the other Jews joined him in this hypocrisy, so that even Barnabas⑤ was led astray by their hypocrisy.

Acts 15:1-2 Then certain individuals② came down [to Antioch]① from Judea and were teaching the brothers, "Unless you are circumcised③ according to the custom of Moses, you cannot be saved." And after Paul and Barnabas had no small dissension④ and debate with them, Paul and Barnabas⑤ and some of the others were appointed to go up to Jerusalem to discuss this question with the apostles and the elders.

Considering Acts to be Luke's perspective on the events, there is little doubt that — according to the canonical reading instruction — Galatians reflects the situation after the dissension in Antioch and before the council in Jerusalem reported in Acts 15:4-29.[15]

Luke explains to his readers that Paul's letter to the Galatians is a literary product of Paul's and Barnabas's campaign to publicize their position on

15. This chain of events was proposed as the most plausible historical solution by William M. Ramsay, *St. Paul the Traveller and the Roman Citizen* (Grand Rapids: Baker, 1982, reprint of 1925 fifteenth edition) 54-60, 152-77.

the issue of circumcision. The distribution of this letter to several churches in Galatia, however, was not their only public activity in this matter. On their way from Antioch to Jerusalem, *"as they passed through both Phoenicia and Samaria, they reported the conversion of the Gentiles, and brought great joy to all the believers"* (Acts 15:3).

V. Conclusion

From a canonical perspective, Acts tries to achieve the same goal that any critical historian would try to achieve: to describe the events that lie behind the text of Paul's letter to the Galatians. The reliability of Luke's information on events of the first century, however, is the object of a long-lasting debate. It is unlikely that this question will be answered convincingly in the near future, and it was not the intention of this study to propose a solution.

However, the canonical perspective — which considers the final form of the New Testament as it was edited and published — is a perspective of the second century, and its historical value should not be overlooked. It describes the view of a readership that strongly believed that Peter and Paul were not opponents and that they both were active missionaries in Rome, where both of them died as martyrs; this belief is expressed by the layout and structure of the canonical edition of the New Testament, and especially by the supporting views of the book of Acts.

The objective of this study was to show that the reading suggested by the canonical edition of the New Testament is still recoverable. In correspondence to the editorial reading instructions of the edition, Luke maintains that Paul wrote his letter to the Galatians after the dissension in Antioch (as reported in Acts 15:1-2 and Gal. 2:11-14) and before he left for the council in Jerusalem (as reported in Acts 15:4-29).

Learning to Narrate Our Lives in Christ

Stephen Fowl

Unlike the vast majority (if not all) of the other contributors to this volume, I was never a student or colleague of Brevard Childs. I am, rather, a representative of an extremely large number of people who found a sort of scholarly liberation from reading Professor Childs's work as a graduate student. As a group we are not formally organized; we do not gather regularly for scholarly meetings. Nevertheless, we share a common experience that as biblical scholars in the making we found the practical, theoretical, and theological limitations of historical criticism extraordinarily frustrating. In the course of working through Childs's commentary on Exodus or his *Introduction to the Old Testament as Scripture* or any number of his essays, we found an alternative that both gave voice to our frustration and helped to relieve it. For many of us, reading Childs allowed us to rethink the possibilities of becoming biblical scholars. We do not consider ourselves to be Childs groupies, but we do recognize that we owe Professor Childs an intellectual debt. This essay is an attempt to begin repayment of that debt.

In this essay I want to offer a theological interpretation of Paul's self-characterizations in Philippians and Galatians. In the course of my account of Paul's self-characterizations I hope to indicate some of the differences between the theological interpretation I offer here and more purely formalist or New Critical approaches to characterization. The aim of this is to address, at least implicitly, one of the arguments John Barton makes in his treatment of Childs's work. In an extended treatment of the "canonical approach" in *Read-*

I am grateful to Lewis Ayres, Greg Jones, and Jim Buckley for comments on earlier versions of this essay.

ing the Old Testament,[1] Barton offers a careful account of Childs's work that combines both cautious appreciation and some rather sharp criticism. Barton eschews many of the superficial and less temperate criticisms of Childs that were common in the first half of the 1980s. Barton thinks that the best way to push the canonical approach forward is to strip it of its theological claims and treat it as a type of New Critical biblical interpretation. While my own theological convictions lie closer to Barton's catholic views than to Childs's Reformed outlook, and while Barton makes some telling criticisms of Childs's theological rationale for the "canonical approach," I think that much would be lost by following Barton's advice. I take Barton's advice as a way of making Childs's work more serviceable as an interpretive method to the bulk of professional biblical scholars. Many people like myself, however, found the importance of Childs's work to lie less in its interpretive method than in its willingness to rise above the limitations of historical criticism and to bring theological concerns to bear rigorously on the interpretation of Scripture. From this perspective, it may be necessary to challenge and argue with Childs's theology at points.[2] To drive a wedge between theological considerations and a formalist approach to the biblical text, however, would be to abandon what seemed most liberating about Childs's work. To argue this point fully would take me far beyond the confines of this essay and require a full-blown engagement with Childs's theological approach to scriptural interpretation. Hence, I will try to make this point by implication as I offer my own theological account of Paul's self-characterizations as an alternative to a New Critical characterization of Paul's self.

My primary aim in presenting Paul's self-characterizations is to show that being able to narrate an account of one's life in Christ is both a literary and a theological task. It involves a variety of rhetorical skills; it requires one

---

1. Philadelphia: Westminster, 1984, chs. 6, 7, and 10 and appendix.

2. To my mind, the best account of Childs's work is Mark Brett's *Biblical Criticism in Crisis?* (Cambridge: Cambridge University Press, 1991). Brett's superiority to Barton lies in his ability to locate Childs's work in a much broader philosophical and literary framework. Brett, too, however, urges that one of the best ways of reconfiguring and advancing Childs's work depends on separating off its theological concerns. For Brett, these theological concerns push Childs towards a hermeneutical or methodological monism that becomes untenable in the light of the obvious coherence of other methods of reading. It seems to me, however, that there is no inherent reason that a variety of theological stances might not be compatible with a variety of interpretive practices. Rather than separate off Childs's theological concerns, one might simply have to engage, criticize, and argue with them in the course of doing one's own theological interpretation. Indeed, Brett does this to some degree, arguing that the closest theological allies available to his reconstructed canonical approach are people like George Lindbeck, Hans Frei, and Ronald Thiemann (see 156-67).

to represent events and relations exterior to oneself as well as interior attitudes and dispositions. What Paul's self-characterizations show to be most important, however, is the theological necessity of setting accounts and representations of exterior events and relations as well as interior attitudes and dispositions within a larger narrative of God's activity in Christ. A standard literary approach to Paul's self-characterizations would not really take account of this theological necessity.[3]

In both Galatians and Philippians this larger Christ-centered narrative is hinted at and inferred more than it is explicitly displayed.[4] Paul presumes that he and his audience share a story about God's activity in Christ and how they are related to that activity. How Paul understands that story is crucial for the ways in which he characterizes himself. Further, Paul's characterizations of himself in the epistles are required to do moral and theological work in relation to that larger story. In both Galatians and Philippians (though in different ways) Paul's account of his self is to be exemplary for the faith and practice of Paul's audience. Hence, some understanding of the relationship Paul desires his audience to have to that larger, largely unnarrated, story will help one understand what is at stake for Paul when he tells his story in one way in Galatians and another way in Philippians.

Due to the limits of space, mine will hardly be a comprehensive account of Paul's self-characterizations.[5] If space permitted, I think that I

---

3. John Darr has noted that, despite a burgeoning of literary readings of the New Testament and of Luke/Acts in particular, relatively little attention has been devoted to character and characterization. In addressing this lack, Darr's work largely focuses on Luke rather than Acts and does not touch on Paul. Nevertheless, Darr's work is an excellent example of a purely literary approach to characterization which is focused on rendering a particular character by compiling and synthesizing a series of direct observations and inferences about a character. These observations and inferences are based on what that character says and does and on what others say about that character. In the course of doing this, it is also common to note the literary techniques used to render characters. See J. Darr, *On Building Character: The Reader, Rhetoric and Characterization in Luke-Acts* (Louisville: Westminster/John Knox, 1992). See also the account of characterization in Adele Berlin's *Poetics and Interpretation of Biblical Narrative* (Sheffield: Almond, 1983): "The reader reconstructs a character from the information provided to him in the discourse; he is told by the statements and evaluations of the narrator and other characters, and he infers from the speech and action of the character himself" (34).

4. Richard Hays has persuasively demonstrated the presence of a "narrative substructure" in Galatians in *The Faith of Jesus Christ* (Chico: Scholars, 1983). I have tried to demonstrate the importance of the story of Christ for Paul's argument in Philippians in *The Story of Christ in the Ethics of Paul* (Sheffield: JSOT, 1991).

5. Further, it must be noted that these accounts are not strictly (auto)biographical. The term autobiography is clearly anachronistic when applied to Paul. The term "auto-

could sustain the points I make about Galatians and Philippians in regard to the Corinthian correspondence as well.[6] In addition, it would be both illustrative and in keeping with a canonical approach to compare these accounts from the epistles with the Paul of Acts. In the interest of space I will confine my comments on this score to a few summary statements along the way.

I. Galatians 1:10–2:21

It is tempting to read Paul's account of himself in Gal. 1:10ff. as part of an overall apologetic strategy. On such a reading Paul, like the Paul of Acts 22–26, renders his character in a primarily defensive context. On this view, Paul in Galatians is defending his apostleship against opponents who do not recognize him (or his message) as the equal of someone like Peter.[7]

In an inportant essay, however, Beverly Gaventa has challenged this way

---

biographical remark" may be a more accurate designation for the self-references found in ancient literature. In regard to Pauline autobiography both B. R. Gaventa, "Galatians 1 and 2: Autobiography as Paradigm" *Novum Testamentum* 28 (1986) 322-326, and George Lyons, *Pauline Autobiography: Toward a New Understanding* (Atlanta: Scholars, 1985), ch. 1, comment on autobiography in antiquity. While Lyons gives a more comprehensive account of autobiography, he focuses too heavily on literature that is not easily comparable to the Pauline epistles. Alternatively, Gaventa shows that the closest parallels to Paul's practice can be found in the autobiographical comments in the letters of Seneca and Pliny, who use self-references for didactic or parenetic purposes. While Gaventa's comments are helpful here, it should also be noted that Paul, like Augustine, is "less interested in telling the reader about himself than he is in narrating how his life has been located in the story of God." For further comments like this on autobiography see L. G. Jones, "For All the Saints: Autobiography in Christian Theology" *Asbury Theological Journal* 47 (1992) 27-42. The quotation here is from p. 34.

6. In the chapter entitled "Humanity: Old and New" in his *Biblical Theology of the Old and New Testaments* (Minneapolis: Fortress, 1992) 580-84, Childs focuses his comments regarding Pauline anthropology on Romans 5–7. It strikes me that the metaphors working in Romans 5–6 in particular indicate that this text has more to do with politics than anthropology. That is, these texts account for how sin (spoken of as a character here) comes to establish a dominion in God's creation and how the coming of Christ establishes an alternative political domain in which the believer enters by baptism. For a fuller argument for this reading see S. Fowl, "Some Uses of Story in Moral Discourse: Reflections on Paul's Moral Discourse and Our Own," *Modern Theology* 4 (1988) 293-308. In this light, I would submit that the Galatians and Philippians texts I will look at here provide a much better account of Pauline views of the self.

7. Lyons devotes an entire chapter to reviewing and rejecting the reasons for this view.

of reading Galatians 1–2.[8] The thrust of her challenge against the apologetic reading of these chapters is that reading them in this light largely divorces them from the theological argument of the rest of the epistle.[9] As a result of being cut loose from the rhetorical unity of the epistle, these chapters have largely been mined for information about the earliest stages of the Christian movement.[10]

As an alternative, Gaventa proposes a reading of these chapters in which the autobiographical comments of Galatians 1–2 can be seen as the implicit basis for the theological argument that follows. "Paul employs events out of his past, events that have to do with the exclusive nature of the gospel's claim on his own life, to urge that same exclusive claim on the Christians in Galatia."[11] Based on Gaventa's reading of the passage, I think one can develop some important insights into Paul's pattern of characterizing himself.

From the opening paragraphs of the epistle, it is clear that Paul is committed to the notion that there is only one gospel (1:6-7). Nothing Paul might say subsequently and nothing said by an angel from heaven can alter this state of affairs.[12] It is this notion of a singular gospel which Paul both proclaims and subjects himself to (1:8) that drives Paul's argument against those who are not simply preaching another gospel but are perverting the one gospel of Christ (1:7).[13]

Having said this, Paul wants to be sure that the Galatians understand that the gospel he proclaims is not his gospel. Rather, it has been given to him by God. This theological claim works rhetorically to allow the divine origin of Paul's gospel to shine through with all of its clarity. In 2:20 he goes so far as to say that, because he has been crucified with Christ, he no longer lives;

8. See "Galatians 1 and 2: Autobiography as Paradigm." Although Gaventa's work and Lyons's work are contemporaneous, and although Lyons's work is more substantial in terms of length and material covered, I find Gaventa's constructive proposal for reading Galatians more persuasive. I find that the real merit of Lyons's work lies in the scholarly consensus that he upsets rather than his own constructive account.

9. Although Lyons does not accept the view that Galatians 1–2 is apologetic, he is not particularly interested in relating chs. 1–2 to chs. 3–4 other than to note that chs. 1–2 provide the foundation for the call to imitate Paul in 4:12-20.

10. See Gaventa, "Galatians 1 and 2," 311-12.

11. *Ibid.*, 313.

12. See John Howard Schütz, *Paul and the Anatomy of Apostolic Authority* (Cambridge: Cambridge University Press, 1975) 118ff.; Gaventa, "Galatians 1 and 2," 314.

13. This is against Lyons, 128, who does not think Paul is as concerned with the possibility of another gospel as with characterizing those proclaiming this "other" gospel as "troublemakers" and the like.

rather Christ lives in him (cf. 6:14). This comes as no surprise when it is remembered that from conception God set Paul, like Isaiah (Isa. 49:1) and Jeremiah (Jer. 1:5), apart for a special task (1:15). Paul is thus able to view his gospel and his mission as a gift (2:9) rather than his own construction. In Galatians Paul wants to be seen, at least in part, as an instrument of God's gracious activity. Indeed, as Paul relates it, this is the view of Paul held by those in Judea who had not seen him but had heard that "the one who formerly was persecuting us is now proclaiming the faith he once tried to destroy" (1:23). God, not Paul, receives the glory for this transformation (1:24).[14]

Paul presents himself to the Galatians as one whose self has been decentered or destabilized by God. That is, Paul claims that in some very significant ways God has supplanted Paul as the locus of Paul's knowing, willing, and desiring. To be sure, Paul's is not the radically unrepresentable, decentered self of certain forms of poststructural philosophy. On the other hand, Paul's self is hardly the autonomous, ahistorical, essentially stable, supremely confident self that critics of modernity have sought to undermine. I will say more about this later.

A self that has been decentered by God in the way Paul's has cannot adequately be characterized simply in the service of autobiographical or New Critical ends. Rather, Paul characterizes himself in ways that primarily say something about God. In fact one can go further and say that Paul's characterization of himself here presupposes a narrative about God's activity in Christ in which Paul presumes both he and the Galatians participate. Without the presumption of this narrative a phrase like "I have been crucified with Christ" is unintelligible.[15] In characterizing himself in a particular way here Paul is implicitly fitting the story of his life into the larger story of the crucified and risen Christ in such a way that this story is seen to be the center of Paul's self.

Paul's decentered self, however, is not a self devoid of particularity. On the contrary, it is only because Paul's self is now located in a narrative of God's action in Christ that he can characterize the particular details of his past as he does. This particularity is crucial both to Paul's character and to his argumentative aims in Galatians. Paul was the most zealous of Jews. He notes his persecution of the church as a mark of his unparalleled advance-

14. See Schütz, 136, who quotes Chrysostom as noting that Paul does not say that "they marveled at me, they praised me, they were struck with admiration of me, but he attributes all to grace."
15. Hays, 5ff., makes similar comments about Paul's claims in Galatians.

ment in Judaism (1:13). With no obvious transition, Paul then goes on to relate that God revealed his Son to him so that Paul might evangelize the Gentiles. This dramatic reversal transforms Paul's past into a "negative mission directed against rather than for the Church."[16] What remains consistent in Paul's portrayal of himself is his zeal. Now, however, this zeal is rightly directed.[17]

It is important to note, however, that although Paul plays on the temporal distinction between his past and his present in 1:10–2:21,[18] his characterization of himself is not simply a juxtaposition of before and after snapshots. Paul's view of his past is also transformed. Indeed, Paul's ability to talk about a former time radically distinct from his present is only conceivable in the light of the transformations that God accomplished in Paul. Further, some of Paul's characterizations of his past are only possible from the perspective of his transforming experience of Christ. For example, prior to his encounter with the resurrected Christ he could not have characterized his actions as "persecuting the church of God" (1:13).[19] Instead, perhaps, he would have said that he was punishing blasphemers. In short, Paul's past is not a self-interpreting story waiting to be juxtaposed to his present life in Christ. It is, rather, a story that must be put together, narrated from a particular point of view.[20]

As Paul moves on from that transforming experience of the resurrected Christ in 1:18ff. he characterizes himself largely through accounts of how others recognized and responded to the life and message of the persecutor turned proclaimer. As 1:24 makes clear, it is still God who is glorified as the source of Paul's transformation. There is, however, also the emphasis on the fact that Paul himself — in the particularity of his life and mission — is recognized as a faithful proclaimer of the one gospel. Indeed, Paul is at pains to stress his independence from the apostles in Jerusalem. At the same time, cit-

---

16. Schütz, 133.

17. Presumably Paul could have characterized his past as he characterizes other Jews in Rom. 10:2, as "having zeal for God, but without knowledge."

18. Lyons, 146-52, nicely displays the "formerly-now" contrast in Galatians. He does not, however, recognize that Paul's account of former things has also been transformed through his encounter with Christ.

19. While Paul could not have said certain things about his past apart from his transforming experience of Christ, I think it distorts Paul's discourse to try to reduce it to an explication of his Damascus Road experience, as Seyoon Kim does in *The Origin of Paul's Gospel* (Grand Rapids: Eerdmans, 1981).

20. An analogous way of thinking about this issue is to imagine the sort of account of his past Augustine would have given on the day he was appointed to his post in Milan and to contrast this with the account he gives in the *Confessions*.

ing the fact that the "pillars" of the Jerusalem church approved of his message and mission certainly supports Paul's claim to be an expositor of the one true gospel.

In 2:11ff. Paul continues to characterize himself in terms of his relations to others. This time, however, it is in the context of his confrontation with Peter in Antioch. Coming immediately after Paul has recounted his reception by the Jerusalem apostles, this passage further emphasizes Paul's personal integrity and consistency as a proclaimer of the one gospel in contrast to Peter (and Barnabas). It is important to remember that the primary accusation against Peter here is not bad theology but hypocrisy (2:13). Peter and the others are "not walking along the straight path of the truth of the gospel" (2:14). As Schütz notes, by phrasing the issue in this way, Paul presents the conflict not as one between two conflicting apostles, but as a conflict over whether Peter will submit to the independent authority of the gospel, as Paul has done.[21] In characterizing Peter in this way Paul is indirectly characterizing himself as one who maintains the singularity of the gospel in word and deed. This passage nicely points out a dual focus in Paul's characterization of himself here in Galatians. On the one hand, he is a selfless servant of God, subject to the truth of the gospel. On the other hand, the particularities of this situation and Paul's specific response to it are to be instructive for the Galatians. I will mention more about this dual focus in a moment.

As Paul's characterization of himself has moved from Galatians 1 into ch. 2 there is a subtle shift of emphasis from Paul's characterization of himself to a characterization of his message. As presented in Galatians, there is no clear distinction to be made between Paul's character and the gospel he proclaims. "In a sense all that the apostle does is a reflection of what the gospel does; all that he is, is a reflection of what the gospel is."[22] This blurring of the differences between Paul and his message is in part accomplished by Paul characterizing himself as one whose self has been decentered by God in the ways I noted above. By presenting himself as an example of what God graciously has done, Paul blurs his personal particularities in a way that makes him an instrument for God's use, a messenger who is subjected to the message.

At the same time, however, Paul says to the Galatians "become as I am" (4:12). Paul wants the Galatians to see him as an example of what the one true

21. "The charge of hypocrisy leveled at Peter accuses him of acting inconsistently, out of accord with an authority he himself means to recognize" (Schütz, 152). See also Bengt Holmberg, *Paul and Power* (Philadelphia: Fortress, 1975) 32.

22. Schütz, 232; see also Gaventa, "Galatians 1 and 2," 317.

gospel can do, and what that gospel demands.[23] The Galatians' zeal for the law ought to be transformed into zeal for God's grace in the same way that Paul's life has been transformed. "To become as Paul is means to allow Christ to live in oneself (cf. 2:20) to the exclusion of the Law or any other tradition or category."[24] Paul seeks the same decentering for the Galatians that God has accomplished in him. This aim, however, requires the particular account that Paul has given of himself. For the demand to "become as I am" to have any bite at all requires a specific "I" (Paul), an "I" that has had a particular experience of God and that stands in a certain relationship to other specific characters, a character who can characterize himself as Paul does. In other words, for the Galatians to become as Paul is they will have to consider the narrative of Christ's work, which is to occupy the center of their selves. Moreover, they will have to fit their particular stories into Christ's story in a manner analogous to the way Paul has embedded his particular story into Christ's in such a way that he no longer lives, but Christ lives in him.

As Paul characterizes himself in Galatians 1–2 he seeks to balance two potentially competing interests. On the one hand, he is unwilling to say anything about himself that would compromise his conviction that he is who he is solely on the basis of God's grace, a grace he now recognizes to have been operative in his life from conception. It is this notion that leads him to claim "it is no longer I who live but Christ who lives in me" (2:20). On the other hand, in seeking to persuade the Galatians to change certain aspects of their faith and practice, he portrays the specificities of his own life as exemplary for the Galatians. To weight one side of this balance too heavily is to risk obliterating Paul's self, thus robbing it of its moral and theological force as an exemplar. To put too much weight on the other side is to risk the view that Paul's transformation and, hence, his gospel are the work of his own zeal and self-discipline. This would, of course, undermine his claims about his apostleship, about the singularity of his gospel, and about his characterization of himself as one who pleases God rather than humans. Achievement of such a balance is, of course, both ongoing and always precarious. Nevertheless, given the ends for which Paul portrays himself in Galatians it would seem that, for Paul, it is not simply a literary and rhetorical, but also a moral and theological, achievement to be able persuasively to characterize oneself in this way.[25]

23. See Gaventa, "Galatians 1 and 2," 314, 319ff.; also Lyons, 164-68.

24. Gaventa, "Galatians 1 and 2," 322; see also Richard Hays, "Christology and Ethics in Galatians: The Law of Christ" *CBQ* 49 (1987) 280ff.

25. Of course we do not know whether and to what extent Paul actually persuaded the churches in Galatia. It would seem, however, that Augustine saw his *Confessions* as engaged in a similar sort of balancing act.

II. Philippians 3:2-17

When Paul comes to characterize himself to the Philippians, he moves away from this attempt at striking a balance between grace and the exemplary particularity of his own life. Instead, he adopts a much more ironic tone. In the early part of the epistle Paul has presented a sustained argument of how the Philippians are to "live in a manner worthy of the gospel of Christ" (1:27) in the face of opposition. This manner of life will entail suffering for the Philippians (1:28). Remaining united in their faith in the gospel and their self-giving love for each other will, however, result in their salvation. This argument is given its direction and force from the narrative about the suffering and exalted Christ presented in 2:6-11.[26] As ch. 3 begins Paul launches a polemical attack against those who would propose a different view of how the Philippians should respond to their situation. Those proposing this alternative way of life do not accept (among other things) Paul's notion that walking in a manner worthy of the gospel of Christ may entail suffering. Paul ultimately comes to call these people enemies of the cross of Christ (3:18).[27]

Paul begins his attack in 3:2 with some strong invective against his opponents. He calls them dogs, malicious workers, and mutilators of the flesh. All these names seem to be designed to belittle the claim to virtue made by Paul's opponents.[28] In short, "their glory is their shame" (3:19). These opponents may have been Jewish Christian missionaries (ἐργάται) who boasted of spiritual attainments as in 2 Corinthians.[29] From Paul's comments in vv. 4ff. it seems that the opponents' claim to spiritual superiority came from keeping the Law to perfection. Their aim would have been for the Philippians to strive after similar spiritual superiority through rigorous adherence to the Law, and, thus, to avoid or transcend persecution.

Against this background, Paul characterizes his own life in 3:4ff. As in Galatians, Paul begins by recounting his zeal and incomparable achievement as a Jew. Again, persecution of the church is seen as a mark of Paul's devotion to God. The achievements in Judaism of which Paul's opponents boast are matched and superseded by Paul's own life.

---

26. See Fowl, *The Story of Christ,* chapters 3-4 for comments on the exegetical details of these passages.

27. It is interesting to note that in Philippians the issue concerns the implications of the gospel. Paul does not need to fight any battles over the singularity of the gospel, as in Galatians.

28. See, for example, Andrew Lincoln's discussion of these terms in *Paradise Now and Not Yet* (Cambridge: Cambridge University Press, 1981) 89.

29. See Helmut Koester, "The Purpose of the Polemic of a Pauline Fragment," *NTS* 8 (1961-62) 321.

While Acts repeatedly expounds an account of Paul's vision of the resurrected Christ, and Galatians at least touches on this event, it is omitted entirely in Paul's characterization of himself here in Philippians. Rather than a transforming experience of the resurrected Christ, what is crucial for Paul here is a transformation in his perceptions about the ends toward which he should order his life. Presumably this was not a transformation that can be as easily identified with a single event. What is crucial here in Philippians is how Paul considers (see the various occurrences of ἡγέομαι in vv. 7-8) his past and his present direction (λογίζομαι is used in v. 13).[30] What he used to consider to be the manner of life worthy of a follower of God is now rubbish. What he previously considered worthy of persecution now provides the *telos* of his life. Clearly, this new *telos* is not simply a mental ideal. Paul's new perspective is not simply an internal state. It both demands action and provides a standard for shaping one's life so that one "can live in a manner worthy of the gospel of Christ." Ironically, however, the manner of life issuing from this new perspective involves suffering. As Paul explains it, this *telos* provides him with power and a place in the eschatological resurrection of the dead, but, most immediately, it also entails a fellowship with Christ's sufferings (3:11).

Here we have a sharp contrast between the Paul of Acts and the Paul rendered in Philippians. In Acts Paul encounters persecution and various trials. This Paul, however, is able to fit them and himself into an ongoing story of God's providential supervision of the gospel. In Acts Paul never gives any hint that his tribulations are anything more than Satan's futile attempts to inhibit the triumph of the gospel. In Philippians Paul views suffering, and his own suffering in particular, as an ironic by-product of "knowing Christ and the power of his resurrection" (3:10).[31] The humiliations suffered in this life are real and the threat they pose to the Christians in Philippi are serious; these humiliations will, however, be transformed at some future point when all things are subjected to Christ (3:21). In more traditional terms, the Paul of Acts fits himself into a theology of glory; the Paul of Philippians considers his life from the viewpoint of a theology of the cross. This cruciform perspective allows Paul the ironic distance he needs to view his early achieve-

---

30. It seems to me now that there are more connections here both to Paul's demand to φρονεῖτε in a particular way in 2:5 and the manner in which Christ considered (ἡγήσατο) his position ἐν μορφῇ θεοῦ than I indicated in my criticisms of Morna Hooker's work on this passage (see *The Story of Christ in the Ethics of Paul*, 77, n. 1). I am still convinced that these connections, however, are not the ones Hooker mentions.

31. Paul does not directly characterize his sufferings in Galatians 1–2, but when he does note them in 6:11ff., he also adopts an ironic perspective, "boasting in the cross of Christ."

ments as "rubbish" and his present sufferings as part of faithful participation in Christ's resurrection, a participation that is ongoing, awaiting completion (3:12).[32]

As in Galatians, Paul presents himself and the transformation of perspective that God has enabled him to achieve as exemplary for the Philippians (3:17ff.). Unlike in Galatians, Paul does not go to such great pains to present his self as decentered by God. Without question, Paul recognizes that he is who he is by God's grace. In 3:12 he notes that his transformed perspective, his new *telos,* is the result of Christ' s prior work. Paul can only make this perspective his own (καταλάβω) because Christ first made Paul his own (κατελήμφθη). Nevertheless, in Philippians Paul does not emphasize his decentered self at the same time that he tries to provide a character substantial and particular enough to be exemplary.[33] Instead, he presents himself as one who has had his perspective on himself and the world transformed through his knowledge of Christ. It is this transformation that he hopes the Philippians will also attain. Such a perspective will allow them, like Paul, to have the ironic distance needed to view both "fleshly" achievements and temporal sufferings as insignificant in the light of the glory that awaits them.[34]

III. Concluding Remarks

In Galatians and Philippians Paul is at pains to characterize himself in certain specific ways so that his convictions, perspectives, and practices can be exemplary for his audience.[35] A narrowly conceived literary or rhetorical ap-

32. This ironic perspective is both clearer and more pointedly polemical in 2 Corinthians 11.

33. This may be due to the more heated nature of his relationship with the churches in Galatia, as Gaventa proposes, "Galatians 1 and 2," p. 322.

34. An ironic perspective is not all they will need. Paul also grounds his demands for a manner of life worthy of the gospel of Christ on a very particular narration of the Christ event in 2:6-11. Nevertheless, it may well be that the ironic perspective needed to endure suffering in the way that Paul wishes the Philippians to do requires Paul to provide a much more stable account of his tranformed self than he gives in Galatians. Perhaps it is the case that certain types of external forces can work to solidify one's self.

35. The obvious exception here is Acts 20:35. This hardly matches the scope of either Galatians or Philippians. Further, one might claim that Acts 26:29 presents Paul as a sort of exemplar for Agrippa, Bernice, and even Festus. The chief difference between Acts and the epistles in this respect is that the Galatians and the Philippians have already responded to the gospel. For them, Paul is an example internal to the body of Christ in a way that he cannot be for Agrippa and the others.

proach to characterization can tend to gloss or leave undeveloped the moral importance attached to Paul's characterization of himself in the epistles. Simply noting what Paul says about himself and how he says it will fail to account for what is at stake morally and theologically in characterizing oneself one way rather than another.

As a way of concluding this essay I would like to touch on two particular points arising from my readings of these passages. First, I want to say a bit more about the importance of being able to narrate an account of one's self. Then I want to return — all too briefly — to the point I made about Paul's decentered self.

Like those who have read these passages in search of historical information, I have noted several differences in the ways Paul characterizes himself in these two texts. Had I examined other texts, particularly Acts, the differences would have been even more pronounced. Given these differences one may be tempted to ask which of these characters (if any) is the "real" Paul? We may be tempted to privilege the Paul of the epistles on the grounds that these are really Paul's accounts of himself rather than accounts that are ultimately dependent on Luke. This is a temptation we should resist. There is no *a priori* reason for preferring the account one gives of oneself to the accounts others might give. In fact, human tendencies to self-deception being what they are might lead one to tilt the scale in favor of an outsider's account. More importantly, I want to argue that to fall prey to this question of the "real Paul," no matter how one answers it, is a mistake. The question presumes that there is something essential and unchanging about Paul (or anybody else) that can be separated from the contingent accounts we have of Paul, some essential core of Paul that can be distilled from the specific narratives of Paul's life that we have looked at. To engage in this quest for the real Paul is to fail to note that character can only be adequately tendered narratively.[36]

Characterizing a person is a narrative achievement. That is, to render a character, one must fit that character into a narrative sequence of actions.[37] This is not to say that one cannot characterize someone or oneself in a single, non-narrative remark. Think, for example, of the characterization "Paul is an apostle." This remark, while not a narrative in itself, presupposes a narratable sequence of events that both display what an apostle is and that involve this character, Paul, in ways that result in the non-narrative judgment that Paul is

---

36. This point is not original to me. Alasdair MacIntyre, Charles Taylor, and Stanley Hauerwas have all made similar claims. For my remarks here I will rely on MacIntyre's account in *After Virtue* (Notre Dame: University of Notre Dame Press, 1984[2]).

37. This is also true of the characterizations I have given of Paul's characterizations of himself.

an apostle. Failure to provide such a narrative when required would lead one to consider this characterization of Paul unintelligible, incorrect, or the result of devious motives. (Of course, all these judgments would require narrative display as well.)

In addition, the claim that the practice of characterization presupposes the ability to narrate is not to say that the narrative always stays the same. Clearly, in all the cases I have examined Paul is an excellent example of someone who revises the narrative he tells about himself. No matter how revisable or unstable the narrative, an intelligible character can only adequately result from narration.[38]

Further, to recognize that characterization is a narrative achievement is also to recognize that characterization is always a contestable practice. To order events in a particular way, to endow them with specific significance, to begin at a certain place and end in another, to embed the life of a character within a larger story all reflect decisions that could be made otherwise.[39] All this is to say that one may be able to articulate standards by which one characterization is seen to be better than another, but there is no intelligible way to claim that one characterization captures the "real" Paul.[40]

Earlier in my discussion of Galatians I proposed that Paul's self was decentered or destabilized by God. I think it is both important to make a claim like this and crucial to qualify that claim. The importance of venturing such a claim lies in being able to show how theological interpretations of Scripture might and (might not) address contemporary moral and theological debates. It becomes theologically crucial to qualify such claims lest Scripture or any other theological resource simply be subsumed within an anti-theological idiom.[41] In

38. So MacIntyre, 216ff.
39. This is a point MacIntyre makes in *After Virtue* 212-13. In this section MacIntyre is attacking historians like Louis Mink who seek to deny the epistemological importance of narrative for historiography. See, for example, Mink's "History and Fiction as Modes of Comprehension," *New Literary History* 1 (1970) 541-58.
40. My account here implies some fairly significant alterations to the way one thinks about and pursues tasks normally associated with theological anthropology. For an outline of some of these alterations see David Kelsey, "Biblical Narrative and Theological Anthropology," in *Scriptural Authority and Narrative Interpretation,* ed. Garrett Green (Philadelphia: Fortress, 1987) 121-43. While Kelsey seems ambivalent about adopting these changes, he does represent them fairly well. It would have certainly changed the account Childs gives in "Humanity: Old and New" if he had engaged in a more systematic way this essay by Kelsey.
41. Ironically, this may be the fate of those who carry on theological anthropology in terms of modernity's account of the self. Even something like Seyla Benhabib's revised account of the modern self in the light of Habermas's "discourse ethics" is clearly

this particular case, a claim that Paul's self was decentered by God indicates the fundamental difference between Paul's conception of humanity and the conception that came to dominate modern discussions of selfhood. The modern self was characterized by presumptions of autonomy, individualism, unencumbered rationality, essential stability, and an absence of historical and social contingency. To the extent that people viewed (and view) themselves this way, Paul's claims about himself will be either misunderstood, rendered unintelligible, or rejected outright.[42] Against these sorts of presumptions, Paul's self can be seen as decentered. It is a self completely enmeshed in historical and cultural contingencies. Through his encounter with the crucified and risen Christ, Paul's standards of rationality are radically undermined and gradually reconstituted in ways that even his fellow Christians have a hard time understanding (see both Phil. 3:2-16 and 1 Corinthians 1–4 for good examples of this). Of course, for Paul, as well as for virtually all other premodern people, the radically autonomous self of modernity would have been an odd, if not dangerous, notion. For Paul, one was never autonomous. The important questions were not about how to achieve autonomy, but about serving the true God as opposed to being in bondage to false gods. Further, as these two passages nicely show, Paul's self is known not by its essence, but by its relationships. These relationships (particularly Paul's relationship to God) are represented in the narratives Paul tells about himself, rather than in a list of essential properties.[43]

Paul's view of the self is not the only opponent of modern concepts of the self. A variety of critics, too diverse to fit under a single rubric such as "postmodern," have offered substantial criticisms of the modern notions of selfhood.[44] Many of these critics of modernity would also speak of the self as

antitheological in all the ways modernity typically has been. See *Situating the Self* (Cambridge: Polity, 1992). For a good example, see chapter 1 and esp. pp. 42-43.

42. Of course, all these things happened to the Pauline writings within the theologies of modernity.

43. Of course, Paul would have recognized a universal claim that all people were created in the image of God. While this claim might sound like an essential characteristic of the self, it receives its intelligibility from the ways it is narrated and reflected on within the biblical traditions.

44. Even those who largely agree with modern notions of selfhood, such as Seyla Benhabib, have had to recognize the substantial critique of modern (Kantian) notions of the self and to make revisions to it (see *Situating the Self*). One of the great virtues of Benhabib's account is that she offers a nuanced account of the various types of opposition to modernity rather than lumping such diverse characters as Richard Rorty, Alasdair MacIntyre, Jacques Derrida, Michel Foucault, and Jacques Lacan all together under the label "postmodern." Whether her revisions to modern views of the self in the light of these criticisms are sufficient is another matter. At the very least they still retain an antitheological stance.

decentered. Moreover, they would also oppose the claim that Paul's self, while decentered by God, was reconstituted in a coherent way under the rule of Christ. As opposed to the Pauline decentered self I have presented, theirs is a self that is simply a collocation of fragments, an a-centered self, a self that is unable to be represented in any stable fashion.

With the critics of modernity, then, Paul's self is decentered, contingent, and known by its relationships rather than its essence. Against these critics of modernity (but still not with the proponents of modernity) Paul's self testifies to the power of God's grace to reconstitute a self under the lordship of Christ. This would indicate that the key issues for any full account of Paul's selfhood should have less to do with issues of interiority, conscience, and the relationships between Paul's inner self and the world. Instead, all these issues would need to be seen as subsidiary to the issue of how they all come to be differently arranged and understood from the perspective of learning to narrate one's life within the economy of God's activity in Christ. I would close by submitting that it is from this position that future theologies of the self need to be articulated.[45]

---

45. For some of the implications of adopting this position see Kelsey, "Biblical Narrative and Theological Anthropology," 136-42. This would also indicate that there is a need to revisit some aspects of Krister Stendahl's arguments about Paul and "the introspective conscience of the West."

The Absence of the Comforter:
Scripture and the Divided Church

Ephraim Radner

I. Does the Holy Spirit Still Illuminate
the Scriptures for the Church?

If one were to view Brevard Childs and his impressive *oeuvre* as a historical phenomenon within the history of the Christian church, what would one perceive? Leaving aside the issue of his particular scholarly proposals and contributions, to what would this phenomenon testify? In a sense, the following essay reflects upon just this question. The manner in which Childs's voice, since the late 1970s, has swept through the field of Biblical Theology and related disciplines, with a resonance matched only by the ruin of its context, has been astonishing. But for someone of my generation, Biblical Theology never seemed so much in "crisis" as already crumbled. And in such an environment, Childs's voice was raised less as a warning for the future than as a sign about the present's inescapable outcome from the past's disarray.

And there is about Childs's language a consistent quality that ties it to the past. There is a sense of valiant striving to hold on to, retrieve, or revive central elements of Christian reading of the Scriptures that not only can be salvaged from the past but can further the salvaging of the past and of the past's present progeny. For Childs this has certainly not involved the reapplication of the past, the refueling of his discipline by central insights and approaches of Luther or Calvin, for instance. That would have been simple nostalgia. Nonetheless, Childs's protest against the present has been sustained by perennial conceptions of the church, of the Holy Spirit, and of

Scripture in their relations, conceptions whose integrity derives from the past, but also whose power of explication has been contradicted by a long devolution of Christian experience.

I am thinking in particular of his frequent deferment to traditional conceptions of Scripture's meaning as something "exposed" to the "church" through the explicit operation of the Spirit.[1] In what follows, I do not intend to argue for or against these conceptions, which tend to follow, in Childs's case, a Reformed shape. But I want only to suggest that their pertinence for reorienting our lives by Scripture may be incapable of reconstruction. If Childs's protest has been valid, as I think it has, the range of its voice may be more colored by the tautened irresolvability of its object than by the intrinsic power for hope with which his positive proposals are fraught. In particular, I want to explore the ways in which it makes sense any longer to speak of the Spirit illuminating Scripture for the Christian community. Perhaps it once made sense, but does it now? And if not, how are we to hold on to the promises of God delivered in the gospel of Christ, a gospel that has traditionally formed the subject matter of scriptural exposition, as well as of biblical theology?

In trying to address these questions, I will revisit some basic notions of pneumatology as they relate to Scripture and the church. Most importantly, I will try to analyze these notions in the context of the reality of a divided church. Certainly, there is a great deal of discussion over the causes and origins of the kind of subversion of, for example, a unified and holistic reading of Christian Scripture, such as Childs has espoused. Seventeenth-century or Enlightenment rationalism are the usually fingered culprits. But a fundamental contributing factor to the situation that has produced a voice like Childs's has surely also been the fragmentation of the church in the West in the wake of the Reformation. And it is a fragmentation that, ironically, informs some of the very conceptualizations of Scripture, church, and Spirit that sustain Childs's work. The frequent and vague references Childs makes to the Christian "community" and to the "church" as the defining agent for whom Scripture's subject matter is given shape are never clearly identified; nor need they be, according to a long post-Reformation Protestant tradition in which such ecclesial referents are deliberately peripheral. But in the contemporary context of communal dispute over the

1. Cf. Brevard S. Childs, *Biblical Theology of the Old and New Testaments: Theological Reflection on the Christian Bible* (Philadelphia: Fortress, 1992) 86-87 or 382 ("if the Church confesses that the spirit of God opens up the text to a perception of its true reality, it also follows that the Spirit also works in applying the reality of God in its fullness to an understanding of the text"). An expanded version of this essay appears as the first chapter of my book *The End of the Church: A Pneumatology of Christian Division in the West* (Grand Rapids: Eerdmans, 1998).

very nature of what Scripture is and of its authority and meaning, this vagueness carries with it an aura of unease that is also not altogether missing from Childs's work. Confusions over Scripture have become linked with confusions over what the Christian church is or where it is to be found, and appeals to the Spirit's guidance in such contexts can appear more desperate than assured. I will have as my paramount concern just this element of ecclesial division as it informs the pneumatological problem of Scripture.[2]

II. The Reformation Crisis: Scriptural Perspicuity and the Church

It is Richard Popkin who has most forcefully of late explored the role of the Reformation division of the church in instigating a range of theological and philosophical responses to the epistemological question of criteria that lie behind so much of modern western philosophy.[3] Specifically, Popkin has argued that the burning problem of how Scripture ought to be interpreted in a divided church helped to ignite a skeptical crisis regarding the source and context for our knowledge in general that has remained with us since the sixteenth century. With the Reformers' denial of the authority of the institutional church in defining the right interpretation of Scripture in favor of various forms of individual pneumatic illumination, Protestants and Catholics were set against each other in a dizzying and always fruitless effort to justify their canons of interpretive criteria. One of the few ways of escaping this impossible argument lay in the adoption of now exposed skeptical postures toward the possibility of justified criteria at all. In the wake of the Reformation, the Christian claim to Scriptural authority lay seemingly mortally assailed, and along with it the claim to Scriptural integrity and meaning.

From the perspective of history, I think Popkin's thesis is unassailable, and the confirming of this history need not concern us here. All we need to

2. Properly, the Great Schism of West and East deserves to form the historical and theological context for what follows. But the Reformation and post-Reformation debates are those that are closest to us in the West and those from which the clearest documents survive and continue to inform our thinking. The parochial nature of the discussion below, however, is granted, although its principles, I would argue, can be extended beyond the Western ecclesial sphere.

3. Cf. Richard H. Popkin's now classic *The History of Scepticism from Erasmus to Spinoza* (Berkeley: University of California Press, 1979), chapter 1. See also "The Role of Scepticism in Modern Philosophy Reconsidered," *Journal of the History of Philosophy* 31 (1993) 501-17.

do here is remind ourselves of at least two of the well-known series of theological oppositions that have been drawn on by the evolving fractured church on the matters, first, of Scripture's perspicuity, and second, of the authorizing locus of scriptural interpretation.

With respect to perspicuity, Popkin uses the Luther-Erasmus debate over free will as the foundational exposition of the skeptical crisis over Scripture that would fuel the exhausting quest of modern philosophy.[4] While Luther's own mature understanding of the relation of Scripture to church is misleadingly gleaned from this encounter, the contrast between him and Erasmus nonetheless accurately establishes the developed polemical set of the post-Reformation controversy over Scripture between Protestant and Catholic. The positions therefore deserve to be restated.

Erasmus prefaces his argument with some straightforward affirmations: first, the Scriptures are filled with obscurities that are not designed by God to be uniformly clarified; if this were otherwise, people would not be arguing over such texts; second, whatever is necessary for a Christian life is made clear enough in Scripture, and all the rest is not worth fighting over; third, it is best to maintain a skeptical attitude toward controverted (and ancillary) points in Scripture; finally, though one can never be sure in such matters, if one is going to believe anybody's interpretation of these obscure passages, one ought to follow the official teachings of the church, since this, at least, furthers peace and harmony.[5]

Luther responds by laying out what will become the classical parameters of the Protestant dogma of Scripture's perspicuity. Christians are not skeptics, he argues, and with regard to matters concerning God and God's will, only the "assertion" of "certainties" will do, "for what is more miserable than uncertainty"?[6] And Scripture itself is perfectly clear as regards its "subject matter," namely Christ and the truths associated with him (e.g., the Incarnation, the Trinity, and Redemption). "Are not these things known and sung even in the highways and byways?" If there are minor obscurities, they are due to purely linguistic ambiguities and are negligible. If there are *dis-*

4. Erasmus, *De Libero Arbitrio* and Luther, *De Servo Arbitrio.* A convenient edition of the two works is contained in *Luther and Erasmus: Free Will and Salvation,* ed. E. Gordon Rupp and Philip S. Watson (Philadelphia: Westminster, 1969).

5. *Ibid.,* 38-47.

6. *Ibid.,* 105ff. For Luther's demand for absolute epistemological certitude in questions of hermeneutics — which was something of a novelty — see Marjorie O'Rourke Boyle, "The Chimera and the Spirit: Luther's Grammar of the Will," in *The Martin Luther Quincentennial,* ed. Gerhard Dünnhaupt (Michigan Germanic Studies; Detroit: Wayne State University Press, 1985) 17-31.

agreements among people regarding the truths taught in Scripture, however, these are due, not to Scripture's intrinsic obscurity, but to the spiritual blindness of the ungodly. "Let miserable men, therefore, stop imputing with blasphemous perversity the darkness and obscurity of their own hearts to the wholly clear Scriptures of God."[7]

Second, it was Luther who firmly set the authority residing in an intrinsically perspicuous Scripture rightly apprehended by the individual over and against the authority of the church's official teaching offices. Luther argued robustly for the evident failures of the church's leadership over time, to the point where he could boldly wonder, "what are we to do? The Church is hidden, the saints are unknown. What and whom are we to believe? [. . .] or who gives us certainty?"[8] If it is certainty we want — and we must in matters that touch our salvation — then only the Scriptures can provide it, and they do so efficaciously. In themselves, of course, the Scriptures are utterly clear and plain in their meaning, so that, "if Satan were not at work, the whole world of men would be converted by a single word of God once heard, and there would be no need of more." But to have a people freed from Satan to apprehend its intrinsic clarity, the Holy Spirit must provide them a special gift of "enlightenment."[9]

As is well known, of course, Luther did not mean somehow to subjectivize the interpretation of Scripture. Especially as he developed his expressions in the ongoing debate with the Anabaptists and "enthusiasts," he came to stress more clearly the pneumatic character of the Word as given through the "means," not only of Scripture's language, but of Scripture's public exposition, through the formal ministry of preaching.[10] Still, as modern Lutheran theologians have been careful to elaborate, this "exterior means" by which the Word speaks in Scripture has more to do with an event of existential presence than of historical tradition. With the theory of Scripture's perspicuous meaning effected through the Spirit's annointing in the

---

7. *Luther and Erasmus,* 111.

8. *Ibid.,* 158. This becomes a standard Protestant platform of attack against Catholics: how can we be sure who are the saints and what constitutes (and where) the True Church over time and space? Since we cannot — that is, since the True Church is, on the basis of historical incertitude regarding its visible integrity, invisible, we must rely on the direct and concrete interpretive action of pneumatically assisted *individuals,* divorced from the fog of time. This is an attack on the knowledge conferred by historical experience. See William Whitaker, *A Disputation on Holy Scripture against the Papists, Especially Bellarmine and Stapleton* [1588], tr. and ed. W. Fitzgerald (Cambridge: Cambridge University Press, 1849) 403, 414, 448-49, 455.

9. *Luther and Erasmus,* 167.

10. Cf. the famous text in the "Smalcald Articles," 3.8.3.

Christian believer, Luther had — in theory, if not in practice — cleanly disposed of the historical teaching tradition of the church as an authoritative guide.[11]

When, a generation later, another celebrated controversy took place, this time between John Calvin and the Catholic bishop Jacopo Sadoleto, who had addressed a letter to the Genevan citizenry appealing for their return to the Roman Church, the terms of the debate had solidified into a more dogmatic form, without however changing much of the substance.[12] Sadoleto had firmed up Erasmus's tepid skepticism with a strong argument for the divinely authoritative character of the undivided Catholic Church, defined according to the Vincentian canon — *quod ubique, quod semper, quod ab omnibus creditum est* — as the interpretive locus of Scripture. The church "brought" the gospel of salvation to the world and suffered for it, and her common faith is now the standard by which the gospel has any saving significance.[13] But what if the church is unfaithful? Calvin, pressing for a more concrete ecclesiology than the early Luther, answered Sadoleto with a redefinition of the church, now seen as a body of faithful people bound by a true scriptural doctrine, that is, as a community subjected, by the Spirit, to the Word of Scripture understood in a uniform manner.[14] But who decides what is the proper exposition of Scripture's Word? What is important to note here is how, on the basis of an argument over the interpretation of Scripture, the issue had been quickly recast into the question "where is the true church?" with each side seeking to found their positions on a criterion internal to their own argument: we know the true meaning of Scripture from Scripture itself, or we know that our interpretation of

11. "All the fathers who interpret Scripture in their own way are refuted, and their interpretation is invalidated. It is forbidden to rely on such interpretation. If Jerome or Augustine or anyone of the fathers has given his own interpretation, we want none of it. [. . .] The Holy Spirit Himself must expound Scripture" (Luther's Commentary on 2 Peter 1:21, in *Luther's Works*, ed. Jaroslav Pelikan and Walter Hansen [St. Louis: Concordia, 1967] XX, 166). Obviously, the promotion of teaching guides like the Smaller and Larger Catechisms, not to mention other authoritative documents, shifts the emphasis away from such sweeping disavowals of tradition. Still, the theory for such disavowals is firmly in place, and they will hold sway in post-Reformation Protestant generalizing about the relation of Scripture and the ecclesial magisterium.

12. See "Letter by Cardinal Sadolet to the Senate and People of Geneva" and Calvin's "Reply to Cardinal Sadolet's Letter" in John Calvin, *Tracts and Treatises on the Reformation of the Church*, tr. Henry Beveridge, introduction and notes by T. F. Torrance (Grand Rapids: Eerdmans, 1958), vol. 1.

13. *Ibid.*, 10.

14. *Ibid.*, 36ff.

Scripture is Spirit-taught from the Spirit's own testimony; or, we know the church's authority over Scripture's interpretation from the church itself or from our need for such a authority.

That two portions of a divided church could never, in the face of their critics or antagonists, persuasively extricate themselves from the circularity of their criteriology was a realization quickly made by both controversialists and religious scoffers. As Popkin has shown, the very project of Christian arguing against separated Christian almost inevitably became enmeshed in methods of discourse that, all sides agreed, reeked of skepticism, but which no one was willing to forgo as long as it was aimed at the oppositon. The most celebrated example of this development is the early seventeenth-century French Jesuit François Veron, whose success at debating his Reformed brethren gained him widespread publication and translation.[15] Veron's most famous "method" (he had many) involved the logical and practical demonstration that no Protestant actually read Scripture without applying to the words *ab initio* some interpretive frame of conceptualization. Even the bare Protestant effort to derive the meaning of biblical texts only from other biblical texts — interpreting "Scripture by Scripture" — demanded the application of a complex system of inductive and deductive logic that is by no means envisioned or implied by Scripture itself and is rather a cultural construct imported to the text by the reader. This seemingly postmodern axiom Veron insisted upon for all readers of Scripture, and the issue for him lay in exposing the challenge that *any* Christian must face of where to find a trustworthy communal context for interpretation.[16]

While Veron himself was aware that simply exposing the challenge did nothing to resolve it — he brought to bear other arguments to show the Ro-

---

15. See Popkin, *The History of Scepticism*, ch. 4, pp. 66ff.

16. Cf. Veron's own epitome of his extended "methods," in his *Abregé des Methodes de Traicter des Controverses de Religion. Enseignées et prattiquées par S. Augustin & les autres SS. Pères; Reduites en art & préceptes* (Paris: Louys Boulanger, 1630) 1-48. Veron himself insists that this method cannot be turned on the Roman Church, since they have never made the claims of Protestants as to the authority of *sola scriptura* divorced from the historical "tradition, authority of the Church, antiquity, miracles, etc." (p. 48). But, as he knew well, the possibility of being roasted on one's own fire was not so easily brushed aside — why is the Roman tradition of interpretation more authoritative than the Reformed? — and Veron elaborated at great length an alternative "method" of disputing with Protestants on the exact basis of *sola scriptura*. On other Roman Catholic attempts at meeting Protestant attacks on the same playing field of the "sole" and "literal" Word of God, cf. Georges Tavard, *La Tadition au XVIIe Siècle en France et en Angleterre* (Paris: Cerf, 1969), esp. 325ff.

man Church's superior interpretive credibility[17] — this kind of approach tended to foster a relativistic assessment concerning the authority of *all* religious communities, let alone of individuals. For some, this situation only besmeared the force of Christian religion and its gospel into weakened unrecognizability, while for others, still driven by a religious conscience, it gave rise to agonies of bewilderment. John Donne, for instance and like many others of the post-Reformation era, ran the gamut, able at once to counsel bemusedly the prospective Christian convert to "doubt wisely" in the face of five major Christian denominations in competition for his soul ("Third Satyre"), and wrenchingly to lament "Shee's dead, shee's dead," of the church's general healing mission within a broken world all "out of joynt" ("First Anniversery").

If Popkin is right as to the ongoing and unresolved character of the Reformation "crisis" over scriptural interpretation brought on by the divided church, then contemporary manifestations of the same set of dilemmas should not surprise us. And, in fact, one of the more publicized recent debates over the these matters took place, not unexpectedly, in the very context of the discussion over the reunion of Protestant and Roman Catholic churches. Shortly before his death in 1984, Karl Rahner, along with Heinrich Fries, made a proposal for the "uniting" of separated churches into a federation of independent bodies that would mutually recognize each other, look to the "Petrine office" as some kind of "guarantor of the unity of the Church in truth and love," and eventually follow a broadly common form of ordination.[18] The main justification for conceiving such an arrangement as possible even now lay in the authors' conviction that "the fundamental truths of Christianity" expressed in Scripture and the creeds were accepted by most major denominations. "Beyond that," as Thesis II of the proposal affirmed, "a realistic principle of faith should apply," that would oblige each "partner" church neither to reject a "dogma" of another nor to impose their "dogma" on another.

It was Rahner's commentary on Thesis II that caused the most contro-

17. Cf. Veron, 49-59, where Veron describes one of his "positive" methods for upholding the Roman Church's claims to interpretive authority, the method of "conjunction," by which Scripture, patristic exposition, conciliar decision, and the present teaching of the church are shown to be mutually consistent. The criterion of "continuity" in teaching was obviously not self-evident, but Veron felt that Protestants at least bore the onus of disproving its weight, given the initiative they took in breaking that continuity.

18. Heinrich Fries and Karl Rahner, *Unity of the Churches: An Actual Possibility* (1983), tr. Ruth C. L. Gritsch and Eric W. Gritsch (Philadelphia: Fortress; New York: Paulist, 1985).

versy. For in it, Rahner outlined a historical theory of knowledge that painted the modern era (implicity identified with the post-Reformation) as one of increasingly fractured and multiplied fields of knowing, which, in their sheer number, now preclude any individual or group from being able to absorb the information necessary to form a "synthesis" of the material at issue. In short, we simply cannot "know" what is what, let alone what another person or group truly thinks is the case; we cannot understand each other, let alone the world, in any common or full sense. Rahner thinks this is a peculiarly pressing problem derived from modernity's pluralistic explosion of information. And given this "intellectual-political situation," Rahner argues that Christians should engage in a form of "epistemological tolerance," which works on the basis of certain accepted fundamentals (i.e. the creeds and some "minimal" common structures of practice) and lets all other issues "slide" in the face of the gospel promise of an eschatological unity of knowledge (this being the only kind we can ever expect).[19]

No less than in the seventeenth century, this kind of reasoning, now at the service of unity, gave immediate rise to charges of "skepticism." And those from both the Protestant and the Roman Catholic sides who viewed the issue of truth as somehow distinct from the issue of the unity of churches — however much they may have been supportive of ecumenical movement toward future unity — denounced the Rahner-Fries proposal just at this point.[20] This,

19. "The basic thesis is: in today's intellectual-political situation, no greater unity of faith is possible than the one proposed, and therefore it must be legitimate if the unity of the churches in faith is not to be abandoned despite all solemn declarations to the contrary [. . .] In the light of a pluralism of thinking which can in no way be integrated into a higher synthesis, it would be totally unrealistic — at least at present and in future — to demand a larger and more tangible unity of faith" (*ibid.,* pp. 39-41).

20. Cf. Cardinal Joseph Ratzinger's discussion of this matter in the "Postscript" to his reprinted interview "Luther and the Unity of the Churches," in his anthology *Church, Ecumenism and Politics: New Essays in Ecclesiology* (New York: Crossroad, 1988) 122-34: "If this [i.e. Rahner's assessment in Thesis 11] is how things are, if in the general fog nobody can see the other and no one sees the truth, then the 'epistemological tolerance' is displayed by the fact that no one contradicts anyone any more. The only thing that is clearly visible in the darkness of the tendencies of our civilization to diminish differences is Christ's command of unity which then becomes fundamentally the only at all clear component. The 'authorities' are now there to bring this unity to realization, and since anyway nobody can judge his or her own thinking, let alone anybody else's, obedience to this instruction should not be too difficult. But what kind of unity is it really? A formal unity without any clear content is fundamentally no unity at all, and a mere linking together of institutions is no value in itself. Unity conceived of in this way is based on common scepticism, not on common knowledge" (p. 131). Ratzinger, however, never evaluates his own rhetorically aimed presuppositions here: what if Rahner *is* correct about the "way things are"?

of course, is the question that the historical demonstration of the Popkin thesis thrusts upon us: is it possible to speak of the gospel's truth apart from the actual unity of the church itself? Does the truth of the gospel become obscured outside the unity of the church? The question, posed this way, is obviously fraught with enormous implications, not only for the small enterprises that make the study of the truth their business — including scholarly enterprises like scriptural studies and theology. The question clearly touches on the very nature of the gospel and of the church that proclaims it. It may be possible, on an abstract level, to construe the arguments of the Protestant-Catholic split over Scripture and the church in terms of a "dialectic," as Childs himself has done.[21] But such a dialectic will itself be "unified" only to the degree that its progress is seen as independent of concrete and concretely divided Christian communities, only as it is idealized according to some ahistorical scheme. In terms of concrete churches, the question of scriptural clarity and ecclesial division remains glaringly unresolved.

III. The Pneumatological Contradiction Inherent in the Post-Reformation Debate over Scripture

The same question is posed, furthermore, by the logical quandary embedded within the historical oppositions taken up in the Reformation debate (if not before), a dilemma involving the work of the Holy Spirit in the interpretation of Scripture in its relation to the church. For the actual Protestant-Catholic antitheses on the question of the Scripture and the church referred to above may or may not be more or less true in their respective assertions. That has always been the fuel of their argument. But they do give rise to a pneumatological contradiction that, from any confessional side, cannot be resolved into some particular position taken by one or another church.

The notion that Scripture is properly understood through the work of the Spirit enlightening the heart and mind was never in itself doubted by either side of the debate. But in what way or in what context did the Spirit illuminate the Scripture? The Protestant-Catholic opposition on this matter took the form of contrasting emphases on individuals and communities respectively. In the classic late sixteenth-century debate between the Puritan William Whitaker and the Jesuit Robert Bellarmine among others, Whitaker, for instance, reasserts the view that, *if* Scripture is properly interpreted through the Spirit, then this Spirit must work individually, through each sep-

21. Cf. Childs, *op. cit.,* 66ff.

arate member of the church without mediation. Did not the Apostle write in 1 John 2:20, "Ye have an unction from the Holy One"?[22] The theological problem of Scripture then turns on the methods the individual might use, either to assure him or herself of the Spirit's guidance (e.g., prayer) or to master the linguistic and conceptual characteristics of Scripture.[23] For Roman Catholics, instead, the Spirit works within the "general" community of the faithful, and only thence speaks to individuals.[24] The communal discernment of the Spirit, with respect to Scripture, then becomes the focus of theological interest, and this leads, not only to orderings of authoritative pronouncement — *sensus fidelium,* theologians, Fathers, councils, Pope in some such order — but to the assessment of holiness in history, in saints and times, which confirm such authorities.[25]

As Puritanism, for instance, developed, theological emphases for many Protestants shifted to the subjective, rather than the literary aspect (in Whitaker's scheme) of pneumatic assurance in the reading of Scripture. Introspective concerns regarding the experiential elements of the Spirit's inspiration took on increasing weight, and the interior shape of *illuminatio* became a major topic.[26] On the Catholic side, this kind of individualism was avoided in favor of a deliberately objective communitarianism, that sought to examine, historically, the characteristics of corporate experience, given in terms of the theorized ecclesial marks of "perpetuity," "continuity," "unity,"

22. William Whitaker, *Disputation on Holy Scripture,* 451f. Bellarmine kept a portrait of Whitaker hanging in his library, commenting to astonished visitors that "although he was a heretic and his adversary, yet he was a learned adversary." See James Brodrick, S.J., *Robert Bellarmine: Saint and Scholar* (London: Burns and Oates, 1961) 84.

23. Cf. Whitaker, *Disputation on Holy Scripture,* 466ff.

24. Cf. St. Francis de Sales: "In a word, it is to the general Church to whom the Spirit immediately addresses its inspirations and persuasions for the common good of Christians; and next, through the preaching of the Church, the Spirit communicates to particular persons. The milk is produced in the Bride, and then the children suckle at her breasts." Discourse 20 of his *Controverses,* in the *Oeuvres complètes de Saint François de Sales* (Paris: Louis Vivès, 1859) VIII, 321.

25. Cf. St. Francis de Sales, 449-519.

26. Cf. John Owen's *Pneumatologia* VI/2, 7, in *The Works of John Owen, D.D.,* ed. W. H. Goold (London and Edinburgh: Johnstone and Hunter, 1852) IV, 202ff. Cf. also John Wilson's *The Scripture's Genuine Interpreter Asserted, or, A Discourse Concerning the Right Interpretation of Scripture* (London, 1678), which although occasioned by a philosophically skeptical account of Scripture's (lack of) perspicuity, by Lodewijk Meijer, is basically a typical anti-Catholic controversial work on the topic, happy to rely on Whitaker's standard categories. By the end of it, however, Wilson feels it necessary to provide an extended and elaborate outline of criteria for subjective pneumatic apprehension.

"apostolicity," etc., all of which, of course, are bound up with the identifiable "visibility" of the church as a social phenomenon.[27] Sadoleto had early on located the Catholic opposition to the Reformers in the former's understanding of *caritas* as central to the work of salvation (including justification). So central was the effective force of *caritas* in historical redemption that "communion," love's greatest work, was made the defining criterion, according to Roman Catholics, for any subsequent theological claim. Associating love with the actual Person of the Holy Spirit, as Sadoleto did (along with the side tradition he represented), he thereby pointed out as axiomatic the way that all positive pneumatic action was tied to the visible Christian community *qua* communion.[28]

How deep were these contrasts? Historically speaking, they have been irresolvable. And that may be because each aspect to the confrontation implies a pneumatology that cannot sustain at once the existence of both sides to the debate, without at the same time denying both in some fundamental manner. Protestants stressed the perspicuity of Scripture, the rules for whose interpretation were made possible by an affirmation of Scripture's unified scope and method. They also linked this conviction, in a logical way, with ecclesiologies of diverse individualities or histories bound together in invisible unities.[29] This set of affirmations implied a particular pneumatology, ac-

27. Thus, Bellarmine's definition that "the Church is an assembly of persons as visible and as palpable as is the assembly of the Roman people or the kingdom of France or the Republic of Venice," which roused Protestant attack because of what today we would call its alleged "sociological" (and thus too purely human) conceptualization of a divine reality. Cf. Jean Claude's singleminded barrage against the whole idea of the church's visible (and hence "perpetual," "continuous," etc.) character, in his ongoing debate with Bossuet, e.g. the *Réponse au livre de Monsieur l'Evesque de Meaux, intitulé Conférence avec M. Claude* (Charenton: Veuve d'Olivier de Varennes, 1683), esp. the long preface. Bossuet, for his part, staked much of his vast anti-Protestant writing on Bellarmine's kind of definition.

28. Cf. Sadoleto, *op. cit.*, 9-10, 20.

29. Cf. John Owen's *A Vindication of the Animadversions on "Fiat Lux"* (1663), in his *Works*, vol. 14, esp. pp. 257-318. Owen's congregationalism flowed easily from his conviction that the Spirit worked, especially in the hearing of the gospel in the Scriptures, primarily through individuals. His notion of the "unity" of the church was necessarily informed by a theology of historical diversity, and Christian unity could therefore have as its only meaningful referent something historically "invisible." His remarks on what "Protestant unity" implies, versus the Roman notion of visible communion, are classic expositions of the unifying force common attitudes to the Bible are seen to wield. They also show in what way this kind of ecclesiology tends toward distorted historical judgments made in the interest of demonstrating an often fictitious minimum standard of agreement between separated Protestant denominations.

cording to which the Holy Spirit's work is diversely determined in history and embodied concretely only in the acts of proper scriptural interpretation, wherever they may take place. If unity exists concretely among Christians, it can be located, according to the Protestant paradigm, only in common ways of reading the Bible. Conversely, with ecclesiologies of effective unity so promiment on the Roman Catholic side, corresponding pneumatologies were implied by which the Holy Spirit was seen as working in a uniformly determined history, embodied immediately in ecclesial communion. According to this Catholic pneumatology, true scriptural interpretation is given only in the living, and hence pneumatic, practice of such unity.

But according to *both* accounts, the genuine existence of the *other* as a truly Christian church constitutes a pneumatological contradiction. From the Protestant point of view, either Catholic interpretation of Scripture is unspiritual, or the principle of pneumatic *illuminatio* is itself invalid, along with the Christian communities formed by the aggregates of its objects. Similarly from the Catholic side, either Protestants are not members of the true church, and hence defective in their teaching about Scripture, or the principle of the pneumatic unity of concrete *caritas* is likewise mistaken. In each case, respective pneumatologies can be sustained only by ruling out the other as objects of pneumatic operation.[30]

---

30. Despite minor concessions here and there as to God's possible saving action within other Christian communities, until quite recently Protestants and Catholics have indeed viewed each other as, in different degrees, somehow not truly "church." Cf. Luther's categorical denial of the Roman Church's pneumatic character, due to its lack of proper teaching concerning Christ, a pneumatic absence that rendered that "church" no true church at all: "Where [the Holy Spirit] does not cause the Word to be preached and does not awaken understanding in the heart, all is lost. This was the case under the papacy, where faith was entirely shoved under the bench and no one recognized Christ as the Lord, or the Holy Spirit as the Sanctifier. That is, no one believed that Christ is our Lord in the sense that he won for us this treasure without our works and merits and made us acceptable to the Father. What was lacking here? There was no Holy Spirit present to reveal this truth and have it preached. Men and evil spirits there were, teaching us to obtain grace and be saved by our works. Therefore there was no Christian church. For where Christ is not preached, there is no Holy Spirit to create, call, and gather the Christian church, and outside it no one can come to the Lord Christ" (*Larger Catechism,* 2.43-46, in *The Book of Concord,* tr. and ed. Theodore G. Tappert [Philadelphia: Fortress, 1959] 416). This kind of exclusion on pneumatological bases has perhaps been more evident among Roman Catholics in recent years than among liberal Protestants. But even among liberal Protestants who participated in the rise of pan-Protestant ecumenical efforts in the nineteenth century, a pneumatology was at work that saw unity in terms of some basic uniformity of scriptural interpretation in a way that contradicts the notion of a visibly pneumatic church altogether. It was the same pneumatology that could have been found two

The intransigence of the post-Reformation debate depended in part on this pneumatological contradiction. And as, with the rise of modern tolerance, the churches have proved more and more unwilling to maintain this rejection of the other party, the long-standing contradiction that has invigorated continued separation has become only more difficult to bear. For if we are not to rule out the other, what are we to make of our presupposed pneumatologies? If the Spirit neither works preeminently to guide our hearing of Scripture nor to forge the common space for that hearing, what are we to say about the Spirit at all in its relation to Scripture and the church? Are we faced, to use Bruce Marshall's term for the relation between gospel credibility and the disunity of the churches, with a "genuine *aporia,* a conceptual problem for which there is no conceptual solution"?[31] Or are the basic pneumatologies in question simply inadequate to the truth, yet capable of reformulation?

The pressure to refashion the traditional Protestant and Catholic pneumatologies has in fact proved to be a major project in contemporary theology. But it has also led to a kind of impasse that has only further accentuated the original problem over the hearing of Scripture and Scripture's gospel. The 1968 WCC Assembly at Uppsala, for instance, produced a report entitled "The Holy Spirit and the Catholicity of the Church," that attempted

---

centuries earlier among Puritan congregationalists like John Owen. Further, the rise of historical criticism from Strauss on can be seen as an odd expression of this Protestant pneumatological paradigm as well, according to which unity in the faith can be achieved through the historically demonstrable and hence uniform reconstruction, not of scriptural texts alone, but of scriptural contexts, from which can be pressed, as juice from a lemon, a common moral orientation by which to unite Christian people.

31. Bruce Marshall, "The Disunity of the Church and the Credibility of the Gospel," *Theology Today* 50 (1993) 86. Marshall states his *aporia* this way: "Four propositions create the *aporia:* (a) the gospel is true; (b) the gospel cannot be true if the church is eucharistically divided [this is a modern version of the mark of visible unity in the faith]; (c) there are eucharistic communities that are divided from one another (do not share the eucharist); (d) each of these communities is genuinely church (even if, in some cases they recognize each other as such with some reservations)." Among these, (d) is obviously the new contemporary factor that creates the dilemma, since for much of the post-Reformation period, the dilemma was avoided simply by denying that other "churches" were truly "church." Marshall himself responds to the *aporia* by pointing out that its only resolution is not conceptual at all, but practical: making (c) "false" by "reuniting now divided eucharistic communities." I am here outlining a pneumatological reality only related to the situation the *aporia* describes. And I shall be proposing, not so much a means to do away with the *aporia,* but a way to make sense of it within the larger meaning of the gospel. Which may well be the same as saying that, if looked at in its pneumatological context, it may not be a genuine *aporia* at all.

what some might think a typical ecumenical task, that is, bringing together two sides of an argument as if no tension between the two ever existed.[32] The report finessed the distinction between community and individual, visible and invisible, present and eschatological aspects of pneumatic existence in relation to the church by simply affirming at the same time elements of all of them and lifting up a specific aspect of the Spirit's work that could conceptually hold all together: the Holy Spirit as "leader."[33] By speaking of the church primarily in terms of being "led," all her traditional marks are transferred into the arena of historical process, which precludes firm judgments of pneumatic presence or absence. Unity, for instance, becomes something that is present to the church in a diversity of ways over time, but by the Spirit remains something to be continually sought after in the future.[34] That this kind of formulation might really hide a lurking pan-Protestant version of the pneumatic church — historically and spatially diverse individualities, reconciled inchoately through some shared fundamental commitment, but now extended to all Christian bodies — was something the Orthodox delegates evidently noted. Has the church existed fully in unity continuously or not since the times of the Apostles? they wanted to know.[35] In any case, the direction taken by Uppsala's response was toward a celebration of pneumatic diversity wherein the significance of particularities — whether held in common or in opposition — became increasingly blurred.

The evolution of the WCC's Study Conferences on the Bible manifest this development.[36] The Wadham Conference of 1949 had nothing to say about the Holy Spirit, Scripture, and the church. It stuck to historical-critical issues. The 1963 Montreal paper adopted a rather Catholic-sounding scheme whereby Scripture was said to "testify" to the "Tradition" of the gospel, which is then witnessed to in the "traditions" of preaching, sacraments, and teaching within the churches. The Holy Spirit's work lay in "guarding" and "guiding" the Tradition's multilayered witness in Scripture and the traditions of the church.[37] But Montreal also shifted emphasis toward the pneumatic rendering of the plural "traditions," which pressed toward "diversity" of

32. See the version in *The Uppsala Report 1968*, ed. Norman Goodall (Geneva: World Council of Churches, 1968) 11-19.

33. Cf., §§1, 3-8, 12, etc.

34. §§5, 17ff.

35. Cf. *Uppsala Report 1968*, 9.

36. See *The Bible: Its Authority and Interpretation in the Ecumenical Movement*, ed. Ellen Flesseman-van Leer (Faith and Order Paper 99; Geneva: World Council of Churches, 1980).

37. *Ibid.*, §45.

scriptural interpretation according to time and place.[38] The "Church," in the course of the document, became "the churches," held together by a common commitment to the singular Tradition mediated by the Spirit. The Bristol Report of 1967, dealing with hermeneutical issues, had little to say about the Spirit specifically; but the conference now extended the reality of diversity to the Scriptures themselves, explicitly drawing the parallel, in Section III, between the diversity of churches and the variety of texts and meanings to be found in the Bible. If there was a unity in either sphere, it was to be discovered (and with difficulty and caution) only under the cover of diversity. This was a significant move. Finally, the 1971 Louvain paper brought all this together by openly tying the Holy Spirit's reality to the granting of authority to diverse Scriptures within diverse communities (Section II). At this point, the work of the Spirit was almost made synonymous with scriptural and ecclesial disintegration.

Taken as a whole, then, the ecumenical path for resolving the post-Reformation pneumatological contradiction was to redefine the Holy Spirit's office into that of mediating visible disunity into an invisible unity. Or, to put it in the terms of the confessional debate, ecumenical theologians and biblical scholars determined to give up both the Protestant demand for scriptural uniformity (a premise upon which perspicuity was based) as well as Catholic visible unity (a premise upon which Scriptural authority was based). And the search for an embodied resolution to this pneumatological problem has thus led to an attempt at cutting its Gordian knot completely by saying, in effect, that there *is no* problem in the first place. Incoherence — with respect to the doctrine of the Spirit, or of the church, or of Scripture's use — in this approach, herein becomes itself a pneumatic virtue. The official ecumenical certification of scriptural diversity as a reflection of the Spirit's own creation of variety only leads to a novel Christian affirmation: that is, that Christian unity — whether visible or defined in terms of some concrete and identifiable attribute of commuion — such unity itself is not a fundamental evangelical imperative, and is mistakenly seen to be so. At the least, lack of such unity or communion is not an efficacious defect. By upholding this position, the activities of ecumenical relationship, the theological understanding that undergirds these activities, and, of course, the practice of the churches themselves who are part of such relationships have

38. *Ibid.*, §§47, 52, 56, 57, and 65. For a pungent analysis of this kind of move in the context of specific dialogues, see Cardinal Joseph Ratzinger's comments on the Anglican-Roman Catholic International Commission's first summary report, in "Anglican-Catholic Dialogue: Its Problems and Hopes," in *Church, Ecumenism and Politics: New Essays in Ecclesiology* (New York: Crossroad, 1988) 79ff.

adopted the patent task, in J.-M.-R. Tillard's phrase, of "managing division." And the character of such management is said to derive from the Holy Spirit's action.

IV. The Figuralist Alternative:
Pneumatic Absence from the Church

Childs himself can be seen as vigorously opposing this kind of maneuver within the disicpline of biblical theology. His reappropriation of patristic and Reformed notions of the unifying *scopus* of Scripture, as well as his reaffirmation of Scripture's "subject matter" of the One Lord as that unifying character stands in explicit contrast to the kinds of textual "diversifications" upon which many ecumenical theorists have based their reflections.[39] But another alternative also exists. To those who refuse to accept the management of division (or incoherence) as a pneumatic vocation, one might also wonder, in surveying theologically the condition of the churches' division today, whether, in fact, the Holy Spirit is *absent*.[40] If we are to grasp what is at stake, pneumatologically, in the existence of separated Christian bodies, this question is among the most important to raise. For to "invoke" the Spirit in a situation of theological and ecclesial incoherence — as the WCC has done in its gatherings, and, indeed, as individuals and churches continue to do in their own daily life — is to call down a voice that bespeaks a confusion; a confusion that involves, in a central fashion, our grasp of Scripture itself. This, I think, is the only path to follow here as we try to assess how the Scripture can speak the gospel to us in a condition of division: the answer being that it *cannot,* except insofar as it unveils our incomprehension.

And I do not think this answer is defeatist about the power of the gospel,

39. Cf. Childs, *op. cit.,* 83ff., 719ff.

40. So Tillard wonders about the WCC Assembly at Canberra earlier this decade, ironically given over to the theme of the Holy Spirit. Was the Holy Spirit even present at the Assembly? Tillard cannot quite bring himself to answer in the negative. But if the Spirit was indeed present — and it certainly was not in the "sermons" and other proclamatory actions of the Council, he claims — it was only in offering (to some few) the "grace of clarity which led to the discovery that the ecumenical movement is beginning to go adrift," without "rudder or anchor." Pneumatic presence was thus fleetingly grasped as the sobering knowledge of a dissipated vocation. Cf. J.-M.-R. Tillard, "Was the Holy Spirit at Canberra?" in *One In Christ* 1993/1, p. 62. The remark on "managing division" is made on p. 57 in the midst of a discussion on the way the original thrust of the WCC's foundational vision for the reestablishment of unity among the churches has increasingly been pushed to the periphery of the Council's concern.

precisely because I believe that it is consistent with a proper evangelical understanding of the Holy Spirit itself, consistent, that is, with how the Holy Spirit does indeed create among us the new life of Christ Jesus. If the post-Reformation Protestant and Catholic construals of the relationship between Spirit, Scripture, and church do in fact result in the positing of some basic pneumatological obstacle, then we can confirm the truth of the Christian gospel only by subsuming such obstacles into our very confession of the Holy Spirit's mission. We must confess, in short, that the "absence of the Paraclete" from within the church is constitutive of historical pneumatology (our understanding of the Holy Spirit's life in time), and that Christian division and scriptural obscurity are themselves pneumatic realities of the historical present. How we do this coherently is what I would like now to explore.

A clue to how we might use Scripture itself[41] to bring into relief a proper pneumatology of absence is given by Joseph Ratzinger in the course of a rather negative assessment of the Anglican-Roman Catholic dialogue in the form of the ARCIC I Reports. Ratzinger writes: "perhaps institutional separation has some share in the significance of salvation history which St. Paul attributes to the division between Israel and the Gentiles — namely that they should make 'each other envious,' vying with each other in coming closer to the Lord (Rom. 11:11)."[42] Several things about this comment, made in passing, deserve to be noted. First, the separation of the churches may properly be seen in terms of "the significance of salvation history": that is, it may be caught up in the sovereign shaping of history by God in a way that must point, intrinsically, to the heart of the gospel of Christ. Second, Ratzinger suggests that the division of the churches in this respect might be related to the division of "Israel and the Gentiles." Related, but how? It is precisely through each reality's sharing in the same divinely "disposed" significance that they are related, that is, brought together in the one gospel of Christ.[43] Each set of divisions plays a part in and reflects the salvation

---

41. It may seem paradoxical to assert that only a particular understanding of Scripture can help explain our inability to understand it. But this, I think, is the case: a certain way of receiving Scripture's elucidation of our history — our history as a broken church — allows us to perceive as well our instrinsic alienation from Scripture's saving significance at the same time. Only by claiming such a continuing role for scriptural speech can we still link Scripture and gospel together, much as Paul insisted that a law whose life-giving purpose had turned to death was still a "spiritual" entity given by God (Romans 7).

42. Cardinal Joseph Ratzinger, "Anglican-Catholic Dialogue: Its Problems and Hopes," 87.

43. In a later essay in the volume, on "The Progress of Ecumenism," Ratzinger explores the same point on the basis of Paul's remark in 1 Cor. 11:19 that "there must be

wrought in Christ in some mysterious fashion. Each set of historical episodes refers to the other — intra-Christian division and Jewish-Gentile division — through the mediating and effecting reality of Christ Jesus, to whom, in fact, each refers in a primary way. In the terms of classical hermeneutics, then, Ratzinger suggests that we adopt a "figuralist" approach to assessing the significance of Christian division.

Such a figuralist approach to Christian division is, I believe, a fruitful one to pursue. Nor is it at all novel, although rarely practiced in our day. Although, for instance, Yves Congar outlined in 1948 the basic shape of, as well as the basic questions raised by, a figuralist construal of the divided Christian church after the type of divided Israel, he did not (nor did anyone else) elaborate his suggestion.[44] At the time of the Reformation, however, theologians were quick to turn to a figuralist interpretation of Scripture to shed light on the astonishing prospect of a disintegrating Christian church laid out before their eyes. To be sure, such methods tended to serve polemical ends, but they were serious nonetheless. Calvin, for instance, already in the *Reply to*

---

factions" (*ibid.*, 138ff.). Moving from comments on this text by Augustine and H. Schlier, Ratzinger suggests that it be taken in terms of "an eschatological and dogmatic proposition," and that "schisms," however they originate in human sin, should be confronted as part of a "dimension that corresponds to God's disposing." Ratzinger has no interest here in the pneumatological implications of such an assertion, in large measure because, for all his sensitivities and indeed openness to Christ's salvific work among Protestant churches — indeed *because* of such sensitivities — he remains a firm Roman Catholic chauvinist: the Spirit's concrete operative mission in the churches, however divided and necessarily including his own, is assumed. This is why he can favor a position on ecumenical relations that counsels "patience" in the midst of division, and argues against attempts to effect communion *in sacris* before communion in doctrine.

44. Yves M.-J. Congar, "Reflections on the Schism of Israel in the Perspective of Christian Divisions," originally in *Proche-Orient chrétien* 1 (1951) and translated and reprinted with additional notes in *Dialogue between Christians* (London: Geoffrey Chapman, 1966) 160-83. This important article assumes, without defending, the figuralist reading of the church elaborated below, and then applies it to the situation of the divided church in particular. Congar spends a good deal of time — perhaps too much, considering the unstable character of such identifications — tracing the socio-historical parallels between Israel's national union and disintegration and the Christian church's. From his Roman Catholic perspective, he also lays great stress on the "privileged" character of the Roman Church vis-à-vis Protestantism, on the basis of the southern kingdom's maintenance of the site of Israel's true worship, vis-à-vis Samaria's idolatrous shrines (Calvin himself applied the same distinction, although he reversed the referents between Protestants and Catholics). Finally, Congar only hints at the nature of Christian reunion suggested by the type of Israel's destruction and exile and has nothing to say about the pneumatological implications of his figuralist scheme. Still, his overall suggestions are in line with the basic thrust of the present argument.

Sadoleto, attempts to explain the apparent "schism" of the Reformers in terms of the figure of the faithful "remnant" of Israelite prophets and their followers who set themselves "against" the corruption of the rulers and priests of the nation. He further characterizes the Roman church as being figured in the Israel of kings Zedekiah and Jehoiakim, far fallen from the purity of David and Solomon's rule, and prophetically destined for dismemberment and destruction at the hands of God's avenging agents.[45] Catholics, for their part, could also make use of divided and assaulted Israel, but in their case to cast the Roman church in the figure of a chosen people victimized by her own children.[46]

This figural construal of the divided church was appropriated by the post-Reformation debate from the early exegesis of the Fathers.[47] Most com-

45. Calvin, *Reply to Sadoleto,* pp. 60 and 38. Cf. the later Puritan John Owen's long description of the Roman Church's "falling" in terms of its conformance to the figure of sinful Israel, against whom the prophets spoke (the "prophets were Protestants — God protested against [Israel] by his prophets") in his *Vindication of the Animadversions on "Fiat Lux,"* Works, XIV, 212ff. Owen later provides the following summary: "She hath fallen by *idolatry* and corruption of life; as did the church of the Jews before captivity. She hath fallen by her *relinquishment* of the written word as the only rule of faith and worship, and by adhereing to the uncertain traditions of men; as did the church of the Jews after their return from captivity. [. . .] She hath fallen by *schism* in herself, — as the Judaical church did when divided into Essenes, Sadducees, and Pharisees, — setting up pope against pope, and council against council, continuing in her intestine broils for some ages together" (p. 224).

46. See below on the ways in which Bellarmine and the Jansenist Jean Hamon describe the figure of "lamenting Israel" in terms of the tears of sorrow engendered by the Protestant agonies: Robert Bellarmine, *De Gemitu Columbae* II, 4 and *passim;* Jean Hamon, *Commentaire sur les Lamentations de Jérémie* (Paris: 1790) 3. Bossuet was among the first Catholics to take strong exception to the limited way in which Reformers made use of the Israel figure to justify their separation from Rome. Cf. his *Seconde Instruction sur les promesses de Jésus-Christ à son Église* (1701), chapters 53-79, in *Oeuvres Complètes* (Guillaume ed.) IV, 129-34. Bossuet argues, against an unnamed Protestant antagonist (probably Jacques Basnage) that the Old Testament figures of "schism," e.g., Jeroboam or the prophets Elijah and Elisha, however applicable to the present time, can only be so under the form of judgment, since Scripture itself evaluates these separations negatively. Certainly Bossuet's exegesis is by far the better in this exchange; but, no less than his Catholic *confrères,* he remains unwilling to transfer the negative aspect of the schismatic figure to the church itself, confining its referent to the church's (Protestant) enemies.

47. This seems more likely than the possibility that medieval uses of the figure were followed. In any case, such uses were rare and were generally adapted to the Western-Eastern schism. Cf. Congar, *op. cit.,* 160, 182-83, who mentions the twelfth-century John of Santa Maria, Joachim of Fiore, Gregory IX, Bonaventure, Humbert of Romans, and Nicholas of Clemanges as all comparing the Greek "schism" to the rebellion of Jeroboam.

mentators from the first centuries of the church worked from a common, though by no means universal, assumption that the Israel of the Old Testament and the Christian church were continuous, even identical bodies, if living under distinct dispensations of the divine economy. Such figural identification of Israel and the church did lean towards supersessionist interpretations, according to which the Apostolic church took the place of a now wholly rejected Jewish Israel.[48] On this reading, the figure of divided Israel and its divinely ordered condition in this state, was applied narrowly to the "unfaithful," and not to the "true" church.[49] This tended to be the tack, as just noted, of later Protestant controversialists like Calvin. But the primary assertion of figural identity by the early church was more fundamental even than its supersessionist temptations, as is proved by the equally pervasive insistence by many patristic commentators that Jewish and Christian Israel be seen as continuous, and therefore that the figure of divided Israel be applied directly to the Christian church as a whole.[50]

48. Cf. the material richly referred to in Marcel Simon's *"Verus Israel": A Study of the Relations between Christians and Jews in the Roman Empire (135-425)* (Oxford: Oxford University Press, 1986), passim, e.g., 76ff.; 169ff.

49. Cf. Jerome's commentary on Jeremiah, on 3:18 and 4:5, or Ephraem's commentary on Isaiah 44:1ff. However regrettable from the standpoint of modern Jewish and Christian history the patristic supersessionist construal of the relation of Jewish Israel and church was, it should be noted that one motivation for this construal lay in the seriousness with which the historical integrity of prophecy was taken, something which today is simply out of our ken. A general criterion applied to the referential interpretation of an Old Testament text acting as a "figure" was whether this prophecy could rightly be called "fulfilled" for the Jews since the captivity. If not, it was best to assume that the Christian church was the "proper" *(proprie)* referent for the figure. While there are limits to this kind of criterion, it is clear that if applied today, given the condition of the Christian church, our figural evaluations would necessarily have to take a different slant. Finally, holding the two — patristic and contemporary — uses of the criterion together, one might arrive at the kind of fuller interpretation here being suggested. In addition to the mainstream patristic use of the divided Israel figure, we should also note the way the figure was used, in anticipation of Protestant-Catholic polemical usage, by the Donatists, who claimed the "southern" or Judah-based privilege of being the true church (cf. Congar, *op. cit.*, 182).

50. Cf. Origen's *Homily IV on Jeremiah*, on 3:6-11, which provides one of the few explicit attempts before the seventeenth century to connect figurally the division of Israel's kingdoms and the relation of Jew and Gentile as given by Paul in Romans 9–11. Cf. also Theodoret's commentary on Isaiah, 49, where Christ himself is made the main figural referent of Israel's distorted life, and only through him the church. On the importance of this kind of interpretive move, see below. With respect to the application of the specific figure of *divided* Israel to the Christian church, there was, however, lack of consensus. Cyprian, for instance, was explicitly clear that the divisions of the kingdom, symbolized in the figure of the

In our day, George Lindbeck has been eloquent in calling for a retrieval of some of the basic hermeneutical presuppositions lying behind this patristic figural identification of the Old Testament's Israel and the Christian church.[51] In suggesting an explicit ecclesiology that takes the Christian church's character as essentially explicated in and through the figure of Israel, Lindbeck has proposed a "narrative" theology of the church that takes the story of Israel as "prior" to any distillation of distinguishing "marks" or "images"; a theology that insists, therefore, on the ecclesial referent of scriptural figure as concrete and "visible" (versus one prominent trend of Reformed theology); and one, finally, that appropriates or applies the "whole" of the figural story to the church, and not just the "favorable" parts divorced from narrative elements of judgment and disease. Significantly, Lindbeck locates the possible working of these elements of a narrative ecclesiology in the mediating reality — the figurating reality, if you will — of Christ himself:

> Thus, despite most later exegesis, the relation of Israel's history to that of the church in the New Testament is not one of shadow to reality, or promise to fulfillment, or type to antitype. Rather, the kingdom already present in Christ alone is the antitype, and both Israel and the church are types. The people of God existing in both the old and the new ages are typologically related to Jesus Christ, and through Christ, Israel is prototypical for the church in much the same way that the exodus story, for example, is seen as prototypical for all later Israelite history by such prophets as Ezekiel.[52]

It is just this insistence upon the central mediating figure of Christ to the relating of the church and Israel that allows for the "whole story" of Israel to touch the church's life in a salvific fashion, whatever the punishing elements of its specific contours. For if Christ lies as the central referent of

---

prophet Ahijah's torn cloak, could not possibly bear figural transference to the church, whose indefectible "unity" was symbolized in the seamless and undivided garment of Jesus at the cross; cf. his *De ecclesiae catholicae unitate*, ch. 7. But just these kinds of distinctions in application pointed to the need for a more rigorous consistency, as did subsequent historical realities that pressed against Cyprian's discriminations.

51. Cf. George Lindbeck, "The Story-Shaped Church: Critical Exegesis and Theological Interpretation," in *Scriptural Authority and Narrative Interpretation,* ed. Garrett Green (Philadelphia: Fortress, 1987), esp. pp. 165-70; and "The Church," in *Keeping the Faith: Essays to Mark the Centenary of "Lux Mundi,"* ed. Geoffrey Wainwright (London: SPCK, 1989). The latter essay appropriates quite closely much of the constructive material of the former and extends its meaning to some specific ecumenical questions.

52. Lindbeck, "Story-Shaped Church," 166.

both Israel's life in the Old Testament, and the Christian church's life, then the drawing of one to the other into a single Israel whose narrative shapes inform each other mutually can be affirmed as manifesting, in whatever mode, the figure of the gospel itself.[53]

This proves an important point if we wish to find a place within that gospel for the reality of the church's division and for the implications this reality embodies regarding the life of the Holy Spirit in our midst. Lindbeck himself has not pursued this question, although he notes that the relation of the Holy Spirit to Israel is consistent through both Testaments — that the Spirit is present and working in the Old Testament Israel as in the New, and that "it departs from the faithless in the present as it did in the past." Pneumatic fullness, in other words, is a "relational attribute refer-

---

53. This christocentric figural claim on Lindbeck's part ought to lessen somewhat Childs's fears that Lindbeck's "narrative" approach has somehow excluded a concern with the "reality outside the text," namely God in Christ Jesus. Cf. Childs's brief comments in *The New Testament as Canon* (Philadelphia: Fortress, 1984) 544-46, and in *Biblical Theology of the Old and New Testaments* (Philadelphia: Fortress, 1992) 21f. It is true that in his discussion of the narrative basis for understanding the church, Lindbeck makes use of critically descriptive categories based on the apparent use of Scripture by the early church, and that this involves the deployment of both literary-critical and sociological tropes that, in themselves, have little reference to "truth-claims." This can result in the use of ambiguous judgments such as that the church's narrative character is "Israel-like." But at the same time Lindbeck claims a primacy for the "narrative" of Jesus in construing the figural relationship of Old and New Testament Israel that itself subverts a casual conception of narrative altogether: the positing of a figural center in the "story" of Jesus — "the uniquely privileged *sensus literalis* of the whole of scripture" — that somehow grants the Christian church access to the "narrative" identity of Israel, back and forth over time in history, is a religious insight, however much it is buttressed by New Testament "exegesis." To claim, as Lindbeck does more consistently, that the church *is* Israel and not simply "Israel-like," derives from reading the Scriptures from a particular standpoint of faith that places the entire discussion in the realm of a Christian discourse whose truth-claims are necessarily presupposed (cf. "Story-Shaped Church," 164, 170). Ecclesiologically, the very notion of a Scripture in which the central "story" of Christ mediates figurally the whole range of specific references to the Old and the new Israel raises into relief the way that, for instance, the figure of the "Body of Christ" operates less as an ancillary "image" of the church (*ibid.*, 165) and more properly as a historical reality whose *res* must escape altogether the scope of literary-critical conceptualization. Childs's own nuanced exegesis of Matt. 21:33-46 offers an example of how a less overtly figuralist reading of the church might nevertheless arrive at some construals of the church's relation to Israel similar in their import to Lindbeck's broad typological appropriations. But Childs is not eager to press this kind of vision in a substantive direction, as is apparent in his more systematic sections on the church as "people of God." Cf. Childs, *Biblical Theology*, 337ff. and 441ff.

ring to what God is making and will make of [the church], not [...] an inherent property."[54]

If not an inherent property, and rather a "relational attribute," the vagaries of the Holy Spirit's operation in the church ought to be traceable according to the figure of Israel. This is the main point I would stress here. And it *is* the case that the figural appropriation of Israel and the Christian church remains one of the few, if not the only means of rooting the present situation of the divided church in Scripture in such a way that Scripture's own place in this "relation" can be more clearly specified. For apart from such a figural location of the problem — one that opens up for "instruction" the "type" of Israel (cf. 1 Cor. 10:11) — the church's division finds little place within the explicit ecclesial referents of the New Testament. In nonfigural terms, the New Testament simply does not envision the entrenched division of the church; it merely points in passing to the eschatological distresses to be suffered by the Christian community at the hands of Satan, only one of which will include factions and schisms (e.g., 1 John 2:18ff.; Jude 17-19). How one understands the church as herself a divided entity is not a topic the New Testament openly broaches.

Small wonder, then, that Reformers and Catholics alike struggled to find alternative scriptural resources for their embattled situation, turning, however imperfectly and limitedly, as we have seen, towards the Old Testament discussion of divided Israel, for example, for help. Yet without grasping the central figurating character of Christ in this process, joining Jewish Israel and the Christian church together as one body narrationally, the kind of truncated attributions of "faithful" and "unfaithful," remnant and sectaries, to one party or the other that we have indicated was inevitable.[55]

In reflecting on the positive meaning of Christian "unity," it is true, it was always possible in the Reformation debate to see the way in which a figural relation of the church to Christ implied some kind of transhistorical constant in signification, that, logically anyway, ought to have tied the Christian community's character to Israel in a more consistent historical fashion. Calvin, for instance, in commenting on John 17:21, in which Jesus prays "that all may be one," is careful to show how intimately tied is the Son's eternal oneness with the Father to our union in Him as historical Mediator. He

54. Lindbeck, "Story-Shaped Church," 168.
55. For a brief discussion of the theological rationale for applying the figure of the divided Israel to the contemporary church, see Ephraim Radner, "The Cost of Communion: A Meditation on Israel and the Divided Church," in *Inhabiting Unity: Theological Perspectives on the Proposed Lutheran-Episcopal Concordat*, ed. Ephraim Radner and R. R. Reno (Grand Rapids: Eerdmans, 1995).

speaks abstractly here — "in order to prevent the *unity* of the Son with the Father from being fruitless and unavailing, the power of that *unity* must be diffused through the whole body of believers."[56] But he at least proposes that the historical shapes of the Christian community's life are properly bound, as fruit on its tree, to a divine reality that reaches over time and therefore, in theory, ought to produce consistently in the history of the faithful, including Israel, concrete forms of its fecundity. The shape of unity, on this account, and its significance in time ought to be visible in the whole history of Israel.

However muddled, the theological tools for grasping the significance of the divided church in terms of the shape of Jewish Israel have been available to the church for some time. But their lack of full deployment has contributed to our stunted ability to comprehend our ecclesial situation. That said, let me now sketch how it might look if we proceeded to apply the approach I have been proposing to the question of pneumatology and the penumatic appropriation of Scripture.

V. The Scriptural Figure of the Pneumatically Abandoned Church

As some controversialists of the Reformation saw, the figure of divided Israel herself provided the locus for confronting the reality of the divided church. Likewise, as they saw, the figure of divided Israel, according to the Old Testament, was embedded in a narrative of divine judgment and cascading disaster. From the time of Jeroboam's rebellion and the rending of Israel into northern and southern kingdoms (1 Kings 12), the people of Israel were dragged down into a steady decline marked by internal apostasy and external victimization. Although there were respites and brief reversals to this pattern — for example, Hezekiah's or Josiah's reigns — both kingdoms eventually succumbed to almost total annihilation at the hands of Assyria and Babylon, and the people were taken into exile and scattered.

But while the polemicists of Christian division have tended to apply this story onesidedly, choosing to identify their particular communities with various righteous "remnants" alluded to in the course of the narrative, it should be stressed that the narrative as a whole forbids such distinguishing of actors within the history. Both kingdoms are ultimately destroyed; the peoples of both are murdered and enslaved; and only the reunion of both as

56. John Calvin, *Commentary on the Gospel According to John,* tr. William Pringle (Grand Rapids: Baker, reprint 1979) 184.

having come through this common ordeal embodies the restoration of Israel
in the public arena of time (cf. Jer. 50:2-4). That there was to be a "remnant"
for whom this restoration was ordered is not in question (cf. Isa. 10:20ff. or
37:34). But to give this remnant some definable status as "the true church,"
granted some continuous character over time as the "elect," literally separated out from the fate of Israel as a whole, is to misconstrue the theology of
the "remainder" altogether. For in the destruction of divided Israel, both the
righteous and unrighteous suffer together, true prophets and false prophets.
The "remnant" — survivors, literally — are thrown by God into the same
cauldron and share the same burdens of destruction and enslavement (cf.
2 Kgs. 17:19-20; Ezek. 5:10). The restoration of the remnant is not the unveiling, let alone the vindication, of the "true church" from amid its travails,
but rather the gracious action of recreating a united people out of the dust of
their past obliteration (cf. Ezek. 11:14-21).[57]

We are dealing, then, with the character and fate of the whole people of
Israel; and whatever distinctions are given to members of that people on the
basis of their division are not such as to remove them from that general character and fate in which their division lies. It is not the case, of course, that the
Old Testament narrative relates the division of Israel to this character and
fate as a cause to its effect. Indeed, the partition of Israel at the time of Jeroboam is itself seen as the punishing effect of earlier and deeper apostasies,
leading back to the time of the exodus itself, and certainly given relief at the
time when Israel clamored for a king (1 Samuel 8). Still, given that the restoration of Israel is to be a patent expression of renewed unity, we must evalu-
ate the previous divisions as being intimately bound to the causal nexus of
the people's sinfulness, which brings upon itself only a deepening embroil-
ment in further unfaithfulness. Not only is the whole people bound to the effects of division, then, but these effects are properly seen in terms of the
whole range of judgments visited upon the people.

By therefore viewing the division of Israel within the integral history of
the people's sin and punishment, we can see that the condition of disunity itself is characterized by the *increase* of sin, by the accelerating inability of the
nation to right itself, to perceive the truth of God's will and call, to heed his
warnings, repent, and seek forgiveness. Just as the sin of the monarchy was
given as a punishment for the desire for a king, so, too, the deadening confusion of competing and self-deceiving claims to truth that mark the evolution

57. Cf. Congar, *op. cit.*, 181: "One is tempted to ask what trials or deportations will
perhaps be necessary before Christians find themselves united once more . . . one begins
to wonder what price we shall perhaps have to pay for the grace of reunion."

of the prophetic and priestly offices were given as a festering of the disease of national fragmentation. According to the scriptural pattern of divine "abandonment" in sin, divided Israel was left to encounter its shattered life on its own.

This fact determines how we are to view the topic at hand: partitioned Israel is "abandoned" Israel; and this Israel, separated among its members, is also separated from the Holy Spirit. This equation between sinfulness, abandonment, and "resistance" to the Spirit is the burden of Stephen's speech in Acts 7 (cf. vv. 42 and 51), and it stands as an explicator to the large number of texts from the prophets where the condition of divided Israel is decribed in the explicit terms of pneumatic absence or antagonism. Isaiah, in particular, offers us a number of examples. 63:10ff., for instance, is part of a prayer for the nation that has much in common with beleaguered rehearsals of Israel's history such as Psalm 106. After extolling God's love in the past, the prophet declares that the people still "rebelled and grieved his holy Spirit; therefore [God] turned to be their enemy, and himself fought against them." Although in the course of the people's history repeated forgiveness is forthcoming, the present conditon of the nation brings the lament, "O Lord, why dost thou make us err from thy ways and harden our heart, so that we fear thee not?" (v. 17).

The sense that opposing the Spirit of God (cf. again Ps. 106:33) carries as one of its effective aspects a divine hardening or a positive dislocation of expected pneumatic assistance, is a common feature of these kinds of texts. In Isa. 6:10; 28:7ff.; and 29:9ff., the normal prophetic efficacy of vision and teaching is described as obscured, and the people become like drunkards and the blind, unable to perceive what God is telling them or might tell them. Yet it is God himself who authors this darkness, and so the Spirit's power is made to reveal itself in its own inefficacy: "Stupefy yourselves and be in a stupor, blind yourselves and be blind! . . . For the Lord has poured out upon you a spirit of deep sleep, and has closed your eyes, the prophets, and covered your heads, the seers. And the vision of all this has become to you like the words of a book that is sealed. When men give it to one who can read, saying 'Read this,' he says, 'I cannot, for it is sealed'" (29:9-11).

Two things at least need to be said about these kinds of texts. First, they are in general set within larger discussions that treat Israel's punishment and restoration. Thus, the themes of pneumatic antagonisms or abandonment and communal blindness to God's Word are explicitly tied, through contrast, to the specific elements of Israel's sinful condition. There will come a time when "the deaf shall hear the words of a book, and out of their gloom and darkness the eyes of the blind shall see" (29:18), but such is precisely the time when God will choose to overturn the present shape of the people, restore to the nation a single and coherent worship. In Ezekiel's terms, the restoration of the Holy Spirit upon the divinely abandoned people of Israel must coincide with their return as a united body (Ezek. 39:25-19). In this way, the prophets make clear that a firm connection exists between the condition of division and the experience of pneumatic deprivation.

Second, we must note that several of these texts from the Old Testament have found a place in the New: for example, Isa. 6:10 in Matt. 13:13-15 and John 12:40, and Isa. 29:9-10 in Rom 11:8-10. Here, the judgment of pneumatic deprivation is linked to Jewish Israel in particular over against the Christian church. And while the circumstances of Paul's and the evangelists' time make that contrast concrete, we must, as Ratzinger also suggested, recognize that the contrast itself is figurally prophetic of Christian Israel too, just because of its participation in the larger christic form that allows for the initial figural transposition through the two Testaments. And given this fact, we are enabled to see how the pneumatic deprivation described by the prophets of beleaguered Israel stands within the entire history of redemption, and how, with the disunity that is its partner, they represent central christological truths. The bitterness of Paul's own struggle with Jewish Israel's "blindness" and "stupor" was manifested in his body as "the marks of Jesus" (Gal. 6:17; cf. 2 Cor. 4:10); yet in this very engagement in opposition was contained a universal "mercy" (Rom. 11:32) and new "life" (2 Cor. 4:12).

Taken together, these two points underscore how the particular aspects of Christian division and pneumatic deprivation — blindness, visionary failure, the deadness of the letter — all these stand as figural realities that themselves, in their conjunction and historical context, indicate the grace of Christ's own cross and resurrection. And we can see, therefore, that to affirm these experiential elements as constitutive of Christian division, and hence, in some sense, as inescapable parameters to our present Christian existence, is not somehow to give up the gospel, let alone to void it.

VI. Ecclesial Implications of Pneumatic Deprivation

If we were to ask, for instance, "where is the true church, in which the gospel is truly preached?" — a question that both a Luther and a Ratzinger would press with varying emphases — it is true that we would have to prescind from a direct answer. For we would now have to say that the true church — even if present and visible — subsists in a relationship to the Holy Spirit and is constituted by the Holy Spirit, not only in the form of division, but of division tied to deafness. Ecumenists of diversity cannot run from this judgment.[58] This is the church's negative visage; but it is inescapably hers. Positively, we would say that this ecclesial constitution by the Spirit is ordered toward the manifestation of Christ, figurally in the form of his Passion, anagogically only in the disclosure of his resurrection.

Nor are we without scriptural support for this suggestion. The pneumatological aspect of this positive visage of the divided and deafened church is perhaps alluded to in Jesus' discussion of the Spirit in John 16. Traditionally, when engaging the topic of church and Scripture, attention has been focused on vv. 12-15 of the chapter, in which Jesus speaks of the "Spirit of truth," come to "guide" the church in all things concerning the Son. But the previous verses (vv. 7-11) set the operational context for this promise of pneumatic leading. They speak of the Spirit's work in "convincing" the world of "sin," "righteousness," and "judgment," which are linked to the disclosure of "unbelief," the departure of the Son, and the sentence of Satan, the "ruler of this world." There seems little doubt that Jesus here is pointing to his death and ascension, in their confrontation with sin, as the acts through which the Spirit performs its mission. And he speaks of these acts of suffering and departure as themselves the manifested embodiments of pneumatic grace, not only in their discrete historical accomplishment, but as the ongoing figure through which the evolving history of the church will live, under and with the truth of the Son's gospel.[59] Though Jesus speaks of the "world"

58. Cf. G. R. Evans, *Problems of Authority in the Reformation Debates* (Cambridge: Cambridge University Press, 1992), who argues that the main stumbling block in the post-Reformation debates and confrontations lay in the inability of the various parties to grasp "the notion of a diversity arising from complementary perceptions of a single and immutable truth" (281). Certainly, this was a problem. But, if, as Evans seems to think, we are all wiser about this notion than in the past, it is a wisdom that yet resides in a context of pneumatically ordered incomprehension that still does not know what to do with this notion, let alone the truth on which it hangs. Realizing that our differences are not really divisive at all, but rather interesting points of view, does not speak to our real condition, which remains one of deafness.

59. Cf. the remarkable discussion of this text by Pope John Paul II in his Encyclical letter of May 18, 1986, on the Holy Spirit (§II). Linking this text to Heb. 9:14, which speaks of the self-offering of Christ on the Cross "through the eternal Spirit," John Paul speaks of the manner in which the Holy Spirit "descends into the depths of the sacrifice" in order to "consummate" it by the "fire of love" (II, 41), and through this act, carried to a universal scope, the "manifestation" or "conviction" of sin of which Jesus speaks in John 16, is given the efficacy of conversionary redemption. The Spirit works by manifesting the eternal sacrifice of Christ in time. John Paul, however, is less interested in the strict ecclesiological implications of this line of thought than in its ability to illumine something of the church's mission in the world.

here, it is of a world confronted by the Spirit of the church. And redemption thus takes place through the form of the cross's pneumatic display, even in the church.

Within the constraints of their era, some earlier Catholic thinkers adopted a similar pneumatology, even to the point of (implicitly anyway) eschewing the chauvinist figuralist readings of the church used by most of their coreligionists. Bellarmine, for instance, in a somewhat odd work entitled *De Gemitu Colombae* ("On the lament of the dove"), structured an entire treatise around the notion that the church, as the place of the Spirit, is a body called to mourning and tears.[60] Divided into three sections, the book first gives a detailed look at the scriptural precedents for such a vocation of sorrow, drawing the Christian community into a figural identity with a wide range of Old Testament prophets and saints. The second section of the volume treats the array of motivations for such sorrowing, the church's disunity being only one of many ills afflicting the body of Christ. Finally, twelve *fructus lacrymarum* are advanced that demonstrate the manner in which the church fulfills its calling to the gospel's new life precisely in dwelling patiently amid its brokenness. Bellarmine, of course, is not questioning the Roman Catholic Church's status as the authoritative locus of the gospel. But in literally identifying that church with the *columba gemens* of Rom. 8:26, he links her to the very infirmity under which the whole of creation labors (v. 22), now taken up, through grace, by a *Deus patiens*.

More marginalized Catholics like the Jansenists took this kind of thinking further in concretizing the historical realm in which the church takes form. In the late seventeenth century, Jean Hamon, the humble doctor of Port-Royal, wrote a commentary on Lamentations for the beleaguered nuns of the convent, in which he embraced the Israel figure of the church rigorously, here in the form of the destroyed city of Jerusalem. Starting from the historical point of the church's interior corruptions and divisions, Hamon turns each of the prophet's sorrows into a description of the Catholic Church, the ultimate integrity of which he can maintain only by recasting its character in the form of its crucified Savior, the "spouse" to the lamenting bride.[61] When, then, he

60. Robert Bellarmine, *De Gemitu Columbae, sive De Bono Lacrymarum,* in his *Opera Omnia,* ed. J. Fèvre (Paris: 1873, reprint Frankfurt: Minerva GMBH, 1965) VIII, 397-484. The title, pregnant with many scriptural allusions, may be taken directly from Isa. 59:11.

61. It is hardly an idiosyncratic insistence. Hamon follows the interpretive line drawn by the seventeenth-century French liturgical elaboration of the *Tenebrae* services, at which portions of Lamentations were methodically sung as figures of the Passion through the repentant voice of the church. For all that, Lamentations was not frequently

comes to the famous verse 1:16, in which the "absence of the Comforter" is asserted, he speaks of the church's necessary figural conformance with its Lord, abandoned in the grip of sin by God upon the cross.[62]

Hamon here points to the direction that Jansenist thinking will later take with respect to the reality of ecclesial division, when, commenting on 1:5, he describes the proper attitude in which the church, and her members, is to suffer her afflictions:

> We must imitate the spirit of the Church, for it is the spirit of her Spouse; and we must never stray from his moderation. She does not oppose those who mistreat her, since she understands that the true cause of her mistreatment are her sins. They are her sins because they are our own. We have nothing else to do but to humble ourselves in the face of all these disorders, to silence ourselves and to groan.[63]

By the end of the seventeenth century, Jansenists and especially those associated with Port-Royal were already aware of their precarious status within the Roman Church. The notion of the church — Christ's bride and hence his body — suffering her own internal attack at the hands of her members seemed an evident reality. Hamon's counsel of suffering moderation, then, became axiomatic for the party. And it was extended to an entire theory regarding the character of dissent within the church that included within it, logically, an evaluation of the Protestant separation as well. Pierre Nicole, for instance, in his celebrated attack on French Calvinists, had contemporaneously put forward the claim that no supposed sin on the part of the church justified the establishment of a new alternative Christian society and ministry. The most that a Christian could ever be pressed, by conscience, to allow was a "simple and negative separation, which consists in the refusal of certain acts of communion, without however involving positive acts of separation against the com-

---

commented on, perhaps because the figural implications so patent in the church's continued use of this text were evidently disturbing. Calvin, who no longer had the liturgical framework as a guide, was free to read Lamentations in a purely "historical" sense, useful for its moral warnings, but with little ongoing prophetic center (see his brief commentary on the book). Other Protestants, like the Irish Anglican John Hull, used the book as a basis for elaborate displays of encyclopedic erudition, drawing on Kabalah, Midrash, Joachimism, the Fathers, and Medieval mystical exegesis to provide a cosmic hermeneutic of divine sovereignty, in contrast to which his few attempts to locate the Churches of Ireland and England within the text fall rather flat. Cf. John Hull, *An Exposition upon a Part of the Lamentations of Ieremie* (1617; London, 1718).

62. Jean Hamon, *Commentaire sur les Lamentations de Jérémie*, 59f.

63. *Ibid.*, 21f.

munity from which one separates."[64] It is best, under such circumstances, that the disaffected remain "without pastors and without an exterior cult, as they wait for God to provide for them in some extraordinary fashion," than that they should erect a distinct ministry.[65] By the eighteenth century, when many Jansenists were deprived of sacraments for their opposition to the Bull *Unigenitus,* this "negative" separation became a fulfilled practice. But *as a practice,* it was possible only because, *contra* Calvin and the Roman Catholic triumphalists together, it was nourished by a vision of the church as a body whose pneumatic indefectability was informed by the reality of the Passion's pneumatic abandonment. No other perspective allowed for the simple suffering of, and hence repentant redemption through, the church's disarray.[66]

VII. Scriptural Implications of Pneumatic Deprivation

Applied to our present era, then, this kind of vision asserts that the pneumatic deprivation implied in the church's division does *not* falsify the truth

---

64. Pierre Nicole, *Préjugez légitimes contre les Calvinistes,* Nouvelle Edition, (Paris, 1725) 137.

65. *Ibid.,* 145.

66. Nicole's argument was in fact quite traditional from a Catholic perspective. It informed most sensible Romanist responses to Protestant separation from the time of people like Erasmus: one might well admit to abuses, indeed horrendous corruption, within the church, but such illnesses were to be borne and opposed from within the church's structures, not from without. Erasmus's weary remark that "there will always be some things good men must endure" points to the sense of a profound suffering of the Body, even in the face of its manifold evils. Cf. the selections of Erasmus on disputes and divisions in the church in *Erasmus and the Seamless Coat of Jesus,* tr. and introduction by Raymond Himelick (Lafayette: Purdue University Studies, 1971) 82 and *passim.* By Nicole's time, this argument was a commonplace. Bossuet, for instance, bases a large part of his famously effective 1655 attack on Paul Ferry's Protestant "Catechism" on just this attitude: only the patent inability of a person to be saved within the church could possibly justify separation from the church. If, as Ferry and most mainstream Protestants allowed, salvation was still to be had in the Roman Church, at least up to 1543, prior to the Council of Trent's decisions, then the whole Reformed separation is condemned from the start, since a basic definition of the true church is that it be a place in which salvation is engendered through Christ. In any situation short of the church's losing that status, Christians must be willing to endure the church's failures. Cf. Bossuet's *Réfutation du Catéchisme du Sieur Paul Ferry,* in the *Oeuvres Complètes* IV, 184ff. "Enduring" the fallen church, however, remained a largely theoretical proposal for most Catholic controversialists (certainly for people like Bossuet). And not until the Jansenists demonstrated what it might mean (and, by extension, what it might have meant for the Reformers of the previous century) did the proposal manifest the depth of its ecclesiological rationale.

of the gospel or its power for salvation. But it nonetheless still leaves unanswered the whole issue of scriptural comprehension within the church, of how we can *hear* God's Word spoken to us. If the hermeneutical incoherence observed earlier is indeed regnant, let alone celebrated, and if it is intrinsically so because of the negative relation existing between Holy Spirit and divided church, then what divine role is Scripture in particular to play in the church, and how are we to receive it?

Theologians from all sides of the confessional divides have always affirmed the pre-Reformation principle — whether we see it as Pauline or Augustinian — that true "understanding" of the Bible is embodied, somehow, in obedience; otherwise Scripture functions, not as a living Word, but as a "dead letter." It is a simple matter of description to observe, on the basis of this principle, that within the divided church Scripture is not, by definition, understood *in general (generaliter)*. That *in particular (in partes)* Scripture is still understood, that specific aspects of Scripture are still evident and still open to accurate apprehension no one would doubt. But in all the debates between Reformers and Romanists, this was *not* ever in doubt, and the Erasmian hermeneutic of erudition, even when leveled to its most basic plane of common-sense reading, was never questioned as a universal possibility among the reprobate or the apostate.[67] The issue turned not on particular understandings, but on the general understanding of Scripture as the gospel of Christ manifest and perceived, on "true hearing." And this possibility, both Protestant and Catholic affirmed together, was tied strictly to the integrity of pneumatic operation. So we must ask, then, if the Scripture is not generally understood, how is it that the Spirit is working through it?

One way of getting at an answer to this question is to examine how Christians have construed more limited examples of the Spirit's absence with respect to the hearing of the gospel. In Catholic spiritual theology, there are the many analyses of pneumatic "aridity." Puritans, for their part, worried about this issue on an individualist basis, as they analyzed situations in which a Christian might no longer receive the proper fruit from, among other things, the reading of Scripture. To take but one example from this wide literature, we can look at the seventeenth-century New England pastor Nehemiah Hobart's attempt to describe the shape of the Holy Spirit's self-distancing from the Christian. It must be admitted that Hobart's firmly Puri-

---

67. Cf. John Owen, *Pneumatologia*, IV/6, 8 (pp. 209-26), on the various means of parsing scriptural discourse clearly, available to all, which yet demand the special work of the Holy Spirit to "perceive the mind of God and Christ therein," available only to "good" and "holy believers."

tan discourse on the *Absence of the Comforter* hardly shared the ecclesiology we have been suggesting is necessary if we are accurately to place divided church and Spirit in relation to one another. For although he apparently believed that the churches of Connecticut were in a bad way spiritually — a fact that motivated his reflections in the first place — he affirmed that the gospel (as against the Law) was still being preached within them and that there was sufficient unity among them to preclude a complete "withdrawing" of the Spirit.[68] Further, writing within the tradition of Congregationalist pneumatology established by John Owen, Hobart's interests were basically focused on the individual Christian. Elements of individual Christian behavior alone seemed to him to signal the possibility of pneumatic deprivation.[69] Nonetheless, the very fact that Hobart chose to provide a kind of dark counterpoint, however unconsciously, to someone like Owen's vast subjectivist pneumatology is worthy of notice, and his remarks on the topic, if projected ecclesially, are pertinent to our argument.[70]

Near the opening of his teatise, Hobart outlines some of the main ways in which the Holy Spirit fulfills its mission as "Comforter." These include, in paradigmatic Puritan fashion, the work of "convicting" a person of sin, conversion, and sanctification. Within this triad, Hobart lays special stress on the role of Comforter in enacting a right and saving relationship between Scripture and Christian: the Spirit comforts by "opening the heart to the truth" of Scripture; by "applying" God's "Promises" to the contexts of Scripture, the gospel, Christ, the future, and the individual heart; and by "reminding" us of God's actions, as given in Scripture. All this constitutes the central pneumatic work of "instruction," on the basis of Neh. 9:20 ("Thou gavest thy good Spirit to instruct them . . .").[71]

The possible and in fact frequent "absence of the Comforter," in contrast, Hobart takes to be axiomatic of much human experience. Such absence, noted literally in Lam. 1:16, is a real fear for the Psalmist in 51:11, and

---

68. Nehemiah Hobart, *The Absence of the Comforter, Described and Lamented* (New London: Timothy Green, 1717) 124ff. Hobart's book was published posthumously under circumstances described in its preface by Eliphalet Adams. As a Congregationalist, furthermore, Hobart (like Owen) saw "unity" as residing in perceived fundamental common doctrines, irrespective of visible differences and antagonisms.

69. *Ibid.,* 134ff.

70. Hobart's project was not, in itself, extraordinary in the context of Puritan introspective analyses that attempted to delineate the shape of interior spiritual health. But the systematic way in which he tried to forge a pneumatological basis for this unveiling of the soul's disease ("soul misery") was, as far as I know, exceptional.

71. *Ibid.,* 34-53.

a real fate for many others in Scripture (e.g., Saul in 1 Sam. 28:15). So obvious and common is this possibility that Hobart does not even bother to describe in any detail its "cause." Instead, having explained the Comforter's mission positively, he spends most of the treatise detailing in what forms the deprivation of that mission will affect either the ungodly[72] or, more importantly and extensively, the godly. Yes, he notes, there is a sense in which the Holy Spirit is never "absent" from either group, working with both in their creation and natural preservation, speaking through "conscience," providing continuously a "carnal offer" of the gospel and "grieving" over sin. For the godly (i.e., the elect), in particular, the Spirit is, in some sense, always present in providing the grace of perseverence, and, in a kind of negative fashion, in rendering them "sensibly dissatisfied" by pneumatic withdrawal.

But although Hobart explicitly affirms the promise made in Isa. 59:21 — "my spirit which is upon you, and my words which I have put in your mouth, shall not depart . . . from this time forth for evermore" — he describes its fulfillment as given in only a hidden fashion under the circumstances of the Comforter's absence. The Isaiah text, of course, offers a clear assertion of the promised relation between Spirit and Word. Yet given that this relation is established in the Spirit's work as "comforter" in particular, the absence of the Comforter must logically alter the embodied form such a relation can take for the Christian. And so Hobart insists that one of the clearest "signs" of the Spirit's "withdrawing" does indeed touch upon the manner in which the Scripture is able to speak to the Christian; that is, it results in "dulness in learning or coming to the distinct understanding of the truth."[73] This is the sum of the matter: when the Spirit withdraws, as it often does, we are dulled to the truth of the Scriptures. There are other signs of the Spirit's absence, too. But for Hobart the reversal of the basic role of the Comforter in "instruction" is linked, as their fundamental source, to the whole range of more particular signs of pneumatic deprivation which manifest themselves in discrete forms of ungodly behavior.[74]

All this is in line with prophetic texts that, as we have seen, speak of pneumatic deprivation and antagonism in terms of "deafness" or "stupor," although now made explicit in its application to the gospel's obscurity within the Scriptures. But does Hobart have some constructive purpose in proposing this analysis? Curiously, his book seems to have little interest in providing directives for "retrieving" the Spirit. There is no attempt to offer

72. *Ibid.*, 62ff.
73. *Ibid.*, 143ff.
74. On the latter, cf. *ibid.*, 87ff.

the Christian a means of "fixing" the "soul-misery" of the Comforter's absence. Rather, Hobart wishes only to alert the Christian to the shape and meaning of this particular pneumatic condition. And the fruit of such awareness will be twofold. First, there will be a knowledge that the absence of the Comforter is consistent with the gospel itself. It is promised in the gospel (understood as underlying the whole of Scripture), and it embodies that gospel insofar as it drives the godly to a new humility and dependence upon God. Much of this talk by Hobart sounds themes commonly found in Puritan discussions about the "profitable" aspects of scriptural obscurity.[75] Awareness of the Comforter's absence offers a second fruit: that a faithful response to such consistency between the gospel and the Spirit's withdrawal is the difficult and patient suffering of it in repentance. All that is left to the pneumatically deprived Christian is an unadorned "listening" to Scripture, unconcerned with any "disputation" of its significance; all that remains is a dogged waiting before the Word, excruciating though its ostensible silence may be.[76]

Projecting Hobart's vision from the individual to the ecclesial spheres, we can say that, in a situation of the Spirit's deprivation, Scripture works, even in and because of its pneumatically rendered obscurity, for the manifestation of a promised condition of spiritual poverty. In a particularized manner parallel to the Spirit's own mission within such a situation, the silence of Scripture in the churches somehow testifies, in a negative fashion, to the reality of Christ, *sub contrario*, in the form of his Passion. The Reformers themselves understood something of this aspect of Scripture's universally effective power, whatever the circumstances of its apprehension. They tended to cast this negative role, however, in terms of bringing into relief the unbelief of the reprobate, thereby "damning" them in the act of their refusal to hear Scripture's truth.[77] From our perspective, however, we can say more properly that the church in which the Scripture is pneumatically rendered obscurely silent

---

75. Cf. William Whitaker, *op. cit.*, 365ff.; John Owen, *Pneumatologia*, IV, 190-91, 197.

76. "Disputation" over Scripture leads to "disunity" in the Christian community. This is one of the only places Hobart actually links — if unreflectedly — the realities of pneumatic withdrawal, the hearing of Scripture, and Christian division. In this case, however, division is a secondary consequence of the former elements, not a primary locus of pneumatic deprivation. But, we noted, Hobart is not really concerned with the possibility of Christian division. Cf. *op, cit.*, 284ff.

77. Cf. Calvin's remarks on Heb. 4:12, in his commentary on that letter: God never speaks "in vain," bringing, through the proclamation of his Word, some to salvation and driving others to perdition.

is the church in which the Word of God reveals the judgment upon sin made manifest in the death of Christ. In doing so, according to John's image, Christ is still and perhaps especially "glorified," even as the church herself stands astounded in the face of such an open act wrought upon her. The gospel proclaimed in such a church is still the gospel, though in a way that escapes the church's explicit testimony. For that the church is formed and lives by grace can be nowhere more evident than here.

Far from contradicting the promise made by Jesus concerning the Holy Spirit's "counsel" in "teaching the truth" to the Church, for example, in John 14, this kind of construal of pneumatic deprivation in the voice of Scripture allows for the continuing fulfillment of that promise amid a community of Christ's followers who have egregiously opposed the fundamental element of the promise's context, "love one another as I have loved you" (John 15:12). By revealing the power of God's justice exercised in the divided church, yet first provided in Christ's self-giving, such justice is made congruent with God's mercy; and despite the church's own practical contradiction of Jesus' exhortation, the Spirit is shown, through its own withdrawal, yet to "bring to remembrance" all that the Lord had spoken (John 14:26).

What then does the Scripture mean to us in the divided church, or what is it destined by God to mean? There is some parallel to this pneumatically deprived functioning of Scripture in Paul's discussion of the nature of the "old covenant"'s and the gospel's significance to the non-Christian Jews (2 Cor. 3:7–4:6). In each case, some scripture or message "spiritual" in itself (cf. Rom. 7:14), fulfills its purpose in a negative way through the Spirit's particular ordering toward its obscurement. And even while Paul clearly does not have in mind in this text the relation of gospel to Christian church, he notes that that relation, even at its most positive, is one borne in an "earthen vessel" designed to make visible the "death of Jesus" in the Christian's body (2 Cor. 4:7-12). Applied to the church as a *divided* whole or in her scattered parts, we can say that the Christian community manifests the death of Christ in her body now to the degree that she becomes as the Jews standing before the veiled gospel. In being confronted by this gospel, there is revealed to the church a limited "splendor"; but what the gospel's full splendor might be, the splendor of the unobscured Word spoken in a pneumatically unobstructed church, cannot yet be imagined. In this way, Christian Israel has indeed been thrust back, through the weight of its present history, upon its unity with Jewish Israel. What I am suggesting, quite bluntly, is that we consider Paul's warning in Rom. 11:21 as a prophecy fulfilled: "For if God did not spare the natural branches, neither will he spare you."

Thus, the figural parallel tentatively drawn by Ratzinger between

Christian division and the division of Christian and Jewish Israel in Romans 9–11, appears to be more than simile. It is a connection rendered organic — fulfilled — in Christ. We do not, because of our condition of pneumatic deprivation, either cease to read the Scriptures or cease to preach upon them. We can still apprehend and proclaim the gospel such as, for instance, Paul describes it in 1 Cor. 15:1-11. Christ's death for our sins according to Scripture, and his resurrection and living appearances to his followers, are not historically obviated by the church's division. Yet our method of reading and applying this gospel and Scripture as a whole must now surely demand a shift from a mode of scriptural authorization (by which we use biblical texts as positive explicators or imperatives) to a mode of "sifting" or "searching," much as the Jewish community in Beroea did (Acts 17), seeking to dwell more knowingly in the realm of listening that explores again the fundamental relationship between "Jewish" and "Christian" Testaments, the "Scriptures" "according" to which the gospel has any significance. We must learn to read the scriptures in a manner parallel to first-century Jewish believers. And though we consider the New Testament's apostolic witness as a now integrated portion of that Scripture, it is still one that stands, in relation to the Old Testament, in a position requiring exegetical testing by the Old.

In doing this, then, Christians will read Scripture, not from a posture of skepticism, but from the conviction that the revelation of God in Christ Jesus takes its meaning from the character of Israel, her promises, and their fulfillment. Thus, if, as Bruce Marshall has potently suggested, the "credibility of the gospel" is tied to the unity of the church, then in our given situation we are called to test, not whether Jesus is Lord, for example, but *how* this conviction is credible in the context of the Scripture's promises, given the state of the church. Much as with the first Jewish Christians, the Scriptures will here function as a grid by which to render coherent an accepted claim about God's work in the world, although in this case, in the face and in the midst of an incoherence the Christian church has herself incarnated. Just as we reappropriate our identity as Israel, witnessed to in Scripture, we are called to use that Scripture, its opacity speaking against us in the form of the Passion, as the basis for a "christodicy": by means of Scripture we must ask, how are the ways of Christ shown to be righteous in the life of the church as it is now constituted?[78] Therefore, although the gospel can still be pro-

---

78. This question — and hence the central role that only Scripture can play in answering it — cannot be resolved simply by applying to the church the character of *simul justus et peccator,* as if the church's failings in, among other things, maintaining unity is to be expected given its human constitution. Cf. Marshall, *op. cit.,* 85: if, as even Calvin supposed, the church's unity instantiates the unity of the trinity, and indeed the church is

claimed, it will speak only to the degree that it is put to the test in describing God's dealing with the church, and in this description revealing the form of Christ.

With respect to the practice of Biblical Theology, the kinds of topics and approaches given by this inescapable role of Scripture in the church are only indirectly suggested in the remarks above. Certainly Brevard Childs has courageously and carefully ordered his own study according to the reality of the Christian church's convoluted obduracy in the face of Scripture's pure speech, an ordering that must remain foundational to the challenge of testing the gospel. And Childs has further begun to speak in terms of a larger vocation that the church has to "search for the Christian Bible," in a way that is perhaps analogous to the present suggestion.[79] Yet such testing of the gospel itself, trying its voice and meaning on the hard surfaces of the church's actual experience of disarray, is not something that has ever been easily assimilated to the scholarly task, within either the biblical or theological disciplines. (The Reformers and their opponents were perhaps among the last scholars to have done this, albeit with a negative outcome!) And it is to be wondered if in fact these are the contexts where such testing can take place at all to any real degree. Perhaps Childs's testament — the "phenomenon" that forms his protest and his insistence — by both unveiling confusions over Scripture and admitting their rootedness, is to orient our patience in another direction.

For the testing of christodicy, by which the scriptural promises of Christ are justified in the life of the church, must ultimately proceed to the sensible embrace of the Spirit's own power at work in the contradiction un-

---

"church" because of this, then its disunity can have nothing to do with the categorically different relationship of human sinfulness to divine grace. Of course, if we wish to understand this latter relationship in figural concert with the sacrifice of Christ, who became sin but knew no sin, we might be able to speak in terms of the church as simultaneously sinner and justified. But even in this case, the compatibility of the church's disunity with its status as "church" would be clear only in terms of the credible ways in which Christ's sacrificial life might be shared with the church through its self-denials. This remains the crucial issue that is avoided in attempts to describe the divisions of the Christian church solely in terms of *inevitable* human frailty. The early Fathers had no trouble denoting the church as sinner, even as "whore," yet they could do so because they saw her condition as one of integral union with the "One who became sin" in the act of redeeming his people from sin; the church's sinfulness, then, did not, in their eyes, undermine its integrity as a people among whom and with whom Christ was to be found, and "separation" from sin could never, contrary to a Puritan view, justify separation from the church. Cf. Y.-M.-J. Congar, *Vraie et Fausse réforme dans l'Église* (Paris: Cerf, 1969) 78-83, for a discussion of this material, with bibliography.

79. Cf. Childs, *op. cit.,* 67.

der question.[80] This has been the province of holiness rather than of learning, of saints rather than savants. In such people, on whom the weight of the Spirit is let down, in presence or in flight, brusquely and forcibly, unexpected paths are pursued, barriers are thrown down, and the Scriptures opened up to the clarity of apprehended hearing. Were there not popes, monks, seminary professors, even tinkers or cobblers — individuals who in the past proved servants of our ecclesial rending, of our spiritual deprivation and of our blindness to the Word? Who knows? It is perhaps time for these offices to be visibly redeemed from their legacies through their use by unexpected individuals of grace. Few today would perhaps care what a Protestant of sanctity did. But were the pope to walk to Wittenberg or Canterbury on his knees in pursuit of the form of Christ, the greatest beneficiary might be the Scriptures. Because of men and women, the church quietly fractured over centuries and then exploded into fragments. Is it too much to expect that the same power that used these limited vessels — individuals of power — to such destruction might not turn them again to another end? For is not this the power "who has torn us to pieces that he might heal us" (Hos. 6:1)?

80. Cf. Ratzinger's remark that "today unity is not to be created through doctrine and discussion alone but only through religious power," in "Luther and the Unity of the Churches," *op. cit.*, 105. This is to be contrasted, in Ratzinger's mind, with a "forced march" approach to ecumenism (allegedly commended by Rahner-Fries) by which church leaders will simply forge reunions not based on real communion of faith, but on hierarchical fiats, expecting flocks to follow. But if the "force" is the bonding example of holiness, how is the freedom of the Spirit thereby contradicted?

Contributors

GARY A. ANDERSON teaches at Harvard Divinity School, Cambridge, Massachusetts

LESLIE BRISMAN teaches in the English Department at Yale University, New Haven, Connecticut

ELLEN F. DAVIS teaches at Virginia Theological Seminary, Alexandria, Virginia

STEPHEN FOWL teaches at Loyola College, Baltimore, Maryland

KATHRYN GREENE-MCCREIGHT teaches at Connecticut College, New London, Connecticut

ROWAN A. GREER is professor emeritus, Yale Divinity School, New Haven, Connecticut

ROY A. HARRISVILLE is professor emeritus, Luther Seminary, Saint Paul, Minnesota

LARRY LYKE teaches at Yale Divinity School, New Haven, Connecticut

GEORGE A. LINDBECK is professor emeritus, Yale Divinity School, New Haven, Connecticut

CLAIRE MATHEWS MCGINNIS teaches at Loyola College, Baltimore, Maryland

PAUL C. MCGLASSON is pastor of Central Presbyterian Church of Stamford, Texas

R. W. L. MOBERLY teaches at the University of Durham, Durham, England

CORRINE PATTON teaches at the University of St. Thomas, St. Paul, Minnesota

EPHRAIM RADNER is rector of the Church of the Ascension, Pueblo, Colorado

CONTRIBUTORS

PETER R. RODGERS is rector of St. John's Episcopal Church, New Haven, Connecticut

CHRISTOPHER SEITZ teaches at University of St. Andrew's, Fife, Scotland

MARK S. SMITH teaches at Saint Joseph's University, Philadelphia, Pennsylvania

DAVID TROBISCH teaches at Bangor Theological Seminary, Bangor, Maine